Contents

Introduction

Marketing is a constantly developing professional discipline, which has become pervasive in business and society throughout the world. It is ubiquitous in our everyday lives. All indications are that marketing will have an even more powerful effect on many aspects of our lives throughout the 21st century. Therefore it is a subject that commands the attention of both the specialist and the non specialist, the student, the business person, and the citizen in every country.

Although there is evidence of advertising in the very earliest societies, in its modern form, as a professional business discipline, marketing is around 100 years old. The first known academic courses in marketing were taught in the American midwest at the beginning of the 20th century. Now, in the 21st century, marketing is taught as part of the core curriculum in business courses at every level all over the world. All major businesses, large and small, and all organizations practise some form of marketing. Marketing as a business discipline has expanded and is no longer confined solely to the business world. Marketing is also a vital element in the work of charities, hospitals, the arts, the armed services, public services, social and environmental causes, countries, cities, regions, political parties, sports teams, and individuals such as actors, entertainers, and top sportspeople. Even secretive organizations have succumbed to the power of marketing: for example the CIA, the FBI, the British monarchy, and the Vatican all have their own promotional websites. These organizations have an overwhelming need to explain themselves, and what they stand for, to the public, their followers, their customers, and their supporters.

The universe of marketing

In our time, marketing is compulsory and compelling. Companies and organizations no longer have any choice, because in order to thrive (and, in some cases, to survive) organizations and individuals simply must be proficient and accomplished in the practice of marketing. My compatriot Robert Louis Stevenson's famous phrase that 'everybody lives by selling something' could now, with some justice, equally be applied to marketing.

There are many sophisticated definitions and complex models of marketing. Fundamentally, however, the practice of marketing still goes to the heart of that most perennial form of human interaction: that people make and exchange resources, goods, and services that are needed or desired, and that they will want to obtain these goods and services at the right time, place, and price, using a convenient method of purchase. All of these factors are in a constant state of transformation. *Marketing is essentially a discipline that studies and looks to exploit changes.* These changes can range from changes in consumer taste to changes in demographics, society, economic growth and decline, technology, business structure, and income distribution. Although an agent of change in business and society, marketing itself, as a professional discipline, has been much slower to change its range of approaches and techniques. In the past decade, however, there have been dramatic changes, particularly those caused to the fundamental methods and techniques of marketing and its sub-disciplines by the rise of the World Wide Web. Marketing is constantly adapting and exploiting the new opportunities for a new age and new market forces. There has never been a better time to immerse oneself in this fascinating subject.

Worldwide spending on marketing activities grows each year, but its focus is shifting. Marketing remains most powerful in consumer goods industries, but a greater proportion is being taken up by service industries. Industrial and manufacturing companies continue to focus on product marketing, expressing their identity through their products and related services. Services companies continue to focus on image, reputation building, and direct customer relationships, expressing themselves through the expertise of their people and their service offerings. Countries and cultures have individually different approaches to marketing. The USA, where modern marketing techniques were pioneered, has been fastest to adapt to the new techniques of marketing. There, marketing is treated as a profession; it enjoys much higher esteem and is better understood as a central factor in economic development than in other countries. The UK has capability in media, communications, consumer goods, and creative advertising, but has always been weak in industrial product marketing and in commercial exploitation of its innovations. Germany, with its strong engineering roots, has majored in product marketing, but continues to be weaker in services marketing, creative advertising, and in its general marketing culture. Japan is skilled in advertising, market research, and product marketing, but does not accord any distinction to marketing as a profession. Russia and China, always strong historically on the uses of image, staged events, and propaganda within their own countries, are now coming to appreciate the necessity of marketing as they start to become major powers in the global economy. India, also using marketing to power its phenomenal growth, continues to be a playground for traditional marketing techniques. For emerging economies, marketing is vital to attract tourist currency and also inward investment. All countries, of whatever size or stage of development, have come to realize the power of the Internet as the marketing tool.

Marketing under fire

Rising power attracts criticism and breeds suspicion. The ubiquitous practice of marketing has become controversial. Marketing stands accused in the West of having become too powerful, too pervasive, and too insidious. Marketing is criticized more than it is praised: whether for its role in the creation of global brands that invade many aspects of public and mental space, or for the intensive hyping that creates artificial economic booms. Marketers are often blamed for being, in fact, successful. Marketers are trained to listen, analyse, and act upon what they hear from the marketplace and from customers, rather than tell the market what they actually think that customers want. For a range of reasons, this has often given marketing a somewhat sinister reputation, suspected of everything from the brainwashing of consumers to the subversion of the democratic process. Frequently, supporters of political parties or campaigns complain that the competing party, campaign, or cause only won because of expensive or well-orchestrated marketing campaigns. 'We were out-marketed' is a more frequent lament of losing politicians these days. Indeed, political parties and governments can help to win elections, and to propagate messages about their policies and actions, by employing superior marketing techniques. This has led to accusations that marketing has fuelled an art of public relations deception (often known as 'spinning'). The net effect of spinning has been to diminish the public's trust in public institutions and politicians and many multinational corporations.

The universe in which marketing has become omnipresent is one of abundant information and fragmented media channels. Public space and culture is perceived as being invaded and colonized by marketing sponsorships and brands. Every major sporting event and sportsman is a major advertising platform. Places like Times Square in New York or central Tokyo or even Mumbai assault the senses with marketing messages and billboards. Advertising and branding have been quick to invade the World Wide Web. The few remaining public service broadcasting channels are always under constant pressure to become more commercial and to use advertising as a revenue source.

In private life, parents tend not to celebrate the creation of global brands, but they do feel the consequences of the persuasive power of those brands through the demands of their children for branded goods. Parents feel that marketers manipulate the young. Fashionable clothes have become wearable billboards for youth-centred brands. For the individual consumer, marketing is held responsible for junk mail, intrusive telemarketing, and aggressive selling of certain products and services to the detriment of consumers and private investors.

Marketing in the new millennium

Despite the criticism levelled at marketing, why has marketing continued its inexorable march into every aspect of life? Since the end of World War II, two major trends have been affecting the practice of marketing: customer power and self-service. Both trends have been accelerated by the Internet. Increasingly, customers are smarter, better informed, better protected, and have a much greater range of choices. Greater choice and information have increased customer sophistication and buying power. Customers can better exploit a world of over-supply to hold down prices. This new power enables customers to negotiate better deals across a vast range of producers. The ways in which customers want to buy goods and services are also changing. Self-service, where companies enable customers to do things for themselves in the name of greater convenience, has been a major factor in the rise of consumer power, particularly in services. We now pour our own petrol, become our own bank teller, pick and pack our own groceries, arrange our own holidays, process and print our own photographs, review books, publish ourselves, broadcast ourselves, analyse markets, buy and sell our own investments directly, and electronically deliver our own mail—activities that previously required a skilled assistant.

The consequence of these changes is that many of the 'classic' functions of marketing—such as mass advertising—are in decline in the West, and their effectiveness is questioned. In the industrial past, the mass market was served by a few mass media that could grab general attention and create demand for mass-produced products. The mass market was characterized by a common culture, a single geographical location, and was served by few but familiar types of media. No longer. The apparent decline in effectiveness of many of the classic marketing techniques is partly attributable to the changes in the market and to the vast range of media now available. With the proliferation of multimedia outlets and channels, there simply is no one medium that can any longer reach a mass audience on a continuous basis in the way that the press, radio, or public broadcaster could have done in the past. For example, as well as the mass media that boomed in the 20th century (such as radio, cinema, telephone, video, satellite and cable television, billboards, the popular printed press, and magazines) there is now the Internet, multimedia, interactive television, iPods and iPads, search engines, and personal mobile communications devices with advanced imaging combined with communications capability. Moreover, digitalization of content enables marketers to use media channels in different ways. Digital content can be distributed faster and wider than its physical counterpart. It can also be updated more rapidly and can be both corrected and replicated endlessly.

Not only are media and content proliferating, markets are simultaneously fragmenting and globalizing. This fragmentation of markets into smaller and smaller segments, but with wider and wider geographical reach, has caused the inexorable decline of what used to be known as the mass audience, or mass market. Within the world of proliferating media channels, the viewers' control and ability to be their own programmers, to create their own viewing choices, and to pause live television has diminished the direct influence of media advertising. The use of the media has also been transformed in the process: people no longer obtain their breaking news from newspaper headlines or radio as they did in the first three-quarters of the 20th century. Now breaking news comes from 24-hour broadcasting channels and websites accessed on mobile devices. Newspapers are now read for analysis and commentary about news that has already been distributed through other more interactive and immediate media. Therefore, the fundamentals of 'classic' marketing in the 20th century—that it served the producer interest and that marketers could, through various 'mixes', control the market—are now of questionable validity. In the early 21st century we have entered a time when marketing has moved from the 'production' or 'sales' era to the 'customer' era and now to the 'interactive' era. Customers can no longer be *talked at*, or sold to, or be told what is good for them, which was the essential marketing characteristic of the industrial production era.

Today, it is the retailers, online and offline, and the customers, individually and in aggregate, and not the producers and their middlemen, who control the market. Consequentially, the old ways of classifying and segmenting the market into producers and buyers are now strained and inadequate to the task of focusing and allocating market resources to a cornucopia of fragmented niches and customer groupings. Philip Kotler, one of the leading thinkers in marketing since the 1960s, summed up very succinctly the two most important changes in marketing in the last 30 years. 'First, marketers have moved from thinking their job is to sell whatever the company makes to thinking that their job is to influence what the company makes. Second, marketers now have tools to focus their efforts on reaching and satisfying niches and individuals.'

Consequently, marketing is now the religion that instructs on how to worship at the altar of the glorified, and ever changing, capricious, global customer. It has helped to extend the concept of customer service beyond simple commercial selling; now governments talk of citizens as customers, hospitals call patients customers, employees call each other internal customers, churches are even encouraged to think of their parishioners as consumers of religious services, and it has even been known for breadwinners to think of their own families as their 'major customers'. All enterprises and organizations are expected to adopt a *marketing orientation* in order to understand, then to serve, customers more efficiently, effectively, and even, in some cases, to delight them. What is this much-sought-after marketing orientation? In simplest terms, it means that companies now have to develop a much deeper *insight* into their customers' wants, needs, and desires and seek to deliver satisfaction beyond their expectations in effective ways. Insight is more than analysing market data or conducting individual and group customer research. It is a deep desire to serve, and willingness to listen to, the marketplace, then to enable customers to define the products and services that they want and need, and then to let them determine how they wish to interact with the company. The customer moves to the centre of everything the company does and makes and determines how it allocates its human and capital resources.

The marketing paradox

Aside from the contemporary polemics, and the fundamental changes of technique, marketing's longer-term problem has always been its perceived lack of professionalism and financial accountability. These are the hard results from marketing activities that accountants and chief financial officers can understand. Many business cultures continue to venerate and promote those who count money over those who help to harvest it. Marketing, with its vague emotional appeal, its intangible benefits, and even its artistic elements, is still viewed as more of an unaccountable art than a measurable science. The ethos of our times demands tangible numerical measurement for everything. The standard measures for a set of marketing programmes—customer awareness and satisfaction, brand strength, product and sales growth, and market share increases—are not the most important to the Chief Executive and his Chief Financial Officer (CFO). They continue to be squarely focused on profit and loss, shareholder value, market capitalization, share price and share dividend, return on assets, and return on investment. This makes marketing a continuous battleground for both belief systems and for everyday investment allocation. For, as long as it remains difficult for marketers to quantify their results in terms that the CFO can understand, they will face an uphill struggle to gain investment for marketing programmes and it will remain an impediment to the ascent of their discipline into full professional status. This problem, perceived or real, has not yet been solved. No one is quite sure if marketing is a necessary operating expense (or, worse, an overhead expense) or a strategic investment. Marketers, particularly of intangible services, are everywhere compelled to produce detailed measurements of their 'added value'. There are some economic models that claim to be able to quantify accurately brand value and equity. These models, however, are not yet agreed upon by standard setting organizations in ways that make an intangible asset like brand or customer value quantifiable on a balance sheet.

Consequently, the value and the professional status of the marketer continue to be a paradox. The discrepancy between the manifest power of marketing in practice, and the relative powerlessness of marketers within companies and organizations, is everywhere observable and, for marketers, it is a constant source of frustration and career dilemma. Marketing does not have the status of a profession with standardized professional qualifications such as those that distinguish law, medicine, and even accountancy. In most companies, marketing is not a board-level function, such as finance and sometimes human resources. It would seem that, despite the success of the practice of marketing, marketers have forgotten to market themselves and their role within their own spheres of influence. We can speculate that all professions undergo a 100-year period of scepticism from their inauguration before they are fully established and accepted. Nevertheless, I confidently predict that marketing will be perceived as a full profession within the next 30 years, with established professional qualifications and higher status, from the traditional West to the rising countries of Asia, South America, and Africa. It is a good time for students to be thinking of marketing as a profession.

I have tried, in compiling this *Dictionary of Marketing*, to reflect the crossroads that marketing has reached, and the tensions within it, as well as its substantial achievements, influence, and possibilities. I have given much space to the new techniques of marketing in this age of the World Wide Web and the information-rich age, without neglecting the tried and tested techniques, models, and assumptions of classic marketing which have served many generations well. I have also adopted a wide view of marketing as an all-encompassing business discipline. By this I mean a multi-dimensional function which involves, and has impact upon, every part of the modern enterprise and organization. I have not confined marketing to the activities of a single-function discipline, or department. As the management guru Peter Drucker said, 'Marketing is so basic that it can't be considered as a separate function on a par with others such as manufacturing or personnel. It is a central dimension of the business. It is the whole business seen from the customer's point of view.'

I have also taken a practitioner's viewpoint in compiling this dictionary, rather than the academic's. Much of the academic theory of marketing is based upon what academics think that professional marketers ought to do, rather than what they really do each day. Marketing is a practitioner's art rather than an academic's subject of study. Readers will, however, find theoretical marketing models in this dictionary, although I have rarely seen complex marketing models and theories used purposefully and effectively in operational practice for the 25 years that I have been a marketing practitioner with several global companies. Nevertheless, I have had many opportunities to observe the interplay between marketing theory and marketing reality, and even attempted to implement complex marketing models in everyday business myself. Both have value, but are better working in combination than studied as separate disciplines. I have tried to do justice to both the practical and to the conceptual aspects of marketing when working in combination. I have used many case studies to illustrate theory turned into reality and the resulting consequences. I have also been struck by how often marketing touches so many other disciplines—economics, finance, history, sociology, psychology, statistics, and the creative arts. It is not possible to develop each of these areas in the depth that they deserve. I have, therefore, defined all related areas which have influence and bearing on the subject and context of marketing, rather than as absolute definitions in their own right.

The format of the dictionary is by subject-based alphabetical entries, with mini essays on major subjects allowing a more in-depth analysis with practical guidance on how they might be used. There are also appendices which chart the history and development of marketing, which give case studies of brands, advertising campaigns, and slogans, and which provide web resources for further study. As with markets, some segments merit more attention than others.

Charles Doyle

Acknowledgements

I am grateful to Vicki Donald for having presented me with the opportunity to create this new edition of the Dictionary of Marketing for Oxford University Press. Rebecca Lane, the commissioning editor, has helped me to raise this edition to the high standards of OUP and has provided excellent advice and counsel throughout the redrafting and redesign of this third edition. I am also grateful to the team of experts assembled to assist me: Clare Jenkins, the production editor, who has deftly managed all aspects of the overall production of the dictionary; Jamie Crowther, the assistant commissioning editor, for his creative and design skills and tenacity in obtaining permissions; Sheila Ferguson, my copy editor, who identified many areas for improvement with her laser-like eye; Judith Colleran the proof reader, who ensured quality in the text, and the vital Marketing and Publicity team of Louise Corless, Kate Farquhar-Thompson and Gabby Fletcher who will use their skills and imagination to make this dictionary, which has marketing as its core subject, available at the right price, the right time, and the right place, to the widest potential world-wide audience.

Much of the knowledge accumulated for this dictionary over the 25 years I have been working on the subject has been learned through the many companies I have worked for and in the daily development and practice of marketing and communications programmes: I would like to thank the marketing and communications professionals that I have worked for over the years in those companies who have helped me to observe marketing in practice and to amass this amount of knowledge on this fascinating and indispensable subject, which I am now pleased to present to a new generation.

Working as a full-time Chief Marketing and Communications Officer whilst compiling a dictionary was a complex task. I was therefore grateful to my research assistants, Katherine Doyle and Caroline Doyle, who both assisted me with great patience, insight, and humour in researching and compiling the new edition of this dictionary. Without their dedicated support, I would have been unable to complete it within our time horizon.

Charles Doyle

My wife, Katherine, and my children, Caroline and Alexander, and to my mother, Catherine, and my sister, Sharon.

abandonment The withdrawal or ending of a *product, usually at the end of its *life cycle or when it can no longer be produced profitably.

ABC A popular sales acronym for Always Be Closing.

above the fold Originally the upper half of the front page of a *newspaper that was visible when the paper was folded, which was the normal presentation format to customers when displayed by newspaper vendors on a stand. This was vital both for selling the newspaper—the key story or photograph would appear there—and also as prime *advertising space. More recently, the term refers to the section of a *web page that is visible without scrolling. This is prime advertising space on the Web. Placements that are higher on the web page are usually preferred by advertisers. If a *banner ad is placed above the structure containing the main content, then the ad can be viewed before the main content loads.

above-the-line A term which now has come to mean mass audience advertising and promotional campaigns—for example, to describe campaigns that are targeted at high volumes of *consumers in a large number of countries using *print and *broadcast media. Originally, the term derived from financial accounting, and referred to those *media and *promotional activities for which an *agency obtained a commission, for example for buying broadcast media space and time on behalf of a client. *See* ADVERTISING; BELOW-THE-LINE; MEDIA.

absolute advantage A theory that a company, a country, or a regional cluster, has an advantage over another if more goods (output) can be produced with the same level and quantity of input. Factors contributing to this advantage may be greater efficiency of production process, lower labour or materials costs, better applied technology or clustering of industry expertise in specific locations (for example Silicon Valley in California, The Pearl River Delta in China, the financial services industry in the City of London, the fashion industry in Milan). *See also* COMPETITION.

absolute income hypothesis A theory developed by John Maynard Keynes which puts forward the idea that consumption will rise as income rises, but not necessarily at the same rate.

absolute link A connection which shows the full *URL of the page being looked at.

absorption The allocation of fixed and variable costs to the goods and services that are produced and marketed by a company. This is usually done to recover all costs of production in the *sale price of the *product.

abstract A summary of the core arguments and main points of an article, a thesis, or a longer work such as a book. This enables the reader to get a quick overview of the line of argument and contents before exploring it in greater detail. The abstract is a traditional instrument of the written word, but is also very important for the search and browsing on the *World Wide Web.

ACASI (Audio Computer Aided Self-administered Interviewing) These are self-administered surveys in which the respondent listens to the questions over headphones. Responses are usually registered using a computer-based questionnaire. If responses are recorded on paper it is known as audio SAQ (Self Administered Questionnaire).

acceptance A positive act by a person accepting an offer so as to bring a contract into effect. It can also mean the acceptance of a new idea or *concept that was not previously understood or known about. Acceptance is the stage beyond *attention and *awareness. Market acceptance, which is a high volume of *sales to a defined *marketplace on a consistent and recurring basis, is the desired outcome of much marketing and sales activity. The opposite of market acceptance is market rejection.

acceptance testing A range of formal tests on a completed system to determine whether or not a system satisfies its acceptance criteria and to enable the *customer to determine whether or not to accept the system. Typically this is for end users to trial a *product or *service in real working conditions with a view to gaining their acceptance. Used widely to test new software applications and *websites. Tests tend to focus on ease of use and intuitiveness rather than if the functions work correctly.

accordion insert An ad inserted in a *magazine, with an accordion-style fold.

account An existing client and their associated revenues and profits. Can also be known as client account. *See also* SALES.

account activity Discussions of accounts won and lost, and re-assignments of existing accounts among the representatives of a *marketing agency.

account director A senior person in an advertising or *marketing services agency, usually focused on a single client or a small group of clients. The account director's main role is to ensure client satisfaction and the maximum amount of billings from the client with the agency. The account director is normally the main point of contact between the agency and the client. *See also* ADVERTISING AGENCY; SALES.

account management The individuals involved in, as well as the processes and techniques of, managing clients, advising on, and developing their creative briefs, in addition to the execution of campaigns on their behalf. *See also* ADVERTISING AGENCY; SALES.

account planning The process of market and client *research, development of a strategy that is specific to the client's needs, and the programmes and creative briefs that address them. The function was developed in UK advertising agencies in the 1960s but is also used widely in the US. The account planning process uses research from potential *consumers in the marketplace to inform *advertising and *message development. The account planner acts as the 'conscience' of the market, and brings to bear the mindset of the end consumer and target audience to the development of advertising messages prior to testing with the actual clients themselves. Recently, account planning has come to describe how *sales personnel plan commercial relations for their major customers. *See also* ADVERTISING; ADVERTISING AGENCY.

account review The process of evaluating and selecting an *advertising agency or selecting a new agency. This process usually culminates in a *pitch to the potential client from the pre-selected, short-listed agencies. These can be among the most stressful preparations in advertising activity.

accreditation A formal evaluation of an organization according to accepted criteria or standards. Accreditation may be conducted by an independent and disinterested professional society, a non-governmental body, or a governmental agency.

acculturation The process by which different ethnic or cultural groups or individuals are exposed, then adapt, to different cultural identities and behaviours, while retaining awareness of their original ethnicity and culture. This is typically the process through which most immigrants go.

accumulation An *audience-counting method, where each person exposed to a specific vehicle is counted once within a certain time period.

acid test A financial liquidity measure of the ability of a company to use its cash, and those assets that can be quickly converted into cash, to repay its current liabilities. Usually this is the sum of current assets less stocks and work-in-progress expressed as a ratio of total current liabilities.

AC Nielsen A pioneer of the *market research industry, founded in Chicago in 1923 by Arthur C *Nielsen. The main expertise is in *consumer marketing and *media research. It opened in the UK in 1939 and more widely in Europe and

Asia after 1945. The company now operates in 100 countries. Nielsen was an early leader in measuring the impact of marketing investments, for example in market share and the 'Nielsen Ratings' which measure television, radio, and newspaper audiences.

ACORN (A Classification Of Residential Neighbourhoods) A geodemographic classification system based upon the *segmentation of *consumers in various types of residential neighbourhoods. It was first developed in the 1970s by CACI (a private data system and research company that conducts ACORN among other surveys) using data from the census. Its primary purpose is for *direct marketing. *See also* DIRECT MARKETING; GEODEMOGRAPHICS.

acquiescence bias in market research The tendency of an interviewee in a *market survey to agree with the questioner in order to appear more positive, even if the questions are contradictory.

active exporting *See* EXPORTING.

activity sampling The technique in which a large number of observations are made over a period of time in order to collect information on the percentages of time spent on activities, without the need to devote the time that would otherwise be required for any continuous observation. One of the great advantages of this technique is that it enables lengthy activities or groups of activities to be studied economically and in a way that produces statistically accurate data.

adaptation The process and practice of adapting otherwise standard *products and *services to meet the needs of varying *customer types, either individually or customer groupings. Adaptation is typically used by practitioners of *international marketing to ensure that the products and services being produced and delivered are relevant and suited to the needs of different national *markets and standards. Conceptually, adaptation is often discussed as an alternative to standardized *marketing strategies and approaches, rather than a refinement of the standard approach. A famous example is how McDonald's have adapted their standard fast-food offerings to different national tastes around the world whilst retaining the central idea of fast and low cost food delivered to the mass market.

ad blocking The blocking of *website advertisements, typically the image in graphical web advertisements. This enables the user to filter out ads while surfing websites. Ad blocking is used by a relatively small percentage of the online population. Ad filtering technology is increasingly bundled into other web applications. Those who favour ad blocking say it improves the speed and convenience of the website to visitors, making it less of a nuisance. Those who oppose it say that it deprives website owners of revenue from advertising, as ad-free surfers use valuable resources without indirectly 'paying' in the form of viewing ads, forcing content owners to consider charging.

ad centre Microsoft's pay-per-click advertising service. *See also* ADWORDS.

adcept A halfway stage of a campaign idea at which it is half advert and half concept: a staging point in the creative process, a time when initial creative ideas are checked with various constituencies, probably including clients, to ensure that the concept is following the overall *message and *position developed in the creative brief.

ad copy A printed text or spoken words in an *advertisement.

added value A reference to the increase in worth of a *product or *service as a result of a particular activity, feature, or *benefit. In the context of marketing, the added value is provided by features and benefits over and above those representing the standard product or service.

ad inserts The enclosures that are used to relate information as part of an overall advertising campaign.

adjacencies The time periods immediately before and after a television programme, normally used as a commercial break between scheduled programmes.

ad network A means of aggregating *buyers and *sellers for online advertising. The network is made up of several *websites that sell online advertising, allowing advertising buyers to reach broad *audiences relatively easily. Advertising networks provide a way for a *media buyer to coordinate buys across multiple websites far more efficiently and more cost-effectively than could be done otherwise. Media buyers usually focus on running ads over a category or an entire network. Advertising networks can also aggregate visitor information.

adnorm A measure of *readership averages for print publications over a two-year period, used as a baseline for comparing specific ads to an average.

adoption *See* DIFFUSION OF INNOVATION.

ad recall The measured ability of *readers or *audiences to remember ads they have viewed in various media and programmes.

AdSense The *Google advertising placement service designed to generate revenue for users. It is a highly targeted system in which the content of the advertisements is relevant to the website. Many websites use AdSense to monetize their content. AdSense has been particularly important for delivering advertising revenue to small *websites that do not have the resources for developing marketing campaigns of their own.

ad space The space on a web page available for advertisements. In the early days of *website design, ad space was not a major factor. Nowadays, it is crucial for sites that are dependent on advertising revenues. One of the challenges of web design is to use ad space in a way that satisfies advertisers without alienating visitors and causing them to leave the site.

ad speak The language, acronyms, and idioms used by people in the *advertising industry. Many of these phrases have become part of idiomatic language.

adstock A technique developed by The Brand Consultancy to measure the effect and performance of an *advertising campaign by focusing on the recall in the minds of target audiences that an advertising campaign has after it has ceased to run.

ad tip-ins Set of inserts placed in a publication, such as extra pages of advertising or subscription return cards.

advertising

The main purpose of advertising is the promotion of ideas, goods or services, or any combination of these, that are paid for by an identifiable sponsor. Advertising is among the most visible, most expensive and most controversial of the elements and techniques of marketing communications. Bruce *Barton, the legendary advertising executive who helped develop the image of General Motors in the 1920s, said that 'the role of advertising is to help corporations to find their soul'. The media philosopher, Marshall *McLuhan, called it the art form of the 20th century. Advertising has attracted artists, intellectuals, movie directors, politicians, poets, hard-headed businessmen . . . and controversy.

One of the dominant techniques of *persuasion and selling in the last century, advertising is now changing in nature, purpose, and form. Advertising content was historically directed through mass media to achieve agreed marketing objectives. The relationship between *media channels and advertising is a symbiotic one in which the nature of the media channel has always been a major determining factor in the development and diffusion of advertising content. The economics of media channels are dependent upon revenues from advertising. The proliferation of new media channels, together with the rise of the *World Wide Web, is the greatest force of change that is bearing down on the advertising industry. Nowadays, there is a greater multiplicity and fragmentation of media channels that can be used for advertising. Traditional media channels have now been challenged by new media channels. This gives a significantly different advertising *media mix, including radio, the press, magazines, posters, brochures and catalogues, telephone, the World Wide Web, broadcast satellite and cable channels, physical objects, apparel, and interactive digital television. New media, such as the World Wide Web, have started a revolution in creative advertising development, distribution, and audience feedback and interaction. New media have also vastly increased consumer choice and consumers' ability to select and customize in receiving information and images. Consequently, this affects the ability of advertising to gain attention and then to persuade audiences to act.

Although advertising can be traced back to the earliest times, making use of all media and visual aids available to it at the time, it has always been a much-debated topic. The role of early 20th-century advertising was to shift products in an age of mass production; later, it became a way of changing public opinion, *lifestyles and *consumer habit. In more recent times it has fuelled the 'personality' of *brands and become something of an art form in its own right. One of the more enduring criticisms of advertising, both as a marketing discipline and as an industry, is its lack of financial accountability and uneven effectiveness. Great minds have been consumed in developing incontrovertible formulas that will one day show exactly how many *sales emerge from each advertising campaign. In an age that likes to have measurable results and analyses for every type of business investment, advertising remains difficult to assess and quantify with agreed metrics. It is both emotional and rational, both an entertainment and a way of conveying information.

Few doubt that advertising is crucial to economic development, market competition, and dynamism. It is most prevalent in economies with the highest standards of living (for example the United States spends roughly three times as much on advertising as the next largest spenders, Japan and India).

It has also been argued that advertising helps to promote and diffuse innovation throughout society and to give stimulus to new product development. Many of the great modern inventions—such as cars, telephones, cameras, record players, air travel, electrical appliances, and computers—were initially promoted through advertising. Because advertising is essentially the consequence of market competition, it can also contribute to lower prices and the prevention of *monopoly. Beyond that, advertising also provides a means by which information on products and issues of interest to society are diffused. It can be an entertainment in its own right (some directors and actors have started their careers in advertising) and it can be used in the promotion of cities, countries, regions, charities, causes, political manifestos, and environmental issues.

Types of advertising

1 **Institutional or corporate advertising,** also known as Image advertising, which promotes an organization's brand, image,

people, capabilities, employment opportunities, ideas, or political issues, or anything that the advertiser wants to publicize.

2 **Product and services advertising** promotes specific goods and services to target audiences.

3 **Location advertising** is advertising by communities, states, cities, or destinations; for example, the 'I Love New York' or 'Glasgow Smiles Better' campaigns were designed to attract tourists and businesses and to revitalize the images of these once maligned cities.

4 **Classified advertising** is for the sale of goods, services, jobs between individuals, usually in smaller locations, without display, in newspapers. It is a $50 bn global market. *See* MEDIA CHANNELS for display methods used in advertising.

Purposes of advertising

Advertising is used for different purposes, among which are:

1 Promotion of the value of products and services, which has tended to be dominated by advertising of consumer products.

2 Promotion of ideas, organizations, and causes. These techniques have also been used in one-party states for political and social purposes, or to 'enlighten' captive populations.

3 Increasing the use of existing products and services. This can also be referred to as category brand advertising, especially when a product or service is already well known and repeat purchase is the goal.

4 Reinforcement or extension of existing brand recognition, awareness, value, and esteem. For example, this is often used when a brand has become 'tired', or subject to declining awareness, or needs to be repositioned in the minds of target audiences, or positioned for the first time in the minds of new audiences.

5 Building a new brand from zero, in which case the goal of advertising is rapid recognition and awareness building for the new brand.

6 Acceleration of revenue, sales growth, or number of buyers—in which case advertising can be more directly measured as a contributor to sales. For example, BT could instantly measure the effect of its television advertising by the number of additional calls over and above the norm that were made during and immediately after its famous advertising campaigns.

7 Increasing total market share—in which case advertising supports other elements of the marketing mix in order to increase share relative to competition.

8 Reaching new markets and buyers—particularly important when entering a new market or country or in expanding the market for an existing product or service.

9 Influencing buying decisions—in which case advertising works on the practicalities of moving buyers to make favourable buying decisions for the product or service that is being advertised. This type of advertising is usually characterized by practical information copy rather than advanced concepts.

10 Increasing sales and supporting sales functions.

11 Developing customer loyalty. This is related to number **4**, but may also be used when customer loyalty is threatened by a competing product or service.

12 Announcing a new offer or sales promotion. This is related to number **5**, but may also provide a 'kicker' to a well-established product range.

13 Announcing a product price or service change.

14 Announcing a company vision, mission or values, or a new company. This is related to number **4**.

15 Announcing a merger of two or more companies. This includes practical information, but usually starts to announce the purpose and values of the new entity.

16 Educating existing customers or new customers and audiences.

17 Attacking or counteracting competition or competitor advertising. This type of advertising used to be banned and even today is used in limited doses. Examples are the battle for the British business traveller waged between Virgin Atlantic and British Airways, or for the Cola drinker between Coke and Pepsi.

18 Making a formal statement or supplying direct information to the public. This is where advertising and public relations merge.

19 Recruiting people for a company, organization, or institution.

20 Correction of an advertised claim that has been found by a regulatory body to be deceptive.

21 Promotion of a product or service under the guise of a learned detached copy or programme: known as advertorial in print or infomercials on broadcast media.

Elements of Advertising

Advertising research The creative development research in which the advertising concept's appropriateness for the market and its target audience is researched. This is usually conducted prior to a full-blown advertising campaign. Pre-production Research Testing involves pre-testing the concept and creative work with representative audience samples and panels. This is usually done before and during a campaign. Post-production Research Testing studies overall reactions after the advertising campaign has run, which contributes to the effectiveness measure. *See also* ADVERTISING RESEARCH; MARKET RESEARCH.

a

Regulation of advertising An activity that is done within a national context and is rooted in the cultural, legal, and social interpretations of fairness, integrity, honesty, and truth in advertising in the particular country. Each country has different nuances and regulation of advertising standards. For example, some countries allow unsubstantiated claims for certain products (such as 'product X improves your health') whereas others do not. Some countries allow the use of the superlative (as in 'Product X is the best product in the world') while others do not. For example, in the UK the beer company Carlsberg had to moderate its claim to be 'the best lager in the world' with 'probably'.

The advent of Internet-based advertising has also presented regulatory authorities with a range of challenges. There is, as yet, no universally guaranteed way of regulating Internet-based advertising or enforcing penalties against illegal advertising. The regulation of promotion activities is largely based on self-regulatory codes of practice rather than statutory law as there is no one act which covers the entire range of promotional activities. There are no internationally agreed laws on consumer protection, competition, and monopoly that can be applied to cyberspace. For example, one of the most exposed areas in the short term is the whole system of quality assurance and control standards of goods and services advertised on the Internet. Goods and services promoted then ordered over the Internet from another country could circumvent the apparatus of quality controls. Quality and safety are national variables. For example, drugs which may be over-the-counter in one country may be available only by prescription in another. The patient may be able to see them advertised on the Internet, then order them remotely and receive them through the mail, thereby bypassing the local regulations and controls. Digitally distributed content, such as software for example, or the Internet's most advertised product, pornography, could be accepted in one country and offensive or banned in another. There is no standards body to arbitrate over misleading or inaccurate advertising.

Agency self-regulation is self-policing by the advertising industry, which may include ethical issues, certification, standards, and reviews and recommendations by the industry-policing bodies regarding allegedly deceptive or fraudulent advertising.

Advertising measurement and effectiveness The several methods of measuring the effectiveness of advertising, which is often referred to as the ROAI, or rate of return on advertising investment. The measurement of advertising effectiveness is a perennial source of controversy and has always cast a shadow of doubt on the effectiveness of the advertising industry.

- **Pre-testing** of advertising is a way of testing how effective it can be prior to full launch, usually involving test groups assessing impact, emotional reaction, communication, image, recall, and originality.
- **Post-test evaluation** of advertising, which may involve a customer survey, recall tests (in which each respondent or test group is asked about what advertisements he or she has seen recently), and recognition tests (in which each respondent or test group is shown the actual advertisement and asked if they recognize or recall it and what it meant to them). This is often divided into tests of aided and unaided recall. In aided recall the test group is prompted with cues or lists of the adverts or brand attributes; in the unaided this is not done.
- **Sales testing** is testing to determine the actual sales or order growth that resulted from the advertising campaign. This is a more difficult type of test because, generally, advertising works more on perception in the customer's mind than on immediate purchase action. It could include sales in total, by customer, or sales by product or service contribution or, in total, by customer and by product and service. It may include a measure of the impact of the campaign on actual expenses versus budgeted expenses on the basis that good advertising ought to lower sales costs. It may measure the number of new leads, or potential customer interests resulting and, ultimately, the number of new customers obtained. It may be a simpler measure of percentage increase in sales after the advertising campaign compared with the period before the advertising campaign.
- **Public reaction testing** aims to determine the overall effectiveness of the campaign by, for example, measuring the amount of media space gained, and the number of articles and favourable comments written and made about the campaign.
- **Offer redemption** refers to the uptake of a special offer promoted in the advertising (such as a discounted product, a special package or deal, a coupon in which the way of reclaiming it is embedded in the advertisement) where the redemption or interest in the offer can be measured directly. *See also* DAGMAR; DAR.

(((●))) SEE WEB LINKS
- Website on advertising
- History of classic British advertising on an online archive

advertising agency The primary responsibility of an advertising agency is to gain an understanding of the client's business strategy and imperatives, then to determine what role advertising can play in supporting them, and then to help them execute and measure the campaign. It is usual for companies, organizations, and even governments to use external agencies for advertising rather than attempt to do it themselves. External agencies are used because the company's own marketing team do not usually have the resources, time, media purchasing power, or expertise to develop the campaign themselves. Agencies are usually selected through competitive tendering that results in a final selection or 'pitch'. Agencies that 'pitch' successfully usually have a distinguished track record and credentials; they can usually demonstrate to the prospective client that they understand their brand and that they have innovative ideas to promote it. Then considerations of price, culture, chemistry between the account team and the marketing group, their international reach and local presence in the prospective clients' target markets are taken into the final selection criteria. Ultimately, business and communications strategies must connect and be mutually re-enforcing.

Types of advertising agency

- **Full service agency** Often known as an integrated or 'one-stop shop' agency, this can offer clients a full range of promotional services from research, advertising, public relations, direct marketing, digital, media planning/buying, and events and promotions as well as account management. These agencies are distinguished by their large range of internal resources that have usually been recruited or else acquired through merger or takeover of other agencies. The trend in recent years is to build full marketing service agencies that continue to have advertising at their core.
- **Specialist agency** These agencies provide a customized service to individual clients. Often this type of agency will focus on the creative aspects of advertising and arrange other parts of the campaign mix through other agencies, affiliated companies, and contractors. These agencies are often eventually acquired by the larger agencies.

Functional departments of an advertising agency

Although each advertising agency is organized differently, there are certain core functional departments that most of the larger agencies would deploy.

- **Planning** is generally the department responsible for trying to discover how advertising is received and interpreted and what people find valuable in products and brands. One of the more important elements of the job is to commission, understand, and interpret market and audience research. Planners tend to be more analytical and empirical than creative.
- **Creative** is the department where the basic campaign strategy—objectives, positioning, themes, messages—are turned into creative concepts in terms of artwork and copy. A creative team is usually composed of a copywriter and an art director. Creative people tend not to be analytical or empirical. Creatives tend to have a different, less regimented culture than the rest of the agency.

- **Production** is the department responsible for turning the creative concepts into reality and making the advertisement. Often there is an element of subcontracting here, as studios, camera crew and actors may be required.
- **Media planning and buying** is the department that selects the optimum *media channels that will have the greatest impact over the longest time period with the intended target, at the lowest possible cost. Having developed that strategy, this department then buys media time and space from the media owner. The media buyers also negotiate slots and prices with the media owners. This area tends to attract tough negotiators.
- **Account management** is dedicated to a particular group of clients or in some cases an individual client. The role of account manager is to be dedicated to individual clients and therefore carry ultimate responsibility for the client's satisfaction. The account manager is also accountable to the agency for revenues and profits generated from their clients. This role has to coordinate all specialist functions and activities. They represent the agency to the client, present the agency's findings and outlook, and they feed back client comments. They also deal with client dissatisfaction. The account team must work closely with the client's marketing department. They receive briefing from the client on the overall positioning and strategy. Often the account manager will attend the client's strategic planning meetings.
- **Traffic** deals with delivering the artwork or film to the magazine or TV station on time. When the promotional campaign involves a number of media channels, this process becomes complicated because accurate timing is crucial to successful execution and cost management.

advertising allowance The money provided by a manufacturer to a distributor for the purpose of advertising a specific product or brand.

advertising budget The money set aside by the advertiser to pay for advertising. There are a variety of methods for determining the most desirable size of an advertising budget.

advertising campaign

An interconnected set of creative executions running across multiple *media channels for an extended period of time, with a singular theme and aimed at a *target audience. This is in contrast to a single advertisement or a series of individual, disconnected adverts.

There are two main types of media strategy that support an advertising campaign:

1 **A burst campaign** is an intensive campaign that concentrates expenditure into promotional 'bursts' of three or six weeks in length. Burst campaigns can be repeated periodically and are often used to launch a new brand or product/service.

2 **A continuous campaign** allows for a constant but less intensive campaign over a longer period of time. This is often used to reinforce an existing brand.

There are several stages of a finite advertising campaign:

- Development of an overall positioning strategy to give focus and consistency to the advertising campaign. Often the campaign will be given a theme or a slogan at this stage.
- Detailed research on the target audience. Development of an identifiable target audience.
- Target audience segmentation based upon the detailed market research and planning.
- Overall positioning programmes of a product or service relative to the overall strategy and the knowledge of the target audience.
- Setting clear and measurable advertising objectives for the campaign, which will later form the basis upon which the campaign's success is measured.
- Developing a set of core messages relative to the overall positioning platform for the campaign.
- Sizing and allocation of budget and resources for the advertising campaign (usually within the context of what the client has said that they are prepared to budget for advertising).
- Writing the creative brief for the campaign that explains what an advertisement or the campaign has as a strategic context, objective, and purpose. It includes the overall objective, desired positioning, the target audience, the core and supporting messages, and the overall desired brand essence and personality.
- Production of various creative options and copy that bring the creative brief to life.
- Testing the various options, usually with a representative cross section of the target audience and the client.
- Selection of the final creative story, artwork, and copy for the campaign.
- Final agreement with the client on the artwork, copy, and media.
- Media strategy and selection of the most appropriate media distribution channel and media purchasing.
- Evaluation of any obligations or constraints in the external environment (e.g. advertising standards or prohibitions of types of advertising, local cultural considerations, competitive activity).
- Post-campaign testing and evaluation, usually with test groups.
- Reporting against campaign metrics, based upon the original objectives set.

For a number of examples of a variety of successful advertising campaigns *see* APPENDIX 1.

advertising elasticity The relationship between a change in advertising budget and the resulting change in product sales. Ideally, more advertising means more sales.

advertising medium A vehicle of communication which enables some form of advertising: print, billboard, television, radio, website, catalogue, direct mail, etc.

advertising page exposure A measure of the opportunity for readers to see a particular print advertisement, whether or not they actually look at the ad.

advertising plan An explicit outline of the goals that an advertising campaign should achieve, how to accomplish those goals, and how to determine whether or not the campaign was successful in achieving the goals.

advertising research A method conducted to determine the efficacy of *advertising. Such research focuses on either the performance of a specific advert, or *advertising campaign, or at a more general understanding of how advertising works or how *consumers use or are influenced by the information in advertising. *See also* ADVERTISING.

advertising specialty *See* PROMOTIONAL PRODUCT.

advertising theory An attempt to explain why advertising successfully persuades *audiences to adopt a preference for a given *product, *service, or *brand and ultimately to make a purchase.

advertising-to-sales ratio The percentage of advertising expenses relative to *sales revenues: often used as a prime measure of *advertising effectiveness, particularly for *consumer products and services.

advertorial A paid-for advertisement made to look like a newspaper or magazine editorial. It is normal practice to label these 'Advertising' or 'This is an Advertisement'. An advertorial is the print equivalent of the TV-based *infomercial. In the printed medium these are fairly easy to distinguish from news or journalism. However, advertorials are now also prevalent on the Internet. The ability to create customized advertising online creates another challenge: many Internet surfers are probably not aware that most of the information they get from technology and business news sites is actually sponsored by a corporation. Many surfers fail to distinguish between advertorial and real editorial. Online magazines work hard to generate an appealing look. These publications try to be consistent and advertisements are often designed to look like the magazine they appear in. Often an advertorial is not labelled as an advertisement (as it is in physical print) but as an Info Site or other misnomer.

advocacy advertising The promotion of a position on a political or social issue. For example, Greenpeace may try to create awareness around nuclear testing in the Pacific.

ad volume The amount of dollars or media units (e.g. hours, number of pages) spent on advertising and marketing efforts.

Adwords *See* GOOGLE ADWORDS.

affiliate directory The categorized listing of affiliate programmes. Affiliate directories are used to find and compare various merchants' programmes. Directories provide simple text listings, but a few offer more advanced search capabilities. Many include articles, newsletters, and forums.

affiliate marketing A specific type of marketing on the World Wide Web that is characterized by revenue sharing between online advertisers or merchants and online publishers or salespeople. Affiliates give wider advertising and sales distribution online to the merchant's products. Typically, an affiliate model works in the following way: a smaller website owner registers with a larger and better known website (e.g. Amazon.com or some other affiliate programme), the website owner then puts various links, banners, and products on their website. The larger website owner pays the smaller website owner when visitors click through on these links and purchase a product. Benefits of affiliate marketing include the potential for automating much of the advertising process (such as accepting and approving applications, generating unique sales links, tracking and reporting of results) and payment by desired results (sales, registrations, clicks). Affiliate compensation can also be based on attention metrics, such as audience size, registrations, subscribers, *click-through and *website access. Paying for performance shifts much of the advertising risk from the merchants to the affiliates, although merchants still assume some risk of fraud from partner sites. Amazon.com uses affiliate marketing techniques very effectively. Affiliates are usually small sites run by individual webmasters. However, there is a growing trend for large companies to use affiliates. Some companies even participate as a merchant of their own programme and as an affiliate of other programmes.

affiliate network An intermediary that provides services, including aggregation, for affiliate merchants and affiliates. These services can include providing tracking, sales reporting, payment processing, and access to a large base of affiliates. For affiliates, services can include providing one-click application to new merchants, reporting tools, and payment aggregation.

affinity marketing The targeting of consumers on the basis of their established buying patterns, or trends, or through their common interests. The web has enabled affinity marketers to define and market to narrow niches of like-minded customers, but on a global scale.

affordability index The standard used in the USA to gauge the financial ability of consumers to buy a home.

agate line A measure of newspaper advertising space, one column wide and $\frac{1}{14}$ th inch deep.

age cycle The consumer spending and behaviour patterns that correlate with their age and lifecycle. This is used extensively in the financial services market to customize financial products related to different age groups.

agency commission The advertising agency's fee for designing and placing advertisements. Historically, this was calculated as 15% of the amount spent to purchase space or time in the various media used for the advertising. In recent years the commission has, in many cases, become negotiable, and may even be based on some measure of the campaign's success.

agent A representative of either the buyer or the seller in a negotiation. *See also* BROKER; WHOLESALER. There are now many different types of agent:

- *manufacturers' agents* are used to represent one or more manufacturers. Their primary role is to sell the manufacturer's goods, particularly for manufacturers who do not have their own direct sales force or who wish to sell their goods in a territory where their direct sales force does not operate. They usually cover pricing, defined distribution area, order handling, fulfilment, post-sales service, guarantees, and commission rates. This type of agent usually handles a number of manufacturers' product lines.
- *purchasing agents* primarily buy for the manufacturer. Often these agents will work for the company buyer. Their main role is to negotiate purchases with suppliers, and to receive, inspect, warehouse, and deliver the goods to the company.
- *commission agents* take possession of goods from manufacturers and sell them, taking a commission and expenses following sale.
- *personal agents* are used for high value individuals in the media, entertainment, and sports areas. Their main purpose is to negotiate the best possible deals for their clients in terms of fees, long-term contacts, advertising, and merchandising and, in sports, transfer fees.
- *intelligent agents* are a new development on the *World Wide Web, referring to a non-human software agent taking instructions from a human to search out the best and most appropriate information on the web, customized to the needs of the individual searcher. In future this intelligent agent will become more sophisticated, using intuition to seek out the best information and make purchases for its 'master'.

aggregate demand

The total of planned expenditure on goods and services in an economy. This economic measure is used by marketers for a number of tasks: in assessing investments in geographical markets; planning campaigns for specific socio-economic groups; to understand and measure the ability, and willingness, of individuals and institutions to purchase goods and services. Aggregate demand is primarily a measure of the *ability to spend* on goods and services at different price levels and is therefore a measure of purchasing power relative to expenditure and income.

There are four key types of expenditure that constitute aggregate demand:

Consumption expenditure

Of the four components of aggregate demand, consumption expenditure is the largest, contributing to between 60% and 70% of total expenditure in any given economy. This category of expenditure includes private spending on durable goods (for example cars, electronic goods, appliances), non-durable goods (food, clothing, books), and services (housing, healthcare, education, entertainment). Consumption expenditure decisions are strongly influenced by household disposable income, household wealth, savings needs and plans, confidence in the future direction of the economy, and interest rates.

Special attention must be given to the service component of consumption expenditure for three reasons. First, services are the largest component, representing at least 50% of spending. Second, services include housing services (e.g. rents being paid from tenant to landlord). Third, services, unlike durable and some non-durable goods, are difficult to accumulate as inventory.

Investment expenditure

Investment expenditure constitutes a smaller share of the total but tends to be the most volatile component contributing to the cyclical behaviour of aggregate demand. This category of expenditure includes fixed non-residential investment (factories, machines, transport equipment), fixed residential investment (new houses and rented flats), and business inventories. Often, the volatility in investment results from fluctuation in inventory levels as a result of changing expectations about business conditions. Because of the sensitivity of investment decisions to changing interest rates, this category of expenditure is directly affected by monetary policies and activity in the financial sector of an economy.

Fixed residential and non-residential investment refers to the creation of income-producing assets. For example, those assets that will generate net-benefits (such as housing services) in the case of owner-occupied housing or generate profits as part of the production process. These net-benefits and profits depend on the expected revenue generated by the asset as well as the costs of acquiring, maintaining, and replacing these assets.

Demand for the production of the asset will directly affect the revenue generated. Strong demand based on preferences, optimism, purchasing power, or demographics will lead to the desire for more investment expenditure.

Acquisition costs include both the purchase price of the asset and the borrowing costs involved, which are both highly sensitive to changes in interest rates and the financial markets. Higher interest rates lead to higher borrowing costs; this, in turn, leads to lower net-benefits or profits. Therefore, the level of aggregate investment expenditure may be reduced. Another factor is the cost of maintenance and replacement costs that are related to the useful life of an asset and also to its rate of depreciation. Assets that wear out very quickly, or become obsolete in a short period of time, have higher costs. This has the same effect on aggregate demand as rising interest rates.

Government expenditure

Government expenditure is a reflection of the fiscal needs and policies of the public sector in a given economy. This type of expenditure might be in reaction to the demand for public infrastructure investment and services by citizens and businesses either through electoral voting or other types of political activity. In addition, government expenditure could be used as a directed public policy to increase incomes in the hope of stimulating aggregate demand. This has been used from time to time (famously in the US in the 1930s and throughout the world in 2007–2009) to help national economies recover from depressions and recessions.

Net export expenditure

Net export expenditure is based directly on service and merchandise flows across international borders as well as capital flows into and out of a particular country. Merchandise flows are sensitive to domestic income levels and preferences for foreign-made goods. In addition, these flows are influenced by exchange rates that determine the domestic price of goods and services produced abroad. Capital flows depend on interest rate differentials among nations as well as exchange rates that affect the domestic price of a foreign asset both at the time of purchase of that asset and at the time of sale.

AIDA (Attention Interest Desire Action) One of many models that analyse and measure the customer's journey from ignorance to purchase. The AIDA model is simple, which partly explains its longevity and widespread use. The model was developed in 1898 by St Elmo Lewis in an attempt to explain how personal selling works. The model laid out a sequence that describes the process a salesperson must lead a potential customer through in order to achieve a sale. The stages, Attention, Interest, Desire, and Action, form a linear hierarchy. In order to be motivated to actually make a purchase, customers must progress from being aware of a product's existence to being interested enough to pay attention to the product's benefits and advantages, to having a desire to benefit from the product. Lewis believed that the fourth stage, Action, would come as a natural result of movement through the first three stages.

Although Lewis's work was primarily focused on helping the personal selling process, it was avidly taken up by marketing and advertising theorists over the next half-century. The action stage became the ultimate goal of all marketing and all advertising. This is also fundamental to the understanding of the *hierarchy of effects theory. Later theories distinguished the role of marketing as moving the consumer to action from that of advertising, whose main purpose was to move the consumer through the sequence towards action.

If the seller can successfully gain the consumer's attention, then the next stage is to stimulate interest in the product. For example, what special features or benefits does the product have? What special needs does it address? How might it satisfy any one of the needs and wants that the consumer might have? During this stage the consumer develops a reaction to the product, usually either favourable or unfavourable. If the response is favourable and the advertisement is successful in awakening interest, it then attempts to create in the consumer's mind a desire to purchase. It does this by successfully connecting the benefits of the product with the consumer's needs and wants. This is often the most difficult aspect of advertising design. Portraying a product in an attractive manner that stimulates interest in consumers is the easier part; it is more difficult to persuade consumers to buy it. Advertising rarely makes the sale on its own. So, this phase of advertising has to both show consumers that there is a product available which will satisfy their needs, and show them that they can satisfy that need by purchasing the product in question. This leads to the final stage, action, where consumers actually get up, go out, actively seek the product, and buy it. *See also* DAGMAR; THREE ORDERS MODEL.

aided recall An assisted memory device, using prompting of respondents' memory through providing ideas or associations or other stimuli.

airdate The first time an advertisement is broadcast.

airtime The actual transmission time or time allocation for an advertisement.

Amazon.com An online seller of goods and services, founded in 1995 by Jeff Bezos, which was mainly focused on selling books. Amazon.com was immediately successful and has a robust business model. Since its inception Amazon.com has consistently enlarged the choice of goods and services offered to customers and expanded its ability to deliver from a worldwide set of warehouses. It has also used technological innovation to get closer to its customers: it also has intelligence software systems that analyse individual customer's preferences and buying patterns and offer them related goods ('Listmania' and 'Wish List'). Amazon.com is primarily an e-commerce platform, and for the past decade has made this available to other vendors. Thousands of world-class retail brands and individual sellers use the Amazon. com e-commerce platform as a sales and distribution channel. Independent software developers also work on Amazon.com's applications ('Amazon Web Services'). *See also* APPENDIX 2.

ambient media Description of unusual objects or places in which *advertising is found, such as light projected into the skies or imposed on any non-traditional physical object such as roofs, pavements and floors, petrol pumps, wastepaper bins, seat covers and cushions, papier-mâché animals on streets and on people's bodies. *See* MEDIA CHANNELS.

ambush marketing The false association of one brand with an overall event or sponsorship for which it is not the official sponsor with full marketing rights (because it has not paid and does not have the legal rights) to conduct advertising or other forms of marketing. This technique is usually prevalent at major sporting events in which one brand, that is not an official sponsor, conducts an 'ambush' to make its branded product prominent to both spectators and television or web audience. The ethics of this approach are debated constantly.

angle The perspective that gives identity and character to a story. Editors and journalists constantly strive to find an 'angle' for their editorial and reportage.

animation A technique for film making, which has developed since its development in the 1920s from hand-drawn, frame-by-frame photography to create the illusion of movement, to computer-generated, three-dimensional figures that imitate life. Landmarks on the animation journey would range from *Snow White and the Seven Dwarfs* by Walt Disney in the 1930s, the first ever full-length feature film animation, but painstakingly drawn by hand, to *Avatar* (2009) which uses the most advanced state of the art 3D computer generated animation.

Ansoff matrix (directional matrix)

A model for analysing the approach to product-market growth strategies developed in 1965 by H Igor Ansoff in his book *Corporate Strategy*. The main axes of the matrix are new or existing products and new or existing markets. The matrix has four quadrants: *market penetration*, existing products and markets; *new product development*, which involves new products introduced into existing markets; *market development*, which involves finding new markets for existing products; and *diversification*, which involves new products in new markets. The modern-day marketing practitioner may find the matrix useful mainly for well-defined markets and tangible products. The matrix framework can be used to develop product strategies for various market growth strategies:

1 **Market penetration strategy,** or penetrating the existent market with existing product, is regarded as the lowest risk strategy. This could involve more aggressive marketing and sales campaigns around the existing product. Results could include increased purchase and usage from existing customers encouraged by attractive pricing or discount offers or discounts on multiple purchases. It could be as a result of more intensive customer research and focused action such as targeted mailing of customers with relevant offers. Alternatively, it could be achieved through aggressive market share building, i.e. winning customers from competitors in the existing market.

2 **Market development,** developing new markets with existing products, is higher risk. This strategic approach seeks out new market sectors that are underdeveloped, or which are less price-conscious than the existing market. This may involve the development of new distribution channels or new retail outlets. It may also involve new geographic markets for the existing products, for example through licensing, agent, or distributor arrangements.

3 **New product development,** developing new products for existing markets, can often be the heaviest investment programme because of the cost involved in producing and marketing a new product. This may involve the development of products based upon new and untried technologies.

4 **Diversification,** developing new markets with new products, is regarded as the highest risk. It will take the company into markets and product development cycles in which it is inexperienced. It may also lead the company into making acquisitions or merging with other companies in order to gain either market or product assets.

Market \ Product	Present	New
Present	Market Penetration	Product Development
New	Market Development	Diversification

Ansoff matrix

anthropomorphic (market research) A research technique in which participants describe a product, service, or brand in terms of a human being with personality traits so that the participants' feelings about the object/brand can be determined.

anti-competitive practice Actions to restrict, block, undermine, diminish, distort, or prevent competition in the production, acquisition, supply, and sale of goods and services.

anticorporatism A protest movement targeted against major international and global corporations, particularly those believed to be using cheap labour to create their primary branded product, those whose operations cause harm to the natural environment or its creatures, and those involved in harmful trades, such as arms, tobacco, or certain types of drugs and chemicals. As the focuses of the protests are those companies who have global brands, this is an important social and political movement and trend for marketers to understand, especially when designing campaigns. It shows that consideration of brand reputation must now go beyond the simply commercial dimension of a company.

The global brand image can be a surprisingly complex business to handle, and can be affected adversely in many ways. Nike, for example, became the focus of worldwide protests when it became apparent that Nike trainers are produced by workers in conditions that are characterized in the media as 'sweatshop labour'. Nike responded to this attack by saying they were providing jobs where no one else was, but also seemed to be saying that in any case most trainer manufacturers produced their shoes in the same way, so why did Nike get the bad publicity. The fact remains that many consumers are now aware of the low pay earned by the workers who manufacture their shoes, and there seems little doubt that Nike has been damaged by the many campaigns on low manufacturing pay in the industry. There is also no question that the growing 'anti-globalization' movement has hurt many firms with an international image that once seemed impregnable, a notable example being the McDonald's chain, which has been particularly attacked for its strong propagation of a fast food culture. Being American, with American values, also comes under attack. This is a factor that has also damaged Coca-Cola in the Middle East, where rival local brands explicitly position themselves as opposed to the all-American appeal of Coke. A classic example of an anticorporate case is the so-called 'McDonald's libel trial'. The case was brought by McDonald's against Greenpeace activists Helen Steel and David Morris after London Greenpeace issued a pamphlet 'What's Wrong with McDonald's? Everything they don't want you to know'. The pamphlet accused McDonald's of a wide range of abuses, from animal welfare failings to the exploitation of children. After a trial lasting 313 days (making it the longest-ever English libel trial) the judge found that McDonald's had indeed been libelled, but also found the company responsible in variable degrees for a wide range of abuses, including animal cruelty, misleading customers about nutrition, paying low wages, and child exploitation. Unsurprisingly, the trial is now widely perceived as a huge PR disaster for McDonald's. The image implications for companies with cases such as the McDonald's libel trial are of course enormous and it can be incredibly difficult to undo the harm done. Similarly, even the most powerful oil company (such as BP and Exxon) will find that its image suffers disastrously every time there is an oil spill. For all the power and spin capacity of large commercial enterprises, a photograph of one oil-drenched seabird has the power to negate massive image-building campaigns.

anti-marketing The attitudes or behaviours, either within an organization, or in society in general, that either reject, or are actively hostile to, a marketing approach. Usually this position is based on a belief that marketing is linked to manipulation or, more pragmatically, that it cannot achieve a desired business outcome.

APIC A set of core marketing management activities defined by Philip *Kotler as Analysis, Planning, Implementation, and Control.

appeal The advertisement's selling message. This is usually based on deep research into the audience as well as a clear understanding of the overall strategic objective being adopted using the advertising messages.

applications service provider (ASP) A type of business characterized by the hosting and distribution of third-party applications or services. These applications or services are distributed over the *Internet to many customers in exchange for a stream of smaller payments as opposed to one fixed, upfront price. The business model is based upon customers paying a monthly service fee to use proprietary software developed by major brands, such as Oracle and Microsoft, instead of licensing software and having to support it themselves. Applications service provider is a very general term; there are many different types of ASPs that share very few common characteristics. Many sub-acronyms are currently being introduced in an attempt to better make distinctions, but few of the terms have gained general or major brand recognition.

applied research A survey that is used to answer a specific question, determine why something failed or succeeded, solve a specific, pragmatic problem, or to gain better understanding.

approvers See BUYER AND BUYING BEHAVIOUR; DECISION-MAKING UNIT.

arbitrage pricing theory The expected returns and prices for financial assets can be modelled as linear functions of multiple factors, especially macroeconomic risk factors. See also PRICING.

architecture The term given to an organization's information technology platform, structure and process but increasingly used as a way of explaining complex marketing concepts and functions, for example 'brand architecture' or 'product architecture'.

area samples Those samples that include specific geographic areas as part of the design.

armchair shopping Purchasing from home without visiting a retail outlet, originally meaning use of mail order catalogues, but now also includes purchase via television channels, telephone, and online shopping.

article A piece of non-fiction text written for inclusion in a journal, newspaper, or other publication.

art proof The artwork for an ad, to be submitted for client approval. This is a visual expression of the overall strategy.

arts marketing The commercial promotion of artistic events (exhibitions, concerts, artistic venues, theatrical productions, collections, arts programmes on media) using marketing techniques. This is rising in importance as a distinctive form of marketing technique. Marketing has become an integral part of artistic institutions. The term can also mean the marketing and sale of objects of art direct to buyers.

artwork The visual components of an ad, not including the typeset text.

aspiration level A projected state in which consumers expect or desire to own or experience a certain level of product or service.

at-home testing The time when a product sample is provided for participants to use at home. The reaction to the product is determined in a follow-up telephone survey, written survey, or in a group session.

atmosphere A part of retail image that is created by a blend of sensory effects intended to create a specific shopping mood.

atmospherics A term coined by Philip Kotler in *Journal of Retailing* in 1973 that described how retail environments could affect shopping behaviour and eventual purchase. There has been much psychological and *market research into the practice and effect of the total shopping experience and how it can be best created. Atmospherics may involve music, lighting, scent, the provision of food and beverages, entertainment, and display. There are now many agencies that specialize in the design of retail interiors around a central concept, and the use of atmospherics is core to the design.

attention concept The capturing and retention of customer attention is an increasingly difficult task that is breeding different types of new marketing technique and practice. In an age of impatience and shortening attention spans, increases in the number of communications channels, and the vast availability of information, the impact of traditional mass marketing has, to some extent, been undermined. Attention grabbing is much more difficult than it used to be; attention holding is even more difficult. We are now in the age of customer attention deficit and new techniques that can gain and hold attention need to be developed. Modern-day users of digital information are faced with a paradox: they are overloaded with information, but are unable to absorb and classify it. Yet, in aggregate, they continue to generate even more for other users. This places a higher premium than ever on the marketers' ability to gain attention. Attention has become a key source of value in the economy of the Information Age. The proponents of the Attention Economy argue that attention is a scarce resource, and therefore has and will increase in economic value. It is causing increasingly creative and outlandish marketing campaigns.

attitude A position that an individual has adopted in response to a theory, belief, object, product, service, event, or another person. It is a relatively consistent predisposition to behave in a certain way. There are three components to an attitude: a *cognitive component* which is what the individual knows or believes about an object or act; an *affective component* which is what the individual feels emotionally about an object or act; a *cognitive component* which is how the individual is disposed to behave towards an object or act. *See also* CONSUMER BEHAVIOUR.

attitude research The study of emotional and psychological response to a product or services (rather than a study of usage and purchase).

attitudinal scaling The understanding of a respondent's feelings or attitudes towards a certain area. In most instances, respondents are asked how they view or rank two different variables in relationship to each other.

attribute positioning *See* POSITIONING.

auction A public sale in which property or items of merchandise are sold to the highest bidder. One of the oldest and most direct forms of marketing in which the price is neither set nor arrived at by negotiation, but is arrived at through a process of competitive, open bidding. Traditionally, this activity is done in a public room with a professional auctioneer. Increasingly, auctions are now conducted online without a public auctioneer and the goods and services (from air travel to legal advice) may be offered for bidding by anyone from anywhere and at any time on websites such as eBay.com. *See also* EBAY.

audience The person or persons who are receiving a transmitted marketing or informational message. All good marketing communications should begin with a thorough understanding of the target audience and the assumptions made about them. In all aspects of marketing communications, the definition of the target audience, the determination of attitude and value systems, and the positioning and development of relevant and appropriate messages for them is critical.

audience duplication The number of people who saw or heard more than one of the programmes or read more than one of the publications in which an ad was placed.

audience loyalty The propensity of a readership, viewership, or listenership to continue to spend time reading, watching, or listening to a specific programme on a recurring basis.

audience profiling The socio-economic characteristics of a readership, viewership, or listenership; audience profiling analyses the spending habits of a particular audience (disposable income, home ownership, leisure spending, geographic location). This information is supplied to the advertiser or advertising agency who uses it to optimize specific campaigns for products and services.

audience research A focus on audience statistics relative to use of various types of media—for example, circulation, readership, demographics, lifestyle, viewership, quality, etc.

audilog A diary kept by selected audience members to record which television programmes they watched, as a means of rating television shows. Used by AC *Nielsen.

audimeter An electronic recording device used by AC *Nielsen to track when a television set is in use, and to what station it is set.

audio SAQ *See* ACASI.

audit The examination and verification of the sale of a product. A method for measuring sales in a store by counting beginning inventory, adding new shipments, and subtracting ending inventory. Also used to determine inventory lost to theft. *See also* MARKETING AUDIT.

augmentation The addition of extra features and benefits to core products and services in order to increase appeal, attractiveness, and differentiation. Examples may be after-sales service, warranties, continuing support, extra features.

autocue A prompting device that displays prepared words for people to read usually when making a speech or a television broadcast, enabling them to look at the audience directly without appearing to read from the printed page.

automatic selling The sale of goods by a machine without human intervention. Example would be a vending machine or ATM.

availability The advertising time on radio or television that is available for purchase, at a specific time.

avatar Originally a Sanskrit word meaning the manifestation of a deity in human or animal or superhuman form. Generally it has come to mean the personification of a concept or an alter ego. In the Internet age it is more commonly known as a computer users' representation of an alter ego in computer games, online games such as Second Life or, more prosaically, an invented name or persona on social media services.

average audience (AA) The number of homes or persons tuned to a television programme during an average minute, or the number of persons who read an average issue of a print publication.

average price strategy *See* PRICING.

average propensity to consume The proportion of annual income spent on consumption of goods and services. To calculate the percentage of average propensity to consume, consumption (C) is divided by income (Y). The identity that defines average propensity to consume is given as: $APC = C / Y$. Demand for goods and services is lower in economies where individual consumers save a considerable part of their income.

awareness *See* DAGMAR; MARKETING COMMUNICATIONS.

awareness-trial-reinforcement (Ehrenberg's process) A process suggesting that a trial purchase may proceed from awareness of a brand, or confrontation with a product in a retail outlet, after which the consumer gets to know the product and develops an attitude towards it.

B

baby boom The increase in births that started in 1945, when World War II ended, and extended into the early 1960s.

baby boomers The large generation born after World War II, particularly those born between 1946 and 1964. In market targeting, the baby boomers are among the wealthier and more influential groups in the advanced economies. For example, baby boomers comprise 15% of the on-line population and control a disproportionate amount of the wealth in North America. They constitute 36% of the cinema audience in North America.

baby bust The decrease in births between 1965 and 1976. People born in this period are often referred to as *Generation X.

Backer, Bill (1926–) During his 25-year career with the *advertising agency McCann-Erickson Worldwide, New York, Backer created some of the more successful *advertising campaigns in history. For example: Campbell's Soup's 'Bring on the Campbell's, Soup is Good Food'; Coca-Cola's 1971 'Hilltop' anthem, 'I'd Like to Buy the World a Coke' and Coke's 'It's the Real Thing' jingle; and Miller Lite's 'Tastes great/less filling' celebrity 'feud' series that ran for years and put Lite atop a new beer category. In 1979, Backer left McCann as vice chairman-creative director and, with Carl Spielvogel, Interpublic vice chairman, opened Backer & Spielvogel. Saatchi & Saatchi acquired the agency in 1985 for $100 m. *See also* ADVERTISING; APPENDIX 2 (Coca-Cola).

back room The room from which client personnel observe and listen to focus group proceedings through a two-way mirror.

back-to-back A sequence of commercial adverts being run one immediately after another.

backward invention The process of redesigning and producing a product for foreign markets after it has become obsolete in advanced economies.

bait advertising A product promotion at a very low price, when it is difficult or even impossible to obtain the product for the price advertised. *See also* BAIT AND SWITCH.

bait and switch The practice of enticing or 'baiting' the potential *customer with a misleading advertisement (e.g. offering goods deceptively cheap) then persuading them to buy something more expensive ('switching') or more than they originally intended. Also known as bait advertising. Bait advertising, specifically, is an alluring but insincere offer to sell a product or service that the advertiser does not really want to sell. The real purpose is to switch consumers from buying the advertised merchandise in order to sell something else, usually at a higher price, which is more advantageous to the advertiser. The primary aim of a bait advertisement is to obtain leads that can be 'switched' to buying something else. A range of techniques are used to cause the potential customer to 'switch'. This practice is now illegal in certain markets, notably the USA. In the USA, advertisements cannot contain an offer to sell a product when the offer is not a bona fide effort to sell the advertised product. No statement or illustration can be used in any advertisement that creates a false impression of the grade, quality, make, value, currency of model, size, colour, usability, or origin of the product offered. Nothing that could lead to a misrepresentation of the actual product is allowed. Interviews or contracts that switch the customer to another product are prohibited. No act or practice to discourage the purchase of the advertised merchandise as part of a bait scheme to sell other merchandise is allowed. *See also* ADVERTISING REGULATION.

banner ad A graphical advertising unit especially created for use on the *World Wide Web. These have become the dominant form of advertising on-line. The accepted standard size is 468×60 pixels. Banner ads were initially measured for performance on the basis of the *click-through rate (CTR) achieved. Banner ads have been controversial with many detractors claiming that they do not achieve the required result. Some of this is related to the demise of the CTR as an effective measure of on-line advertising. Consequently, banner ads have declined in price. On-line marketers now seek to combine low-cost banner ad rates with above-average response rates as their prime return on investment metric in this medium. *See also* ADVERTISING; INTERACTIVE MARKETING; POP-UP WINDOW.

banner blindness The tendency of web visitors to ignore banner ads, even when the banner ads contain information visitors are actively looking for. This is a major issue for online advertisers to overcome.

banner exchange A network where participating sites display banner ads in exchange for credits that are converted (using a predetermined exchange rate) into ads to be displayed on other sites.

bargain A discounted price for a product or service or a high-value product or service at a good price relative to competitor prices. Bargains can often be an important part of consumer marketing. Non-financial factors, such as the concept of fairness, play an important role in bargain hunting and consumer satisfaction. Consumers often derive pleasure or satisfaction from the idea that they are paying a fair price rather than a highly reduced price. They can derive pleasure or satisfaction from getting a good deal or 'fair' price even when there was no major cost saving at stake. Price discounts are important in creating a sense of fairness: the percentage discount offered is an important factor in consumer satisfaction and sense of value. Even if the amount of money involved in a discount is relatively small, a higher percentage discount, 40% for example, leads people to infer that they are getting a fair price.

bargain basement The name given, originally, to the lower floor of a department store where excess or end-of-line merchandise was offered to the public at prices well below that which they had when they were on the other floors of the store. It has since become a generic term for low or sell-off prices.

barriers to entry The economic or technical factors or costs that make it difficult for new firms to enter a market against other competitors. The term was popularized by Michael Porter in his classic works *Competitive Strategy* (1980) and *Competitive Advantage* (1985). Companies with high barriers to entry and high market share are in a stronger position than companies with high market share in which barriers to entry are much lower. This is an important element in overall marketing strategy. Barriers to entry reduce the level of competition in a market, often enabling higher-than-competitive prices.

Some factors that prevent competitors from entering a particular market are:

- *cost advantages* on the part of the company with market leadership, or costs that are so high that they prevent major new entrants. For example, it is relatively easy to enter the retail industry, either through purchase of a retail outlet or, increasingly, setting up as an online retailer. On the opposite extreme, entering the oil business or car production business requires a level of capital investment that deters most new entrants. Only large companies, often backed by governments, can meet the entry costs into such industries. For example, there have been relatively few new entrants to the oil, aerospace, or car manufacturing industries over and above those already established since the war.
- *sunk costs* (those that aren't recoverable) can often be a barrier to entry. If a railway owns a rail track or a water company owns a reservoir, it is very difficult for a competitor to enter the marketplace. This makes certain types of business a 'natural monopoly'—such as the provision of drinking water to a certain region. To some extent, sunk costs represent the difference between the purchase price and the resale price of capital equipment and the costs of advertising. High sunk costs will act as a barrier to entry as the cost of failure is so great. Conversely, low sunk costs will encourage firms to enter an industry, as they will have little to lose.
- *marketing costs*, as huge spending by firms leads to consumer loyalty. New entrants have to at least match this level of marketing if they wish to persuade consumers to buy their product. High marketing spending makes

it prohibitively expensive for new companies to enter the market and establish themselves. For example, the movie industry increasingly now spends equally high amounts on the marketing and merchandising of movies as it does in producing them. This makes it very difficult for small or independent movie studios to recapture their investments in movie making because they normally don't have the marketing power to secure major audiences. The vast amount spent by the perfume industry to merchandise and market its products, relative to the costs of production of a bottle of perfume, makes new entrance prohibitively expensive.

- *technological advantage*, often protected by patents, prevents competitors catching up. Increasingly, however, simple technological advantage is unlikely to be a sustainable barrier to entry unless a continuous stream of innovation supplements it.

- *monopolistic or oligopolistic practices* governing strong distribution channels that give access to end-users. An example of this has been the failure of the cable companies and telecom start-ups in Europe to compete effectively against the former state monopoly telecom providers. One of the reasons that is often cited for this is the fact that the former monopolies controlled the local loop, which was the 'last mile' of local exchange and distribution channel to domestic customers. Another example is the diamond industry, which even managed to shut out GE when it discovered a synthetic, low cost way to make diamonds.

- *the vast economies of scale* that some incumbents in industries are able to establish, meaning that the minimum efficient scale (MES) barrier to new entrants is very large. It would take many years to reach the necessary level of output. Existing firms who have the lower costs would be able to win any price war against a new entrant.

- *legislative barriers*, often created by government licences, can prevent other firms from providing services, for example, commercial television and radio, the national lottery, and the production of nuclear energy. Additionally, tariffs and quotas imposed by governments on imported goods and services can act as a barrier to entry as they prevent firms from competing in a particular national market.

- *restrictive practices*, for example a manufacturer's refusing to supply a retailer who stocks a competitor's product, or a firm refusing to sell one product unless the buyer purchases a whole range of goods.

- *pricing*, with firms lowering the price so much that competitors are driven out of the market. Also known as predatory pricing. *See also* COMPETITION; MARKET STRATEGY; PORTER, MICHAEL.

Barton, Bruce (1886–1967) A pioneer of the advertising industry in North America who worked for Batten, Barton, Durstine & Osborn (BBDO) Agency, New York. He discovered the iconic American artist Norman Rockwell and, during World War I, worked on United War Work campaigns with copywriters

Roy Durstine and Alex Osborn. They opened their ad agency in 1918, merging it in 1928 with George Batten Co. to create BBDO. BBDO became known for writing hard-hitting copy. Barton's 1925 bestseller, *The Man Nobody Knows* portrayed Jesus Christ as an advertising salesman. He also wrote many newspaper columns as well as other books and had a political career. After surviving a sensational blackmail scandal, Barton returned to BBDO in 1940.

basic human needs The amalgamation of human wants and desires in the individual, which unconsciously dictate behaviours and attitudes. At a fundamental level food, water, shelter, safety and clothing are the most basic of physical human needs. *See also* HIERARCHY OF NEEDS.

basing point pricing (delivered pricing) A system in which a buyer must pay a price for a product inclusive of freight costs that does not depend on the location of the seller. In this system, the final retail price can be the same nationally, calculated on the cost of manufacturing and packaging, but including a variable cost of transportation from storage point to retail outlet, to insure uniformity of price at point of sale.

Bayesian decision theory A statistical approach for quantifying trade-offs between various decisions using probabilities and costs that accompany such decisions. This technique is used by marketers (using statistics and probability) to make decisions, when there is lack of information or certainty on which to judge outcomes.

Beaverbrook, 1st Baron (William Maxwell Aitken) (1879–1964) Canadian-born British newspaper proprietor and Conservative politician. Born in New Brunswick, his newspapers included the *Daily Express*, which became, under his rule, one of the bestselling newspapers in the world, as well as the *Sunday Express* and the *Evening Standard*. *Hearst commented that Beaverbrook applied tabloid method to broadsheets. Beaverbrook's papers notoriously reflected his own political agenda quite closely (notably on imperial Free Trade and in favour of Edward VIII during the abdication crisis). He boasted that his newspapers were run for influence, not for profit. He said that the modern press was 'a flaming sword that will cut through any political armour'. The journalist Malcolm Muggeridge claimed that, whenever Beaverbrook felt unease at the thought of dying, his editors would commission articles proving the existence of life after death. Beaverbrook would then read the articles and be relieved of his fears. Beaverbrook was a war reporter for the Canadian government in World War I, then served in the British Cabinet as Minister for Propaganda and Information. He was elevated to the peerage by Lloyd George. Lady Astor dismissed him as 'Lord Been-A-Crook'. During World War II, he served in Churchill's war cabinet as Minister of Aircraft Production during the Battle of Britain (1940), Minister of Supply (1941–42), Minister of War Production (1942) and Lord Privy Seal (1943–45). His newspaper group was dismembered after his death in 1964. *See also* MEDIA POWER.

b

belief The underpinning value of *brand image. The set of beliefs that the consumer holds about the brand determine its overall brand image. The beliefs that the consumer holds about a brand are not necessarily aligned to what he thinks are the most important attributes of the brand. Loss of belief in a brand is perhaps more dangerous than temporary falling sales of a brand. *See also* BRAND; CONSUMER MARKETING.

below-the-line Promotions that use directly targeted marketing techniques (such as *direct selling initiatives, *database marketing, *direct mail marketing, *telemarketing and, increasingly, *interactive or 'permission' based techniques using the *Internet) as opposed to advertising in *mass media channels. Certain aspects of public relations can also qualify as below-the-line promotions. In the late 20th century, total spending on below-the-line promotions came to exceed *above-the-line promotions in the mass media. *See also* ADVERTISING; DIRECT MARKETING; PERSONAL SELLING.

benchmark A source against which one compares the area that is being researched. For example, one may compare the results of a study in one region to the results of the nation as a whole.

benchmarking A technique by which a company tries to emulate or exceed standards achieved, or processes adopted, by another company in order to improve its own performance. Sometimes referred to as best practices, exemplary practices, or business excellence, benchmarking is used in marketing to decide on *comparative advantages of *competitors and to advise on gaps in the marketplace between competitors. It can also be a collaborative process among a group of companies to focus on specific operating practices, compare measures and results and identify improved processes within their organizations. In more recent times it has become an analytical tool to help companies improve their business processes. Most business processes can be benchmarked. One of the main benefits of benchmarking is that it encourages companies to look externally and comparatively in order to find best practice and high performance and then to measure actual business operations against those goals. One of the mistakes people make when beginning their benchmarking project is that they only look to benchmark some company within their own industry. Worse yet, some people think they must benchmark their main competitor. The danger here is that the competitor is often a lower performer than the company doing the benchmarking. Therefore, only companies that show excellent performance and are well known for being a good model ought to be benchmarked. Companies initiating a benchmarking study have to decide on the most compatible company to benchmark, who they need to conduct a full benchmark study, and the best format for conducting the survey (in person, by telephone, by e-mail, or by survey instrument). Most business processes are common throughout industry. For example NASA has the same fundamental Human Resources requirements for hiring and developing employees, as does American Express. British Telecom has the same Customer Satisfaction Survey process as Brooklyn Union Gas. These processes, from different industries, are similar and can be benchmarked very effectively.

Key components of benchmarking
- data gathering in the form of detailed surveys of measures and processes;
- identification of best performers; and
- site visits to the best companies.

Benchmarking and best practices
- internally among divisions;
- within the industry; and
- outside the industry.

See also MARKET RESEARCH.

benefit The principal or major benefits sought by customers in making a *purchase decision. These benefits are different depending on the *customer segment, each of which perceives different benefits from the same *product or *service and ascribes a different values to them. Ultimately, benefits must be seen to satisfy an unmet portion of *customer need.

benefit positioning *See* POSITIONING.

benefit segmentation The idea that consumers can be grouped according to the principal benefits that they seek from products or services. Different people buy the same or similar *products for different reasons. For example, women may purchase a Volvo car for safety and comfort; men may purchase it for it durability and practicality. Use of different types of *segmentation variables could lead to the conclusion that the main criterion for segmentation is the *principal benefit sought*. Hence, although this approach acknowledges the fact that no single variable is likely to be of sufficient discriminatory power to segment a market on its own, it regards the *benefit sought* as the main variable. *See also* MARKET SEGMENTATION.

Bernays, Edward L (1891–1995) The founding father of public relations. Lacking his uncle's renown outside the world of business history, this nephew of Sigmund Freud was among the most influential people in the 20th century. Well versed in the then-new science of psychiatry and mass psychology, Bernays, from the 1920s onwards, helped to consolidate a fateful marriage between theories of mass psychology (that had previously been used by government *propaganda agencies) and schemes of corporate and political persuasion and the creation of popular consent for causes, products, and ideas. While there had been major press agencies before Bernays, he was the first to adapt the theories of psychology to the formation of mass public opinion. He defined public relations as 'a vocation applied by a social scientist who advises a client or employer on the social attitudes and actions to take to win the support of the public upon whom the viability of the client or employer depends'. He viewed the public relations professional as one of the intellectual elite shaping the opinions and consent of a democratic society. He founded his own public relations firm in New York in 1919 and he gave the first-ever lectures in public relations in New York University in the 1920s and published the seminal *Crystallizing Public Opinion* in 1923 as well as *Propaganda* (1928) and *The Engineering of Consent* (1947). Bernays, in his career, advised US Presidents Coolidge, Wilson, Hoover, and Eisenhower, legendary individuals such as Edison, Henry Ford, Eleanor Roosevelt, Freud, Caruso, Diaghilev, and Nijinsky, as well as large corporations such as General Motors, Procter & Gamble, RH Macy & Company, Cartier, MGM, and heads of government outside the US. His legendary public relations campaigns included creating favourable public opinion to America's entry into World War I, a campaign to get children to like soap, the election of Herbert Hoover, the building of Route 66 across America, the joys of having bacon for breakfast, convincing women to like Lucky Strike cigarettes in the 1930s, then in a famous volte-face, creating anti-smoking campaigns when the link between smoking and cancer was made in the 1960s.

Bernays, who died aged 103 in 1995, became extremely concerned at the 'monster' that he had helped to create. 'Public relations today is horrible. Any dope, any nitwit, any idiot can call him or herself a public relations practitioner. Some people just use public relations as a euphemism for press agentry,' he declared. 'A firm sends articles or press releases to newspapers to win favour for a client and it usually ends up in the trash. It's not only not good PR; it intensifies the antagonism toward the product. I'm pleased to be known as the father of public relations when the field is taken seriously, like law or architecture.' *See also* PUBLIC RELATIONS.

Bernbach, William (1911–82) The joint founder of the Doyle Dane Bernbach agency in New York in 1949. Often regarded as the most influential figure in the 20th-century advertising industry, Bernbach is remembered for his creative campaigns characterized by their freshness, relevance, lack of pretension, and tonal harmony between product and copy. 'Advertising doesn't create a product advantage. It can only convey it', was a typical Bernbach view of the advertising industry. He was an advocate of advertising as an art form and the (then) radical notion that the general public was intelligent. Underlying respect for the public, in his view, would encourage favourable reactions to intelligent and imaginative advertising. Bernbach always insisted on first learning how his client's products related to their users, and what human qualities and emotions came into play. The next stage was to decide on how best to communicate those elements to the consumers through various media channels, gaining the consumers' understanding and support. His most legendary campaign was for Volkswagen's introduction to the USA, involving a range of print and TV commercials. In print, VW's 'Think Small' ad challenged the acquisitive tendencies that had been characteristic of American advertising in the 1950s. The Beetle became the first successful import car and the ad campaign altered the overall approach to advertising for all time. He had very successful TV advertising campaigns: Volkswagen's 'Funeral' and 'Snow plow' stories as part of the overall Volkswagen campaign; 'Mamma mia' and 'Poached oyster' for Alka-Seltzer; 'Visit to Grandpa' plus Laurence Olivier for Polaroid; 'Italian wedding' for Rheingold beer; 'Mikey' for Life cereal; 'Gorilla' for American Tourister luggage; 'Card game' and 'Sharing,' with Jack Gilford, for Cracker Jack; 'Burning egg' for GTE; and stop-motion 'Contrasts' for the Jamaica Tourist Board. *See also* ADVERTISING; BRAND. *See* APPENDIX 2 for more on the Volkswagen campaign.

beyond-the-banner Online advertising not involving standard GIF and JPEG banner ads. *See also* BANNER AD; POP-UP WINDOWS.

bias The opposite of detached objectivity. There can be biased questions, biased responses, or biased samples within market research. Biased questions occur when the questions are slanted in such a way as to elicit a particular response from the *respondent. Biased questions can occur from the way the questions are phrased. Bias can also be introduced from an interviewer's facial or body expressions. A biased response occurs when the respondent says something that is not true. Biased responses can be made consciously or subconsciously. A biased sample occurs when the sample used is not representative of the population. *See also* MARKET RESEARCH.

bidding The process in which potential suppliers submit their offers (or tenders) in response to a published requirement. This process is normally competitive. Competitive bidding is one dimension of selling, particularly in a *business-to-business market. There are always judgements to be made around the balance of value, price, actual cost, and the desire to win the contract. For many, the physical and oral presentation of the tender to the potential client is the 'sharp end' of marketing, when the potential client judges all attributes of the potential supplier, including the specific proposal. Competitive bidding principally benefits the *buyer, given that it creates an impartial environment that is likely to drive value for money efficiency. It also helps to 'educate' the buyer by giving him a lot of information on various *competitors and their offerings. This process is increasing for large-scale purchases, and is almost mandatory for large government contracts. *See also* SALES.

billboard The board on which posters, or bills, are pasted. It can also be known as a hoarding or *poster site. Billboards can be placed at the side of buildings on a near-permanent basis. They are often used in conjunction with other media. The billboard is one of the oldest *advertising media and is still among the most popular.

billing A marketing term that tends to be used as a measure of a marketing agency's (particularly an advertising agency's) total revenues. In an advertising agency it is the term used for the total value of business undertaken by the agency.

billing rate The individual price of each expert in an agency charged externally, usually on an hourly or a daily basis.

bipolar scale A scale used for a range of responses with the extremes at opposite ends and more moderate responses in the middle.

It forces the *respondent to make some sort of choice rather than to stay neutral. An example of a bipolar scale would be the following choices:

1 Unacceptable;
2 Somewhat unacceptable;
3 Somewhat acceptable;
4 Very acceptable.

A four-point scale is useful if what is being measured does not have absolutes. Many researchers stay away from five-point scales because respondents frequently choose the middle (3) or average response if they do not have a strong leaning one way or another.

bivariate data A data set where there are two sets of variables.

black box A model of consumer behaviour in which the mind of the consumer is likened to a 'black box' that cannot be penetrated to find out what is inside. Such models focus on the input or stimulus (for example, advertising) and the response or output (purchase behaviour). *See also* CONSUMER BEHAVIOUR.

black hat SEO (black hat search engine optimization) A set of techniques that is used to get higher search rankings in an unethical manner and designed to obtain short-term gains in terms of search rankings. If discovered, the use of this technique carries the risk of being penalized by search engines. Some examples of black hat SEO techniques include keyword stuffing, invisible text, and doorway pages. Spamdexing is a typical frequently used black hat SEO practice. *See also* WHITE HAT SEO.

blanket coverage Promotions and *advertising without prior *market segmentation or targeting of a specific audience or type of customer. Typically used in mass consumer goods or *awareness creation campaigns.

bleed A picture or ad that extends beyond the normal margins of print on a page, to the edge of the page.

blind product testing An evaluation of a product based on an opinion formed by the *respondent who is unaware of the brand.

bliss point The equilibrium point of a *consumer's total satisfaction for a good that is consumed within their budget limit.

blitzkrieg advertising A technique used in advertising in which an advertising placement is concentrated in the media for an intensive and short period of time. This is used to gain rapid awareness or a quick response from an audience. *See also* ADVERTISING.

blog An abbreviated term for a weblog. A blog, or the act of 'blogging' is defined by its existence and transmission rather than by a predetermined format. In essence, it is a highly personalized point of view, usually written chronologically, on a defined subject area, and posted on a website that hosts fellow 'bloggers'. A blog can take the form of a personal log, journal, or diary, and often intersperses personal emotions with the specific subject matter. Most 'blogging' discussions are moderated. The benefit to the 'blogger' is the sharp and near instant feedback received from fellow bloggers. Blogging can be interpreted as 'Internet journalism' (many leading print journalists now have personal blogs), or how the *Internet has enabled individuals to go beyond the traditional journalism of the printed page, or, less favourably, as vanity publishing enabled by the Internet and the World Wide Web. *See also* WEB 2.0.

blogosphere The online community of people who write *blogs, known as bloggers, whose principal motivations are self expression and sharing of expertise and personal experiences. The term blogosphere was coined by Brad Graham in 1999 and propagated more widely by William Quirk. The blogosphere is constantly expanding as *blogging has become ubiquitous, effective, and authentic; the blogosphere is important to both *opinion forming and promotion of expertise. Inhabitants of the blogosphere universe are both amateur and professional. A recent element of the blogosphere's expansion is the use of social media, such as *Twitter to promote individual blogs, particularly by professional bloggers.

bluetooth A technology that wirelessly connects devices and lets them share information such as music and pictures.

blurb A short description of a book that appears on the cover. It can also mean the effusive endorsements of a book or a play, or a film that are usually printed on the cover or poster.

body copy The text of a print ad, not including the headline, logo, or subscript material.

body language The movement and gestures of the body that communicate to another person non-verbally. There are two aspects of body language; voluntary and involuntary. Voluntary body language comprises movements, gestures, and poses that a person makes with full or partial intention (for example smiling or hand movements). Involuntary body language often takes the form of a facial expression. This suggests that one is engaged with the emotions of the person one is communicating with (for example raising the eyebrow often means one is skeptical or surprised). Body language is very important for marketers to study and understand, particularly those engaged in *customer research and interviewing.

BOGOFF The acronym of 'buy one get one free' and mnemonic phrase for a promotional practice in which when one product is purchased another is given to the *consumer for free.

boilerplate A standard copy used in different formats, such as company descriptions in *press releases and marketing documents. Boilerplate copy tends to be reproduced in multiple formats and for multiple reasons.

bonus pack A product that comes with an additional smaller package of its kind, but sold at the price originally set for the standard pack.

booklet A small and concise version of a larger text, often presented in bound or leaflet form. Alternatively, it could be a short piece of presentational material summarizing essential features and benefits.

bookmark A link stored in a web browser for future reference. It is the main way in which people personalize their favourite sources of information on the vast *World Wide Web.

boom *See* BUSINESS CYCLE.

boomerang effect A strong counter-reaction when there is a deliberate attempt to change an *attitude (resulting in a strengthening or adoption of the attitude that the marketer was attempting to change) or, when a *product is marketed very hard, it can sometimes alienate the consumer so much that it results in them deliberately purchasing an alternative or rival product.

booth An exhibition stand in which products and services or other information are displayed or demonstrated. A whole section of the marketing industry has grown out of the renting and display of conference booths—it is particularly important in both consumer products and services and industrial business-to-business markets.

bootlegging Originally slang for the concealment of contraband goods inside a boot, the term has come to be applied to the illicit distribution of regulated or copyrighted material. Bootlegging remains a practice in many areas where there is strong regulatory activity or prohibition is in force. Most recently the bootlegging or 'piracy' of CDs and *DVDs or music recording and films has become an illicit trade on a global scale. The

*Internet has created many more options for bootlegging and has caused its proliferation.

Boston Consulting Group (BCG) matrix

A model developed by the consultancy of the same name in the 1970s. It is focused on the cash flows generated by products' and businesses' portfolios as a result of relative market share and growth. Market share is measured relative to the product's largest competitor. This technique became a staple of market strategies in the 1980s. In the Boston matrix products are classified according to their ability to either generate or to consume cash. These are the main categories with their famous labels for each dimension of the matrix.

- **Cash cow,** a product or business with high market share and low market growth;
- **Dog,** one with a low market share and low growth;
- **Problem child** (or **question mark**), one with low market share and high growth potential;
- **Star,** one having high growth and growing market share, but not as high a share and therefore not as cash generative as a cash cow.

The matrix is not static and the interrelationship between the various classifications makes the model very useful, particularly for developing market strategies. For example: stars are businesses or products with outstanding opportunities that do not generate excess cash because they are still growing market share in face of competition. They may well be self-financing. Stars of today may become the cash cows of the future. Excess cash is provided by the cash cows that are entering a period of low growth in mature markets but which need relatively little cash investment. Cash cows are assumed to enjoy lower cost, economies of scale, and high profit margins. Dogs, by contrast, have low market shares in low-growth markets and tend to generate either a loss or a relatively low profit. They typically take up more management time than warranted and, unless they can be strategically justified, such as contributing to overheads, are potential candidates for divestment. Problem children (or question marks) need considerable cash investment because they have a low relative share but high growth prospects. They are therefore cash users and could become stars of the future. Management must choose between further speculative investment and even withdrawal, depending on their prospects in their target markets.

The BCG remains a useful framework for portfolio analysis. It has, since the 1980s, been subject to various criticisms of its shortcomings and has become less reliable as a framework for practical marketing action. The main criticism levelled at the matrix is the assumption that all of a company's products and business units work in an interconnected life

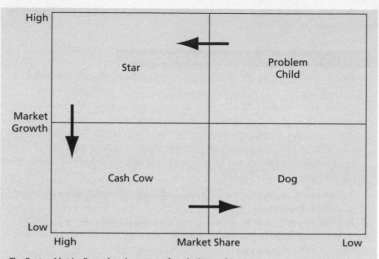

The Boston Matrix. Reproduced courtesy of marketingteacher.com

cycle. In this life cycle, the mature and profitable funds and fuels the new and growing while the old falters and eventually is terminated. Another one of the problems that practitioners have with the BCG matrix is that it is difficult to delineate and define what a 'market' is, and, consequently, to measure market share precisely. It does not take into account technological discontinuities that can alter the entire shape and dynamics of a marketplace within a very short space of time. Beyond that, some critics have also pointed out the underlying assumption that cash generation is always organic with a company and does not take into account many other 'inorganic' or external cash generating instruments that are available which could affect a portfolio and market position. Also, one would have to be careful in its uses—particularly using it as a guide to divestments and product withdrawals—as it offers an overly simplistic formula to determine 'dog' status. General Electric Corporation developed a more sophisticated analytical matrix model (known as the GE matrix) that used *industry attractiveness* and *business strengths* as the main axes of analysis.

bounce rate A term used in *website traffic analysis. It represents the percentage of initial visitors to a site who 'bounce' away to a different site, rather than continue on to other pages within the same site. The formula used to calculate bounce rate is: Bounce Rate = Total Number of Visits Viewing Only One Page divided by Total Number of Visits.

boutique A specialist agency or consultancy that employs experts and creative specialists who offer a range of discrete marketing and professional services, such as market strategy, branding, or creative writing.

boycott The refusal of a government or public groups and consumers to buy certain goods from a country or company.

brainstorming A technique both for concept generation and creative problem-solving. It tends to involve a group of people who generate ideas related to a particular topic or issue. When in a group brainstorm, participants are expected and encouraged to share their ideas as soon as they are generated, and the others in the group are not expected to pass critical judgement or comment in order to allow a free flow of ideas. The essence of brainstorming is to allow the imaginative thought process to run freely, and as an idea comes to mind it is captured and then used as a stimulant for the development of additional and better ideas. The aim is to list as many ideas as possible and no criticism or discussion is allowed until all ideas are gathered. These ideas are then reviewed critically after the brainstorming session. The session is usually moderated by a facilitator whose role is to encourage and to capture ideas.

brand

A combination of attributes that gives a company, organization product, service concept, or even an individual, a distinctive identity and value relative to its competitors, its advocates, its stakeholders, and its customers. The attributes that make a brand are both tangible and intangible: a name, a visual logo or trademark, products, services, people, a personality, reputation, brand loyalty, mental associations, culture, and inherent values which, together, create a memorable, reassuring, and relevant brand image in the eye and mind of the beholder. The overall value of brand to the business results in what is often known as *brand equity.

The relationship between consumer and brand is often emotional rather than rational. The brand is often something that lives as a perception in the mind of the beholder. As the famous advertising guru Leo Burnett said in 1955, 'Before you can have share of market, you must have share of mind'. Branding facilitates memory recall, thus contributing to preferred selection and improving customer loyalty. Also, brands can be more enduring. *Products have life cycles; brands can last forever.* That was the argument made in 1931 by Neil McElroy to executives of Procter & Gamble Co. when he advanced the vision that each brand within the package-goods company needed to be managed by a team whose sole focus was driving that brand into a No. 1 position in its category. At the time this was a revolutionary idea, because until then

b

marketing had been about pushing products through retail channels to customers—and branding was viewed as making this an easier process. This would make the brand an area of marketing promotions against which investments were made in order to create the supreme market position. Moreover, and this certainly proved to be the case with Procter & Gamble, it assured certain brands enduring distinctiveness. This formed the basis of what is now known as *brand management, one of the more powerful functions of marketing.

In the 1990s brands took on a new dimension of meaning. Branding became the most powerful aspect of the marketing mix. Advertising spending, which increased exponentially after the early 1990s' recession, fuelled the cult of branding. Brand expanded its frontiers. Companies used advertising and sponsorship to develop *brand meaning* rather than simply using brand to push products and services. Companies invested heavily in brand to the extent that their products and services (once the centrepiece of their marketing efforts) became merely tools in promoting the overall brand values, experience, and personality. For example, companies such as Nike, Apple, and the Body Shop developed the notion in the 1990s that buying their otherwise ordinary and basic products was a lifestyle statement and choice, endowed with higher meaning than simple satisfaction of customer need for simple consumable goods. Branding started to extend beyond the product and services themselves and into the entire retail outlet and often the public space itself. Suddenly, there appeared entire stores dedicated to Nike, the Gap, and Disney, selling only one branded range. More and more ingenious ways are found to completely encircle the consumer with the brand experience and personality. The management guru, Tom Peters, even produced a book advising on how to make oneself a brand.

Distinctive and successful brands usually have the following qualities:

1 They are differentiated from competing brands. In an age of increased customer choice, over-supply, and growing clutter and clamour in the marketplace, a differentiated brand (and the investment that is required to build and grow it) is necessary to survival and prosperity. The more that brands can meet, and even exceed expectations that customers have of them, the deeper the trust; the longer the survival, the greater the value of the brand.

2 They are both relevant and desirable to their target market. They have a deep emotional resonance with their customers (rather than just vast recognition and awareness of name and logo). Great brands are usually perceived to have some involvement in the fabric of consumers' lives by the consumers themselves. GE always promoted the idea that its products and services touched multiple aspects of American daily lives and made them easier.

3 They enjoy public esteem and have a 'legendary' status, perhaps having passed from generation to generation. There is constant investment in keeping them fresh without departing from the core values of the brand. Occasionally, their decline and revival contribute to the mythology of the brand. Examples include Perrier's perilous situation when benzene was discovered in the drink and it was recalled; Coca-Cola's near-disastrous attempt to change its flavour and its dramatic recovery of its position after mass protest; and Apple's role in the creation of the PC market, then its decline, followed by its revival in the late 1990s with the innovative iMac designs then followed by their development of the iPod, iPhone, iPad, iTunes range.

4 The very great brand can dominate and change the nature of an entire segment of the market. Examples are IBM's domination of the information technology market for most of the second half of the 20th century; Kodak's domination of camera film processing; and Disney's constant pushing back the frontiers of family entertainment since the 1930s.

5 At the more advanced levels the greatest brands ultimately become global brands, even if their origins are very national. For example, Kodak, Coca-Cola, McDonald's, Sony, Disney, Microsoft, Rolls-Royce, BMW, Volkswagen, Gucci, Ferrari, the BBC, Mercedes, Nike, and Intel all began as domestic, national brand names and have now become global.

Brands that have such emotional resonance, personality, and customer connection can have huge power and economic value. A typical measure of such brand strength is the ability to command a price premium, to inspire customer loyalty, or to dominate a market through higher market share.

There are many reasons to have a strong brand and branding strategy. A strong brand gives a product or service a sustainable advantage in a competitive market, market share increase and, often, economies of scale and improved profitability. Brands differentiate and subsume products and services. Brand helps to create an acceptance of and intimacy with the product and service in the target consumer. Brand reduces price pressures, particularly against competing products of similar quality. They ensure longevity and repeatability and diminish risk. For marketing management purposes, a strong brand enables greater negotiating power with channels of distribution; display space is more easily obtained and point-of-sale promotions for branded product can be made more prominent in retail outlets. Companies can use strong brand names to increase their shareholder value. The brand is the bellwether of a company's reputation. Some of the most recognized brands such as

Disney, Microsoft, Dell, Sony, Nike, and Mercedes Benz have vastly
increased their market value. Nike, for example, during the promotion of
the Just Do It advertising campaign, saw its market value increase from
$750 m in 1987 to $4 bn in 1994.

In addition to regular advertising activities, companies also use
corporate sponsorship to increase brand awareness. Companies sponsor
charity events, the arts, sporting events and venues, as well as various
tournaments. Corporate sponsorship provides a double dose of
advertising and brand awareness. People attending the event become
more aware of the corporate brand. In addition, as a corporate sponsor, a
company will typically have access to special lounges or areas or may
have a table at a dinner. This provides a good opportunity to bring
existing or potential clients to these events and build a rapport that can
also lead to more business.

Other advantages of branding include obtaining legal protection for
products and services. Branding also makes it easier to link advertising to
other marketing communication programmes and it can reduce the
overall cost of personal selling and persuasion. Finally, a strong brand
gives a foundation from which a company can launch new products and
services as extensions of the brand. For further cases of iconic brand case
studies *see* APPENDIX 2.

brand cannibalization The extent to which one brand gains recognition
and esteem at the expense of other similar brands from the same company.

brand collaboration (brand co-branding) The bringing together of two
well-known brands to endorse a new product or service in which they have a
mutual interest.

brand descriptor A specific attribute, offering, or benefit of the *brand.

brand environment The physical manifestations of the brand, such as the
graphics, logo, and their application to physical space. It is important for a
brand to have consistency of design, look, and feel, whatever the environment
in which it is projected. A brand has to be displayed in the right environment
and in the right media. There has to be harmony between them.

brand equity The value added to a range of products and services that is
over and above the net book value of the company, or the cash flow from
products and services with the brand name compared with the cash flow
without the brand name. The effects of strong equity can manifest
themselves in the overall value of a company or in the higher prices that a
company can charge for its products and services. Brand strength has a
direct impact on revenues and profits and can only be sustained with

appropriate levels of investments in sustaining and growing it. So far, despite multiple models that can quantify brand valuation in monetary values, there is as yet no single, universally agreed methodology to measure the value of a brand.

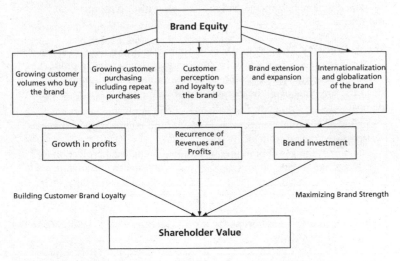

Brand Equity Components

brand equity The total value that the brand brings to a company over and above its net book value.

brand essence The expression of the total attributes, tangible and intangible, of a brand as a core concept.

brand experience The total experience the customers have of the branded product and service. For example, Virgin Atlantic view the total customer experience for business class customers as an end-to-end experience. Customers are picked up from their departure point by a limousine, they are checked in without leaving the car, they go to the well-branded Virgin lounges where they enjoy complimentary food, drinks, shoeshines, massages, haircuts, manicures, and pedicures; where they can listen to music, work on their computer, use a small office, make calls, surf the Internet, and read in the library. In the flight itself, there is also a complimentary massage and manicure service. Some planes have an open stand-up bar, as well as a wide range of food that can be taken at any time, innovative entertainment, and then a complimentary limousine pick-up after checking through customs to go to the final destination.

brand extension The use of an existing brand for a new product or service offering a distinctive benefit to a new set of target customers.

The belief is that the core attributes and essence of the original brand can be transferred to a new product or service. French couturiers such as Dior and Chanel have been particularly adept at extending their brand name to perfume and retail goods and apparel. Disney has extended its brand, developed in film, into theme parks, holidays, cruise ships, merchandise, and resorts.

brand identity The way in which various elements of a brand are made to appear externally, by means of a corporate logo or symbol, a product, service, packaging, slogan, or a physical environment. This can also mean the sum total of all the elements of branding that make the unique identity.

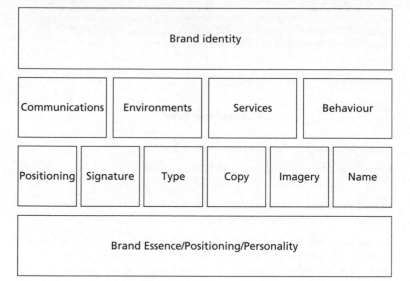

Fundamental Elements of Brand Management Systems

brand identity model This was developed by David A Aaker, leading *brand theorist, in his 1996 book *Building Strong Brands*. Aaker developed a planning model which outlines four dimensions of brand identity:

Brand as product can be a single *product, or set of products, which will affect the type of associations of the brand that *customers experience. For customers, the *attributes directly related to the purchase or use of a product can be both functional benefits and emotional benefits. Examples may be Kleenex tissues, or Band Aid, or Gillette razors. A product-related attribute can create a *value proposition by offering extras like features or services. Aaker argues, however, that the goal of linking a brand with a product is for customers to remember the brand when they have a need that can be met by the product's attributes.

Brand as an organization focuses on organizational attributes such as, for example, *innovation, quality, and safety, that are created by people, culture, values, and programmes within the company. Aaker states that organizational attributes are more enduring and resistant to *competitors than *product attributes. Examples may be IBM, Kodak, and Exxon.

Brand as a person where the brand is perceived as having a personal dimension, with a unique personality similar to an individual. Aaker cites three ways a brand personality can create a stronger brand: a) a vehicle for customers to express their own personalities; b) forming the basis of a relationship between customers and the brand; and c) helping to communicate a product or service attribute in a personal way. An example may be Tiger Woods exemplifying mastery, Mercedes exemplifying elegant status and accomplishment, Apple exemplifying innovation, or Nike conveying energy and determination to succeed.

Brand as a symbol Aaker describes this dimension as three types of symbols: a) visual imagery, b) metaphors, and c) the brand heritage. A memorable symbol can provide cohesion and structure to a brand identity and make it much easier to gain *recognition and *recall. Its presence can be a key ingredient of brand development and its absence can be a substantial handicap. Elevating symbols to the status of being part of the identity reflects their potential power. Examples could be the Olympic rings for a movement or where a symbol epitomizes the company, such as the Ronald McDonald clown for McDonald's, the Jolly Green Giant, or the meerkats in Comparethemarket.com

The purpose of the brand identity planning system is to use the different brand elements and patterns that can help enrich and *differentiate a brand identity. Aaker summarized his Brand Identity System as a model.

Each brand can employ one or many of these dimensions of identity. Each organization should, however, consider all of the dimensions in the development of a differentiated brand identity.

Brand identity consists of a core identity and an extended *identity. The former represents the timeless essence of the brand. This is central to both the meaning and success of the brand, and contains the associations that are most likely to remain constant. The extended identity includes elements that provide 'texture and completeness'.

brand image The perception of the brand in the minds of consumers. One of the major roles of *brand management is to create positive perceptions in the minds of target customer groups; these perceptions constitute the brand image. A key measure of the success of the brand image is the preference that customers show towards this brand over other competing brands. This is closely connected to *brand loyalty and repeat purchases of the branded products and services by the customer.

brand interactive (interactive branding) The use of websites and interactive techniques to enhance the overall power of the brand.

brand loyalty A measure of the consumers' unwillingness to switch to a competing product or service. Successful brands are characterized by high levels of customer satisfaction and repeat purchases of the branded goods or service by existing customers over a long period of time. The cost of winning new customers is much higher than retaining and cross selling to existing customers, so brand loyalty is an important economic factor in profitable brand development. There are several methods of measuring customers' brand loyalty and preference, but few of the methods have managed to capture all the factors involved in the decision. For example, straightforward repeat purchase measurement does not always capture customers' purchase of other brands. Also, customers may be loyal to a brand because choice is limited, special pricing deals are used, or the brand dominates a given channel of distribution.

brand loyalty segmentation *See* MARKET SEGMENTATION.

brand management A range of marketing disciplines focused on treating the brand as a managed asset. This is indispensable to the longevity of a brand. Brands do not 'naturally' survive and prosper; they have to be actively managed and invested in. The brand is perishable unless investment continues and it is actively managed through a range of appropriate managed programmes. The brand can act as the focal point for the entire range of marketing activities. Successful brands have a strong, well-integrated brand management system that covers all aspects and dimensions of the brand as an asset, as a guide to action and behaviour, and with a full range of protection over the use of the brand both by the brand owner and by associated third parties.

brand mark (brand icon, brand symbol) The part of an overall brand that can be recognized but which is not written as the brand name. These symbols or characters give instant recognition of the brand. Examples are the Metro-Goldwyn-Mayer roaring lion, the Nike swoosh, Mickey Mouse, the Marlboro Man, Tony the Tiger, the Coca-Cola dynamic curve, and the Michelin man (from 1898).

brand name Letters, words or groups of words, which can be written or spoken. Names can include a manufacturer's name in which the brand name is owned by the company making the individual branded product (e.g. Dulux, Persil, Maxwell House); a family brand name in which the brand is projected onto all products sold by the company (e.g. Microsoft, Kodak, Heinz, Campbell's); a category brand name for a range of products within the same category, such as household appliances (e.g. Hotpoint, Hoover, Whirlpool) or a specific product name combined with the company name (e.g. Mars Bar, Hershey Bar, Kellogg's Corn Flakes). A private label brand is one in which the company making the product does not have title to the brand name.

Most brand names are legally protected trademarks. One of the more famous brands, Coca-Cola, is fiercely protected, but it cannot have exclusive use of the second part of the name, cola, because this is viewed as a generic category name that is now used by many competitors. Generic names are difficult to protect because legal and regulatory authorities view them as being in the public domain. The same applies to names of cities, rivers, countries, and mountains.

Selection of new brand names has become increasingly complex. A new brand name with trademark now must also be registered for use as a website or domain name on the *Internet. There are hundreds of millions of commercial domain names already registered on the Internet. This narrows the chances of creating a new name that is clear and descriptive of the product or service. As a result, new or rebranded companies often sport a range of fanciful or compound names with no direct relevance to the product or service delivered. *See also* LOGO; TRADEMARK.

brand revitalization The injection by a company of new energy into its brand, either by changing its overall positioning, or by investment in regenerating the various types of brand execution. Inevitably, all brands become tired and revitalization becomes necessary. For example, Volkswagen AG's new brand strategy for Audi is to market it as a sportier brand. In the past, Audi had been viewed as too conservative. Audi is now developing high-performance cars that challenge BMW as part of a brand revitalization strategy to make Audi a premium luxury brand in Europe, thereby differentiating itself from the other VW brands. Lucozade, formerly perceived as a medicinal drink usually administered to people recovering from colds and flu, was completely revitalized and repositioned and is now known as a high-energy drink for athletes. Harley-Davidson, once the motorbike of choice of Hell's Angels, then languishing in the shadow of Japanese and European motorcycle brands, kicked itself into life as a lifestyle choice for prosperous, active, middle-aged Americans, with an entire range of Harley-Davidson clothes, accessories, restaurants, and retail outlets.

brand strategy A necessary element in the development of a successful brand. The brand must be closely aligned to the company's overall business strategy and market positioning. It must be integrated into all other marketing and communications programmes. Objectives for the brand are set and an investment plan for the brand is created. Positioning, or repositioning, is at the heart of a successful brand strategy. A full brand communication strategy and programme is developed to build awareness of the brand attributes. If it is a consumer brand, this will involve a sales incentive programme, trade promotions, merchandising, and retail display to create brand recognition and customer demand for the brand. A wide distribution network must be built up and the brand must be made known and understandable to the retailers. Finally, full ranges of evaluations are put in place in including sales volumes, cost efficiencies, volume building, and improved profits.

brand switching The movement from one brand preference to another. Potential reasons for brand switching are: dissatisfaction with the current brand and its experiences; curiosity about another brand, possibly a newer one; an inducement to move from one brand to another; availability of a new or substitute brand, often making claims of superior performance or benefit; a move to multiple brand choices for reasons of variety, risk management, price consciousness, or simple indifference; coping with multiple preferences in the buyer group or as a way of capitalizing on various brand promotions at the same time.

brand valuation The premium attributed over and above a company's net book value, often taken as a part of the goodwill value of a company. This collection of intangible value added is often known as the brand value, or equity. In the modern economy, brand is one of the major intangible assets to which marketers can directly contribute. There is much debate on the right way to value a brand, and this is compounded by the fact that there are different methods and standards of accounting in each country. Although there are many theories and techniques for valuing a brand, there is no single agreed method of valuation that is supported by accountants to include it on the balance sheet. A method for this is Interbrand Brand Equity Model and Young and Rub. *See also* BRAND EQUITY.

(⊕) SEE WEB LINKS

• Interbrand list of the world's most valuable brands using their valuation methods

breakeven analysis The study of the interrelationships between costs, sales volume, and prices at various levels of activity. The breakeven point is the time at which the fixed and variable costs involved in the production and distribution of a product are matched by its overall sales: the point at which total costs are exactly equal to revenues. Beyond this point, when revenues exceed total costs, there lies profitability.

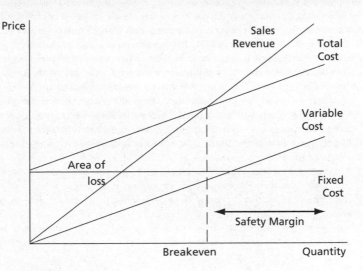

Breakeven analysis

To understand the breakeven analysis it is necessary to appreciate fixed and variable costs:

Examples of costs that are typically 'fixed':

- salaries of personnel
- sales administration
- advertising investments ('*above-the-line')
- capital costs, such as building and plant

Examples of costs that are typically 'variable':

- commissions to agents and brokers and salesmen
- delivery costs
- after-sales maintenance and service
- credit
- order processing
- invoicing
- non-advertising marketing costs ('*below-the-line')

In physical volume terms, the usual formula for the breakeven point is:

$$\text{breakeven point} = \frac{\text{Fixed cost}}{(\text{Sales revenue} - \text{Variable cost})/\text{Units sold}}$$

The main purposes of a breakeven analysis for a marketer are to provide information about cost behaviour for new product marketing activities and to determine specific decision-making. A marketer of a new product needs to know what volume of sales is needed at any given budgeted sales price in order to break even. The product marketer needs to identify the 'risk' in the budget by measuring the margin and to calculate the effects on profit of changes in variable cost, cost of sales ratios, sales price, and volume and product mix.

Care should be taken in applying the breakeven analysis to real-life marketing, particularly in a dynamic market environment. The breakeven point contains some risky assumptions: for example, sales prices are assumed to be constant and fixed costs are assumed to remain stable. A breakeven calculation only holds for circumstances where efficiency remains constant, notwithstanding increased productivity. Since there is a direct relationship between purchases and sales, then all that is manufactured can actually be sold and the sales and marketing mix will be maintained at the same levels throughout the initial launch.

Although the breakeven analysis lends itself to product marketing, it can also be applied to services. For example, if a company is arranging a large entertainment event, it is important to know how the fixed and variable costs of producing and marketing the event are linked to the sale of tickets to the event. Dividing the fixed and variable costs of an event will give an indication of how many tickets need to be sold and at what price in order to make the event break even.

bridge A transition from one scene to another in a commercial advertisement or programme.

brief A concise and short statement of strategy, positioning, objectives, factual information that is agreed between a client organization and its marketing agency as a prerequisite to a campaign being formulated. *See also* ADVERTISING.

Brin, Sergey (1973–) A Russian-American computer scientist and businessman who, along with Larry *Page, is best known as the co-founder of *Google, Inc., the world's largest *Internet search and database company. *See also* APPENDIX 2 on Google.

broadband The various transmission technologies that enable users to view content across the *Internet such as large files and multimedia such as video, audio, and 3D. Broadband can also refer to an increased ability to do so. (The term narrowband can refer to the inability to do so.) A user's broadband capability is typically governed by the connection to the home, the connection between the service provider and the user. As broadband becomes more widely available to consumers and businesses, it will enable new types of media and marketing techniques, as well as becoming a much more widely used commercial channel for the delivery of digitized products and services. The advent of mass availability of broadband connections at increasingly higher speeds that are 'always on' has had a profound effect on direct marketing.

broadcast media An *advertising technique that uses media such as radio and television that reach target audiences using airwaves as the transmission medium. Broadcast media advertising remains the most expensive form of advertising because it reaches the largest audiences. *See* MEDIA CHANNELS.

broadsheet A British term for a quality newspaper, usually to contrast with the lower quality 'tabloid'. The terms originally referred to the size of the newspaper, a broadsheet newspaper being twice the size of a tabloid. The broadsheet places its emphasis on the information, features, and analysis of national public affairs, international stories, business, culture, arts, and intellectual and sports commentary. The distinction between the two types of newspapers is beginning to become blurred as publishers of quality newspapers such as the *Guardian*, the *Independent*, and *The Times* in the UK have realized that tabloid newspapers are easier to read and hold and that, in general, fewer people buy newspapers for news headlines and bulletins, and that attention spans of readers are shortening.

brochures An everyday form of *advertising. Like *catalogues, they are usually portable, either mailed directly or handed over in person. This medium is very dominant for physical products, professional services, and tourist holiday sales. *See* MEDIA CHANNELS.

broker A market intermediary whose function is to bring buyers and sellers together and to assist in negotiation. A broker assumes no risk, does not finance deals, and does not take title to goods. The party on whose initiative they are acting usually pays them. *See also* AGENTS; CHANNELS OF DISTRIBUTION.

brown goods A term, now largely outdated, to describe those domestic appliances that used to be encased in brown veneer, such as old radios, televisions, and Hi-Fi systems. With the advent of multi-coloured plastics this term has only historical interest. This contrasts with *white goods, which continues to be a relevant term for domestic appliances.

browser Abbreviation of 'web browser', a software application used to locate and display *web pages. Currently, the two most popular browsers are Internet Explorer and Firefox. Both of these are graphical browsers, meaning that they can display graphics as well as text. In addition, most modern browsers can present multimedia information, including sound and video.

B2B (business to business) A term referring to an enterprise that sells products or provides services to other businesses rather than to consumers. Examples would be an aerospace engine company such as Rolls-Royce or GE selling aircraft engines to the world's leading airline carriers, or a management consultancy selling strategic advice to major banks or industrial manufacturers. Intel is also a business-to-business company that sells semiconductor components for information machines and systems, yet manages to have a visible brand.

B2C (business to consumer) A term referring to a business that sells products or provides services to the end-user consumers or audiences. Examples would be food retailers, cinemas, domestic appliance retailers, or individual life insurance providers.

built-in obsolescence (planned obsolescence) A policy of deliberately planning or designing a product with a finite lifespan, so it will become obsolete or non-functional after a certain period. Planned obsolescence is often used to tempt the customer to purchase again. Cars, computers, and software are good examples of products with built-in obsolescence.

bundling (bundle pricing) The technique of combining different products and services at a unified price in order to achieve market prominence, to outsmart or destabilize a competitor, or to reward valuable customers or buyers. Bundling involves combinations of products, or products and services (for example 'free' software bundled with a PC), often at discounted or tiered prices. In service businesses the need to add greater value to the customer often leads to 'extras' being bundled into the price of the core service offering. For example, a cable company may offer free telephone services and Internet connection time to those subscribers who buy a digital television package. However, at another extreme, some service industries, seeing the larger profit potential, go in for 'unbundling' of services in which individual services are separated out and priced, allowing consumers to mix and match their service purchases. *See also* PRICING.

buried position The position of an ad between other ads in a print publication, so that readers are less likely to see it.

Burnett, Leo (1892–1971) The founder of the Leo Burnett Advertising Agency, headquartered in Chicago, in 1935. Founder of the 'Chicago School' of advertising, Burnett, brought drama to advertising through shared emotions and experiences drawn from mid-western American values. He created such famous brand icons as the Jolly Green Giant, Pillsbury Doughboy, Charlie the Tuna, and Tony the Tiger. His Marlboro campaign, a legendary, if controversial, example of advertising's power to build a global brand, ultimately became a target for legislative restrictions on tobacco industry marketing. *See also* ADVERTISING.

burst campaign *See* ADVERTISING.

business cycle (trade cycle) The periodic fluctuation of levels of economic activity that affects overall output, profitability, productivity, and employment. At a macroeconomic level the business cycle is the cyclical, periodic, or regular fluctuations of economic activity and income through boom, downturn, recession, and upturn. Finally, the business cycle can be a definition of the progression of events from business formation that starts with the establishment of a new business, products, or services and continues through their growth, maturity, and decline. It has many parallels with the *product life cycle.

An understanding of the business cycle is particularly important to market planning and investment. Below are general elements and characteristics of the business cycle and the different types of marketing management technique that may be used in its various phases:

- *downturn* is a period when consumer demand starts to fall away and markets stop growing. Consumer confidence starts to decline and there is rising job insecurity. Prices stabilize or start to fall. As demand drops, there is heavy discounting in the marketplace and consequently business profit falls. Marketing managers must in this period be very attentive to the balancing of supply and demand. The major danger in this period for a product business is the accumulation of excess unsold inventory; for a service business, excess capacity and people without enough fee-earning work. This is a time to review product and service portfolios and channels of distribution. Recruitment of new marketing staff should be halted and no further long-term commitment taken on.

- *recession* is technically a stage that is reached in the business cycle where Gross Domestic Product has fallen for two consecutive quarters. Domestic consumption falls off. Company investment becomes very tightly controlled as companies struggle to maintain sales volumes and profit margins. Speculative investments are usually cancelled and productive capacity is brought in line with decline in market demand. Lay-offs are frequent and overall unemployment rises. Inevitably, some businesses fail completely and are either taken over or seek protection from bankruptcy. During this time marketing usually focuses on fundamentals, such as directing marketing investment to core markets and clients and being on constant alert for signs of economic and market recovery. It is important during this period to retain core skills and assets. Strong management and cost control over suppliers, agencies, and contractors is also advisable in this period.

- *recovery* is characterized by returning consumer confidence, then spending, then rising market demand. New investment begins. Employment rises, although slowly at first, as employment usually lags behind a recovery by one year. Profits rise for companies that are able to take early advantage of the recovery. Overall business confidence grows and is often witnessed by mergers and takeovers. Prices start to rise. Marketers must be ready to take immediate advantage of the upswing. Those in product marketing should start to build up their stock in anticipation and to sell off their redundant stock to discounters, perhaps by organizing special sales initiatives. They can take advantage of lower prices for stock and for resource contracts. Marketing programmes should be aggressive and confident. This may also be a time to attack competitors who have been very weakened in the recession.

- *boom* is characterized by consumer spending rising so fast that it is fuelling concerns about inflation and rising debt. Productive capacity rises and there are key skills shortages. Productivity gains are sought to offset labour shortages and market demands. Investment spending is high and frequently speculative. Use of external contractors and agencies is much less controlled than hitherto. Increases in market demand now stimulate price rises and, consequently, profits rise. Marketers should encourage the sale of surplus in order to realize top prices. Retention of top quality marketing skills is at a premium. New market entry and new product or service line introduction may be explored. However, the marketer should be judicious in the expansion knowing that a downturn will inevitably follow.

business ethics An enquiry into the moral dimensions of business activities and conduct, an increasingly important aspect of corporate governance and public reputation. Business ethics are notoriously difficult to define in a standardized way and do vary from culture to culture. With the recent wave of accountancy scandals, however, business ethics and financial probity has become an international issue of major importance, both in terms of markets and economic systems and beliefs. For example, an unethical business would be prepared to go to any lengths and to condone any actions that contribute to the achievement of its corporate aims and objectives. Other organizations respect the laws but not necessarily the spirit of the law, if that conflicts with economic performance. Other companies, believing that there is much to be gained from ethical behaviour, actually communicate their ethical behaviour and in some cases actively market it. Other organizations take an active (rather than reactive) interest in ethical issues. (An example would be the Body Shop.) At the most advanced level, some organizations are entirely driven by an ethical platform, informing everything that the company does and involving a commitment on the part of everyone to carefully selected core values.

business plan A statement of the way in which a company intends to be operated, what its main goals are, how much money it will take to achieve the goals, what activities will be performed and what investments will be made to achieve the goals. Marketing is an integral activity in a business plan.

business presentation *See* MARKETING PLAN.

business to business *See* B2B.

business-to-business advertising Advertising directed to other businesses, rather than to consumers.

business-to-business (B2B) marketing The targeting, packaging, and promotion of products and services to other businesses or organizations rather than to individual consumers. It can also be known as industrial, commercial, trade, organizational, or institutional marketing. This type of marketing requires a different set of techniques and analysis from consumer marketing. The main difference is that the buyer in the industrial market does not purchase for final consumption. Purchases in the business-to-business market are made for further processing, for adding value, or for incorporation into finished products. The target buyers are not end consumers, but those in the supply chain that reach the final consumer, such as manufacturers who make the products, internal users within companies, wholesalers who buy the products in bulk and distribute them, and retailers who merchandise and sell them to final consumers. This determines an entirely different type of segmentation, channel, and pricing strategy from those engaged in consumer marketing.

The business-to-business market has different dynamics from the consumer market. It is characterized by larger purchasers, fewer buyers and by different types of demand: for example, derived, volatile, and concentrated. Derived demand means that the demand for the product and services of another business is ultimately determined by demand from the final consumer. Volatile demand in business-to-business markets—as we often see in oil or aero engines—is much greater than volatility in consumer markets. Economists calculate that a 20% rise in consumer demand can cause an increase in industrial demand by up to 200%. For example, if demand for PCs or mobile phones rises by 20%, this can cause a current rise of 200% for microchips. Business-to-business markets are also more prone to concentrated demand than consumer markets—largely because many industries are more geographically concentrated than consumer industries. This tends to cluster industrial buyers in specific geographies.

Buyers in business-to-business markets tend to be expert buyers, knowledgeable in the product area, and highly trained. Committees of experts make buying decisions. This, in turn, requires a more sophisticated form of personal selling and salesperson to address and negotiate with these types of buyers.

Also, in business-to-business marketing, there are different ways of obtaining the product apart from straightforward purchase—for example leasing is quite normal for industrial equipment. In some markets, without stable currencies, there is counter-trading, in which one form of good is exchanged for others in lieu of monetary purchase.

There are several ways of segmenting the business-to-business market, the most common of which is to use the standard industrial classification code that divides industries into various generic markets. Another way is to segment the industrial market by type of manufacturing: capital equipment, batch, discrete, and process manufacturing.

The key elements, approaches and techniques of business-to-business marketing are:

- a heavier emphasis on relationship marketing—an unremitting focus on retaining customers through building trust and commitment.
- a deployment of a key account manager for large customers who has excellent communications, problem-solving, and negotiation skills.
- additional services such as technical advice and technical specification are required in business-to-business marketing.
- because the preparation and negotiation of competitive tenders to win new orders is at a premium, there must be experienced sales and sales support teams with the requisite skills in these areas.
- prices are usually negotiated rather than set in advance, with a high emphasis on discounting and loss leaders.
- there is a high skill requirement for sophisticated personal selling.
- promotion is focused on trade press, specialized advertising, exhibitions, trade shows, and business press publicity rather than mass media outlets.
- image building is usually focused on individual customers or small clusters of customers rather than to mass audiences. *See also* BUYER AND BUYING BEHAVIOUR.

business to consumer *See* B2C.

button ad A graphical advertising unit used on the *World Wide Web that is smaller than a *banner ad. Button ads measure typically 120 × 90, 120 × 60, 125 × 125, and 88 × 31 pixels. Whereas banners are often placed at the top or bottom of a page, buttons are often placed towards the middle of a page on the left or right sides. *See also* ADVERTISING.

button exchange A network where participating sites on the *World Wide Web display button ads in exchange for credits, which are converted (using a predetermined exchange rate) into ads to be displayed on other sites. *See also* ADVERTISING; FREE WEBSITE PROMOTION.

buyer and buying behaviour (industrial and consumer)

Buyer and buying behaviour is one of the more fervently studied subjects in marketing. To understand buyer behaviour is the ultimate goal of all marketers. Buyers are crucial in managing the relationship between an organization of the company, the enterprise, and its suppliers. Effective marketing plans and programmes must be based upon a sound and thorough understanding of the buyer, the buyer's behaviour, and the buyer's values. While complete knowledge of buyer behaviour is unattainable, this has not prevented many marketers, academics, and psychologists from attempting to model repeatable buyer behaviour.

Buyers in consumer markets

Philip *Kotler (in his book *Marketing Management*) identified several
types who can play a role in an overall buying decision in a consumer
market:

- **The Initiator** who can first suggest the idea of buying a product or
  service;
- **The Influencer** whose personal authority or knowledge can
  influence the outcome of the buying decision;
- **The Decider** who eventually decides on whether to buy, what to buy,
  where to buy from, and how to buy;
- **The Buyer** is the person who actually makes the buying transaction;
- **The User** is the person who actually uses the product or consumes
  the service.

A marketer, equipped with knowledge of the various roles that people
play in the buying process, can shape his marketing programmes around
these buyer types. We see, for example, huge effort expended on
marketing toys to children during children's television commercial
breaks, in the complete knowledge that the child is unlikely to be either
the decider or buyer, but is most certainly going to be the initiator,
possibly the influencer, through pestering the parent, and certainly the
final user.

Kotler also outlined a five-stage model for the buying process:

- **problem recognition,** the first stage of the buyer's decision process
  in which the consumer recognizes a problem or need. The
  recognition of the need becomes a drive to satisfy that need. The task
  for the marketer at this stage is to identify the circumstances and
  stimuli that trigger that particular need and use this knowledge to
  develop marketing strategies and plans to develop consumer
  interest.
- **information search,** the stage of the buyer decision process in
  which the consumer is aroused to search for more information. The
  intensity of the information search is partly determined by the level
  of the consumers' drive to satisfy their need. For example, the
  consumer may simply have heightened attention or may conduct an
  intensive information search. The task of the marketer is to decide
  which major information sources the customer will use at this stage:
  for example a) personal sources (such as friends, family, neighbours,
  workmates), who may be the most trusted sources but may not
  be the most expert; b) commercial sources (such as salespeople,
  websites, dealers, advertising or marketing information), which may
  be the most expert sources but not necessarily the most trusted;
  c) public sources (such as published studies that evaluate various
  products on behalf of consumers); d) experiential (such as personal

use of the product during a demonstration or a trial period);
this could be the final stage when the buyer decides to 'see for
himself'.

- **alternative evaluation,** the stage of the buyer decision process in
  which the consumer searches out and uses information to
  evaluate alternative brands. It is vital for the marketer to know what
  attributes are important to the buyer during this stage. In fact it is
  possible, if the knowledge is deep enough, to segment buyers
  according to the importance they place on each product or service
  attribute. Also, some marketers attempt to predict, using statistical
  probabilities and game theories, what the buyer will actually
  choose given a set of options and variables. The actions that
  professional marketers might follow at this stage in the buying
  process are to obtain as much information directly from potential
  buyers about what attributes that they value in specific branded
  products and services. Having analysed the responses, the
  marketer can:

a) modify the existing brand by altering beliefs about the brand
   (*repositioning*);
b) alter beliefs about the competitor's brands (*competitive
   depositioning*);
c) alter the buyers' weighting of attributes by trying to persuade the
   buyer to attach more importance to the key attributes of their
   company's brand;
d) call attention to attributes that have been neglected, perhaps
   because of imperfect information or knowledge, or, most difficult
   of all;
e) attempt to shift the buyer's ideas, beliefs, and perceptions of the
   brand (*psychological repositioning*).

- **purchase decision,** the final stage in the buying process. The
  purchase decision follows from the evaluation of alternatives stage
  during which a purchasing intent is made. Between the formation of
  a purchasing intent and the completion of a purchasing decision the
  buyer can again change course and make different choices. Another
  party can influence the buyer, either positively or negatively, and this
  can result in a changed choice of brand. Unanticipated factors can
  also occur that did not exist when the purchasing intent was made,
  such as a change in financial circumstances. Kotler points out that a
  buyer making a final purchasing decision actually makes five
  decisions, or sub-decisions: they choose a brand; they choose a
  retailer or dealer; they make a decision on quantity; then the timing
  of the purchase; finally the payment method.

- **post-purchase behaviour,** the stage of the process in which the buyer takes further action after purchase based on their satisfaction or dissatisfaction with their purchase. If they are dissatisfied, they may return the product, complain, or else avoid repurchase; if they are satisfied, or if their initial expectations are exceeded, then they may repeat the purchase, or, in a best case for a marketer, become a living advert for the product and spread the word to their friends and associates. Buyer satisfaction depends upon the alignment of initial expectations and the perceived product or service performance. In some cases the buyer expectation could have been set too high (for example by the salesman 'overselling' the product or service). The marketer's role must extend into this period, as it is a crucial determinant of the buyers' repurchase decisions. They ought to be aware of the ways in which buyers express dissatisfaction and be prepared to handle the various ways in which a buyer will demonstrate dissatisfaction. Post-purchase communication with the buyer is vital.

Factors influencing consumer buyer behaviour

Consumers' buying behaviour and the resulting purchase decision is strongly influenced by cultural, social, personal, and psychological characteristics. An understanding of the influence of these factors is essential for marketers in order to develop suitable marketing mixes to appeal to the target customer:

- Factors include a consumer's culture, subculture, and social class. These factors are often inherent in our values and decision processes.
- Factors include groups (reference groups, aspirational groups, and member groups), family, roles, and status. This explains the outside influences of others on our purchase decisions either directly or indirectly.
- Factors include such variables as age and life-cycle stage, occupation, economic circumstances, lifestyle (activities, interests, opinions, and demographics), personality, and self-concept. These may explain why our preferences often change as our 'situation' changes.
- Factors affecting our purchase decision include motivation (Maslow's *hierarchy of needs), perception, learning, beliefs, and attitudes.

Types of consumer buying

Buying tends to be more complex with the size of the purchase. The size of the purchase usually determines the number of people involved in the buying process.

Consumers buy in different ways:

- **complex buying,** when the consumer is highly involved in the purchase and has much information about different brands and is aware of differences between them. This buyer spends much time in evaluation and choice selection;
- **habitual buying,** when the consumer has low involvement and is not aware of significant differences between the brands. Brands are usually bought on the basis of their familiarity rather than their perceived attributes;
- **variety buying,** when the consumer has low involvement in the purchase but is aware of high brand differences. These consumers tend to switch brands frequently.

Buyer types have also been divided into various categories among which are:

- **the loyal,** who repeat purchase the same brand for long periods;
- **the opportunistic,** who change brands and suppliers on the basis of their own long-term interests;
- **the dealer,** who concentrates on the best deal available at the time;
- **the creative,** who ask the seller to customize the product, service, and price precisely to their needs;
- **the trader,** who asks for extras and mutual favours in exchange for their purchase;
- **the negotiator,** who constantly demands extra discounts on pricing;
- **the no-frills buyer,** who buys products on the basis of the quality of their construction.

Buying decisions

As the table shows, the consumer is subject to several influences in the pathway to a final decision or group of decisions.

There are two overall types of buyer influence:

1 The marketing input that introduces the product or service to the buyer and draws the buyer's attention. If this is done well it should appeal to the buyer's needs, wants, and desires. How the product or service is packaged, priced, and distributed are also key influences in the final buying decision.

2 Secondly, and more intangible, are the psychological factors that include cultural (such as the culture of the country of the buyer, perhaps the subculture, religion, and social class); social (such as peer group, the family, social reference groups that confer status, education, and socio-economic groups); psychological (such as needs, motivation, perception, learning, beliefs, and attitude); personal factors (such as the buyer's age and where they are in their

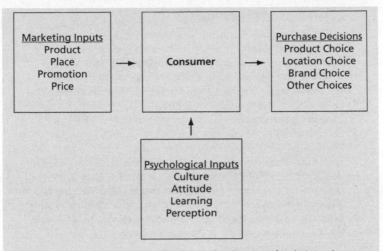

Buyer Decision Process based on Cohen (1991). Reproduced courtesy of marketingteacher.com

life cycle, their occupation, their economic status, their personality, and how they view themselves in terms of lifestyle).

Buyers in organizations

In an organization a buyer is the person or group responsible for the purchasing policies and management of the purchasing functions of the organization. A buyer can be an individual, a department within a company, or a group from various parts of the company that is brought together to make a buying decision. This is often referred to as the buying group or the buying centre. The buyer, or buyers, can be a direct purchaser themselves for their individual use (for example an Information Technology manager buying a range of PCs for his own staff); they can be influencers (for example an Information Technology manager who provides an evaluation of various PC suppliers to management to supply the entire organization); deciders (for example an Information Technology manager who decides on the entire supply of PCs on behalf of his organization based upon the evaluations and recommendations of third parties, or perhaps a competitive tendering process); or they can be gatekeepers (past whom a PC supplier must go in order to gain access to management who can decide on the overall purchase).

Different types and size of purchase will require different types of buyer and buying process. Normally, the larger the purchase, the more buyers become involved and the more complex the buying process.

Industrial (organizational) buying

- **Industrial market,** the acquisition of goods and services that enter into the production of other products and services that are sold, rented, or supplied to others. Goods and services are usually purchased for organizations. There are few buyers but many decision-makers. Buying volume can be very large and there are close supplier-customer relationships.

- **Industry structure,** the organizational and competitive characteristics of an industry including the number and size distribution of buyers and sellers, the nature of the product, and the size of any barriers to entry. There are both fragmented industries that are populated by a large number of small and medium-sized companies and concentrated industries that differ from fragmented industries in that they are dominated by a small number of large firms. These concentrated firms are able to exercise a significant buying influence over the market as a whole.

Types of industrial/organization buyer

Organizational buyers can be:

- manufacturers,
- wholesalers,
- operational users, or
- retailers.

Retailers are the last destination before the final user. Physical retailers buy, display, merchandize, service, and sell the products to the final user and give it local context and a highly targeted approach to local buyers. Online retailers, whilst losing the local point of presence and sale, can develop direct relationships with their buyers based on a number of indirect channels (phone, Internet/e-mail, websites). Online retailers normally sell at a discount to physical retailers.

Wholesalers are in the stage before the retailers in the value chain. The characteristic of the wholesale purchase of products is high volume. The purpose of the wholesaler is to be able to access the retail markets in a cost-effective way. Wholesalers sell to the retailer, either physical or online.

Buying process for organizations or industrial buyers

Kotler identified the following stages in the industrial buying process:

- **problem recognition,** the first stage of the industrial buying process in which someone in the company recognizes a problem or need that can be met by acquiring a good or a service.

- **general need description,** the stage at which the company describes the general characteristics and quantity of a needed item.

- **product or service specification,** the stage at which the buying organization decides on and specifies the best technical product characteristics for a needed product or service. The major activity is the design and development of product specifications designed to solve the problem previously identified. Often this will involve assistance from third parties prior to this being put out to contract.

- **products and suppliers search,** the stage at which the buyer looks to match suppliers with the detailed specification. This is the point at which the reputation, track record, and awareness of potential suppliers becomes important.

- **proposal solicitation,** the stage in which the buyer invites qualified suppliers to submit proposals. This is the stage at which the selling abilities of the supplier organization are vitally important. This may also involve the issuing of an invitation to tender, depending on the size and scale of the purchase.

- **selection and ordering,** the stage at which a selected group of suppliers is assessed by the decision-making unit (see below) which tends to involve several experts—purchasing, legal, selling, commercial contracts, and finance. Terms are negotiated, selection made, and contracts offered.

- **performance review** (evaluating the product and supplier), the stage at which the buyer rates their satisfaction with suppliers, deciding whether to continue, modify, or drop them.

The **decision-making unit** (DMU) in an industrial purchasing process consists of all those individuals and groups who participate in the buying decision, all of whom share some common goals and are knowledgeable about the risks arising from decisions.

Although each decision-making unit is different, these are the usual roles:

- **Initiators** are a group within the DMU who begin the process of considering a purchase. This group help the decision-makers by gathering information.

- **Influencers** are a group within the DMU who help define the specification and also provide an input into the process of evaluating the available alternatives.

- **Deciders** are a group within the DMU who have the responsibility for deciding on product requirements and suppliers.

- **Approvers** are a group within the DMU who authorize the proposals of deciders and buyers.

- **Gatekeepers** are a group within the DMU who, by controlling the flow of information, may be able to stop sellers from reaching individuals within the buying centre.

- **Buyers** are a group within the DMU who have the formal authority for the selection of suppliers and negotiating purchase terms.

- **Users** are a group within the DMU who may initiate the buying process and help define purchase specifications.

Functionally, these decision-makers might be Operation Managers who use the product in the organization's processes and who are seeking greater efficiency and effectiveness; Technical Managers who might test and approve the product and who will be seeking quality and reliability; the Senior Executive who may approve major expenditure or choice of supplier; the Purchasing or Commercial Manager who negotiates terms, approves conditions of purchase and monitors supplier performance; the Legal Manager who draws up or approves legal contracts with the supplier; or the Finance Manager who approves expenditure and controls.

Types of organizational buying
- **New task purchase** when the organization is facing a need or a problem for the first time and the full organizational buying process will probably occur.
- **Modified re-buy purchase** when something about the buying situation has changed, but a lot still remains the same.
- **Straight re-buy** when the buyer routinely purchases the same product under the same terms of sale.

Contrast between industrial/organizational and consumer market buying
There are fundamental differences between the individual consumer buying process and the organizational buying process.

- Individual buyers are normally spending their own money; in organizational, or industrial buying, the purchase is made with organizational money.
- The number of customers is much smaller in industrial markets.
- The buying decision in organizations and industries is more complex and the influences are different.
- Those in consumer markets tend to be individual or family-based with fewer decision points.
- Organizational purchases tend to be larger than individual consumer purchases.
- Purchases in industrial markets tend to be contract-based rather than straightforward money or credit purchases. Price decisions in industrial markets are negotiated beforehand and terms are important whereas in consumer markets prices are normally pre-set and fixed and bargain discounts are important.
- Suppliers to industrial markets tend to have deeper, longer-term relationships with organizations than they do with individuals.
- The nature of demand in industrial markets is dependent on demand in consumer markets. This is usually known as derived or

joint demand (in consumer markets this is known as primary demand).

- Buying motivations in industrial markets are usually in support of a company's operations and its longer range needs, while those in consumer markets are for immediate individual or family needs.
- Product specifications in industrial markets are usually technically sophisticated whereas in the consumer market the technical content is lower.
- In terms of marketing and sales the emphasis in industrial markets is on personal selling, whereas in consumer markets the emphasis is on mass media advertising.
- Distribution decisions: in industrial markets there are a limited number of large buyers and simple channels; in consumer markets there are a large number of small buyers and complex channels.
- Customer service: this is critical to success in industrial markets and less important in consumer markets.

buy-feel-learn model A technique for analysing the impulse purchasing and/or new brands. Attitudes, knowledge, and preference are developed after the purchasing of the product rather than before. Buying often precedes the creation or reinforcement of feelings about the product. Traditionally, it was thought that logically the process happened in reverse. *See also* AIDA; HIERARCHY OF EFFECTS.

buying association An informal group of retailers, usually in a specific geographic locality, who group together to enjoy the economies of scale accruing from bulk purchases from wholesalers and manufacturers.

buzzword A short-lived word or phrase that is used more to impress than explain. A buzzword may be a newly coined word or an old word used in a new way. Buzzwords are part of the fashion of a living language, more about style than substance. Some buzzwords are actually useful for a period of time, but the object they describe eventually becomes less useful. Other buzzwords are simply confusing or inaccurate. A buzzword spends only a fraction of its lifespan being used; the rest of the time it is being abused. The result is a phenomenon known as buzzword backlash, whereby the tide turns against a buzzword and it starts to fade from usage.

by-product pricing *See* PRICING.

cable An important medium for direct advertising, interactive marketing and *Internet access. Increasingly cable is the focus of 'triple play' offers— telephony, digital television, and high-speed Internet access. *See also* BROADBAND.

caching The storage of web files for later re-use at a point more quickly accessed by the end user. Caching can happen at many places, for example the user's local computer. The objective is to make efficient use of resources and speed the delivery of content to the end user. While caching can have a positive impact on the user's experience, it can have a negative impact for site publishers, resulting in undercounts of page views and ad impressions. In response to this problem, sites have implemented various cache-busting techniques to better ensure that all performance statistics are accurately measured.

call planning The detailed preparations made by a salesman in preparation for a client meeting. Call planning can almost be viewed as a type of single campaign for a single client on a single occasion. *See also* PERSONAL SELLING.

call to action An advertising phrase that attracts buyers or users to take immediate and explicit action. It is designed to be a single focused command to a potential customer, usually with an incentive to buy within a defined time frame.

camera-ready art The artwork that is in sufficiently finished form to be photographed for printing.

campaigns *See* ADVERTISING.

canned presentation A prepared and tested sales or advertising campaign demonstration that is committed to memory and used consistently for all prospects.

cannibalization The situation when a new product or service line takes away sales or market share from other products in the existing product or service line of the same company. It is incumbent upon marketers to guide their range of products and services away from cannibalization, which is very damaging to their portfolio.

canvass To look for potential new customers for a product or service. Canvassing is typically done in person rather than over the phone or via other channels.

CAPI (computer-aided personal interviewing) Interviewer-administered surveying using a computer-based questionnaire.

capital equipment Those industrial machinery, tools, office equipment, or transport vehicles that are purchased infrequently and are used to produce goods, to provide a service, or to support the day-to-day operation of an organization.

capital items Those industrial goods that enter or become part of the finished product, including installations and accessory equipment.

caption An advertisement's headline or the text accompanying an illustration or photograph.

captive product pricing *See* PRICING.

card rate The media advertising rates published by a broadcast station or print publication on a 'rate card'. This is typically the highest rate charged by a vehicle.

cartel An association of suppliers whose purpose in cooperating is the fixing of variables, such as price and output levels. This places a limitation on free market competition and pricing. Cartels are subject to legislative action in the major economies. Although becoming a cartel would make a marketer's life much easier, cartels are inimical to the marketing profession and process.

cash and carry A bulk and large-quantity retail or wholesale outlet that offers discounted goods and limited or no service or packaging. There are usually no credit terms available to buyers.

cash cow *See* BOSTON CONSULTING GROUP MATRIX.

cash discount The price reduction for *buyers who pay their bills promptly or to buyers who pay their bills in cash rather than on credit. This is used as an instrument of competitive marketing as well as financial management.

cash refund offer (cash rebate) A guarantee to refund part of the purchase price of a product after the purchase to consumers who produce a 'proof of purchase' such as an original receipt. This can often be a market differentiator for retailers whose policies create good word of mouth marketing, such as Marks and Spencer in the UK or Nordstrom in the US.

CASI (computer-aided self-administered interviewing) (market research) Self-administered surveying using a computer-based questionnaire.

catalogue An important channel of direct marketing and also one of the earliest ways in marketing techniques for increasing distribution channel and reach, particularly to those buyers who were unable to visit the retail store or factory outlet. Catalogues display a variety of merchandise available from a manufacturer or retailer. Originally intended to service remote and rural areas that were far from department stores, catalogues have now entered a new era of commercial development. Electronic catalogues are also available on the *World Wide Web and this has extended their reach even further, enabling even more direct marketing than ever.

catalogue marketing An example of direct marketing using catalogues mailed to a select list of customers or made available in retail outlets. Retail catalogues often employ agents at a local level who organize purchase and delivery of goods as well as collecting and remitting moneys in exchange for commission from the catalogue company. *See also* DIRECT MARKETING.

catalogue showroom A retail operation that sells a wide selection of consumer goods (usually at discount prices) that can be identified in the retail catalogue. This is, in the age of electronic shopping, a surprisingly popular way of shopping.

catchphrase A mnemonic device usually in the form of a slogan and used in advertising. Many memorable catch phrases enter the language as everyday phrases used outside the original purpose. *See* APPENDIX 3 on Slogans.

category development index (CDI) A comparison of the percentage of sales of a product category in a market, to the percentage of population in that market.

category killer A term used to describe a huge range of products concentrated in a single outlet which far exceeds that of smaller outlets who cannot supply such a range in such depth, or with such price discounts or with such efficiency and ability to attract large numbers of potential buyers. Large discount toy chains, sporting goods chains, home improvement and office supply chains are examples of category killers.

category positioning *See* POSITIONING.

CATI (computer-aided telephone interviewing) Interviewer-administered telephone surveying using a computer-based questionnaire.

causal research Research that helps marketers identify a specific factor that causes an effect in the marketplace. *See also* MARKET RESEARCH; DIRECT MARKETING.

causation The inference that a change in one variable is responsible for an observed change in another variable.

cause-related marketing A strategic positioning and marketing approach that links a company or brand to a relevant social cause, for the mutual benefit of sponsor and sponsored. The term was copyrighted by the American Express Corporation and it specifically refers to promotional programmes that link charitable contributions to sales of a specific good or service bought with a credit card. A certain percentage of the purchase price of a good or service is contributed to a defined charity. In a broader sense, the term has also come to mean the sponsorship of causes by major corporations, or groups of corporations, which enables the company to associate its brand with a worthy cause. As business ethics and corporate responsibility climb higher up the agendas of major companies, cause-related and not-for-profit marketing are taking on new dimensions of importance. *See also* CHARITY (OR NOT-FOR-PROFIT) MARKETING.

caveat emptor Latin for 'let the buyer beware', from the principle that the buyer alone is responsible if dissatisfied.

caveat venditor Latin for 'let the seller beware'.

CD-ROM A compact disc with read-only memory, forming a cost-effective and secure information storage device with multimedia capabilities. *See also* DIRECT MARKETING.

celebrity endorsement An advertisement or promotion featuring testimonials for products by a well-known personality from the field of entertainment, sport, and politics. *See also* ADVERTISING.

celebrity marketing The strategic use of a widely known person to promote goods, services, places, ideas, or causes. Examples may be Tiger Woods promoting Nike, or a range of Hollywood actresses promoting French perfumes and cosmetics.

chain store Multiple outlets that are commonly owned and controlled, have central buying and merchandising, and sell similar lines of merchandise. The most common type is the corporate chain store that is made up of retail outlets that are owned by a single company. Marketing is usually done centrally. Wal-Mart, Tesco, and Sainsbury are examples of such chain stores. The next most common type of chain store is the franchise outlet such as Burger King or McDonald's.

change agent *See* ADOPTION.

change aide *See* ADOPTION.

channel conflict *See* CHANNELS OF DISTRIBUTION.

channel marketing The specific promotional activities focused on distributors, wholesalers, retailers, trade affiliates, and business partners in a channel of distribution, usually for physical goods. A channel marketing programmes does not directly address or communicate with the end consumer.

channel of communication The general description of any linked way of communicating between the producer, the *middleman, and the end customer in a marketing programme.

channels of distribution

Channels of distribution are the means by which a seller of goods or services connects with their target customers. The management and development of these channels is a key part of the marketing mix. There are wholesale and retail channels, direct and indirect channels, narrow channels, and broad channels. A distribution channel can be any channel used by the product or service creator to get produce to the end customer. Distribution is a key element of the marketing mix. There are direct and indirect channels of distribution. Marketers can use multiple channels to get their products and services to market, but must avoid channel confusion or conflict in order that the channels work efficiently.

Direct channels

Direct channels are characterized by the producers of goods and services interacting directly with the end consumer. Examples include:

- personal selling;
- retail selling;
- direct mailing;
- mail order;
- telesales;
- taking orders over the Internet.

The direct sales force is among the oldest channels. Although declining as a volume channel relative to other channels to market, the personal sales channel is one of the more effective and most expensive to run. Increasingly, direct personal selling is being used for major complex sales rather than the sales of consumer goods and services.

The retail channel markets, sells, and services consumers directly. They will often offer credit to the customers. The retail channel determines the final price of the good or service to the customer. Retail channels can take the form of stores, catalogues, franchises, websites, telesales, mail order, and home shopping channels. Retailers act as a channel for multiple brands, but can themselves also be a brand—sometimes much more powerful than the brands that they distribute and sell. *See also* BRAND; CONSUMER MARKETING. The retail channel is highly managed and often controls other parts of the supply chain. For example, an in-store *eftpos (Electronic Funds Transfer at Point of Sale) system can immediately collect and transfer information about purchases to warehouse and distribution centres that can dispatch new supplies when they are needed in the retail store. This system eliminates the need for stockrooms within the retail outlet and allows the entire space to become a retail outlet serving customers. Retail channels can exercise enormous power over pricing and product design and quality.

The *Internet represents a powerful intermediary channel. It has possibly the widest geographical reach of the channels to market. It can enable niche products to reach a vast audience. It is a relatively low-cost channel with low entry barriers. It uses online payments to enable purchase.

Indirect distribution

Indirect distribution channels are characterized by using a third party as an intermediary between the producer of the goods and services and the end consumer. Examples are:

- wholesalers;
- agents;
- brokers;
- resellers;
- dealers;
- aggregators.

Indirect distribution channels are used most efficiently when they can access either more customers than retailers or can sell more efficiently (such as to a diverse base of smaller retailers in a large geographical area) or can add more value (such as customization of product) for the retail outlet that serves end customers.

A wholesale distribution channel is formed between the producer and the retailer: wholesalers generally do not sell to the end consumer, but to the retail channel. Wholesalers take ownership, or title, to the goods that they buy. They provide storage facilities. Wholesalers usually buy goods from a range of manufacturers at a substantial discount and then sell on to retailers who in turn sell them to end consumers. Wholesalers can service multiple small retailers who do not have sufficient purchasing power on their own to deal directly with the manufacturer. Occasionally, wholesalers produce marketing materials, such as brochures, catalogues, websites, and price lists, but they are not so active as the retailer.

Another type of indirect distribution is agents and brokers, who largely sell on behalf of the producer without taking possession of and title to the products: they bring together the producer and the buyer and they are mainly compensated on a commission basis. Agents secure orders and take commission but do not take ownership or title to the goods themselves.

Resellers tend to be used for international marketing. *See* INTERNATIONAL MARKETING.

The chief purpose of the dealer is to buy goods, add value to them, then resell them with post-sales service.

Channel conflict

Channel conflict is disagreement among marketing channel members on goals and roles in a channel of distribution: on who should cover which territory, who should sell what, to whom, and for what rewards. It can also occur between manufacturers and retailers over who controls volumes and pricing in a specific channel. It can involve field sales forces who have to sell different products by different means in the same territory. Examples of industries facing significant channel conflict include insurance, music, airlines, computer manufacturers, appliances, furniture, and securities trading.

Channel conflict is not a new business phenomenon. For example, during the 1980s manufacturers faced channel conflicts when outlet and discount superstores expanded and started to harm the trade of traditional department stores. Recognizing the demand for outlet stores, manufacturers began to use them to reach new customers and sell different products, creating mutual benefit for themselves and their distribution channels.

On the other hand, companies that control their own channels risk cannibalizing offline revenues with online revenues. This takes customers away from existing channels, decreasing the older channels' profitability. For example, as more consumers use online banking, commercial banks have been unable to justify maintaining as many physical branches. There have been waves of bank branch closures in the UK retail-banking sector.

However, in the Internet economy, channel conflicts are intensified by the unique characteristics of the electronic marketplace. Companies now have to contend with a business environment characterized by new consumer expectations, new competitors, and a faster time to market. Ideally companies facing channel conflict will devise strategies to minimize it, while simultaneously creating value on the Internet. To do this, companies need to determine the level of channel conflict they may incur.

Some products and services are appropriate for electronic channels, and some are not. For example, books and music sell easily on the Internet. However, service businesses, such as hair salons and car repairs, cannot transfer entirely to the Internet, but might use it for customer service, marketing, or appointment setting.

The level of channel control that a company exercises is also important. Channel control can be defined in two different ways. For manufacturers, channel control is the extent to which they control the relationship with their retail channels. For retailers, channel control is better defined as the power they have in the market in which they compete. Companies with easily transferable businesses, and little control over their channels, may face significant channel conflicts. Companies with easily transferable businesses, but high channel control, face moderate levels of channel conflict, most often related to cannibalization of existing channels. Industries in this area include many retail chains (e.g., office supplies, books, toys), mobile telephone providers, and many franchise organizations. Companies in this category often *link* their existing channels with the online channels to enhance the benefit of having all channels together.

Companies with businesses that do not transfer to the Internet, and that have little control over channels, face minimal channel conflict. These companies' channels will likely view electronic commerce as a threat to their control of the customer relationship. It is unlikely that companies that have control over their channels, but do not easily transfer to the Internet, will experience channel conflict. Examples of industries in this area include: pharmaceutical companies, law firms, accounting firms, and other professional service firms.

New channels of distribution and channel conflict

Both Amazon.com and E-Trade.com have demonstrated that they can grow an online business in a market that had been hitherto dominated by physical, non-electronic distribution channels. Amazon does not support a chain of bricks-and-mortar bookstores. Amazon was able to avoid channel conflict because the company developed new channels. The degree and type of channel conflict in the electronic marketplace varies across industries and individual companies. The key for these companies was to develop strategies that minimize the impact of channel conflict. However, both of these successes caused the traditional competitors to develop online distribution and marketing channels to implement their physical businesses.

See also DISTRIBUTION.

character symbol A historical figure, animated character, animal, or object used to advertise a brand and that comes to be associated with the brand, e.g. 'Joe Camel' for Camel cigarettes, the lion in MGM movies, Tony the Tiger for Exxon, Charlie Chaplin (played by an actor) in 1980s IBM ads. *See also* BRAND.

charity (or not-for-profit) marketing Use of promotional and communications techniques to assist charities to gain greater exposure for their cause and greater support for it. Charities are primarily using marketing not for profit, but for contributions. In recent years, organizations such as Médecins Sans Frontières, OXFAM, and Save the Children have become increasingly assertive in their advertising and sponsorship-seeking efforts. Increasingly, charities seek out corporate sponsorships in order to improve their funding; corporations seek out charities to improve their reputation. *See also* CAUSE-RELATED MARKETING.

cherry picking An elitist or top quality approach either to buying or selling. For example, when a buyer selects only a few top quality items from one vendor's line and a few from another line. A marketing campaign can attempt to 'cherry pick' the best markets and customers with advanced targeting.

Chiat, Jay (1931–2002) Founder of Chiat/Day Agency, New York. Jay Chiat created an innovative style of advertising fused with popular culture that revolutionized the industry in the 1970s and '80s. His agency, Chiat/Day, grew from its single Los Angeles office in 1968, to an international agency with 1,200 employees and billings of $1.3 bn in the early '90s. Chiat/Day, known for creativity and innovation, introduced the British discipline of account planning to the US; he set up unconventional work environments like the 'virtual agency' in the company's New York offices.

Born Morton Jay Chiat in the Bronx on 25 October 1931, he worked on recruitment advertising for Aerojet General, an Air Force contractor, and then joined a small advertising agency in Orange County, California. He opened Jay Chiat & Associates in 1962 before merging with another small agency, Faust/Day, in 1968, which became Chiat/Day. He sold his advertising agency to the Omnicom Group in 1995. Chiat/Day earned the coveted title of agency of the decade from *Advertising Age* magazine, as well as agency of the year in 1980 and 1988. In 1998, Chiat became acting chief executive of Screaming Media, an *Internet content distributor, and took on the role of chairman in 1999. *Advertising Age* named him one of the top 10 on a list of 100 top players who had shaped the course of advertising history.

Chiat introduced Apple Computers' Macintosh PC to millions of viewers with his celebrated '1984' commercial during Super Bowl XVIII (*see also* ADVERTISING). While the mini-film was shown on national television only once, it set the tone for future Super Bowl commercials. With Chiat's influence, Nike became the 'unofficial' footwear of the 1984 Summer Olympics after he ran a campaign that featured Randy Newman singing 'I Love LA'. Five years later, he made the popular Energizer bunny commercial.

choice A consumer attribute benefit by suppliers. One of the greatest dynamics behind consumerism in the post-war period. In recent time consumer choice has been greatly widened through the advent of global markets and the *Internet. Greater access to information on products and services has not only given consumers greater choice, it has also given them greater power. This power shift has resulted in an increased focus on the consumers rather than the producer. Consequently, marketing is starting to transform the entire range of its techniques, which were originally developed to serve the producer interest. *See also* CONSUMERISM.

churn The percentage of customers who have no product loyalty and who will switch to a competing product.

cinema advertising A major medium and outlet for marketing programmes. Advertising is an obvious beneficiary of cinema. The advantages of using advertising through cinema are that the audience, although relatively small compared to a television audience, is captive and has a higher attention span. The size of the screen and the audio quality can have a memorable impact on the audience. Often, the type of movie being shown enables the advertiser to target the messages and the ad to the audience. Advertising can be customized to either regional or local culture in the local cinema area in which the movie is being shown. The cinema can also be an advertising location for the company that owns the cinema, such as Warner Brothers.

Increasingly, as product merchandising (such as T-shirts, dolls, computer games and derivatives) is becoming an important element in the total marketing of a movie, the cinema can often act as a retail outlet for merchandised goods. Increasing percentages of the total budget of a movie are being spent on advertising. In the last few years, *websites have become part of the marketing mix for the promotion of new films by movie companies. Major films these days reach the local cinema with a website promoting the film concurrently. It is a much less expensive promotional technique than traditional media. The cost of creating these websites is a fraction of the cost of a full TV or radio advertising campaign. There is a high correlation between Internet users and moviegoers, making websites a targeted and cost-effective medium for creating awareness for their films. Unlike a traditional promotion, a website can continue to generate awareness over a sustained period. Movie websites are not only building awareness for a movie before and during the cinema distribution, they continue to promote once the mass media advertisements have stopped running and the movies have moved on to ancillary markets. In addition to generating buzz and hype, film websites can also engage the viewer and enhance the experience. These communities are where visitors can find more information, take part in interactive activities, subscribe to newsletters, and chat with other like-minded individuals, with the eventual aim of creating greater audience loyalty. *See* MEDIA.

circulation The number of copies of a publication that is sold both directly and through subscription. The circulation number remains one of the main measures of the success of newspapers. The reason for this is that the circulation number is directly linked to advertising rates: the greater the circulation to an identifiable audience, the greater the advertising rate that can be charged.

There are frequent outbreaks of 'circulation wars', or extreme competition between newspapers. Weapons in these wars can involve 'scoop' stories, shock stories, eye-catching features, an increased number of extra sections, lowered prices, competitions and games, or even poaching well-known journalists and writers from each other.

clarifying A follow-up technique for getting complete responses to open-ended *questions by asking respondents to explain general terms in their answers.

classified advertising The print advertising that is limited to certain classes of goods and services, such as household goods, local services, and personal ads, usually limited in size and content and usually in black and white. They are paid for on a per-word, per-line, or per-inch basis. Although very different and less glamorous in style, content, and cost from display advertising, the classified advertising market is worth around $50 bn worldwide. *See also* ADVERTISING.

clearance The process by which an advertising standards body or media channel reviews an advertisement for legal, ethical, and taste standards, before accepting the ad for publication.

click-through The process of clicking through an online advertisement to the advertiser's destination, such as a *website or online service. The click-through is the most common way in which online visitors connect with an advertiser's website. Alternatively, visitors can also choose to visit the website directly by typing the *URL directly into the browser bar, or typing the company's name into a *search engine.

click-through rate (CTR) The most immediate response to an advertisement as well as the prime measure of an online ad's success. Accurate counting methods of click-throughs are very important when CTR is used as the measurement on which online advertisers' payments are based. *See also* ADVERTISING.

client account *See* ACCOUNT.

clincher An additional inducement offered to a potential buyer by a salesperson in order to close a sale. Inducements might include price discounts, rebates, extended credit, reduced delivery charges, etc.

clinical focus group A group that explores subconscious motivation. Psychologists are frequently used as facilitators on these focus groups to interpret the buyer behaviour patterns.

clipping service An agency service for extracting and reporting on relevant news items or advertisements concerning a company or a product in return for a fee. In past times this meant literally cutting media mentions from newspapers and pasting them into a reporting book. Nowadays this reporting is done electronically, and crosses all types of media, both online and offline. Many services are now globally organized given the globalization of news and information.

cloacking A *black hat search engine optimization (SEO) technique in which the content presented to the search engine *spider is different to that presented to the user's browser. The purpose of cloaking is to deceive search engines so they display the page when it would not otherwise be displayed. *See also* BLACK HAT SEO.

closed-ended question A question that asks the *respondent to choose from a limited number of pre-listed answers. *See* QUESTIONS.

closing date The day that final copy and other materials must be at the vehicle in order to appear in a specific issue or time slot.

closing skill The ability of a salesperson to obtain the buyer's commitment to the purchase. *See also* SELLING.

closing techniques The methods employed by a salesperson when asking for an order and aimed at obtaining a favourable response from a buyer.

cluster analysis A multivariate statistical classification technique for discovering whether the individuals of a population fall into different groups by making quantitative comparisons of multiple characteristics. The differences within any group should be less than the differences between groups. This analytical technique is often used for consumer segmentation and brand positioning. Cluster analysis is used in *market research when the sample is divided into different groups based upon various types of data or facts that are similar, or where there are very small differences. Cluster analysis is typically used for brand research or consumer segmentation. This would simplify the analysis process since large clusters rather than many small pieces of data only would need to be analysed. The differences within a particular cluster must be smaller than the differences between different clusters. Once the clusters or segments are identified, marketing themes can be identified for each specific segment or cluster. *See* GEODEMOGRAPHIC SEGMENTATION.

cluster sampling The selecting of clusters of units in a population and then performing a census on each cluster. The selection of clusters could be based on some desired feature of the population or could be a random sample of clusters in the population. *See* SAMPLING.

cluster theory The various theories on geographic concentrations of interconnected companies or expertise which includes specialized suppliers, service providers, firms in related industries, and associate institutions, and where the companies are in a particular field that both competes and cooperates. Strong geographic clusters can give *competitive advantage to nations or areas, such as Silicon Valley in California for high technology, the Pearl River Delta in China for manufacturing, the City in London for financial services.

clutter All non-programming time on radio and TV; this includes time given to advertising commercials, station or channel promotions, station or channel identifications, and programme credits. Excessively high clutter levels may result in audience dissatisfaction or alienation. *See also* ATTENTION; ADVERTISING.

code of ethics The ethical standards that are adopted by an organization and expected to be followed by its employees. Well known voluntary codes of ethics exist in many multinational companies and are used frequently in the public and not-for-profit sectors.

code of practice A voluntary guideline to encourage desirable modes of behaviour. *See also* ADVERTISING.

co-efficient of variation The standard deviation of a distribution of values divided by its arithmetical mean. This is used to compare frequency distributions and their variables.

cognitive dissonance A theory concerned with the relationships among cognitions developed by Leon Festinger, a social scientist from Stanford University, in 1957. Cognition is any type of knowledge. The knowledge may be about an attitude, an emotion, behaviour, a value. People hold a multitude of cognitions simultaneously, and these cognitions form irrelevant, consonant, or dissonant relationships with one another. Festinger considered the human need to avoid dissonance as basic as the need for safety or the need to satisfy hunger. (*See also* HIERARCHY OF NEEDS.) It is an aversive drive that pushes us to be consistent. He claimed that people avoid information that is likely to increase dissonance. Not only do we tend to select reading material and television programmes that are consistent with our existing beliefs, we usually choose to be with people who are like us. The tension of dissonance motivates us to change either our behaviour or our beliefs in an effort to avoid a distressing feeling. The more important the issue, and the greater the discrepancy between behaviour and belief, the higher the magnitude of dissonance that we will feel. In a marketing context, cognitive dissonance arises after a major purchase when alternatives are recommended, or if dislikes emerge after the purchase choice has been made. To eliminate the discomfort of dissonance, the consumer will seek to rationalize the original choice, in other words, find positive advantages and ignore negatives.

coincidental survey A survey of viewers or listeners of broadcast programming, conducted during the programme.

cold calling The practice of making a sales call on a client without an appointment. This can be done either in person or by telephone. Cold calling is often seen as a necessity to make new sales or to develop new prospects, but it is often a source of major criticism, particularly when made through telesales, obtrusively, and at unwelcome times. Examples are double-glazing and replacement windows salespeople in the UK or telephony services supplies in the US. *See also* DIRECT MARKETING.

Cold calling gives the sales world a very unpalatable reputation. The consumer generally detests cold calling. Equally, few practising sales people actually like cold calling, at best seeing it as a means to an end. It is the type of selling that has the highest rejection rate and often incurs hostility. So why does cold calling exist? Here are some potential reasons:

* Sales managers think that cold calling develops character and technique among salespeople. Those making cold calls have to deal with rejection and often hostility. In the sales mindset this is good for personal growth and development.
* Cold calling is supposed to keep the salespeople sharp and involved.
* Cold calling is a way to educate and teach salespeople in the fundamentals.
* Cold calls are a supplement to other marketing and sales approaches. Frequently, the purpose of cold calling is to get an appointment for a salesperson; in fact it enables direct personal selling.
* Cold calling is often a way to establish the needs and problems of a group of clients. Once these are established, a more effective way of marketing, based on detailed knowledge, can be adapted.
* If the information gleaned from cold calling is analysed on a database, one can track changing needs. This tracking can open new market potential. Today's modern sales process requires multiple contacts.
* Cold calling can actually be used as a form of market research. Depending on the industry, gathering information by cold calling gives first-hand customer and competitive intelligence.
* It is a way in which some sales managers track the performance of their salespeople in advance of selling.

collage A selection of objects mounted on a surface to create a pictorial illusion, often in abstract form.

collateral marketing strategies A case in which a market segmentation strategy accidently addresses the wrong target market.

colour An extremely important dimension of marketing, particularly in branding. Much of marketing is visual as well as psychological. Colour is a powerful means of communicating emotion, which is a driving force behind decision-making. Colour is used in logos, signage, marketing packages and material, graphics, and illustrations. Company brand systems usually ascribe different moods and meanings to colour. For example, the Kodak logo is inextricably linked to the yellow background, IBM to a blue logo, Coca-Cola to red, Marks and Spencer to green in either background or foreground. Colour also has different connotations in different cultures.

colour proof An early full-colour print of a finished advertisement, used to evaluate the ad's final appearance.

column inch A common unit of measure by newspapers, whereby ad space is purchased by the width, in columns, and the depth, in inches. For example, an ad that is three standard columns wide and five inches tall (or deep) would be 15 column inches.

combination rate A special media pricing arrangement that involves purchasing space or time on more than one vehicle, in a package deal. This is frequently offered where different vehicles share a common owner.

commission The money paid to the salesperson after the successful completion of a sale. Commissions are typically predetermined and can be a percentage of sales or the number of units sold.

commoditization The process of becoming a commodity, meaning higher volumes, less differentiation, wider availability, and usually lower prices. It has been argued by some economists that in today's economy the process of commoditization will become increasingly common due to the faster pace of innovation.

communications

Communications is one of the more important elements of the marketing mix. Marketing communications usually constitutes the largest component of an overall communications budget, but an important element is also corporate communications, which had its roots in the public relations industry, and whose primary purpose is to educate investors, consumers, and the general public about what this company is, what it does, and what it stands for. Towards the end of the 20th century, with the fragmentation of markets and the introduction of new communications media and technologies, communications were able to be more customized, more targeted, and more interactive than the classic forms of mass communication. Some companies have attempted to integrate all communications in support of the overall brand rather than seeing them as separate functional domains. In recent times, in terms of expenditure, direct marketing communications have surpassed all other forms of marketing. The advent of globalization has also posed some challenges for communications, in terms of language, medium, culture, and tone. More and more communications systems have become global while the messages and content are adapted to local language and culture. The phenomenon of globalization has placed greater emphasis on the communication of the global brand, which can often transcend cultural and geographical barriers.

There are multiple types of communication, both external to an enterprise and internal to it, those based upon mass communications systems and those based upon more direct, interpersonal communications. In the broadest sense, it covers the transmission or exchange of information to a target audience. In the context of marketing, the substance of communications is all-encompassing, covering all advertising, press releases, press and analyst communication and interaction, internal communications, websites, marketing materials, sales presentations, management communications, formal documents such as the company annual report, all branded materials and messages that present the company and its products and services internally and externally, price lists, product catalogues, service descriptions and guarantees, market research questionnaires, letters, interviews on all forms of media, internal and external formal announcements, presentations to investors, recruitment literature and the conduct of recruitment campaigns, and speeches by company staff as well as all external publications by and on behalf of the company. In short, the totality of how the company, its people, services, and products are made known internally and externally. For the marketer, communications is the way in which the company or enterprise communicates the benefits and differences to target markets and customers.

Increasingly, modern communications techniques attempt to share meaning within a defined context. Each market demands a different type of communication message, context of meaning and medium. For example, industrial markets demand a higher level of personal communication (such as personal selling) than consumer markets that demand a higher degree of non-personal communications (such as advertising). There is an increasing number of communications media that have dramatically broadened the ways in which audiences receive and understand meaning and messages. These have complicated greatly the techniques of the marketer and public relations expert in the transmission of messages to target audiences.

The communications media available to the marketer have grown significantly in the past years, and this has changed the nature of marketing communications. The array of media available often outpaces the ability of the marketer and public relations expert to adapt messages in the right format. Messages can be transmitted through face-to-face communication, formal meetings, conferences, events, interviews, oral communication, the telephone, and the multiparty conference call, long, short, and FM wave and internet-based radio, television, videoconferencing, written communication (in physical and in electronic format), letters, external mail system, internal mail system, e-mail, chat lines, formal reports and memoranda, forms, lists, catalogues, notice boards, journals, newspapers, internal bulletins, newsletters, broadcasts, webcasts, narrowcasts, manuals, visual communication aids (static, pictorial, and animated), presentation charts, films, corporate videos, electronic data interchange. At the beginning of the 21st century, the average consumer in the advanced economies can be exposed to an average of 3000 commercial messages a day.

Despite the multiplicity of media and the vast amplification of 'noise' created by modern communications, the purposes of communications remain relatively constant: to inform, to initiate actions, to communicate decisions, to motivate people, to find out, then make known, needs and requirements, to exchange information, ideas, attitudes, and beliefs, to establish understanding and sometimes meaning, and also to initiate, develop, and maintain relations.

Schramm's Communication model outlines a simple model and process for communications flow:

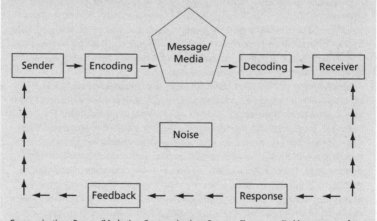

Communications Process/Marketing Communications Process. Figure supplied by courtesy of marketingteacher.com

The process begins with a desire to communicate: the *sender* sends the message to the other party. The sender is alternatively known as the *communicator* or the *source*. It is normal at this stage to have a purpose, or target destination, for the message. The *encoding* stage of the process imbues meaning with symbolic form (such as words, signs, sounds, etc.). At this stage, it is important to understand both the context—which gives meaning to the message—and also the audience whom the final message is intended to reach and to influence. The next stage is the selection of the *media*, that is the communication channel or channels through which the message moves from sender to receiver. It is vital at this stage to select the most important medium to enhance the message. A good message can often be undermined by a poor communications medium. *Decoding* is a process carried out by the *receiver* who converts the symbolic forms transmitted by the sender into a form that has meaning and that makes sense to him. This is one of the more difficult stages in the communications process, as much can change between message transmission and message reception. Often the best-crafted messages through the most impactful communications medium will have an altogether different effect from that intended by the sender. The *receiver* is the party who receives the message, also known as the *audience* or the *destination*. They will often interpret the message and its meaning in their own context and their own circumstances. This often results in a single message having multiple meanings to the same audience. The impact and effect of the message is gauged by the *response* process that measures the reaction of the receiver to the message communicated. This is when the receiver can be transposed into the sender.

Often there is polling of a sample audience immediately after a keynote political speech to determine if the messages transmitted had any resonance in the minds of the receiver. This leads to the *feedback* stage, which is the part of the receiver's response that the receiver communicates back to the sender. *Noise* is a modern description of all those factors that prevent the decoding of a message by the receiver in the way intended by the sender. This is also known as message distortion.

In communications, much can go wrong between the transmission of the message and its reception. One of the core problems faced by the modern marketer is that the attention span of the receiver is either short or very selective, given that the receiver is bombarded by a constant stream of messages on a daily basis (*see also* ATTENTION). The second problem is that the receivers, being human, have a complex array of cultures, preconceived notions, beliefs and opinions that are unique to them and which cause them to distort the information or messages received in order to fit into their belief or value system. The next problem is the receivers' memories—both the short-term memory and the permanent memory. Studies have shown that receivers retain in their permanent memory only a small fraction of the messages that reach them. Beyond that is the more complex phenomenon of message rehearsal, a phenomenon in communication whereby the receiver elaborates on the meaning of the message in a way that brings related thoughts from the long-term memory into the short-term memory.

Fundamental types of communication

- **one-to-many,** this type of communication is normal for mass communication. Content is generated from a single broadcast point and is then made available over airwaves or in mass print runs. One-to-many is an appropriate model for news distribution and other situations in which discussion and dialogue are not necessarily desirable. It is not interactive or tailored to individuals.

- **many-to-one,** many-to-one is often linked to one-to-many communications. Examples include a freefone number, an invitation to return a pre-paid envelope, or a reply button on an e-mail: all techniques of engendering bi-directional communication from mass communications.

- **one-to-one,** the most intensive communication 'transactions' occur at a one-to-one level. For example, a sales presentation, a negotiation over price, or direct delivery is almost always done on a one-to-one basis. For value-based products and services one-to-one communication is preferred. Most one-to-one communications take place face to face. On the Internet the most common type of one-to-one communication takes place in transaction-centred e-mail, where a buyer and seller communicate directly. Another example is instant message 'chat' channels, which are becoming hugely popular in business.

- **many-to-many,** on the Internet the main outlet for many-to-many communications has been in community building such as online forums, real-time chat rooms, 'blogging' websites, discussion boards on issues of common interest. The principal value of many-to-many comes from the participants' ability to exchange ideas and experiences.

- **immediacy and longevity,** each type of communication is time-based. All the communications models listed above lend themselves naturally to different types of 'time'. Some communications fade quickly from memory; others linger longer and have lasting impact. For example, one-to-one communication channels tend to be focused on the here-and-now. At the other extreme, many-to-many channels tend to focus less on urgency and more on reference. Meanwhile, many-to-one and one-to-many have varying levels of immediacy, but almost never have any sort of permanence. These two dimensions, immediacy and longevity, are responsible for defining the underlying *value* of any communications medium.

The tools available in the many-to-many category have the broadest range of time-based attributes. Real-time chat offers immediate communications with almost no inherent longevity at all, while discussion boards and moderated newsgroups offer slow interaction. Newsgroups and on-line forums also offer a certain amount of archival capabilities, providing other users with an additional source of knowledge and expertise. A website is by definition a one-to-many forum, while real-time chat is an immediate, impermanent, many-to-many tool.

company culture An intangible system of values, collective personality, and beliefs shared by people in an organization: the company's collective identity and meaning, often described to outsiders as 'the way we do things around here'. This can be the product of the company's history or of a strong leader or founder. A company's culture shapes the way that it treats its customers and goes to market. This is important for the business-to-business marketer to understand in the same way that the consumer marketer seeks to understand the mind of the individual consumer. *See also* CORPORATE CULTURE.

company forecast The expected level of sales for the company based on a chosen marketing plan and an assumed marketing environment. Frequently these forecasts are given within a relative context, such as market share, or measured against previous years' growth.

comparative advantage The principle that companies and countries are best employed in activities that they undertake and execute relatively better than their competitors. For example, in the economics of international trade, a country has a comparative advantage in producing good X over good Y if it can produce good X at a low opportunity cost relative to good Y. It follows that a country will benefit from specializing in producing goods in which it has a comparative advantage over other countries. *See also* COMPETITION AND COMPETITIVENESS; COMPETITIVE ADVANTAGE; FIVE FORCES MODEL.

comparative advertising An explicit comparison of one product brand with a competitive brand. An example would be the Cola wars in which Pepsi 'challenges' consumers to compare the taste of Pepsi to Coca-Cola. Nowadays some advertising directly and indirectly attacks competitors, such as Virgin Atlantic and British Airways. For a long time comparative advertising was prohibited.

comparative influence A type of influence exerted on consumers by their reference and peer groups. Comparative influence occurs when the reference group provides the means by which consumers compare their beliefs, attitudes, and behaviour. When there is similarity between a consumer's opinions and those of the peer or reference group, the greater the comparative influence of that group. *See also* CONSUMER BEHAVIOUR.

competition

The rival activities between enterprises trying to increase sales, profits, or market share while addressing the same set of customers within a similar target market. Competition is critical in a free-market economy and is the dynamic that drives marketing processes.

A market displaying characteristics of *perfect competition* (which rarely ever exists) would include the following assumptions:

- There are many companies each selling an identical or indistinguishable product (lack of differentiation is much more difficult in the area of services, which are delivered mainly through people, all of whom are different).
- There are many buyers for these products.
- There are no restrictions on entry to the industry or marketplace.
- Firms in the industry have no advantage over potential new entrants.
- Firms and buyers have complete information about the market.

Since in *perfect competition* there are many firms selling a homogenous product, no single firm can influence the market to a greater extent than any other. Therefore, all firms must accept the 'natural' market price for their product.

The short run and the long run

The short run, under perfect competition, is the period during which there is too little time for new firms to enter the industry. In the short run, the total number of firms is fixed. Firms could be making large or small profits, breaking even, or making a loss.

The long run under perfect competition is the period of time that is long enough for new firms to enter the industry.

- In the long run the level of profit will affect the entry or exit of firms.
- Normal profit is the level of profit just sufficient to persuade firms to stay in the industry, but not high enough to attract new firms. This level of normal profit will vary from one industry to another.
- Supernormal profit is any profit above normal profit. If economic profits are being made, new firms will be attracted into the industry in the long run. This will have the effect of increasing supply and reducing price and profit for those firms already in the industry.

Short run equilibrium of the firm

The diagram below shows the short run equilibrium for a firm in perfect competition.

- **Price** is determined by industry supply and demand curves. The firm in a market of perfect competition faces a horizontal demand curve (or average revenue) at this price.

  In the diagram, the y axis represents the natural market (Price) and the x axis (Quantity) represents supply.

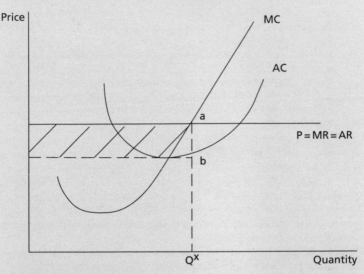

Profit graph

- **Output** profits will be maximized where marginal cost (MC) equals marginal revenue (MR). Whilst MR is greater than MC total revenue is increasing at a faster rate than total cost, thus profits will be increasing. Where marginal cost is greater than marginal revenue, total cost is increasing more quickly than total revenue and therefore profits are declining.
- **Profit**—at the profit maximizing output average cost (AC) (which includes normal profit) is below average revenue and therefore the firm is making supernormal profits. The firm's short run supply curve will be its (short run) marginal cost curve. A supply curve relates quantity to marginal cost.

Long run equilibrium of the firm

In the long run, if typical firms are making economic profits, new firms will be attracted into the industry or existing firms will increase the scale of their operations. The industry supply curve will shift to the right, leading to a fall in price. Supply will go on increasing and price falling until firms are only making normal profits. This will be where the demand

c

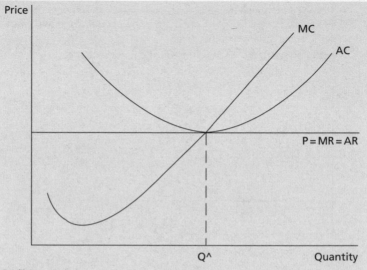

Equilibrium graph

curve for the firm touches the lowest point of its average cost curve. This can be seen in the second diagram.

In the long run if the price falls below the average cost of producing the goods, then firms will make a loss and will leave the industry. If firms leave the industry, supply will decrease and the price will rise until firms are just making normal profit, that is where the demand curve touches the lowest point of the average cost curve. Therefore, under perfect competition output will always tend towards this long run equilibrium. Long run equilibrium is therefore where AR=MR=MC=AC.

Exit point

We can find the short run breakeven price, and the short run exit price, by comparing the price with average variable total costs. Profit maximization occurs where MC=MR. Since the average total cost (ATC) includes all the relevant opportunity costs, this equilibrium is the short run breakeven point where normal profits (zero economic profits) are being made. As the price falls, the firm will carry on producing, but will only be achieving below normal profit. However, if the price falls below the average variable costs, then it will not be worth the firm producing any more products, as they will be making a loss larger than their fixed costs. The exit point from an industry therefore comes when average revenue (AR) is equal to average variable cost (AR=AVC). *See also* BREAKEVEN ANALYSIS; PRICING.

Perfect competition and the public interest

The nature of competition is very important to the overall economy and therefore to the public interest of a country or grouping of nations. Perfect competition carries both advantages and disadvantages:

Advantages

- Price equals marginal cost. Given that price equals marginal utility (that is, how much satisfaction a consumer places on a good), marginal utility will equal marginal costs.
- If a firm is less efficient than other firms it will make less than normal profit and be driven out of business. If it is more efficient it will earn supernormal profits. Thus competition will act as an incentive to efficiency within an industry.
- The desire to earn supernormal profits and to avoid making a loss will encourage the development of new management techniques, processes, and technology.
- The lack of advertising (all goods are homogenous) will lower the firm's costs.
- The long run equilibrium is at the bottom of the firm's long run average cost curve and, therefore, will produce at the lowest cost output.
- The consumer gains from lower prices, since not only are costs low, but there are no long run supernormal profits.
- If consumer attitude towards a product changes, the price change will lead to the firm responding.

These last two points are said to lead to the dominance of the consumer. Consumers through the market decide what, and how much, is produced.

Disadvantages

- Even though firms may have developed new technology, they may not be able to afford the necessary research and development.
- Perfectly competitive industries produce undifferentiated products. This lack of variety may be seen as a disadvantage to the consumer.

Obstacles to efficiency

The two main obstacles to efficiency are:

- External costs and benefits, and
- Existence of monopoly.

The model of perfect competition allows us to understand important features of real world markets even though most markets do not have perfect competition.

competitive activity The actions taken by businesses to improve their profitability at the expense of rivals. Marketing activity should always be considered in a relative position to that of competition. Often the marketing activities of one company (such as price discounting, new product introduction, or market expansion) may trigger a reaction in competitors.

competitive advantage The factor which enables a firm to compete successfully with competitors on a sustained basis particularly to satisfy consumer needs and wants. This leading theory and models of competitive advantage (both of industries, and then of nations) were advanced by Michael Porter in the 1980s. They have had an enormous influence on market strategy and planning.

There are many sources of competitive advantage, among which are:

- superior skills, or resources, such as salespeople;
- expenditure on advertising and sales promotion;
- range and reach of *channels of distribution;
- expenditure on, and successful exploitation of, research and development;
- the scale and efficiency of productive capacity;
- financial resources, such as deep reserves of investment capital or strong cash flows;
- powerful *brand equity;
- market relevant capabilities and expertise;
- a superior supply chain with world-class in-bound and out-bound physical distribution;
- cost-effective and low-cost operations;
- effective marketing;
- excellent customer service;
- efficient procurement and low cost sourcing;
- valuable use of technology to improve business process;
- recruitment of the best people;
- a solid enabling infrastructure.

competitive (and anti-competitive) behaviour The conduct of businesses in market situations involving actions and reactions to achieve advantage over rivals. Strong competition is usually beneficial to the consumer. Most governments in the advanced economies are dedicated to inculcating competitive behaviour and discouraging anti-competitive behaviour (such as *monopoly, *cartels, collusion to limit supply, predatory pricing to drive competitors out of business, and price fixing). Strong and unbiased enforcement of competition policy is one of the key elements in the creation of a modern market economy. Effective marketing depends upon a strong climate of competition and effective regulation of anti-competitive practices that are inimical to consumer interests. The EU and the US have learned from experience that lively domestic competition leads to greater international competitiveness. Weak enforcement of competition policy all too often hinders innovation or else leads to inefficient allocation of resources in the economy and high input costs for business, and hits the defenceless consumer hardest. EU regulatory bodies on competition can fine a company up to 10% of its total world turnover for anti-competitive behaviour and actions.

competitive bidding A process in which buyers request potential suppliers, who are direct competitors, for a proposed purchase or contract. There is usually a short list of suppliers who are requested to submit bids simultaneously by means of a request for proposal. The request for proposal usually includes a detailed specification of the requirement, the standards sought, the terms of delivery, the contract, and the due date of the bid. This is the usual way of winning business in a business-to-business environment and less used in a consumer environment. Competitive bidding is the preferred way of government and public authorities' buying processes. It is usually accompanied by intensive negotiations and presentations.

competitive depositioning A set of actions attempting to change the beliefs of buyers about the attributes of a competitor's product. The attempt may be especially useful in cases where buyers generally have an inflated perception of the quality of a competitor's product. This can also involve comparative advertising. *See* MARKET POSITIONING.

competitive environment Where other firms are vying for the same market. The competitive environment is also a description of how the companies compete within a defined market place—the distribution channels, collaborations between suppliers, competitors, and distributors, the pricing methods, the level of promotion, etc. It is determined by how the competing companies are positioned relative to the *five forces.

competitive equilibrium A market situation of relatively stable competitive position and activity.

competitive forces (Porter's five forces) *See* COMPETITIVE STRATEGY; PORTER, MICHAEL.

competitive myopia Cases of short-sightedness in regard to the activities of competitors by incumbent market players. For example, this may involve an over-concentration on a single competitor to the exclusion of, say, new competitors or rising competitors or it could also mean completely ignoring competition in the marketplace. Often, existing competitors become so fixated by each other that they fail to see new competitors entering their markets in unexpected ways.

competitive niche A defined segment in a market in which a company can compete effectively and possibly win a major share of the market. Here an organization focuses effort and resources on a narrow, delimited segment of a market in which competitors have less strength. Competitive advantage is generated specifically for that market niche. Smaller firms often use a niche strategy. A company could use either a cost focus or a differentiation focus. With a cost focus a firm aims at being the lowest cost producer in that niche or segment. With a differentiation focus a firm creates competitive advantage through differentiation within the niche or segment. There can also be potential problems with the niche approach; for example, if the niche is so small or so specialized that it does not give an adequate return to the companies that serve the niche. *See also* COMPETITIVE STRATEGY; FIVE FORCES MODEL.

competitive parity A method of determining an advertising budget, in which the image, awareness, share of voice, and general perceptions of competitors are compared. The rationale is that one company can improve its brand and image awareness by spending more on advertising than another. Although this theory does not always prove accurate in practice, it is used within numerous companies to argue in favour of investing more in advertising.

competitive parity budgeting A method of allocating a promotion budget based on matching the activity of a major competitor.

competitive position (competitiveness) A range of measures that assesses the overall competitiveness of one company relative to another company operating in a defined market. Traditionally, competitive position can be measured by means of a combination of the following variables:

1 *Relative market share of the competitors.* Here it is important to emphasize relativeness: the reason for this is that an apparently high market share of say 20% can be relatively weak if the nearest competitors have 40% and 35% of the same market; alternatively an apparently low share, of say 8%, can be the dominant share in a highly fragmented market where no one commands more than 10% of the total market.
2 *Costs* (either of production, running the enterprise, or marketing and selling, or a combination of all three), which are particularly important in price-sensitive and mature markets where consumers are looking for higher quality at lower cost.
3 *Price of goods and/or services.* Although this depends on the price elasticity of the market, prices have always tended towards affordability as the market expands. Only the most exclusive luxury brands and services can afford to ignore prices.
4 *Quality of goods and services.* As has often been said, the memory of price fades faster than the memory of poor quality; equally, exceptional quality will quickly erode the memory of high prices.

5 *Accumulated experience* of a service delivery or product, which factors into a lower and more effective way to serve the market. Experience and expertise in products and service delivery is a distinct competitive advantage, which can often enable higher prices to be charged for a rival product and particularly a service. 'They're not cheap, but they are good' is a familiar refrain for this type of company.

6 *R & D performance*: good research and development is critical to the development of good products. The linkage between marketing and research and development (R&D) is often neglected, given that marketing, being in regular touch with the market, can often inform where and how research investment ought to be spent. This prevents what is often known as an 'engineering' or 'technology' centric culture, that emphasizes the technical features and benefits of the product rather than tuning it to the needs of the marketplace. This mindset turns marketing and sales into blind functionaries who have to market and sell whatever is developed. There is always a fine line to tread between slavishly following the market and allowing research that leads to innovative products. The sales and marketing community is often fond of pointing out the examples of technically good products that, because they were developed in a market vacuum (e.g. K_5, Ford Edsel, Concorde, nuclear power stations, Betamax, Visicalc, the Apple Newton), were market failures, whereas the engineers can point to the Sony Walkman, the laser, penicillin, the telephone, etc. that were developed without the assistance of market research and analyses.

7 *Production effectiveness and capacity.* Again, the efficiency of production determines the price and therefore the market competitiveness. A good product cannot survive if the costs of production exceed the amount of return that can be gained from the product. *See also* BREAKEVEN ANALYSIS.

8 *Distribution channel and network*: effective distribution is crucial to effective marketing, particularly for products in either consumer or business-to-business markets. Good products need to reach their target audience at the right time, place, and cost. Increasingly, there are many new channels of distribution, or new ways of reaching audiences, such as the *World Wide Web, that can reduce the costs of engaging audiences with products on a worldwide scale that were previously beyond the reach of a single country or local producer. *See also* CHANNELS OF DISTRIBUTION.

9 *Brand and image reputation* relative to competition; in a world where it is increasingly difficult to sustain product and service differentiation, and where consumers are increasingly discerning and better informed, the image and brand of a company are vital to retaining customer loyalty. A powerful brand and reputation in professional services is now an indispensable necessity to be able to compete. The recent fate of Andersen shows how a once venerable business can be completely wiped out in a very short space of time when trust in the brand is lost in the minds of clients and markets.

10 *Competitive scope*, meaning, for example, the breadth or narrowness, of an organization's focus as measured horizontally by the range of industries, market segments, or geographical regions that the company targets, with its range of products and services. Alternatively, competitive scope can also refer to the degree of *vertical integration that a company has relative to other competitors in the same marketplace. For example, one company in the paper industry may be vertically integrated if it owns the forests, pulp mills, paper-making factories, distribution systems, and outlets for its paper products relative to another competitor that only manufactures paper but does not own the raw materials or the means of distribution and sale.

11 *Competitive dynamics*, which means the overall standing of a company or organization in its markets, relative to the standing of its competitors, when all competitors are described in terms of their size, resources, capabilities, product range and quality, marketing strategies, opportunities, goals, intentions, behaviour, and similar variables. Usually the dynamics of a market are those special or unique ingredients that cause the market to operate as it does and which tend to favour one competitor over another. Also, competitive market dynamics are constantly changing, therefore competitiveness can often be defined by the company that adapts more efficiently to changing market dynamics. *See also* COMPETITIVE ADVANTAGE.

competitive strategy The way in which a company chooses to compete in the marketplace and the method and approach that a company adopts relative to its competitors' strategies. For example, a Competitive Attack Strategy uses various methods for attacking a competitor, many of which are derived from military strategy, including a frontal attack (head-on), a flanking attack (attack at a point of weakness), an encirclement attack (attack on several fronts at once), a by-pass attack (attack by diversifying into new territories, products or technologies), and a guerrilla attack (attack by waging small, intermittent skirmishes with unconventional marketing methods).

Michael *Porter has defined several strategic approaches to competitive strategy:

- *Differentiation* is an approach which offers leadership or focus products which can be regarded as unique in areas which are highly valued by the consumer, creating consumer loyalty which protects the firm from competition. This enables the producer to sell at premium price to consumers who perceive deep value in the product or service.

- *Niche focus* is an approach to serve particularly attractive or suitable segments or niches (to differentiate within one or a small number of target market segments).

- *Cost leadership* attempts to control the market through being the low-cost producer in a given market.

SUMMARY OF PORTER'S COMPETITIVE STRATEGY CLASSIFICATIONS

TYPE OF COMPETITIVE STRATEGY	SKILLS & RESOURCES	ORGANIZATIONAL DIMENSION	ASSOCIATED RISKS
Overall Cost Leadership	Sustained capital investment and access to capital. Outstanding process engineering skills. Intensive supervision of labour by management. Products designed for ease of manufacture. Low-cost distribution system to access the market.	Tight cost control. Frequent, detailed reports on costs and productivity. Structured organization and detailed responsibilities. Incentives based on meeting strict quantitative targets, usually financial.	Technological change that nullifies past investments or learning. Low-cost learning by industry newcomers or followers through imitation, or through their ability to invest in state-of-the-art facilities. Inability to see required product, service or marketing change because of the attention placed on cost. Organization becomes too tactical, run by short-term financial considerations. Inflation in costs that narrow the firm's ability to maintain enough of a price differential to offset competitors' brand images or other approaches to differentiation.
Differentiation	Strong marketing capability. Product design and engineering. Creative flair and innovation.	Strong coordination among functions in R&D, product development, and marketing.	The cost differential between low-cost competitors and the differentiated firm becomes too great for differentiation to hold brand loyalty.
Differentiation	Strong capability in basic research. Corporate reputation for quality or technological leadership.	Subjective measurement and incentives instead of quantitative measures. Amenities to attract highly skilled labour, scientists, or creative people.	Buyers thus sacrifice some of the features, services, or image possessed by the differentiated firm for large cost savings. Buyers' need for the differentiating factor falls. This can occur as buyers become more sophisticated.

	Long tradition in the industry or unique combination of skills drawn from other businesses. Strong cooperation from channels.	Focus on unique competencies of the organization.	Imitation narrows perceived differentiation, a common occurrence as industries mature.
Focus	Combination of the above policies directed at the particular strategic market target.	Combination of the above policies directed at the particular strategic market target.	The cost differential between broad-range competitors and the focused firm widens to eliminate the cost advantages of serving a narrow target, or, to offset the differentiation achieved by focus. The differences in desired products or services between the strategic target and the market as a whole narrows. Competitors find niche markets and sub-segments within the strategic target and out-focus the focuser.

Other individual elements that can be included in a competitive strategy or that may affect the nature of competition:

- *Creation of *cartels* (International cartels: OPEC (oil), and De Beers (diamonds));
- *Product differentiation* through design, quality, packaging, brand name, delivery, after-sales service: for example Dell and Apple computers;
- *Price*. Using customer credit and payment terms, credit allowances, and trade-in values;
- *Promotion* that supports differentiation: for example, sales force, advertising;
- *Distribution* in which one company can dominate a market through superior *channels of distribution, reaching a greater number of customers than their competitors can;
- *Acquisitions*, mergers, and economies of scale;
- *Creation of barriers to entry* to other competitors: for example, the world's top oil companies;
- *Innovation*: for example 3M, Sony, Xerox.

competitor analysis An analysis of competitors' strengths and weaknesses, strategies, assumptions, resources, and *market positioning from all available sources of information, in order to identify suitable market strategies. Competitor analysis is an integral part of market planning. *See also* COMPETITOR INTELLIGENCE; MARKET RESEARCH. The process of competitor analysis involves the following steps:

- Identify competitors within a target market (products, product substitutes, services, generics, new entrants);
- Audit competitor capabilities (financial, technical, managerial, marketing assets, strengths and weaknesses);
- Relate the competitor capabilities to those of the enterprise to determine competitive advantages and disadvantages. Infer competitor objectives and strategic thrust of competitor;
- Deduce competitor strategies (target segments, differential advantages, competitive scope, cost leadership);
- Estimate competitor response pattern to the company's marketing strategy (retaliatory, complacent, hemmed-in, selective, unpredictable). *See also* COMPETITIVE ADVANTAGE; MARKETING PLAN (section on SWOT ANALYSIS); MARKET RESEARCH.

competitor intelligence The systematic collection and analysis of data about a firm's competitors, with the goals of understanding the competitors' positions in the market and of formulating strategies in response. Competitor intelligence is also the process of monitoring the competitive environment. It enables senior managers in companies of all sizes to make informed decisions about everything from marketing and research and development (R&D) to investments and long-term business strategies. Effective competitor intelligence is a continuous process involving the legal and ethical collection of information, analysis, and controlled dissemination of actionable intelligence to decision-makers. It is also important to study the competitor's likely responses to a given course of actions as well as the facts and data about its actual performance.

competitor positioning *See* POSITIONING.

complaint An expression of customer dissatisfaction which can directly affect the company or organization's permanent reputation. The management and handling of complaints is increasingly the focus of marketing interest because the way in which complaints are handled and resolved is critical to the image and reputation of a company or organization in the eyes of its customers. One badly handled situation with a customer complaint can forever injure the reputation of the company with that customer. *See also* CUSTOMER LOYALTY.

complementary products Goods that are sold separately from each other, but which, however, depend on each other for their sales performance.

complements Goods are complements of each other if changes in the demand for one will have a complementary effect on the demand for the other: for example, compact disc players and compact discs, cars and petrol, printers and ink.

comprehensive layout A draft layout of an ad designed for presentation only, but so detailed as to appear very much like the finished ad.

computer-aided personal interviewing *See* CAPI.

computer-aided self-administered interviewing *See* CASI.

computer-aided telephone interviewing *See* CATI.

concentrated marketing Promotional activities focused on a small part of the market with a single or limited line of similar products. It can be used by firms with limited resources or in markets with specialized customer segments. It enables deep concentration of resources in a highly defined market space, with the objective of gaining leadership. It is better known now as *niche marketing. *See also* MARKETING.

concentration ratios The proportion of firms holding most of the market (e.g. the top two firms hold 20%). In the United States, the US Census Bureau covers this.

concept development A process of successively refining, amplifying and enhancing the basic idea of the product. While concept development is often conducted haphazardly, it can and should be a highly organized process:

1. Assess the present situation You must thoroughly understand what people are doing now. You want to know their present satisfaction levels, whether they perceive a problem for which your product may be a solution, and what are their present beliefs, misconceptions, attitudes, and emotions. Look particularly for the issues that they have the most energy around, rather than what they tell you is important. You want to know the words they use, and the way they categorize and conceptualize the area. More often than not, people will not make the same distinctions and discriminations the manufacturers make. Users' concepts will be much more use- and function-oriented. The manufacturers' concepts will be more product- and feature-oriented. Sometimes people say that they don't need the product when it is the kind of product that solves a problem that they don't see, or are embarrassed about, or don't want to acknowledge. Such a response does not mean that your concept is dead. One of the roles of the experienced marketer is to get them to acknowledge that there is a problem. Product rejection is a normal initial reaction, when the respondents take professional pride in their ability to overcome the difficulties that your products will eliminate.

2. Concept statement This step is the most difficult in the concept development and testing process. The way the concept is presented is crucial.

The statement ought to be more than just a straightforward 'objective' description of the features of the product, and it should not make claims that cannot be backed up in reality. Instead, a balance must be struck between a specification and a sales document. It should begin with a brief description of the present situation, in words the target audience uses. It is usually best to describe the concept as a solution to a problem; then the product or the service itself, and, importantly, how the product's claims will be substantiated.

3. Refine and elaborate the statement with subsequent testing with different groups The concept statement is written and rewritten, for successive groups, continually taking into account what has been learned before. Each time it is presented, the marketer will elicit qualms, objections, and concerns as well as praise, new uses, and new ways of describing it. You take the positives and incorporate them into the concept statement. With the negatives, the marketer will look for ways to turn them into benefits. The marketer will find out directly from participants how the product can be made more appealing.

Almost every good concept starts off with strong scepticism, which can be devastating to the client unless the process is understood. Sometimes concept testing is unfortunately stopped at this initial flood of objections. However, objections are actually desirable, because in the first sessions you want to understand people's concerns. As successive focus groups begin to become more positive, it is important to reiterate the negatives encountered in former groups and ask them how they would answer such objections. Shifts of opinion, however subtle or implicit, should be closely monitored. These shifts of opinion, either from positive to negative or vice versa, are often intimations of how the product will be received in the real marketplace.

For concept work, a skilled marketer or facilitator is needed—especially someone with experience of product introductions, successful as well as unsuccessful. The facilitator should also have extensive experience in creative idea generation sessions.

What to avoid in a concept development focus group

- letting the participants take a product, rather than market, focus;
- using a moderator inexperienced in concept development;
- adopting a 'Testing' mindset rather than one focused on concept development;
- testing products that are not comprehensible to the focus group, such as products that can't be produced in prototype, or ideas that are so vague that they cannot yet be communicated meaningfully;
- waiting until it is too late to do concept development. This is sometimes the case in the pharmaceutical industry where many products are tested only after the clinical trials are arranged;
- killing the concept at the first sign of either negative or sceptical reaction;
- taking votes for the purpose of projecting whether the concept will be successful. Much can be extrapolated from groups, but this ought to be based on opinions and reactions;

- taking what people say at face value, rather than looking for deeper reactions and contexts for what they are saying. *See also* MARKET RESEARCH.

concept testing The testing of a new product concept with a group of target consumers to learn whether the concepts have the wrong consumer appeal and should be developed further. *See also* MARKET RESEARCH. Fundamentally, concept testing and development are techniques that attempt to predict the success of a new product idea before it is actually marketed in order to mitigate the risk of a misplaced launch. The research usually involves getting people's reactions to a statement describing the basic idea of the product. The concept is ultimately 'bought' in the minds of people who will not be the ultimate consumers. It is also important to gauge the reaction of those who will ultimately influence the product concept.

Care should be taken with concept testing that the original idea is not lost: a more fruitful approach is to use testing as part of the gradual development and refinement of new ideas into a form that is most likely to be accepted in the marketplace. Testing can also provide guidance for the communication of relevant benefits, uses, packaging, advertising, sales approaches, product information, distribution, and pricing. People find it more difficult to hypothesize and, generally, test groups react better to actual products than to conceptual ideas about new products. Also, they tend to be sceptical about new ideas, and often hostile to them. Radically new products shake up people's established way of doing things, putting them at or over the edge of their own incompetence. So, new ideas are unsettling at best, and a threat at worst. People often do not have the imagination to see how the new product would benefit them.

For these reasons, good ideas which were ultimate successes, like automated teller machines, extended battery-life pacemakers, VCRs, and the Walkman had major problems when they were first described to people in the concept testing stage of development. New product ideas presented in the form of a half-page concept statement run a terrible risk of being killed prematurely. Concept testing is sometimes practised rather naïvely. All too often, a couple of *focus groups are assembled, read a simple description of the concept and people are then asked for their reactions. This approach can often be dangerous. Many underdeveloped, defenceless concepts are killed in their early stages by being concept tested by only a few groups of people.

However, concept testing can be a very powerful tool. It has saved hundreds of millions in investments. It helps marketers avoid false starts, wrong positioning, poor strategy, and selling in a misdirected way to the wrong parts of the market. It is not only vital insurance, but also more importantly, it acts as a guide throughout the entire concept development process, from original thinking to successful launch. The idea is not the product. It is disastrous to believe that a new product will sell itself. It is absolutely necessary to see the product from the point of view of the customers. A new product is unsettling to most people. It usually requires a new way of doing things.

Consumers only change to new products when they perceive that there is a significant benefit or gain. They have to believe it is more valuable than the money, time, and comfort that they will have to give up in order to purchase it. Marketers have to convince people that it will ultimately be an improvement over what they have now, it is worth changing from what they already have, there is a relatively simple way to verify its superiority, and that it will live up to the promises implicit in the claims made for it. Marginal improvements rarely succeed in displacing a market leader. Different people will perceive even the most straightforward product differently. It can be seen from various perspectives, used for a variety of purposes, in different contexts, and with different expectations. Most products require a prototype and initial testing in the real world.

conditioning Learning to associate a stimulus with a response.

condition reflexes The reaction of consumers following a reminder stimulus to the earlier brand conditioning.

conglomerate diversification The making or acquiring of new products for new markets, particularly in a large and diverse company with multiple products in multiple markets. A conglomerate diversification merger or takeover is where businesses in completely different industries merge together, for example if a leisure company merged with a computer firm.

conjoint analysis A versatile market research technique that can provide valuable information for market segmentation, new product development, forecasting and pricing decisions. The technique is important in competitive positioning of new products and in new product development. It seeks to determine the relative importance and strength of various combinations of product attributes in the minds of target customers. The background research on conjoint analysis focuses on combinations rather than individual attributes of products and services. Respondents are asked to evaluate various combinations of attributes, and then asked to evaluate them overall. The objective is to find the right combination for the right target market. For example, the perfect combination for the British middle-class buyer of a Volvo may be safety and durability, rather than safety and style. In a real purchase situation, buyers examine and evaluate a range of features or attributes in making their final purchase choice. Conjoint analysis examines these evaluations and exchanges to determine what features are most valued by buyers. Once data is collected the researcher can conduct a number of 'choice simulations' to estimate market share for products with different attributes/features. This lets the researcher know which products or services will be successful before the product is introduced to the market.

conjoint association A moderation technique in which participants are asked to choose between two hypothetical products or services, each of which has different attributes. The objective is to stimulate discussion about the various attributes in order to gain insight into the relative value of each.

conspicuous consumption A term coined by US economist Thorstein Veblen in 1899 to describe the practice of buying goods which will impress the social group to which the purchaser aspires, and which creates an outward impression of a materially and socially successful lifestyle.

consumer The end user of a product or service. The consumer may or may not be the actual buying customer. A consumer is different from either retail or wholesale buyers in that the consumer tends to buy for personal use rather than for resale. Consumer activity, in terms of saving and spending, is a bellwether of confidence that is much observed and studied in the modern economy. *See also* BUYER AND BUYING BEHAVIOUR.

consumer advertising Promotions directed at a person who will actually use the product for their own benefit (rather than business-to-business or organizational advertising). *See also* CONSUMER MARKETING.

consumer behaviour and motivations models

Consumer behaviour is a process through which an identifiable group of consumers actually make buying decisions. Any study of consumer buying behaviour must also include the forces that influence them in making their decisions in their final choice of a brand at a given time, place, and price. Deep study of consumer behaviour is a separate discipline within marketing and has grown in sophistication since its origins in the 1960s.

In the quest of understanding why consumers behave as they do, what their mental processes are, and what influences them, many academic models and theories of consumer behaviour have been elaborated. These various models show how the consumer develops and grows towards a decision, using information, knowledge, and experience, and then how these decisions are either reinforced or rejected over time. Many of these models go into the roots of human psychology, sociology, economics, and learning. Some models involve differential calculus, mathematical modelling, computer simulation techniques, econometrics, Freudian analysis, sociology, statistical analysis, and even game theory.

The theories of consumer behaviour explore the various drivers, fundamental and secondary, that impel consumers towards their choices. Some of these choices can be highly rational, in that they seek to satisfy their needs within their disposable income range to the best of their knowledge; others are more emotional, in that they are actually attempting to satisfy some subconscious desire deep within their psyche.

Consumer behaviour is analysed using one or several of the following general models:

- **The Stimulus-Response Model** Behaviour is determined by learned experience through exposure to a set of stimuli and their associations. There is a focus on human drives—both primary and secondary. Secondary drives are learned drives (pride, covetousness, status, fear) that are acquired in order to satisfy primary drives (safety, need to belong, etc.). Various stimuli are focused on satisfying these drives and can result in brand loyalty. These stimuli (including those created by marketing) activate the drives and the response made by the consumer to these various stimuli. Various types of reinforcement also condition the consumer to respond in similar ways again over time, for example to buy the same brand again.

- **Psychological Models** These theories attribute complex motives to buying, including an intermingling of functional and symbolic drivers. For example, someone who buys a Rolex watch may say that the motive is for the precision of its timekeeping whilst the real reason is to display social status. The fundamental role of the psyche is, therefore, not always made known to marketers with various research survey instruments, because consumers are not always prepared, or not always conditioned, to say what their deeper psyche is really wanting. This may account for some of the many new product launches that fail, despite market research giving every indication of potential success. *See also* HIERARCHY OF NEEDS.

- **Sociological Model** This model espouses the view that consumers' behaviour is primarily determined by the social forces that act upon them. These are, for example, the culture and value system of the society that the consumer lives within; the subculture which is a group within the dominant culture whose values are somewhat at variance with the mainstream. Social class is a grouping where individuals in a given society share similar values, education, income levels, and lifestyles; reference groups which shape the individual's behaviour and from whom the individual seeks validation.

- **Economic Model** This model is founded on the concept of utility maximization, in which the individual seeks to maximize their self-interest within their economic means. This model views the consumer as mainly rational, and one who tends to spend within reason and according to their means.

Many of these consumer behaviour theories are predicated upon the availability of information to the consumer and various other stimuli that are derived from the industrial world. They make assumptions in that context about how the consumers are equipped to analyse and evaluate available information and then make choices and final purchase decisions. However, many of these models and theories were developed before the commercialization of the *Internet via the *World Wide Web. In the present times, the Internet has made the consumer much more powerful in terms of information, accessibility, and range of buying choices available, but it is too early to tell if it has made buying decisions more rational. Consumers often delegate the processing of available information and the evaluation of competing products and services because their knowledge is imperfect, and often the glut of information has made the buyer less sure of their overall knowledge and, as a result, has modified their decision-making processes.

consumer demand The total number of customers who want to buy a specific product or service create consumer demand. Manufacturers often deliberately under-produce much-sought-after goods in order to intensify consumer demand, as in, for example, the intentional under-supplying of the must-have Christmas presents.

consumer goods Goods made for the household consumer, which can be used without any further commercial processing. Convenience goods are generally purchased in small units of low value (e.g. milk, sweets). Shopping goods have higher unit values and are bought less frequently (e.g. clothes, furniture). Speciality goods are those of high value, which a customer will know by name and go out of their way to purchase. *See also* CONSUMER MARKETING; MARKETING.

consumerism 1 The advocacy of the rights of consumers, as against the efforts of advertisers and producers (*see* CONSUMER RIGHTS).
  2 The emphasis of advertising, public relations, and marketing efforts towards creating consumers (*see* CONSUMER SOCIETY).
  These two definitions are almost opposite in meaning, but the former is commonly used today, while the latter was common prior to the 1970s.

consumerists Groups and organizations who exert legal, moral, and economic pressure on businesses to make them more accountable for the interests of their consumers over their profits.

consumer jury test A method of testing advertisements that involves asking consumers to compare, rank, and otherwise evaluate the ads. *See also* MARKET RESEARCH.

consumer market A market characterized by the purchase of goods for personal consumption by single, or very few, buyers each buying a small volume of goods but which, in aggregate, leads to mass numbers of total goods sold in the market. In this type of market, the consumer purchases directly from the *retailer.

consumer marketing The promoting and selling of goods directly to the consumer for personal consumption. In contrast to the *business-to-business marketer, the consumer marketer must address a market of many buyers with very few decision-makers in the overall pattern of purchasing. The amounts are usually relatively small and there is little direct contact or communication between the producer and the end customer. Consumer goods are largely sold through retailers and intermediaries rather than directly, which makes pricing and channel management very important components of the consumer marketing mix. *See also* BUSINESS-TO-BUSINESS MARKETING; BUYER AND BUYING BEHAVIOUR; CONSUMER BEHAVIOUR AND MOTIVATIONS MODELS.

consumer panel A form of sample surveying where data is collected from the sample of consumers on more than one occasion. These panels are used to test new products or to modify or improve existing ones. These can often happen in person as well as remotely. Information technology has made the job of the panel members a lot easier. *See* CONCEPT DEVELOPMENT; CONCEPT TESTING; MARKET RESEARCH.

consumer products *See* PRODUCT.

consumer rights Those rights designed for the benefit and protection of consumers and to force the producers and providers to take the consumer's perspective. Various laws and protective bodies augment the rights and powers of consumers in relation to sellers up to the point where the consumer is able to defend his interests.

An example is John F Kennedy's Consumer Bill of Rights in 1962, which is the landmark legislation in this area and defines the four fundamental principles and rights of the consumer:

1 The right of consumers to be protected from defective goods and services and unscrupulous or illegal traders.
2 The right of consumers to be informed about what they are buying, the price, quality, contents, and guarantees for the product or service.
3 The consumer's right to choose and to have a range of competing choices and prices.
4 The consumer's right to be heard by producers and retailers and to have means of redress against them if required.

Consumers' rights are, in the advanced economies, becoming as important as political, social, and human rights, and have gained a further stimulus as a result of new trading patterns resulting from *globalization and the *Internet.

Consumers' Association A UK interest group representing consumers; it conducts product tests and comparisons, and lobbies government. It also publishes a range of consumer publications.

consumer satisfaction The evaluation of a product or service as meeting or exceeding the consumer need and expectation. This is a key measure of *brand loyalty.

consumer society The organized pursuit of getting and spending on a mass scale: a social and economic phenomenon that expanded continuously throughout the 20th century. The United Nations reports that world consumption expanded at an unprecedented pace over the 20th century, with private and public consumption expenditures reaching $24 trillion in 1998, twice the level of 1975 and six times that of 1950. In 1900 real consumption expenditure was $1.5 trillion.

Prior to the 20th century, consumerism as a lifestyle activity was confined to social elites. For the mass of the people, buying was based on necessities. Cultures and religions were not favourable to consumer society. Many Christian denominations frowned upon 'luxury' and encouraged frugality. Gradually, some religions and belief systems promoted some limited, careful consumption for all and protested disparities in consumption between rich and poor. Excessive or conspicuous consumption, particularly by the rich, was often recognized and criticized in pre-industrial societies.

The rise in mass consumerism that started in the late 19th century and continued throughout the 20th was caused by over-production of goods by new technologies without enough people to buy them. Resources were scarce prior to systematic and mass production of goods. However, technological advances and innovations in production changed the situation from dearth to one of abundance. Raw materials and resources become more accessible than ever before. These advances were supplemented by the expansion of new trade routes with modern transport, military conquest, the growth of urban centres, and the wealthier nation states experiencing second waves of industrialization.

Convincing people to buy more goods beyond those needed to sustain them, by generating a new ideology of pleasure and leisure, was part of the birth of modern marketing. Active consumption was encouraged. The barriers to a consumer society were gradually removed; there were changes in attitude and lifestyle, higher standards of living, a new approach to international commerce, as well as changes in the law, and, notably, higher wages and the extension of mass credit. The effect of this credit was to increase consumer debt, while creating mass markets for consumer goods that stimulated economic growth.

The role of marketing was to promote the idea that those goods that were previously regarded as luxuries of the rich, were now necessities for everyone. (For example, *see* APPENDIX 2—Luxury Goods, the case on De Beer's A Diamond is Forever campaign.) This was a trend that has continued, fuelled by marketing, up to the present day. Conspicuous consumption became the hallmark of wealthy countries and their citizens.

One of the early engines of mass consumer society was the *department store. Department stores were created to constantly display goods on a scale never previously imagined and to encourage people to buy them. There were also developments in the concept and practice of 'customer service'—where people who bought in department stores were flattered with levels of service hitherto reserved for the social elite. The shopping malls that succeeded the department store, and the hypermarkets that succeeded the supermarket, are carefully designed to create appropriate moods to indirectly encourage buying. Also, as home ownership rose, the home and the family became a focus of mass consumption. Shopping was done increasingly from the home—through catalogues, by mail, by telephone, by television, and latterly over the Internet.

Also, the profession and the techniques of advertising grew rapidly in, and helped to shape, a new commercial culture aimed at the masses. In the United States in 1880, only $30 m was spent on advertising; by 1910, $600 m (then 4% of national income) was spent; today the US spends $120 bn and worldwide $250 bn is spent on advertising. Advertisers helped to create the concepts of fashion and fashionability and obsolescence—creating a constant restlessness about needing to have new and up-to-date possessions; buying for style rather than for need, in order to remain 'fashionable'. *See also* ADVERTISING.

Education services also began to embrace business and to create learning in marketing, sales, accounting, and communications. Governments set up departments and chambers of commerce to promote consumption of commodities. In the US, government-sponsored consumer research began in the 1920s; in the UK, it did not begin until the 1950s. These surveys detailed what citizens consumed and where and how they purchased.

Consumerism and the cult of individualism became intertwined. The discipline of psychology, pioneered in the 20th century, contributed to understanding and promoting individualism. From its social and political activism beginnings, individualism became used and understood by corporations to create more diverse products for consumers. There is overwhelming pressure to consume and to be seen to be consuming. Some people resort to what psychologists term as 'compensatory consumption', that is, consuming even more to feel better, or as it has become popularly known, retail therapy.

Individualism became good for business and marketing shaped its messages around this new individualism. Corporations supported individualism, but detached it from strong political and social activism. The 1960s generation, once concerned with social issues, started to focus on exploring and fulfilling their individual desires through the purchase of material goods. Consumption became a definition of identity: 'I shop, therefore I am.' Democratic participation increasingly became about expressing needs and wants rather than supporting great causes.

The consumer society has evolved in such a way that consumption and consumerism (for good and bad) is identified as being at the core of a modern culture and society. Right-wing governments in Europe and America continued to champion and support individualism throughout the 1980s. The collapse of the Soviet Union and the Soviet bloc was seen in the west as much as a triumph of consumerism, and people's desire to go shopping, as much as of ideology. China opened its markets and encouraged a far greater degree of consumer demand than hitherto. Corporations began to globalize. Consumerism became a global phenomenon rather than just the preserve of the wealthy nations. Global brands, global production and distribution were everywhere. Governments now constantly monitor consumer debt and behaviour as this has the power to destabilize—or in some cases, prop up—an overall modern economy.

The rise of consumer society has had many critics, both in the capitalist and non-capitalist worlds. In the 20th century a worldwide battle for access to and control of consumable resources has driven many conflicts and conquests. Conquest and control of oil supplies, for example, was a major factor in the military and political strategies of combatants in both world wars. Unequal trade between unequal regions has led to a massive imbalance that is reflected in differentials in consumption. There has been much protest that the poorer countries end up servicing the consumption of the wealthier countries. Globally, 20% of the world's people in the highest-income countries account for 86% of total private consumption expenditures; the poorest 20% a minuscule 1.3%. The richest 20% of the world consume 45% of all meat and fish, the poorest 20%, only 5%. The richest fifth consume 58% of total energy, the poorest fifth less than 4%. The richest fifth have 74% of all telephone lines, the poorest fifth only 1.5%. The richest fifth consume 84% of all paper, the poorest fifth 1.1%. And the richest fifth own 87% of the world's cars while the poorest fifth less than 1%.

In the 1960s, there were growing student-based and civil rights movements in the advanced consumer economies among whose targets were corporations who were exploitative in their drive for profits, and who encouraged mass consumerism that was creating conformity. With increasing activism, this had a possibility of threatening political stability for power holders, and economic stability for corporations in nation states, as students and the young are the consumers of the future.

In the early 21st century there is in the advanced economies another backlash—similar in some ways to the 1960s' backlash against the materialist, mass consumer society—but now it is more focused on globalization, particularly its effect on the environment, global resources, the exacerbation of inequality, and on the destruction of local ways of life. How we consume, and for what purposes, drives how we extract resources, create products, and produce pollution and waste. Issues relating to consumption also affect environmental degradation, poverty, hunger, and even the rise in obesity. Global brands— particularly those that use low-paid foreign labour in the manufacture of their products—are particularly vilified. Marketing, seen as the handmaiden of the consumer society, has also suffered in the backlash against global brands and the cult of 'spin'. *See also* ANTICORPORATION; PUBLIC RELATIONS.

consumer stimulants The promotional efforts designed to stimulate short-term purchasing behaviour. Coupons offering price discounts, premiums, two-for-one offers, special sales, and samples are examples of consumer stimulants.

consumer-to-business (c2b) The (mainly) online practice where the consumer offers, for example, a service, product, or product idea to a company. This is a reversal of the more traditional model, and is facilitated by the *Internet.

consumer-to-consumer (c2c) The online practice where one consumer conducts a transaction with another consumer, usually through a third party who will charge a fee, as in eBay.com.

consumer unit All related members of a particular household; a person living alone or sharing a household with others, who is financially independent; two or more persons living together who pool their incomes to make joint purchases.

consumption expenditure *See* AGGREGATE DEMAND.

contest A promotion, such as a sweepstake, prize draw, lottery, or quiz, that offers a prize and may or may not require a purchase for prize eligibility. These are often linked to direct *below-the-line marketing.

contextual advertising The online practice of scanning *keywords in the website the user is viewing and displaying advertisements related to that subject.

contingency The action with a marketing plan to be implemented only upon the occurrence of future events other than those in the accepted plan.

continuity The scheduling of advertisements to appear in media channels at regular intervals over a period of time.

continuous advertising The scheduling of advertisements to appear regularly, even during times when consumers are not likely to purchase the product or service, so that consumers are constantly reminded of the brand.

continuous research A research activity planned to provide regular information from systematic ongoing data collection from key sources. This could, for example, include: sales quantity and value by individual customer; sales quantity and value by product; profitability by customer; profitability by product. This research is then used to inform and shape marketing programmes. *See also* MARKET RESEARCH.

contractual marketing system A system defined by Philip *Kotler as *vertical marketing in which independent firms at different levels of production and distribution join together through contracts to obtain more economies or sales impact than they could achieve alone.

contribution A financial measure of sales value less variable cost of sales. More generally it can be anything that adds value or benefit, either tangible or intangible.

contributions centre A profit centre where expenditure is reported on a marginal or direct cost basis.

control group *See* REFERENCE GROUP.

controlled circulation The publications, generally business-oriented, that are delivered only to readers who have some special qualifications or positions. Generally, publications are free to the qualified recipients. An example is the *McKinsey Quarterly*.

convenience goods Those consumer goods that the customer usually buys frequently, immediately, and with the minimum of comparison and buying effort. Alternatively they are relatively inexpensive products that buyers or users choose frequently with a minimum of thought and effort. *See also* BUYER AND BUYING BEHAVIOUR; CONSUMER MARKETING.

convenience sampling *See* SAMPLING.

convenience store A small-scale retail outlet, usually located near a residential area, serving a local market, open long hours, seven days a week, and carrying a limited line of high-turnover goods that are more convenient for customers to buy locally than in a major supermarket or mall. *See also* BUYER AND BUYING BEHAVIOUR; CONSUMER MARKETING.

conventional distribution channel A channel consisting of one or more independent producers, wholesalers, and retailers, each a separate business seeking to maximize its own profits even at the expense of profits for the system as a whole. *See also* CHANNELS OF DISTRIBUTION.

conversion rate A measure of the number of online visitors to a *website who take a specified action (expressed as a percentage of the total number of visitors). These actions could typically be sales of products, membership registrations, newsletter subscriptions, software downloads, or polling. A high conversion rate depends on several factors, such as the attractiveness of the site, the offer, the interest level of the visitor, the ease of using the buttons, the quality of the navigation guides, and speed of loading. *See also* INTERACTIVE MARKETING.

cookie The information stored on a user's computer by a *website in order that website preferences are remembered on future requests. Cookies are passed from a web server through a web browser to the user's hard drive. This information is essential for many of the features taken for granted on the *Web, such as shopping cart credit information and personalized portals. Privacy advocates and guardians have raised concerns over the role of cookies in online advertisements. They fear that large companies could piece together information that could be used against individuals, especially if offline information is merged with online information. Cookies are not universally used. Estimates vary, but some percentage of the web population browses with cookies turned off. Cookies can be blocked completely via the browser, or selectively via a cookie manager.

cooperative advertising (co-op advertising) A system by which ad costs are divided between two or more parties. Usually, such programmes are offered by manufacturers to their wholesalers or retailers, as a means of encouraging them to advertise the products themselves.

cooperative campaign A collaboration of two or more advertisers and advertising in which the manufacturer of a product provides materials to and reimburses a retailer for part or all of the retailer's advertising expenditures. *See also* ADVERTISING.

cooperative marketing The practice whereby several companies in the same marketing area combine in order to create or increase demand for a specific product, for the benefit of all.

co-op payment (honorarium, incentive) The payment provided to participants as an incentive to come to the *focus group or answer surveys. The amount varies dramatically, based on the difficulty of recruiting the participants.

copy The spoken or written words that make up the substance of all advertisements. It does not include artwork and graphics although in more recent times copy is often used to mean the finished work. *See also* ADVERTISING.

copy date The date at which the finished advert must be delivered to the publisher or broadcaster.

copyright The exclusive legal right to reproduce, publish, and sell the matter and form of a literary, musical, or artistic work. Copyright laws were developed over the last century for the physical, controllable world; however, the world of the *Internet with instant publication and vast distribution channel has challenged the existing copyright laws and the copyright owners' ability to police and enforce them. An example of the new threat to old copyright processes was the huge popularity of the free music file-sharing Napster website and its major challenge to the assumptions of the music industry. Napster, which itself was bought by a large media conglomerate, raised many questions about the nature of artistic property rights in a digital medium where copying and file sharing are made possible on a massive scale.

copy testing Research to determine an advert's effectiveness, based on consumer responses to the ad, or special panels used to evaluate the ad, before or after it is printed or broadcast. Copy testing is an integral part of the creative development process.

copywriter The person in an advertising agency who writes the words that are in an advert.

core customers A company's more important customers, distinguished from the rest by their long-term value to the company. The standard wisdom is that the core customers never usually constitute more that 20% of the total customer base of a company. *See also* CUSTOMER LOYALTY.

cornering the market The practice of a company gaining control of a market sector at a point where there is high demand and little competition, taking advantage of the opportunity to set prices and erect entrance barriers to new entrants.

corporate appraisal A critical assessment of the strengths and weaknesses, opportunities and threats in relation to the internal and environmental factors affecting an entity in order to establish its condition prior to the preparation of the long-term plan. *See also* MARKETING PLAN (section on SWOT ANALYSIS).

corporate culture The culture of an organization, perhaps influenced by its founder, dominant group, history, structure and systems, leadership, and management style. It is often described as 'the way we do things here'.

corporate marketing The development and maintenance of a company's image and reputation at the institutional level and combining a range of disciplines such as *brand development, *public relations, investor communications, crisis communications, corporate website, corporate *advertising, *marketing strategy. It is often the role of corporate marketing to ensure the cohesion and integration of marketing across all the various marketing programmes that exist at the product and divisional level of a corporation.

corporate marketing research department The group that oversees and/or conducts research to support the firm's present or future marketing efforts, particularly overall positioning and market strategy.

corporate sponsorship The corporate financial backing for a project or event, in return for public exposure and goodwill. Often referred to as 'as brought to you by company X' in the advertisements for cultural events. This is now seen to be a field of mutual interest. The UK national lottery, for example, the largest business to consumer business in the UK, donates the majority of its profits to good causes that might otherwise be funded by private charity or the taxpayer. *See also* MARKETING.

corporate strategy A total strategy for the business as a whole, including all strategic objectives and all aspects of investment and execution programmes, including marketing. Successful marketing is usually deeply integrated into the corporate strategy.

corrective advertising An advertisement or messages within advertisements for the purpose of correcting consumers' mistaken impressions created by prior advertising. Public authorities, such as the advertising standards agency in the given country, usually order this type of advertising.

co-sponsorship To sponsor an event with another sponsor, so that the event owner has benefits from the additional sponsorship fees and the individual sponsors benefit from the juxtaposition, or that a less prestigious sponsor benefits from juxtaposition alongside a more prestigious company.

cost-based pricing *See* PRICING.

cost benefit analysis A method of measuring resources used in an activity and comparing them with the value of benefits. Marketing is frequently one of the costs measured and its benefit is not always easily expressed in straightforward financial terms.

cost efficiency The balance, for a media schedule or purchase, of reaching target audiences at the right frequency relative to the business goals and at the lowest price.

cost leadership The attempt to control the market through being the low cost producer (lowest cost position). *See also* COMPETITIVE ADVANTAGE; COMPETITIVE STRATEGY; POSITIONING.

A business obtains low cost leadership by focusing attention on it at every functional level of the organization. Low cost leaders typically:
1 optimize the operating efficiency of facilities;
2 pursue cost reductions through tight procedural controls, and avoidance or elimination of marginal customer accounts; and
3 minimize costs in areas like research and development.

Many businesses have grown from small to very big over the years using low cost leadership as a strategic tool. Some of the more famous examples include Briggs and Stratton, Texas Instruments, Black and Decker, Du Pont, and Wal-Mart. Low cost leadership is certainly a proven approach to successful competition in the marketplace.

cost of ownership The total cost of acquiring and owning a product; it includes the search costs, the purchase price, and any other expenses related to installation, maintenance, service, and replacement. It is traditionally used by business to help control costs and make strategic decisions. Product salesmen often use it, particularly those selling computer systems, to indicate total costs to potential customers.

cost of sales The sum or variable cost of the total value of the goods and services that were sold to customers. Typically, this refers to businesses that buy inventory for resale or a manufacturer who builds items for resale. Total revenue less cost of goods sold equals gross profit.

cost per action (CPA) An online advertising payment model in which payment is based solely on qualifying actions such as sales or registrations.

cost per click (CPC) The cost or cost-equivalent paid per *click-through on a *website.

cost per inquiry The cost of prompting one person to inquire about your product or service. This is a standard used in direct response advertising.

cost per rating point (CPP) The cost, per 1% of a target audience, of buying advertising space in a given media vehicle.

cost per thousand A measure of media and advertising cost-effectiveness, in terms of the price paid to reach a target audience of one thousand readers. *See also* ADVERTISING.

cost plus pricing A method of determining the price of a good by adding a percentage mark-up to the average variable cost. *See also* PRICING.

cost pool A group of all costs that are associated with the same activity or cost driver.

cost-push inflation An increase in the costs of production of goods and services, either from prices of imported raw materials or from salary increases.

cost unit A unit of product or service in relation to which costs are ascertained.

counter-advertising A contrary position to an advertising message that preceded it. Such advertising may be used to take an opposing position on a polemical subject in a public debate, or to counter an impression that might be made by another party's advertising.

counterpurchasing *See* COUNTERTRADE.

countertrade A reciprocal and compensatory trade agreement in the purchase of goods or services between the seller and the buyer of a product, or when the seller assists the buyer in reducing the amount of net cost of the purchase through some form of compensatory financing. Countertrading is now a sophisticated international activity with multiple types of trading activity determined by the trading party and the economies in which they trade. It has been compared to a modern type of the barter system which was one of the older forms of international trading. For example, in trading with countries that do not have 'hard' currencies, exchange of goods or services of equivalent value can take place without the use of currency. A computer system may be sold in exchange for uranium, nickel, wood, or rubber. One of the main uses of countertrade is in defence and aerospace deals. For example, advanced industrial economies will often use reciprocal trade agreements using industrial goods and services in compensation for military-related export sales and services. This is known as an *offset deal* and can be divided into two categories, *indirect offset* and *direct offset*. The former is when goods and services unrelated to the aerospace or defence material are sold in exchange; the latter is when compensation is in related goods and usually involves a licence or joint venture. Another type of agreement is one in which the exporter either buys, or undertakes to find a buyer for, a specified amount or value of unrelated goods from the initial importer during a specified time period. This is known as counterpurchasing. Also, often as part of an offset agreement, other than co-production or licensed production, some level of technology transfer is agreed. It may be in the form of research and development, technical assistance and training, or patent exchange. This is important to many Third World enterprises, both public and private. *See also* EXPORTING; INTERNATIONAL MARKETING.

coupon A legal certificate offered by manufacturers or retailers that entitles the bearer to a discount on an item at the time of purchase; includes rebates. Alternatively, they can be certificates that give buyers a saving when they purchase a product. A coupon is a very frequent technique in consumer goods marketing. It usually takes the form of a voucher with money off the purchase price, with the purpose of encouraging greater amounts of purchase or else as a way of rewarding consumer loyalty. There is always a vast disparity between the number of coupons issued and the number redeemed, usually in the range of 10–15%, suggesting that this is not a very efficient way of marketing.

coverage (reach) A measure of the percentage of the specified target that see an advertisement at least once during a defined time period of an advertising campaign. *See also* ADVERTISING.

crawl frequency The rate at which a *website is crawled. High rates of crawling, by, say a 'spider' like that of *Google, is a mark of the website's status and trustworthiness. Sites which are well trusted or frequently updated may be crawled more frequently than sites with low trust scores and limited *link authority. *See also* SPIDER.

creaming (the market) The deliberate selling of a product or service at a high price before substitutes appear and reduce the price, by which time the market will have been 'creamed'. *See also* PRICING.

creatives The art directors, designers, and copywriters in an ad agency, often distinguished from the 'suits' (such as account directors) by their unique culture and attitude.

creative strategy An outline of the positioning message: to whom it should be conveyed, together with tone, substance, and objective. This is usually set down in a document called a creative brief, and provides the guiding principles for copywriters and art directors who are assigned to develop the advertisement from a concept to full copy, artwork, and campaign. Within the context of that assignment, any ad that is then created should conform to that strategy and creative brief.

credentials Evidence proving the truth of stated facts, concerning the individual qualifications and relevant experience.

credibility gap The lack of correlation between the level of performance actually achieved and the greater expectations created by exaggerated or unrealistic claims made for an individual company, product, or service.

credit (and the availability of credit) A component of market demand. The rise of easily available credit to individuals and to business has gone hand in hand with the rise of the *consumer society. Governments and their economic agencies now closely monitor the levels of consumer credit and debt—partly with a view to controlling inflation. Raising interest rates is one way of controlling spiralling credit; reducing interest rates, or easing credit might be to encourage a higher promotion of bad debts or to increase sales volume. As advanced economies have moved from a cash to a credit economy this has created different types of commercial relations between buyers and sellers and consequently, different approaches to marketing. *See also* CONSUMERISM.

credit crunch Same as *credit squeeze but a more recent terminology related to the recession of 2007–09.

creditor A person or company who extends credit and to whom money is owed.

credit squeeze Government and banking measures implemented to restrict the ease at which credit facilities are available, in order to curb inflation. *See also* CREDIT CRUNCH.

crisis communications The immediate actions taken by a company or organization to maintain its credibility and good reputation after a situation has occurred that may adversely affect the company and its reputation, increasingly a core activity of the corporate communications or public relations team. Often the failure of a company to communicate effectively in a crisis can cause immeasurable damage. The process, characterized by rapidity of response, involves: the fast identification of the problem; articulating the problem in a way that both addresses the problem and mitigates risk to the company or organization's reputation without altering or covering up the facts; identification of the right level of spokesperson; speech and message development for key spokespersons; the development of a full media briefing plan and interview; media explanations and articulation of a plan for future prevention or mitigation. Two extreme examples of crisis communications and how they were handled (badly in these cases) from the oil industry are how Exxon handled the Valdez incident in Alaska and how BP handled the sub sea oil leakage in the Gulf of Mexico. *See also* COMMUNICATION; PUBLIC RELATIONS.

crisis management *See* PUBLIC RELATIONS.

critical path analysis (CPA) A project management technique, often used on large scale marketing projects, that maps the sequential relationships between different tasks in a project in order to assist planning, and to find the shortest possible time for doing them and to manage costs effectively. The main benefit of the CPA approach is to create the shortest possible time horizon for a project by identifying activities to schedule simultaneously. This, in turn, enables the most effective allocation of resources to the various strands of the project.

CRM *See* CUSTOMER RELATIONSHIP MARKETING.

crop To eliminate or cut off specific portions of a photograph or illustration.

crop marks The marks inserted on a photograph or illustration to indicate which portions are to be used, and which are to be eliminated.

cross elasticity The extent to which products are substitutes for one another. Marketers use differentiation and quality to seek to minimize cross elasticity and thus it could be seen as part of brand equity or marketing effectiveness.

cross elasticity of demand A measure of the responsiveness of demand for one good to changes in the price of another: the percentage change in the quantity demanded of one good divided by the percentage change in the price of the other good. Elasticity is also a measure of responsiveness. It tells how much one thing changes when you change something else that affects it. For example, the elasticity of demand tells us how much the quantity demanded changes when the price changes. The elasticity of demand measures the responsiveness of quantity demanded to changes in the price charged. *See also* PRICING (section on PRICE ELASTICITY).

cross impact analysis A qualitative forecasting technique that involves the assessment of the impact of key trends. This is a relatively inexpensive technique that allows regular updates as situations develop. *See also* MARKET RESEARCH.

cross selling Selling by a salesperson of some part of the company's total product range for which another division or salesperson has prime responsibility. This is a frequently used technique to increase total sales volume to the same customer. *See also* DIRECT MARKETING; SALES.

cross-tabulation A table that shows the number of times a variable may occur. Cross-tabulation is the most popular of all multivariate and bivariate statistical procedures. It is used to show the link, or correlation, between variables and can be easily set up. This method of analysis is frequently used for analysing demographic data. An example would be the correlation between age and neighbourhood location.

crowdsourcing A fusion of 'crowds' and 'outsourcing' coined by Mark Robinson and Jeff Howe in an article in *Wired* magazine in June 2006. Essentially this involves taking a function performed by employees and outsourcing it to a large network of people in the form of an open call. This often takes the form of collaborative working, particularly on software development.

((🌐)) SEE WEB LINKS

• Original article in *Wired* magazine

cue A signal communicated by a person, a product, or a service, usually non-verbally.

cultural environment A combination of the various institutions and other forces that control and affect society's basic values, perceptions, preferences, and behaviours.

culture A high determining factor in marketing, particularly in the interplay between international and local marketing. Marketers must be sensitive to the reigning aspects and dimensions of culture: shared values, beliefs, religion, language, laws, rituals, attitudes of mind, traditions, customs, and behaviours learned by members of society from family and other important institutions. In some societies, religion is the dominant cultural force; in others, it is institutions; in others, the family. There are multiple examples in consumer and industrial goods of products failing in one country that have been successfully marketed in another because of culture. There are many well-documented cases of McDonald's having to modify highly standardized fast-food packages because of very different eating habits around the world. Even in services, this can also be prevalent. For example, the marketing of professional advisory services that are intangible, such as management consultancy, is very difficult in Asia because local cultures do not normally pay for discrete advisory services; they are normally given 'free' as part of a more tangible purchase.

cumes An abbreviation for 'net cumulative audience' for broadcast media. This refers to the number of unduplicated people or homes in a broadcast programme's audience within a specified time period. AC *Nielsen uses this term. It is also used by many advertising practitioners to refer to the unduplicated audience of a print vehicle, or an entire media schedule.

current awareness Up-to-date information relevant to key results or areas of interest usually accessed online or via a website.

current demand The willingness of customers to pay the custom market price for a service or product.

customer The actual or intended purchaser of a product or service. The customer is always the buyer, although not always necessarily the consumer. *See also* CONSUMER. There have been several extensions of the customer concept, even within an organization, in which employees are also seen as customers of the various internal services of the company, or where citizens are viewed as customers of government services.

customer acquisition cost A calculation of dividing total costs of acquiring a new customer by the total number of customers. Generally, it is much less expensive to develop and grow an existing customer than to acquire a new one. This, of course, varies from market to market and by channel for accessing customers.

customer care A fundamental approach to the standards of customer service quality. It covers every aspect of a company's operations, from the design of a product or service, to how it is packaged, delivered, and serviced, for the pre- and post-sales periods. Governments and their agencies have ensured a steady stream of laws and regulations (for example, in air travel, financial services, communications, energy supply) to improve customer choice, to deregulate previous monopolies, and to encourage competition. This has brought increased benefit, choice, and strength to the customer. It is now recognized that customer care directly affects continuing profits and brand strength. Therefore, the company is highly dependent upon the customer service agents who deal regularly with the customers as well as the systems that support them in dealing with customers. These systems can be call centres, customer databases, or electronic information systems. It is now an all-too-frequent occurrence for customer service agents to deal with their computer rather than directly with the customer. Consequently, customer care has become one of the toughest competitive battlegrounds in modern business, particularly in those businesses whose products and services are otherwise undifferentiated from those of their competitors. Suppliers of customer care systems have themselves become major businesses in their own right. Customers, increasingly powerful, are very aware of their multiple choices and have rising expectations of excellent customer care. To some extent, that which delights customers today becomes a standard expectation tomorrow. Therefore, customer care is something that requires continuous attention and work. It is particularly important to care for long-term customers and to work assiduously at building long-term relationships with them. The cost of growing revenues from existing customers is far smaller than the cost of acquiring new customers. Good customer care means repeat customers and customers who will buy more products and services. *See also* CUSTOMER LOYALTY; RELATIONSHIP MARKETING.

The essential elements of superior customer care are a mindset of putting the customer first and at the centre of all operations of the company, gaining a deep knowledge, understanding, and insight into the customer, a high degree of sensitivity to customer needs supported by good ability and willingness to listen to customers and to respond to what is heard, a general persuasion to please the customer at all times and be accessible whenever and however the customer needs service, and be generally easy to interact with. The higher dimension of customer service is when the customer is actually delighted rather than merely satisfied. Many organizations appoint a very senior director, who has responsibility for customer service and who regularly monitors performance, as well as a dedicated staff who are fully trained, have expertise, and are always available to handle customer issues, complaints, and requests for information. All contemporary evidence suggests that customers prefer to speak directly to another person rather than to use automated information systems. It is important to resolve customers' problems as fast as possible, with resolution being made closest to where the complaints originate by staff with the power to resolve them. Additionally, there ought to be a published customer service policy that is well understood and acted upon, backed up by a customer charter, and a code of practice that is adhered to. Finally, it is important to have a continuous dialogue and feedback from customers and to act upon—and to be seen to be acting upon—their suggestions.

customer churn The attrition, or the loss of customers, usually occurs where there are high levels of price-based competition among providers of services, for example Internet service providers, mobile phone companies, and insurance companies.

customer database A centralized collection of consumer purchasing information from which lifestyle choices can be deduced by the marketer, and the customer accurately targeted.

customer delight A term to describe the result of delivering product or service which is not merely satisfactory but goes beyond the customer expectations.

customer driven A marketing process where all plans and strategies are based on the customer's demands and expectations.

customer lifetime value A technique for analysing all the potential purchase values from a single customer over the lifetime of a relationship with a supplier or service provider. This moves the focus away from looking at customers in terms of single purchasing transactions and, equally, gives an assessment of the cost of losing a potentially lifetime customer. Lifetime value calculations depend upon a thorough understanding for the target customers' life cycles because customer behaviour changes over time. Even though a transaction, or 'snapshot' approach to customer value behaviour can be modelled at a given point in time, it is far more powerful to look at the total value over a time period. The old ways of mass marketing were predicated on treating all customers the same—and consequently offering the same price and promotions to everyone. When a sale or promotion is launched, everyone gets the sale price—loyal customers and occasional transaction buyers. New techniques of marketing, notably the use of customer research and databases, have caused a more sophisticated approach to customer targeting. For example, some retail outlets are now issuing their customers with proprietary shopping cards and rewarding them for using them. The cards then become the basis of the store's customer database. With the database set up, the retailers can ensure that different customers receive different offers. Occasional, unknown customers pay full price. Loyal, regular customers pay a lower price on certain merchandise, or on all merchandise. Furthermore, the loyal customers are made aware that they are the favoured. They are treated like gold card customers on major airlines. Retailers have discovered that they can modify customer behaviour by appropriate application of rewards. Customer lifetime value stresses that existing customers should be encouraged to spend more with the same supplier over a longer lifetime. This is different to the more traditional approach of taking customers away from competitors. Marketers using lifetime value approaches to customers tend to reduce their advertising outlay because they know the low profitability and low loyalty of the promiscuous shoppers who are attracted to their stores by heavy advertising. This leads to an approach in which low margin offers are not made to unprofitable customers. The best customers get offered the most aggressive pricing and special promotions and are treated more specially.

customer loyalty The ability to retain customers and to keep them buying what is on offer over a longer period of time than competitors. Recent trends point to growing customer dissatisfaction and turnover. Loyal customers are increasingly hard to develop and keep. Aspects of building customer loyalty include delivering a quality product or service which meets the customer expectation, and ensuring that customers are valued and looked after effectively. As far as the benefits of customer loyalty are concerned, research has shown that it can be up to six times more expensive to acquire a new customer than it is to retain an existing one. Customer loyalty is extremely important and highly profitable to a company. A continuous dialogue with customers gives increased contact and knowledge of customer needs and this understanding of customer needs means fewer returns and complaints and costs. Happy customers generate positive word of mouth recommendation that improves a company's competitive position and lowers marketing costs. Finally, well-serviced and satisfied customers are always less sensitive to price, enabling greater profitability.

customer orientation A management philosophy, and often a culture, based on the idea that the customer is central to everything the company does and that the processes of a company begin with, and are designed around, the customer. A customer orientation is not necessarily the same as a market orientation: often a market orientation begins with the producer and examines the best way, using various channels, to get products and services to the customers. A customer orientation adapts to the way that the customer wishes to deal with and interact with the producer or supplier. Some companies have detailed customer measurement systems indicating their share of total customer expenditure that they are able to address and detailed revenue and profit from each customer relationship.

customer relationship marketing (CRM) **1** A systematic fostering of good reciprocal relationships with existing customers, on the basis that this will provide new or ongoing business from that customer with more ease and speed, and less cost, than winning and developing new customers.
2 An information system for gathering and analysing information and intelligence on existing clients with a view to deepening knowledge, improving relationships, and growing sales to that customer.

customer satisfaction The measurement of quality and effectiveness of the customer care delivery system. There can be measures of both meeting customer expectations and also, which is more desirable, exceeding expectations. This gives management an immediate view of the organization's performance relative to customer expectations, and enables them to track customer response and perception over time, which helps with market planning. It also enables cross-comparison of customer service centres and, in some cases, can help with remuneration schemes, where remuneration is connected to excellent customer service. Those with the better customer satisfaction scores are given bonuses. Services can usually only be measured for customer satisfaction after consumption. Also, as customers become aware of, or actually experience, alternatives, their expectations will change and rise over time. Jan Carlzon, when CEO of the SAS airline, called the encounter between a service provider and the customer a 'moment of truth'. These are the crucial interactions or touch points at which the customer forms an impression of the service provider; for example, at an airline check-in desk, being greeted at a restaurant, or dealing with a bank teller.

customer satisfaction research The measure of overall satisfaction with a product or service and satisfaction with specific elements of the product or service. Increasingly, many companies use this research as part of the compensation for their executives responsible for serving customers.

customer value analysis An analysis conducted to determine which benefits or features target customers value and how they rate the relative value of various competitors' offers. *See also* CONJOINT ANALYSIS; MARKET RESEARCH.

customized marketing The means by which marketers can customize products and services for individual customers. This is specifically when a supplier creates a product or service for an individual customer that did not exist before. This can exist in both personal service markets as well as in business-to-business markets. *See also* CUSTOMER; MASS CUSTOMIZATION; RELATIONSHIP MARKETING.

customs Long-established business practices and modes of customer behaviour (e.g. half-day closing, religious holidays, social taboos). They represent culturally approved ways of responding to given situations: usual and acceptable ways of behaving. They comprise folk history, idioms, literature, song, conventions, mores, and laws. These can often determine the success or failure of a marketing programme conducted from outside the territory. Global marketing often becomes a series of adaptations to local customs and cultures.

cut throat competition The practice of suppliers in a specific market undercutting one another, often to prices below cost, in order to eliminate competition, usually as a result of supply exceeding demand.

cyberspace Word derived from the Greek kybernētēs meaning 'steersman' or 'pilot' or 'rudder', and in modern times a fusion word of cybernetics and space coined by William Gibson, the Canadian science fiction writer, in his 1982 novel *Neuromancer*. It signifies a 'virtual' meeting place of computer networks, where online communication and interaction take place with their own etiquette, rules, and standards.

cybersquatting The practice of acquiring a domain name for the purpose of trading it at a profit at a later date with a large company.

cycle analysis A time series correction technique that adjusts forecasts for movements in the overall economy. *See also* BUSINESS CYCLE; DEMAND.

D

DAGMAR (Defining Advertising Goals for Measured Advertising Results) A method developed by Russell Colley in 1961, its purpose is the measurement of advertising effectiveness. Its central idea is that the audience moves through phases of awareness of an advertising campaign to comprehension, to conviction that the product can meet their needs, to eventual action, or purchase. *See also* ADVERTISING CAMPAIGN; AIDA; DESIRE.

daily activities A report or record of a salesperson's activities on a day-by-day basis, showing clients visited, products presented, and results. It may also include reasons for the failure to sell and is often used as a measure of *sales productivity before measurement moves to actual tangibles such as orders and revenues. *See also* SALES.

daily sales plan A record of a *salesperson's intended sales calls on a day-by-day basis, listing the clients to be visited, the objectives of each call, and the anticipated outcomes.

dailies (rushes) An unedited film, so called because, typically, the film from a single day's shooting is viewed, even if the final commercial or programme will take many days or weeks of shooting and editing with computers.

DAR (day-after recall) A method for analysing and assessing the impact of *television advertising one day after it was first broadcast. *See also* ADVERTISING.

database marketing A form of targeted marketing that makes use of *customer data captured through customer transactions and communications. This data may be used independently or in conjunction with outside data to guide targeted customer prospecting, customer retention, promotions, and other marketing efforts. For example, a database may have a collection of available information on past and current customers together with future prospects, structured to allow for implementation of effective *marketing strategies. *Consumer goods and *services companies as well as political parties and organizations use these widely for various campaigns.

Database marketing began in the mid-1980s as computers and software became quite sophisticated and economical. It was possible to store information about customers, and use the information to build lasting relationships with them. As a result, it was possible to increase sales and profits by:

- analysing *customer buying behaviour;
- promoting *cross sales, repeat sales and upgrades;
- computing *customer lifetime value and using it in strategy evaluation;
- creating referrals and *customer loyalty.

Database marketing progressed in sophistication and applications throughout the 1990s to become *one-to-one, or *customized marketing. Toll-free numbers with customer service agents advanced. Customer service agents began using computers to obtain the information asked for by customers from the database. They read the answers off the screen over the phone to the customers. Then they typed into the customer database what happened and what was discussed during the call. It was a big advance on previous customer service, but customers started to complain that the service sounded wooden and robotic. In practice and in reality very few companies ever achieved effective one-to-one marketing. To devise a different marketing strategy for each person who would be treated as a 'market of one' was really beyond the capability of any but the most sophisticated marketers with the most advanced systems. The advent of the *Internet, however, transformed and evolved the pursuit of highly customized marketing and the databases that supported these activities. It took several years before most marketers realized the potential of the Internet, but when they did they saw that the Internet had created a huge and inexhaustible database marketing system with worldwide ubiquity and scope. Using the Internet, it became possible to do things that were only dreamed about in the early database marketing days, for example:

1 Focusing on new prospects;
2 Evaluating new prospects;
3 Cross-selling related products;
4 Launching new products to potential prospects;
5 Identifying new distribution channels;
6 Building customer loyalty;
7 Generating enquiries and follow-up sales;
8 Targeting niche markets.

With the Web, the approach to customer service is now about empowering the customer with *self service. Companies are giving customers web access to the same screens that the customer service agents see. Customers are now enabled to do their own searches and get their own answers. Customers can now get much more information over the Web than they could ever get from a live operator with a computer. Companies now put page after page of technical data, product specifications, descriptions, services, special offers, and details on their websites with adequate indexing so that any customer or prospect can get all the information they want or need. This is valuable to the customer and the company for the following reasons:

d

- There is no long-distance call to pay for.
- There is no Customer Service Agent to pay for (an Internet enquiry costs a bank only 10% of the processing cost for a customer service agent to handle the call 'live').
- The system is open for business 24 hours a day.
- The company can track what information people want and who wants it.
- Once the system is set up, the variable costs are almost nothing.

For the Web to succeed it must be very value-added to customers. Some companies are using collaborative filtering with special software to make product suggestions to their customers both on the phone and on the Web. This software, linked to your customer database, starts to 'sense' and understand customer preferences based upon previous purchases and enquiries. *Amazon.com has excelled in this technique and is able to make book and other recommendations whenever a returning customer comes to their website.

data collection A compilation of relevant information or informed observations and analysis. Collecting good and valid data is crucial to marketing since it drives strategic and tactical decisions. When gathering data, it is important to determine the source of the data as well as the context the data has come from. Not all sources of data are reliable, so it is necessary to understand how the data was gathered, where it was gathered from, what means and techniques were used, and what was included in the data set in order to draw correct conclusions. Data is usually the raw and untreated facts and opinions that have been gathered through the data gathering process. Hard data is the scientific collection of the latter; soft data is more a collection of emotions and opinions around the same subject that have been collected anecdotally. Also, in the context of *market research there are primary and secondary data. Primary data is that which is collected directly from the target respondent group, for example by means of a structured interview or questionnaire. Secondary data is information that has been gathered for another purpose, neither directly by the user nor specifically for the user, often under conditions not known to the user. Secondary data, for example, may include government reports, economic information, industry analyst information, and trade associations' reports. Banks, stockbrokers, and market research reports are other potential sources of information. International secondary data can be collected in the home country or in the country to be researched. Non-governmental sources include consultants and international agencies. There is also internal data that is specific to and generated by the organization, for example, sales statistics (by customer, by product), financial data such as profitability (by product, by customer), customer complaints, inventory levels, or debtor information. Secondary and internal data are useful background and context settings for primary research. With the tools available today, it can be gathered very quickly, and is much lower-cost than primary data collection.

database An ordered collection of data, stored on a computer with a dedicated software program, that can be used for multiple purposes. The advent of the database has transformed various marketing techniques and channels to market. For example, the increasing sophistication of databases has enabled marketers to gather and process data with greater precision on different types of customers. In particular, *market analysts can clearly see the differences between high spending and low spending *customers. Such depth of knowledge enables marketers not only to see patterns more clearly, it also allows more targeted *marketing programmes to be executed. See, for example, DIRECT MARKETING; E-MAIL MARKETING; GOOGLE; INTERACTIVE MARKETING.

data mining The process of gathering or locating pertinent information from a database. This is particularly key to customer marketing as it enables multiple combinations, for example customers who bought a certain type of car at a certain location in a certain time period. The key to data mining is to understand what data you are trying to collect and to go through all the combinations and variable data until you find that which is needed.

data processing The organization of data for the purpose of producing desired information, involving recording, classifying, sorting, summarizing, calculating, disseminating, and storing data.

data protection A range of security measures used to protect valuable data. Gathered data on a database needs to be protected against hackers as well as software and network system failures. Many software packages exist which password-protect information and also provide data back-ups so that important information will not be lost.

data warehouse A collection of data designed to support management decision-making. Data warehouses contain a wide variety of data that present a coherent picture of business conditions at a single point in time. Development of a data warehouse includes development of systems to extract data from operating systems plus installation of a warehouse database system that provides managers with flexible access to the data. The term data warehousing generally refers to combining many different databases across an entire enterprise. *See also* MARKET RESEARCH.

day part Any of the standard time periods into which the day is divided by broadcast media. Cost of purchasing advertising time on a vehicle varies by the day part selected.

dealer A general name for someone who trades, purchases, and maintains an inventory of goods to be sold. Can be either an individual, a *middleman, or a *franchisee established or operated under an authorization to sell or distribute a company's goods or services.

dealer network A group of mutually supportive individuals helping each other in the *buying and *selling process or a part of a wider *distribution network, either directly owned by the producer or buying and selling products and services on behalf of the producer or owner while retaining independence to market those of other producers.

decay constant An estimate of the decline in *product sales if *advertising were discontinued or reduced.

deceptive advertising Type of *copy intended to deceive *consumers with false or misleading claims. This is prohibited in most of the advanced economies. *See* ADVERTISING.

deceptive packaging Method intended to deceive the purchaser; for example excessive ullage creates the impression that the volume of the contents is greater than it actually is.

deceptive pricing The pricing of goods and *services in such a way as to cause a customer to be misled. An example of deceptive pricing is *bait-and-switch pricing.

decision criteria Set of documented rules or standards for evaluating alternatives and selecting a preferred option. Good decision is determined by identifying the most relevant factors and ranking them in terms of importance.

decision-makers *See* BUYER AND BUYING BEHAVIOUR.

decision-making unit (DMU) Individuals and groups participating in a *buying decision in an *industrial purchasing process. They share some common goals and are knowledgeable about the risks arising from decisions. Members of the group may be initiators, influencers, deciders, approvers, gatekeepers, buyers, or users. *See* BUYER AND BUYING BEHAVIOUR.

decision theory A branch of statistical theory that enables problem-solving and which leads to decisions about the most advantageous course of action under the given conditions, particularly conditions of uncertainty. Decision theory divides decisions into three classes: 1) Decisions under certainty; 2) Decisions under conflict; 3) Decisions under uncertainty. *See also* GAME THEORY.

decision tree An analytical tool for classifying the choices, risks, objectives, gains, and information needs involved in different courses of action.

defensive marketing A focused plan and actions intended to protect (rather than expand) a company's *market position including its *market share, *reputation, profitability, *product and *service position, and *customer base. Many of these techniques are adapted from military strategy.

deflation The decrease of price levels for goods and services in an economy. Deflation usually occurs when an economy is lacking in money supply, or the economic fundamentals are failing.

delayed gratification The psychological condition which enables the individual to wait patiently for future benefits instead of demanding something that they desire instantly and acting accordingly. The condition is contrary to *instant gratification, and is important to marketers as it directly affects the *buying behaviour of customers, separating those who delay purchases from those who buy on impulse.

Delphi technique A forecasting method in which a coordinator seeks predictions from experts who revise their opinions in light of the opinions of the others until some degree of consensus is reached. The technique is based on the Hegelian principle of achieving a consensus through a three-step process of thesis, antithesis, and synthesis. In thesis and antithesis, all present their opinion or vision on a given subject, establishing views and opposing views. In synthesis, opposites are brought together to form the new thesis. All participants must then accept ownership of the new thesis and support it, changing their own views to align with the new thesis. Through a continual process of evolution, a consensus or oneness of vision occurs. This technique uses expert judgement and anticipation of the future without empirical hard data, for example long-term strategic planning using scenarios of future events. Stage 1 is to poll experts, anonymously and separately. In stage 2, the results are consolidated and fed back to the experts as a group. Stage 3 polls them individually again, in the light of peer group opinion. A forecast of the future is prepared which has the acceptance of all or most of the panel of experts. When there is some uncertainty among the experts, probability weightings might be given to different possible future scenarios or events.

demand

The stimulations that lead to the acquisition of new customers, keeping existing customers, and growing the overall demand of each customer for the company or organization's products and services. This may also include increasing demand by taking an innovative approach to the way in which traditional products and services are delivered to customers, which has the effect of expanding demand. For example, Amazon.com delivers traditional products in an innovative way, thereby increasing its total market demand to a far greater level than a local or national bookseller. It can also involve extending the company's brand into new products and services that are based upon its core competence. For example, Disney has a core competence in entertainment that started in animated films, then extended into general movie production, theme parks, music and book publishing, television broadcasting, retailing and merchandising, tourist and holiday packages (such as cruises), and property development, such as resort timeshares. The Disney brand is used to develop new market areas and generate overall demand for the Disney Company's overall products and services.

The assessment of demand is also crucial, particularly in terms of strategy and pricing. There are five types of demand:

- *Historic demand* is based on the extrapolation of historical market demand data from customers who have bought a product or service in the past, and is often used as a guide to future demand, which can cause problems, as it does not take into account discontinuity in market demand.

- *Existing demand* uses data from customers who are currently buying the products and services.

- *Latent demand* is a reference to inactivated demand that could be developed if certain marketing strategies and programmes were developed but which otherwise remains dormant.

- *Potential demand* makes a forecast based upon customers who might buy products and services in the foreseeable future if the circumstances (such as their disposable income, or special offers, or prices) are right and the market environment is favourable.

- *Price-related demand* is the main instrument available to marketers to convert latent or potential demand into existing demand. This makes use of the instrument of pricing to increase market demand for given products and services. The law of demand states that quantity demanded varies inversely with price. Economists expect that demand will diminish if prices increase. The maximum price a buyer is willing to pay for a good or a service, rather than do without, is called the *reservation price*. As a group, buyers' reservation prices for a given quantity of a good can vary because of differences in their preference for the good or service, their knowledge of the price of substitute or complementary goods and services, their disposable income, and their expectations about what will happen to their income or the price of the good in the near future. The quantity of a good demanded by buyers in a market varies with market price, if all these other influences are held constant. As market price rises, fewer buyers will have a reservation price high enough to make the purchase worthwhile. That's because as price rises, *substitutes for the good* start to look more attractive. As price falls, more buyers will have a reservation price low enough to make the purchase worthwhile. That's because as price falls, *substitute uses for this good* start to look more attractive.

Demand can vary over time and according to the changing nature of markets, technologies, and lifestyles. Historic demand is always an imperfect source of demand information and trends for the marketer. Equally, an innovative new product or service will have no historical demand data or trends, and the marketer must therefore use other techniques—including guesswork, hope, and instinct. *See also* AGGREGATE DEMAND; COMPETITION; COMPETITIVE ADVANTAGE; DISPOSABLE INCOME; PRICING.

d

demarketing An attempt to temporarily or permanently reduce demand and limit future growth. It is mainly an inverse marketing technique to dissuade the public from doing something, for example government warnings concerning smoking, drugs, drinking and driving, AIDS prevention, or overuse of water during a drought. Special interest groups can also launch campaigns to dissuade the public from buying certain types of good or service, for example from a totalitarian regime. It may also be used if a product is found to be faulty and the producers of the good do not wish to risk their reputation by continuing to sell it—for example in the recall of benzene-infected Perrier Water or Tylenol in the US or the recall of Toyota cars with faulty controls.

demographic segmentation *See* MARKET SEGMENTATION.

demography The study of human populations in terms of size, density, location, age, sex, race, occupation, and other statistics. It is also the description of the vital statistics or objective and quantifiable characteristics of an audience or population. Demographic designators include age, marital status, income, family size, occupation, and personal or household characteristics such as age, sex, income, or educational level. Demographics are used extensively in *marketing. *See also* GEODEMOGRAPHICS.

density A measure that is computed by dividing the total population of a geographic unit by its land area measured in square miles or square kilometres.

department store A retail organization that carries a wide variety of product lines, typically clothing, home furnishings, personal care products, accessories, and household goods; each line is operated as a separate department managed by specialist buyers or merchandisers. For the first time merchandise was displayed with fixed prices and were linked to various income levels of the customers. Department stores were not places to haggle about prices, as the small stores and markets that existed at the time were known for. The department store was an invention of the 19th century that has survived into the 21st century despite many competing retail outlets, both physical and online. The world's first department store, *Au Bon Marché*, was opened in Paris in 1852 and by 1877 had become the world's largest department store. *See also* CONSUMERISM; CONSUMER MARKETING.

depreciation A measure of the loss of value due to wear and tear, consumption, or other reduction in the useful economic life of a fixed asset, whether arising from use, affliction of time, or obsolescence through technological or market changes. In accounting, it is an allowance made for a loss in value of property, such as a machine or vehicle. To encourage companies to maintain their capital stock, governments usually allow for depreciation when calculating corporation tax. In economics, it is the reduction in the purchasing value of money. *See also* CONSUMER SOCIETY.

depth interview A one-on-one interview that probes and elicits detailed answers to questions, often using nondirective techniques to uncover hidden motivations.

derived demand The mechanism through which demand for industrial goods is derived from consumer market demand. If demand for end-product consumer goods falls, then this has an effect along the production supply line to all the inputs. Derived demand emphasizes the relationship between the price of the industrial good, and the quantity of the good demanded by firms employing it in production of the final product. It is directly dependent on consumer demand for the final product(s) the industrial good is used to produce.

For example: if, for some reason, the demand for personal computers increases so that more PCs than before can be sold at any given price, then the derived demand for semiconductor chips used in making PCs will also increase. As a result, semiconductor manufacturers will be able to sell more chips at any given price. The key is the change in the price of the final product brought about by the shift in demand for it. If the demand curve for personal computers shifts upwards and the supply curve remains unchanged, then the equilibrium price and quantity in the PC market will now involve both a higher price for PCs and a larger quantity of PCs being produced and sold to the public. Because of the price rise, the marginal revenues earned by the manufacturers per additional PC sold will be higher. So, consequently, their desire to maximize profits will lead them to produce additional PCs until the marginal cost for the last PC rises to equal the new higher price. Producing more PCs than before will require more production capacity than before, which they will want to purchase from their suppliers, shifting the demand curves for each of the semiconductors upwards. This increase in demand for the semiconductors in turn will tend to raise their prices and to increase the quantity of chips sold, which then affects the semiconductor manufacturers' demand for their own necessary inputs (such as silicone and gallium arsenide) and brings about further price-and-quantity adjustments throughout the economy in an ever-widening, derived demand ripple effect. *See also* BUYER AND BUYING BEHAVIOUR; DEMAND.

description tag A tag used by *website page authors to provide a description for search engine listings.

design A generic skill that can be applied in many different professions and contexts and has at its core the visualization of ideas, concepts, drawings, plans, and models and turning them into real and desirable things. Design quality and profitability are directly linked. In marketing, these design skills can be applied to the creation of an overall advertising or publicity campaign, a corporate identity, a brand logo, an exhibition space, a brochure, a poster, a product, a website. Design is extremely important to *product differentiation. For marketers, design is often what brings the intangible to life. The management of design gives a company a visual way of expressing the nature of the organization. Design is very closely linked to *brand management. Packaging, advertising, company logo, merchandise, products, buildings, office space layout, staff uniforms, and collateral, should all be designed with an overall theme and with a view to projecting the personality and essence of the company.

designer label A company *logo usually attached to a piece of apparel or *merchandise to indicate a higher value product that comes from a top quality designer. The French couturiers have been especially adept at extending the designer label concept across a range of fashion items. At some point between the 1970s and 1990s marketers convinced the public to wear these labels (previously worn on the inside) to the outside, making each consumer a walking advertisement. *See also* APPENDIX 2 (Luxury Goods section).

desire The phase in a marketing sequence that follows from the creation of *awareness, then *interest and is usually the stage when the *customer actually deeply wants the product or service that is being marketed. Desire is the state viewed as being a precursor to actual purchase. *See also* AIDA.

desk research A type of secondary research, literally done at a desk from secondary sources. *See* MARKET RESEARCH.

desktop publishing The digital process of combining text with visuals and graphics to create *brochures, newsletters, *magazines, *newspapers, *logos, electronic slides, and other published work using a computer.

devaluation An official lowering of a nation's currency; a decrease in the value of a country's currency relative to that of foreign countries which usually occurs when the national government lowers the value of the exchange rate from one fixed rate to another. Devaluation is a tool that has been used by national governments to increase international *exports, but is can also lead to inflation domestically.

deviation A variation that deviates from the standard or norm often known as 'the deviation from the mean'.

diary panel A survey in which the same *respondents keep a diary of what they watch, listen to, or buy, etc., over a specified period of time.

differential sampling A market research technique in which increased samples are taken from a defined *segment of the market out of proportion to their relative size and scale within the overall group in order to highlight specific issues, needs, or wants within that group.

differentiation A concept that originally applied to the main differences and unique benefits of a given *product over another competing product that made it more attractive to a *target market; the concept is now all encompassing in marketing and can apply to *services, companies, *brands, cultures, and individuals. Differentiation is vital to creating *competitive advantage. Achieving differentiation can be based on the creation and supply of advanced products and services, on superior *client service, *market niche focus, the expertise or culture of an organization, the reputation and strength of a *brand, higher value, lower cost, or some combination of all of these factors. An additional task of marketing is not only to help create the features of differentiation, but also to communicate these elements of differentiation.

differentiated marketing An advanced method of segmentation involving the division of a heterogeneous market into relatively homogeneous segments so that the needs and wants of the different *segments might be served in a different and more dedicated way than competitors can. Often referred to as multisegment marketing.

diffusion of innovation

An enduring theory concerning the adoption process through which an individual passes, from first hearing about an innovation to final adoption, via the intermediate psychological stages of *awareness and interest, to the final stages of evaluation and trial. The usual purpose of the adoption model is to determine the process for buying either a new or previously unknown product or service. The rate and speed of adoption varies from product to product and depends upon the different types of *consumer. These consumers are divided into the categories described below which indicate the extent to which people are prepared to innovate and try out new products. The adoption curve for innovation, developed by Everett M Rogers in 1962, provides a stage-by-stage analysis to show how new products and services spread through markets.

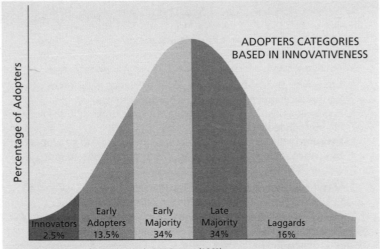

The Adoption Curve (For Innovation). E M Rogers (1962)

The original diffusion research was done as early as 1903 by the French sociologist Gabriel Tarde who plotted the original S-shaped diffusion curve. In Tarde's model some innovations diffuse rapidly, creating a steep S-curve; other innovations have a slower rate of adoption, creating a more gradual slope of the S-curve. As Tarde says in *The Laws of Imitation*, 'A slow advance in the beginning, followed by rapid and uniformly accelerated progress, followed again by progress that continues to slacken until it finally stops: These are the three ages of . . . invention . . . if taken as a guide by the statistician and by the sociologists, (they) would save many illusions.' These observations are as valid today as they were 100 years ago.

In the 1940s, the sociologists Bryce Ryan and Neal Gross published their 'seminal' study of the 'diffusion of hybrid seed among Iowa farmers' renewing interest in the diffusion of innovation S-curve. This now infamous hybrid-corn study resulted in a renewed wave of research. The rate of adoption curve was similar to the S-shaped diffusion curve graphed by Tarde forty years earlier. As the technological advances of the late 19th and early 20th centuries became commercial realities in the everyday lives of consumers, the rate at which technology turned into marketable goods was a compelling subject. The rate of adoption, or diffusion rate, has become an important area of research to sociologists, and more specifically, to advertisers and marketers of new products.

In his book *Diffusion of Innovations* (1983) Everett Rogers defines diffusion as the process by which an innovation is communicated through certain channels over time among the members of a social system.

The stages through which a technological innovation passes are:

- **Knowledge** (including exposure to the existence of the innovation, leading to an understanding of its functionality and uses);
- **Persuasion** (involving the formation of a favourable attitude towards the innovation by potential consumers);
- **Decision** (where the consumer becomes committed to its adoption);
- **Implementation** (where the consumer puts the innovation to use and starts to feel its effects in their everyday lives);
- **Confirmation** (the reinforcement of the decision to have purchased the innovation based on the positive outcomes from it).

Early adopters are generally more highly educated, have higher social status, are more open to both mass media and interpersonal channels of communication, and have more contact with change agents. Mass media channels are relatively more important at the knowledge stage, whereas interpersonal channels are relatively more important at the persuasion stage. Innovation decisions may be optional (where the person or organization has a real opportunity to adopt or reject the idea), collective (where a decision is reached by consensus among the members of a system), or authority-based (where a decision is imposed by another person or organization possessing the requisite power, status, or technical expertise).

Important characteristics of an innovation include:

- **Relative advantage** (the degree to which it is perceived to be better than what it supersedes or replaces; for example, the telephone was perceived to be an improvement both on the postal system and the telegraph);
- **Compatibility** (meaning a consistency with existing values, past experiences, and needs);
- **Complexity** (difficulty of understanding and use, which is one of the major inhibitors to early uptake);
- **Trial** (the degree to which the innovation can be experimented with, or tried and tested, on a limited basis and for a defined time period);
- **Observability** (the visibility and tangibility of its results. All innovations thrive and become adopted by a critical mass of consumers when they can be shown, whatever their complexity, to have practical and useful purposes. An example is the PC, which became a mass product only when it had practical uses such as word processing, spreadsheets, design, databases, and entertainment).

The different adopter categories are identified as:

- **Innovators** (who are bold, risk-taking, and venturesome);
- **Early adopters** (who are socially respectable);
- **Early majority** (who are cautious and deliberate);
- **Late majority** (who are sceptical and difficult to convince);
- **Laggards** (who are traditional).

See detailed descriptions below.

The adoption of the innovation process is characterized by important roles that include:

- **Opinion leaders** (who have relatively frequent informal influence over the behaviour of others);
- **Change agents** (who positively influence innovation decisions, by mediating between the change agency and the relevant social system);
- **Change aides** (who complement the change agent, by having more intensive contact with clients, and who have less competence credibility but more safety or trustworthiness credibility).

The change agent's roles are to:

- **Develop** a need for change on the part of the client;
- **Establish** an information-exchange relationship;
- **Diagnose** the client's problems;
- **Create** intent to change in the client's culture;
- **Translate** this intent into action;
- **Stabilize** adoption and prevent discontinuity; and
- **Shift** the client from reliance on the change agent to self-reliance, and to adopt the innovation themselves.

Rogers' definition contains four crucial elements that are present in the diffusion of innovation process. The four main elements are:

1. Innovation—an idea, practice, technique, method, or object that is perceived as new by an individual or other group.
2. Communication channels, or the means by which messages get transmitted from one individual to another about the innovation and its benefits.
3. Time, of which the major parts are a) the innovation-decision process itself; b) the relative time with which an innovation is adopted by an individual or group in a market or society; and c) the innovation's rate of adoption in the marketplace.
4. Social system—which is an important set of interrelated groups that are engaged in joint problem-solving to accomplish a common goal.

Also, Rogers categorized the type of people who constitute the various segments of the market who make up the overall curve: although additional names and titles for the adopters of an innovation have been used in other research studies, Rogers' original labels for the five adopter categories are now standard for the industry.

Why is the Adoption Process of any relevance to marketers and advertisers? A primary purpose of marketing and advertising is to increase sales. It is through analysing and understanding the adoption process that marketers and advertisers are able to develop fully integrated marketing and communication plans against each stage of the adoption process to ensure an appropriate return on the original product investment. Moreover, the specific characteristics that Rogers identifies for each adopter category is of significance to advertisers and marketers interested in creating an integrated marketing plan targeting a specific audience at defined stages in the process. *See also* AIDA; BUYER AND BUYING BEHAVIOUR; HIERARCHY OF EFFECTS.

Descriptions
Innovators A group active early in the adoption process and tending to be a small (typically less than 5% of the market) risk-taking group. They are characterized by their zeal for new ideas and new products. They tend to have higher disposable incomes. They are anxious to be in the lead and to avoid being followers. Therefore, they tend to gain their information from expert sources rather than from their peers and social group.

Rogers identifies the following characteristics dominant in the innovator type:

- venturesomeness, desire for the rash, the daring, and the risky;
- control of substantial financial resources to absorb possible loss from an unprofitable innovation;
- ability to understand and apply complex technical knowledge;
- ability to cope with a high degree of uncertainty about an innovation.

Early adopters buy the product or service early in its life cycle. They represent a slightly larger part of the market (typically around 12–15%). Not as zealous for newness as the Innovators, they will seek information and approval from their peers and group. Earlier adopting individuals tend not to be different in age, but to have more years of education, higher social status, and upward social mobility, or are working in larger organizations, have greater empathy, less dogmatism, and a greater ability to deal with abstractions than the later majority adopters. They have greater rationality, intelligence, ability to cope with uncertainty and risk, higher aspirations, more contact with other people, greater exposure to both mass media and interpersonal communications channels, and engage in more active information seeking. The Early adopters are likely to be more socially integrated and conscious than the Innovators: they are also likely to be able to influence larger groups. However, taken together, the Innovators and Early adopters are the minority when it comes to the marketing stakes—a starter gunner in the race that leads to the mass market. They are often regarded as crucial to the launch of the new product or service, because of their ability to influence the next, and potentially much larger, segment of the market, which is known as the Early and Late majority.

Early majority is one of the larger segments of the market (typically 30–35%). Those within this segment are characterized by their cautious and thoughtful approach to new products and services. They will tend to analyse the product or service by collecting more information and making comparative evaluation of existing, competing, or alternative brands than will the Early adopters. The Early majority have frequent interactions with their social peers, which helps in the communications process. Although they seldom lead opinions, they do tend to influence others in moving towards a decision. Reaching this segment of the market will take longer; the process of adoption is slower. However, this is a critical part of the market as they perform two vital roles: they vastly increase the take-up of the product or service (that is usually marked by a price reduction) and they also form a bridge between the early and later adopters.

Late majority (typically 35–40%) tend to adopt only after their Early majority peer group has already done so. The reasons for this range from economic (they were waiting for the price to come down) to scepticism (they remained unconvinced about the benefits for a longer period of time than the other groups) to lack of confidence and caution (they tend to conform to peer and group pressure in decision-making). Typically, this group is older with lower disposable income. Often they will buy the innovation out of economic necessity—for example they may have purchased an early television because it was cheaper than going to the cinema or theatre. This group tends to receive information by word of mouth rather than from expert sources.

Laggards (typically 15–20%) are usually the last people in the marketplace to adopt a new product or service. They bear some resemblance to the Innovator type because peer and group pressure does not sway them. However, while the Innovator is fixed upon the future, the Laggard tends to consider the past and tradition before making decisions. They are suspicious of the future and of innovation. Usually with a low disposable income, the product or service is no longer an innovation by the time they adopt it. They have no opinion leadership and are often quite isolated from their peers, for example older people living on their own.

diffusion process The stages through which a product innovation spreads throughout a market from one customer to another. It is the overall cycle from creation to use. Successful diffusion leads to acceptance and to eventual adoption. *See* ADOPTION.

digital marketing (online marketing, web marketing) The use of digital technology, including web and multimedia and processes in the development, distribution, and promotion of products and services. Digital technologies include *Internet media such as websites and *e-mail as well as other digital media such as wireless or mobile and media for delivering digital television, both cable and satellite.

diminishing marginal utility (law of) An economic concept that holds that with each unit of good consumed by an individual, less and less value and incremental benefit is derived from the *consumption.

diminishing returns (law of) An economic concept that holds that if one factor of production is fixed (e.g. land, machinery, buildings) and one is variable (e.g. number of workers, length of hours in which they work), and if the variable factor (e.g. increase in the number of workers or increase in length of their working day through overtime) of production is increased, there comes a point where initial gains in production, and in productivity, will eventually level out and then start to decline. The marginal returns to successive small increases in the variable factor of production start to diminish, and then eventually the overall average returns per unit of the variable input will start decreasing. This law tends to cover short-term production, as, in the long run, all costs become variable.

direct computer interviewing Method in which consumers are intercepted in a shopping mall or other central location and interviewed using a computer that asks questions and accepts responses.

direct exporting *See* EXPORTING.

directional matrix *See* ANSOFF MATRIX.

direct mail A form of marketing involving the sending of *promotional material directly to the home address or electronic mailbox of the target *consumer. It is seen as a lower cost way of promoting goods and services and it eliminates the *middleman. Traditionally a form of print medium, direct mail consists of items such as *catalogues, *brochures, free samples, newsletters, fly sheets, or special offers sent directly through the mail to the potential *buyer from the producer or sales point, accompanied by contact and payment details supplied by the advertiser. It can also be personalized to the individual *consumer. Direct mailing is also done by e-mail, either on a targeted or untargeted basis. However, consumers tend to reject the bulk of what they describe as *junk mail and few direct mail campaigns ever reach higher than a 5% response rate. *See* BELOW-THE-LINE; DATABASE MARKETING; DIRECT MARKETING; E-MAIL SPAM; MEDIA CHANNELS.

direct marketing A technique rather than a *communications channel or marketing medium. It is an aspect of total marketing that is characterized by measurability and accountability, with heavy reliance on lists and data and uses several types of media (*direct mail, *catalogues, printed material, telephone, fax, *text message, *e-mail) to effect a measurable customer response and, in some cases, a commercial transaction. The main purpose is to make a sale or to obtain a *sales lead in a highly targeted but low-cost way. The direct marketing explosion has been partly created by increasingly sophisticated *databases and database trading between companies who sell address and e-mail lists to each other. Additionally, the increase in the number of delivery services and high use of credit cards has also created greater channel range for the sale and delivery of goods directly. There are also some lifestyle components to this phenomenon: people increasingly have less time to shop and are equipped with computers and credit cards to make purchases from their homes. The *Internet has also extended massively the power and reach of direct marketing. *See also* DATABASE MARKETING; INTERNET, THE.

directory A printed or electronic listing, in alphabetic order, usually of businesses in a local area. Typically, a business directory or *Yellow Pages* is an important form of local *classified advertising. Increasingly, business service and product directories are moving to electronic database and can be used interactively. Electronic directories can achieve far greater reach and coverage than the printed versions. *See* MEDIA CHANNELS.

directory advertising Copy that appears in a *directory, such as a telephone directory, Yellow Pages style directory, or reference brochure.

direct response Promotions that enable or request *consumers to respond directly to the *advertiser, by mail, telephone, *e-mail, or some other means of communication. *See also* DIRECT MARKETING.

direct response marketing A range of promotions sent directly to *consumers, by mail, catalogue, or other home delivery, attempting to solicit orders by mail or a toll-free number. This can also include advertising through any medium designed to generate a direct, measurable response. *See also* DATABASE MARKETING; DIRECT MARKETING.

direct selling The process whereby the producer sells to the end users, final consumer, or *retailer without intervening middlemen such as *wholesalers, retailers, or *brokers outside of a fixed retail location and usually in the home or workplace of the potential *buyer. This typically involves face to face presentation, communication, negotiation, and persuasion using a *direct sales force. It is probably the oldest form of commercial distribution, and, with the growth of the *Internet, its importance is diminishing for *consumer goods and commodity *services but is still important in the sale of specialized goods and services. *See also* SALES.

Dirichlet Model A measure of *repeat buying behaviour which makes some simple assumptions e.g. that consumers tend to have split loyalties to each of several *brands. Named after the German mathematician Peter Gustav Dirichlet (1805–59), the model was developed for use in marketing in the 1980s and is used to predicts future *sales performance, to analyse the extent of *brand cannibalization, possible success factors for new brands, and the impact of *brand loyalty programmes. Key outputs of the model are analysis and prediction on penetration of *category, frequency of buying and buying behaviour (*see* BUYER AND BUYING BEHAVIOUR), number of brands bought, and *market share. The model is numerical and does not assess the emotional reasons for brand switching. The Dirichlet Model of repeat-purchase behaviour stands out as probably the most widely validated model in *consumer marketing. *See also* DOUBLE JEOPARDY.

discount Any reduction from normal list price offered to *customers. Negotiated *discounting is more a feature of *industrial markets; price discounts on goods are more of a feature of *consumer markets. The main purposes of discounting are: to encourage greater volume sales; to get rid of end of line or discontinued stock; to try to win market share from competitors, or to respond to competitor price cutting; to increase purchase in low season periods (such as winter holidays or January sales); or to provide an incentive for another 'bundled' product (for example, if consumers buy a certain product they get a discount on another product or service). *See also* BARGAIN; PRICING.

discount store A type of *department store, which sells *merchandise at prices lower than those of traditional department stores and other traditional retail outlets. Many stores that began as discount stores, have grown into vast commercial retail empires, such as Tesco or Wal Mart.

discriminant analysis A multivariate technique for analysing the predictive value of a set of independent variables. *See* MARKET RESEARCH.

disintermediation The removal or supplanting of the *middleman in any commercial supply and demand chain. The elimination of middlemen was seen as one of the dividends of the new network economy; the *Internet would enable a direct path from producer to consumer with consequent cost advantages for the producer (who no longer had to pay intermediaries' commission) and price advantages for the consumer (who was not paying higher prices that producers passed on to customers to cover the costs of the middlemen). This new form of commerce particularly altered the model for selling basic financial services such as banking and insurance. However, the new economy did not eliminate the intermediary; it simply caused intermediaries to adapt and form new types of intermediary in the new economy, such as the information aggregator and the *portal site. Following the demise of many of the dot.com companies, it is now evident that disintermediation has not doomed distributors, retailers, wholesalers, and all other intermediaries between producers and the ultimate customer. The Internet has transformed but has not eliminated intermediary *channels of distribution. The reality is that customers need a significant amount of value to be added to most products before they can buy and use them.

For example, the car industry is an example of the change in emphasis rather than the total disintermediation that was predicted at one time. During the dot.com boom many online companies started with the intention of offering customers direct sale of cars at much lower prices than traditional car dealers, who were viewed as inflating the prices of cars. However, customers still wanted to test-drive cars, despite being concerned about dealers' mark-ups and often their sales methods. So the car-buying customer tended to research cars using the Internet then did a test drive at a dealer, ordered it over the Internet from the manufacturer who built it to order, then collected it from the dealership which provided local servicing of the car over its lifetime. As dealerships make more profit from servicing cars than they do from selling them, the actual value created by the dealer buying the vehicle from the manufacturer and then reselling it to the customer is lower that the ongoing servicing relationship. Instead of making profit on a car sale transaction, the dealership will be paid a commission by the manufacturer as a reward for the services it provides. Therefore, the dealership is not eliminated; it simply adds value in a different way, in this case by test driving, collection, and servicing. It is a demonstration centre rather than a sales point, a delivery site, and a service centre.

disparaging copy (knocking copy in the UK) An advertising copy which is critical of another company's products, services, actions, or the company itself.

dispersion A degree of scatter in a statistical analysis as measured against the mean or *standard deviation.

display advertisement Any advertisement in print media other than a classified ad, or an ad that stands alone, such as a window sign or a billboard. *See also* ADVERTISING.

displays Any form of *merchandising combined with the use of *posters, *billboards, or other similar formats at *trade shows and *exhibitions or *retail outlets. *See* MEDIA CHANNELS.

disposable income The financial means which are available to persons for spending or saving after taxes have been deducted. A subset of disposable income is discretionary income, which is the portion most often targeted by marketers. Encouraging *target consumers to spend a greater percentage of their discretionary income is the target of most consumer marketers. It can vary from market to market and is closely related to demographic changes in markets. For example, the over-40s market (*see also* BABY BOOMERS) has the highest percentage of disposable and discretionary income and has not until recently been targeted by advertisers.

d

disruptive technology A specific technology that can fundamentally change not only established technologies but also the rules and business models of a given market, and often business and society overall. The *Internet is the best known example in recent times; the personal computer and telephone in previous generations.

The term was coined by Clay Christensen, a Harvard Business School professor, in his 1997 book, *The Innovator's Dilemma*. Disruptive technology often has problems because it is new, appeals to a limited *audience, and may not yet have a proven practical application. Often, established users have trouble capitalizing on the new marketing opportunities created by low-margin disruptive technologies. Often industries are changed by an 'outsider' using a disruptive technology: for example, the Apple iPod and its iTune service is a good example of how a technology 'disrupted' the music industry establishment and traditional business model.

dissolve A fade from one scene to another in a film, video, multimedia, or television production.

dissonance-attribution model A part of an overall *consumer response model that shows how *consumers act in a specific way after the purchase of a *product to gather positive information and feelings in support of their purchase which supports their *buying behaviour and portrays their decision to buy as one of independent judgement uninfluenced by information from *advertising, peers, salespeople, etc. *See also* COGNITIVE DISSONANCE.

dissonance hierarchy *See* THREE ORDERS MODEL.

distribution An element of the marketing mix which describes the function of delivering goods and services to the *marketplace and to *customers. Distribution is part of an overall *supply chain which connects the overall production of the goods, or the origination of the service, to the packaging, storage, wholesaling, retailing, transportation, marketing, selling to the end customer. Distribution can be part of a complex supply chain system (such as automobiles or movies) or it can be a simple distribution (such as a bakery selling bread). *See also* CHANNELS OF DISTRIBUTION.

distributor's brand (own label) The brand used by the distributor or in-store retailers usually to promote outlet loyalty rather than individual brand product loyalty.

divergent marketing The creation of individual *brand management and profit centres within a company for each product group, each with separate marketing goals.

diversification *See* ANSOFF MATRIX.

documentary Either television, film, video, or radio programme dealing with factual material rather than fictional material, usually with some defined goal to create new insight or exposure to facts.

domain name The identity and location of an entity on the *Internet. There are different levels of domain, and examples are as follows:

Top-level (TLD): .com, .net, .org, .edu, .gov
2nd-level: business, shopping, search (2nd-level may contain letters, numbers, and hyphens)
3rd-level: www1, www2, keyword (optional)

The selection of domain names is a major consideration when doing business online, and it is often one of the first issues to be addressed. While a good domain name will not guarantee success, it can have a positive (or negative) impact on almost every aspect of online business. A good domain name is one that is easy to remember and minimizes confusion. The most logical variations are non-hyphenated and hyphenated variations, along with words that are phonetically similar and common misspellings. With the commercialization of the *World Wide Web it is estimated that there are around 50 million commercial domain names registered, making domain names an increasingly valuable commodity.

domination The undisputed market leadership, or concentration of *product marketing or *media promotion in a single niche or channel in order to dominate either the market or the medium.

door opener A product or *advertising speciality, usually given free by a salesperson to consumers to induce them to listen to a sales pitch. The worst examples of this are free gifts given by timeshare salesmen to induce potential customers to listen to a high-pressure sales pitch.

doorway An *Internet domain used specifically to rank the addressee well in *search engines for particular *keywords, serving as an entry point through which visitors pass to the main domain.

doorway page A *website page made specifically to rank well in search engines for particular *keywords, serving as an entry point through which visitors pass to the main content.

double exposure (cinema; video) The technique of superimposing one shot upon another.

double jeopardy A term for a marketing problem in which smaller brands are bought both less frequently and by fewer people. This usually marks the beginning of a spiral of *brand decline. Brands with a large *market share have a huge benefit over smaller brands in stable markets. This results from the 'double jeopardy' effect that demonstrates how big brands that have more *customers (who buy more often) have the double benefit effect and smaller brands have the double jeopardy effect. Buyers buy from portfolios of brands in most market categories. This tends to be in a fixed ratio in which their favourite brand is bought the most often and their third or fourth favourite only 10% or so of the time. In a stable market, the biggest *buyers are buying a number of brands and the marketer's goal is to get them to buy their brand repeatedly. Therefore, brands that are lower than fourth preference for the bulk of buyers inevitably fail to gain any real share. The benefits for big brands ensure that new small brands simply have no real chance, unless they truly disrupt the market. *See also* DIRICHLET MODEL.

double page spread Two pages in a newspaper, magazine, or other print publication which are facing each other. Often used for promotional material.

double sampling A collection of data through an inexpensive sampling technique for a sample larger than the final desired sample size. A subsample of this group is then selected and sampled, usually with a more expensive technique.

double truck A two-page spread in a print publication, where the ad runs across the middle gutter.

download A technique of distribution of electronic material, such as software, from one system to another. Downloading has become one of the principal distribution channels of electronic commerce.

downmarket A description of something or some place that is seen to be for *mass consumers, low priced, and low quality. Both *upmarket and downmarket are based on the simplistic notion that markets have upper and lower ends and that quality and exclusivity are at the top and cheapness and mass accessibility are at the bottom.

downturn *See* BUSINESS CYCLE.

draft An unrefined and partially edited copy in need of further comment, editing, additional material.

draw The money paid to a *salesperson before the sale is actually completed. The draw is then applied towards the commissions earned from future sales. Draws are used for salespeople where income is based entirely upon a commission. Draws can be either recoverable or non-recoverable. Recoverable draws occur when the salesperson is required to reimburse the company if the commission targets are not met; non-recoverable draws cannot be recovered if the targets are not met. *See also* SALES.

drip advertising A *campaign with infrequent use of *advertising over a long period of time. *See* ADVERTISING.

drive time A time band used in *radio advertising, which refers to morning and afternoon times when *consumers are driving to and from work.

drop out rate The number of people who begin an *Internet-based survey but who do not complete it and also the number of people who abandon the process of online purchasing, usually between placing something in their online 'shopping cart' and eventual purchase.

dummy copy An incomplete ad, or even blank sheets of paper, provided to a printer or artist as an example of the size, colour, or other aspect of the ad to be produced.

dumping An export practice in international trade involving selling goods in an overseas market at a much lower price than in the domestic market. The World Trade Organization has prohibited this practice. *See also* INTERNATIONAL MARKETING.

duplication The extent of overlap of readership, viewership, listenership, or circulation between *media.

duplicated audience The portion of an audience that is reached by more than one media vehicle.

Dutch auction (descending price auction) Commercial terms are initially offered at a high price and are moved progressively lower until a buyer is found.

DVD (Digital Video Disk) A digital storage format for reading information from a laser disk using a DVD, a DVD player, and a personal computer. For a decade the DVD has been the dominant format for movie and other multimedia content; however, its position is now under threat from direct *multimedia *downloading over the Web direct to personal multimedia devices such as iPods and iPhones.

dynamic obsolescence The deliberate redesign of goods or services intended to render established goods and services outdated and eventually obsolete.

dynamic pricing *See* PRICING.

E

early adopters *See* DIFFUSION OF INNOVATION.

earned rate A discounted media rate, based on volume or frequency of media placement. *See also* ADVERTISING.

EAV (Equivalent Advertising Value) The degree of editorial exposure resulting from a *media relations campaign, expressed in items of what the cost would have been if the exposure generated by the media campaign had been purchased as advertising space. *See also* ADVERTISING.

eBay An online auction *website where individuals or businesses can sell goods and services worldwide. *See* APPENDIX 2 (eBay case study).

e-commerce The short term for electronic commerce. This refers to commerce, such as the buying, selling, and trading of information, goods, and services, over the *Internet by means of the *World Wide Web. Electronic commerce has risen dramatically since the commercialization of the Internet in the mid-1990s. It can include retailing over the Internet (known as e-tailing), *business-to-business commerce (*B2B), *business-to-consumer (*B2C), *intranets and *extranets, *online marketing, and online presences of any form that are used for some type of commercial relations (for example, *customer loyalty programmes and customer services).

economic environment The external elements that must be taken into consideration in the environmental section of *market strategy and planning. The economic environment ought to include macro- and microeconomic factors, as well as global, regional, national, and local economic environments. It is important to set the wider context of macroeconomics even when developing the most focused marketing plans in very specific market segments. Macroeconomic factors can affect many dimensions of marketing, most specifically demand. *See also* MARKETING PLAN.

editorial A leader article in any medium, usually expressing the opinion of the editor or managing group. Alternatively, it can refer to the entire text of a *newspaper or *magazine and the angle or bias of the opinion.

editorial calendar A printed and dated schedule of the main editorial features planned for future editions of a publication, issued to attract relevant *advertisers.

editorial column The sections of a publication comprised of editorial as opposed to advertising or news reporting content.

editorial policy The guidance set by the editor, newspaper owner, or group regarding the political stance, news angle, writing style, ethics, and legal and operating procedures of the group.

editorial publicity Publicizing or discussing of a product or service in a publication, at the editors' discretion, also simply known as 'publicity'.

editorial write up A journalistic story or feature about a company, service, product, or individual.

educational advertising Copy devoted to informing consumers about a new or extended product or service, particularly useful for the *advertiser when the product or service is recent and its details are not well known. Also refers simply to advertisements concerning educational matters, such as marketing a university to potential students.

effectiveness of advertising *See* ADVERTISING (advertising measurement and effectiveness).

eftpos (Electronic Funds Transfer at Point Of Sale) A networked system through which funds are transferred electronically from the customer's account to the retailer's account, usually involving some sort of credit or debit card. Developed in the mid-1980s, this has become indispensable both for retailers and customers in the sale and purchase of goods and services. For example, these systems are linked to epos (Electronic Point Of Sale) systems that record the goods sold by reading the barcodes on the goods. This enables management information to be transmitted to help with in-store merchandising, rapid replenishment of goods that are selling fast, as well as overall inventory and cash flow control. Retailing has become much more efficient as a result of these systems. It has also helped marketers analyse how and what each customer spends, on what and with what frequency, and where.

Ehrenberg's process *See* AWARENESS-TRIAL-REINFORCEMENT.

elasticity of demand (price elasticity of demand) The measurement of *consumer demand for a *product and how such demand responds to changes in price. If demand is elastic, then a decrease in price results in an increase in purchase, and if inelastic then the reduction results in a decrease in purchase. This is hugely important to *pricing of all goods, from luxury to *commodity goods.

electric spectacular This refers to outdoor signs or billboards composed largely of lighting or other electrical components.

electronic bulletin board A computerized system which allows participants and subscribers to read each other's messages and post new messages and files for other users.

electronic commerce *See* E-COMMERCE.

electronic media Those channels which are used in electronic communication; media which uses electronics or electromechanical energy for the specific audience to access the content such as computer games, digital radio as well as media that can store digital or electronic data such as CD ROMS, SD cards, hard drives, memory sticks, and DVDs. *See also* MULTIMEDIA.

electronic shopping The direct marketing through a two-way system that links consumers with the seller's computerized catalogue by cable or telephone lines.

elephant A potential customer who would bring in a good amount of revenue if successfully converted to a fully paying customer. *See also* WHALE.

e-mail The short name for electronic mail, probably the most successful, and certainly the most widely used, application on the *Internet since its inception. E-mail, is, quite simply, electronically transmitted mail on a computer. E-mail is a very versatile medium. Its speed and broadcasting abilities give it numerous advantages over traditional mail. Unlike traditional physical mail, e-mail enables instantaneous transmission of messages anywhere in the world, at any time, to anyone for less money than it would cost to mail a letter or call someone on the telephone. Linked by high-speed data connections that create a global network, e-mail permits message composition and transmission in seconds to one or more recipients. Businesses and consumers have enthusiastically and universally adopted e-mail across the world. It has become a new means of communication and is a major marketing tool. *See also* INTERACTIVE MARKETING.

e-mail marketing The use of e-mail to market goods and services. E-mail marketing content can be either general or customized. Frequency of transmission to targets can consist of fixed, frequent intervals or sporadic intervals, occurring only when there is something newsworthy to communicate, or else be based upon agreed permissions and registered interest from the receiver. Sophistication (and cost) can be very low or very high. E-mail can also be used to confirm orders of existing customers made through *websites and to *cross sell to existing customers. E-mail is a new and convenient development of *direct marketing. Along with the marketing power of e-mail however, comes the abuse of e-mail, commonly known as *spamming, which is unwanted and unsolicited e-mail. While some users fail to distinguish between permission marketing and e-mail spam, spamming is actually a major threat to legitimate e-mail marketers, as a glut of messages could make the entire e-mail medium less effective. It is the online equivalent of junk mail and is starting to be regarded as a public nuisance, but its global medium makes it much more difficult to regulate than junk mail which is delivered through national postal services and can be regulated by national consumer bodies. It is also known as i-marketing, *online marketing, *digital marketing or web-marketing. *See also* DATABASE MARKETING; DIRECT MARKETING; E-MAIL SPAM; INTERACTIVE MARKETING.

e-mail spam An unwanted, unsolicited *e-mail, especially unsolicited commercial messages sent in bulk by organizations and people usually unknown to the receiver. (spamming refers to the process of sending this.) There is no agreed-upon definition of e-mail spam because it is in the eye of the individual beholder. Some argue that e-mail spam is the electronic equivalent of traditional *junk mail, however it is much cheaper than junk mail. The cost of sending e-mail spam is very small, and people other than the sender pay most of the costs. The lack of significant *barriers to entry (i.e. cost of sending) is often cited as a key problem with e-mail spam. It has bred a range of hucksters and fraudsters on the *Internet. With traditional junk mail, a direct marketer must ensure that the offer and the response from customer targets are enough to offset the costs of mailing. With e-mail spam there is no such accountability. Spamming has been used unscrupulously to defraud online consumers. It is one of the negative by-products of the Internet age.

embargo A prohibition on the export of a particular good or classes of goods to certain countries, usually for political reasons. This can have significant impact on international trade and the economic wellbeing of a country. It is closely linked to foreign policy. For example, the continuing US embargo of Cuba, which originated in the politics of the Cold War, is a major controversy at present. There are many embargos placed upon regimes regarded as dangerous to international security, such as the various embargos on weapons technology to Iraq in the aftermath of the Gulf War of the early 1990s. *See also* EXPORTING.

emergency purchases *See* PRODUCT.

emotional model A model developed in 1984 by Peggy Kreshel, a professor of advertising theory, to examine the influence of emotions on *buying behaviour. This extended the range of prior models, such as the *hierarchy of effects model, that had emphasized cognition as the spring source of purchasing behaviour. In the 1980s there was a growing recognition that many of the academic models had, for the most part, ignored emotion as a significant factor in consumer response. Throughout the 1980s numerous new models of consumer response were created which held emotion to be the underlying element that shaped all subsequent responses. Peggy Kreshel suggested that cognition could alter affect (as in previous models) only because of the affective connotations carried by the cognitive process. In other words, information is relevant primarily because of its affective impact. Or, put another way, it is impossible to separate our emotional connections to a stimulus from the stimulus itself. *See also* ADVERTISING; AIDA; BUYER AND BUYING BEHAVIOUR; DAGMAR; HIERARCHY OF EFFECTS.

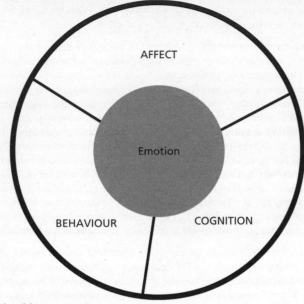

Emotional model

empirical research An investigation that produces results based on direct observation rather than theory and preconceived models.

empiricism A method and approach in *market research based on the belief that knowledge derives from fact, experience, and observation rather than theory.

employee communications The process of communication, personal and non-personal, between a company and its employees, the purpose of which is to inform, educate and motivate the employees.

empty nesters Families whose children have left home and set up their own homes. This is a group with high disposable and discretionary income, caused by no longer having to support children and also possibly from the sale of the original or inherited family property. Increasingly, marketers target this once ignored group because of their rising economic power as well as their more active lifestyles and aspirations following the departure of their children. *See also* LIFESTYLE.

endorsement The overt and explicit support for a *product or *service, usually from a well-known or famous individual, but sometimes an organization, who has normally an association with some field connected with the product or service, and who will be recognized by the *target audience.

end user The person who actually uses a product and service. The end user is not necessarily always the *customer. For example, end users include children who are bought toys and clothes by their parents, or business users who have their equipment and services bought for them by their company purchasing departments. End users always certainly influence the purchasing decision, even if they do not always make it themselves. This is an important element for marketers to understand as they segment their markets and target their campaigns.

Engel's Laws The differences, noted more than a century ago by Ernst Engel, in how people shift their spending across food, housing, transportation, healthcare, and other goods and services categories as family income rises.

enlightened marketing A marketing philosophy holding that a company's marketing should embody the five principles of enlightened marketing:

- **Consumer-oriented marketing** A principle of enlightened marketing that holds that a company should view and organize its marketing activities from the consumers' point of view and place the customer at the centre of everything a company does.
- **Innovative marketing** A principle of enlightened marketing that requires that a company seeks real product and marketing improvements that are of benefit to mankind.
- **Value marketing** A principle of enlightened marketing that holds that a company should put most of its resources into value-building marketing investments over the longer term.
- **Sense-of-mission marketing** A principle of enlightened marketing that holds that a company should define its mission in broad social terms rather than narrow product or profit terms.
- **Societal marketing** A principle of enlightened marketing that holds that a company should make marketing decisions by considering consumers' needs, the consumers' long-run interests together with society's long-term interests.

  See also ETHICAL MARKETING; NON-PROFIT MARKETING.

enquiries The consumer response to a company's *advertising or other promotional activities, such as *coupons. Used for measuring the effectiveness of some promotions.

entry barriers The restrictions or factors which make it difficult for new entrants to expand into lucrative markets. These barriers can be, for example, the need for initial large capital input to develop an infrastructure (for example, transport services), or economies of scale of more established organizations (for example, oil operations), or large marketing expenditure (for example well established consumer brands), or control of massive databases (for example Internet search companies). *See also* COMPETITION; COMPETITIVE ADVANTAGE.

entry page The first page seen by a user on visiting a particular *website.

envelope stuffer A direct mail advertisement included with another mailed message (such as a bill). For example, gas and electricity companies are using their mailing lists to advertise either their own products and services or those of others. *See also* DIRECT MARKETING.

environmentalism An ethos that puts fundamental importance on the relationship between human beings and their actions with the physical environment. *Consumers are showing an increasing desire for environmentally friendly products and are prepared to pay a premium price for them. The reputations of companies can be injured if they damage the environment and their reputations can be enhanced if they are perceived as helping the environment. Environmentalism must therefore be a major consideration for all marketing and corporate reputation building. Products that are perceived to be harmful to the environment will prove increasingly difficult, if not impossible, to market.

environmental scanning An activity taken as part of the overall *market planning process to understand the overall dynamics of the external environment within which market opportunities are to be determined. It will include, for example, *market trends, sizes, *demographics, economics, resources, environment, technology, politics, culture, and *competition. Analysing the external environment gives context and substance to various marketing strategies and plans. It is indispensable in today's complex and ever-changing markets in a globalizing economy. *See also* MARKETING PLAN; MARKETING STRATEGY.

equivalent advertising The amount of free publicity created by editorial coverage in a media or press-relations campaign, expressed as the cost that would have been incurred if it had been purchased as advertising space. *See also* ADVERTISING; BELOW-THE-LINE; EAV.

ergonomics The study of the effect that the physical environment of the workplace has on the physical and psychological wellbeing of the employee, and hence his or her output, with the objective of ensuring comfort, safety, and productivity. Additionally, ergonomics has also come to mean the design of products to suit human needs, with an emphasis on ease of use and adaptability.

e-tailing See E-COMMERCE.

ethical marketing The making and implementing of ethical decisions at all times, conforming to morally sound practice and policies, and communicating these to internal and external audiences. *See also* ENLIGHTENED MARKETING.

ethnic marketing The targeting of a product or service at a specific ethnic group which has *disposable income, sometimes in the language of that group, and aligning with the attitudes and lifestyles of that group. Increasingly important as developed economies are more multi-ethnic than hitherto and cultural norms can no longer be taken for granted as in past times.

ethnocentrism An attitude of mind that holds a single culture to be superior to such a degree that other cultures are denied any importance. In *international marketing terms, an ethnocentric company will often view overseas operations as secondary to domestic operations, often using the overseas operations as a means of dumping excess domestic stock. For global marketing, ethnocentrism is a very dangerous attitude and limits the scope of operation. *See also* GLOBALIZATION.

even price effect The effect on *sales of a price ending in an even digit, particularly zeros. In the psychology of pricing linked to purchase, some research suggests that even price endings affect sales favourably. However there is also a view that prices ending in odd numbers, particularly nines ($9.99 rather than $10) have a more favourable effect on buyers than even number prices. *See also* PRICING.

event marketing A disciplined promotional activity, large scale or small, for events both inside and outside a *sponsorship—such as a major client event, a product launch, a charity event, a concert, or a sports tournament, an art exhibition, a movie launch, a store launch, a book tour, a political rally or convention, a visit—aimed at consumers who have an interest in that specific area. *See also* PUBLIC RELATIONS.

excess capacity The supply, expertise, or manufacturing production exceeding the amount required to fulfil the current market demand.

excess demand Market demand exceeding the amount of supply, expertise, and manufacturing production currently available.

exclusive agency agreement (exclusive dealership agreement) An agreement involving a product, service, geographical area, or market, which bonds a principle and an agent for a specific period of time, restricting either one from making a deal with the other's competitors.

exclusive distribution The right given by a producer to a retailer or other type of distributor to be the sole *distribution channel in a determined territory. In return, exclusive distributors or *retailers are usually required to provide exceptional and far-reaching service to customers.

exclusivity A binding contract term in which one party grants another party sole rights with regard to a particular business function. Some *advertising networks demand exclusivity with a client. Some do not demand exclusivity, but offer a higher rate for an exclusive deal than the standard rate given to non-exclusive deals. Most reputable firms require exclusivity as a result of the in-depth relationships they have with publishers. Some demand exclusivity when sponsoring events or charities. A couple of affiliate networks demand exclusivity of their merchants, but other affiliate networks have tried to exploit this by promoting their non-exclusive terms. Some affiliate programmes demand exclusivity within their product category, but they are exceptions, as few affiliate programmes are in a position to make extra demands.

exhibit (external stimuli) Anything that is shown to *respondents during an interview. Examples might be a *print advertisement, a card listing income categories, or a new package for familiar products. *See also* MARKET RESEARCH.

exhibition

A large-scale venue for the demonstration of goods and services from numerous producers usually brought together around a single theme or industry. These are an effective part of the overall *marketing promotional mix. Exhibitions are dominated by *business-to-business (B2B) marketing, although there are many exhibitions for consumers also. In the US the trade show is an indispensable part of marketing. There are several factors that determine whether or not it is a good use of resources to get involved in exhibitions:

- The right location: there are some places that excel at exhibitions, such as Las Vegas and Orlando.
- The exhibition hall or show area has to be impressive and well laid-out.
- The stands, including the documentation, advice, personnel, gifts, and interactive displays have to be attractive and compelling.
- The exhibitors have to be worth seeing—either for their products and services or even for the quality of their stand.
- The quality and quantity of the visitors is important: how many of them could be prospective clients? How many existing clients? How many

buyers? How many potential visitors will see my competitors' goods if
we do not exhibit?
- The technological and industrial environment: does it make
  attendance at a trade show compelling? Are important new products
  going to be on display or launched?

exit barriers The obstacles, usually financial, legal, or emotional,
preventing an organization from leaving a particular market or sector. *See also*
COMPETITION; ENTRY BARRIERS; MARKETING STRATEGY.

expectations The customers' needs and wants of goods and services
measured against a certain standard that they hold. Expectations for
information are rising all the time and it is the task of the marketer both to
anticipate customer expectation and to manage their expectations. There are
few more damaging consequences for a company than disappointed or
unfulfilled expectations.

expected value The mean of a probability distribution. It is the value of the
probability distribution we would expect in the long run. *See also* MARKET
RESEARCH.

experience curve A model developed to show that real unit costs decline
systematically with increases in cumulative volume production. The
antecedent of the experience curve is the production learning curve, first
observed in the 1930s, as a systematic decline in the number of man-hours
required to produce an aeroplane in American factories. It was only in the
mid-1960s that the notion of the learning curve was generalized by the *Boston
Consulting Group to encompass the behaviour of all value-added costs and
prices as cumulative volume or experience increases. Complete acceptance of
this model is now waning. The application problems were always formidable,
but now there is a growing suspicion that some of the key strategic
implications may be invalid. The rise of innovative technologies that can
substitute for human experience accumulation have undermined the universal
application of the model.

experiencing focus groups The panels that enable a client to observe
and listen to how consumers think and feel about products and services.

experimental unit *See* RESPONDENT.

exploratory focus groups The panels that aid in the precise definition of
the problem, in pilot testing, or in generating hypotheses for testing or
concepts for further market research.

exploratory research The preliminary research to clarify the exact nature of the problem to be solved.

exponential smoothing *See* TIME SERIES ANALYSIS.

exporting

A discipline within *international marketing that concentrates mainly on the *sale of products created in the domestic market to overseas markets. Exporting is usually the first stage in full-scale international marketing and foreign market entry. Exporting is also a central component of international trade negotiations as well as multilateral and bilateral trade agreements. Exporting is also a barometer of the strength or weakness of the domestic economy and partly determines the balance of trade. There are several ways to export. The way in which a company chooses to export its products can have a significant effect on its international market strategies. The basic categories of exporting all relate to the exporter's level of involvement in the export process. There are at least three approaches, which may be used alone or in combination:

- **Passive exporting,** in this approach, orders are received from foreign buyers and fulfilled domestically and shipped to the buyer. Alternatively, sales are made to domestic buyers who then export the product to overseas buyers. These sales are indistinguishable from other domestic sales as far as the original manufacturer is concerned. Someone else has decided that the product in question meets foreign demand. That party takes all the risk and handles all of the exporting details, in some cases without even the awareness of the original seller.
- **Active exporting,** this approach is when the company seeks out domestic export merchants or agents or companies who represent foreign customers. These buyers are a large customer market for a wide variety of goods and services. In this case, a company knows that its product is being exported, but it is still the intermediary who assumes the risk and handles the details of exporting. This is known as *indirect exporting*. The chief characteristic of indirect exporting is that the export of products is carried out through intermediaries. It is also a lower risk and lower cost option for international exporting. It involves no direct investment in the foreign markets. With this approach, a company engages the services of an intermediary firm, agents, or merchants capable of finding foreign markets and buyers for its products. Export management companies, export trading companies, international trade consultants, and other intermediaries can give the exporter access to well-established expertise and trade contacts.
- **Direct exporting,** this approach is the most ambitious and most difficult, since the exporter personally handles every aspect of the exporting process from market research and planning to foreign

distribution, fulfilment, and collections. Consequently, a significant commitment of management time and attention is required to achieve good results. It also requires greater investment and research to be successful. However, this approach may also be the best way to achieve maximum profits and long-term growth and grow into a fully international company. The direct exporting company will most likely set up an export department within its own company. Additionally, the company will set up sales offices in foreign markets to handle storage, distribution, sales, servicing, and marketing. Alternatively, the company may recruit foreign sales agents who exclusively represent the product in that territory.

There are also potential combinations of export strategy. For example, a company may choose to export to adjacent or neighbouring markets, or an economic free trade area, or economic community zone, directly, then use export agents and intermediaries where it is less familiar with the culture and language and customs, or where the market potential is smaller but still significant.

Other approaches to exporting may involve *licensing products, processes, trademarks, patents, and intellectual property in exchange for a royalty or fee. This is lower risk than setting up a full infrastructure in the foreign territory. It can also be lower risk for the licensee as the expertise or product is already tried and tested.

Deciding when to export

There are several ways to gauge the overseas market potential of products and services.

Domestic success of a product or service is no guarantee for success overseas. Market differences may inhibit repeatability of success that was known in domestic markets. Those differences may be cultural, environmental, or social factors. There may be problems with local availability of raw materials or product alternatives. There may be lower wage costs or lower purchasing power. There could be a lack of convertible currency or the availability of foreign exchange (rather than hard currencies like the dollar, the British pound, and the Japanese yen). There could be government import controls or restrictive labour laws.

Some countries impose tariffs on foreign exports in order to protect their domestic markets or to raise revenues. Some countries have strict import quotas in order to protect their domestic markets or to preserve their foreign currency reserves. At worse, the exporter can face an embargo, or total ban, on foreign imports. There are also non-tariff barriers, such as demanding extraordinary safety features that it is impossible for certain exporters to provide, that have the effect of discriminating against certain export products from foreign countries.

If a product is unique or has important features that are hard to duplicate abroad, the chances of finding an export market overseas may be good. For a unique product, competition may be nonexistent or very slight, while demand may be quite high.

If sales of a product are declining in the domestic market, sizeable export markets may exist, especially if the product once did well in the domestic market but is now losing market share to more technically advanced products. Countries that are less developed than the domestic market may not need more advanced products and may be unable to afford the more advanced and expensive products. Such markets may instead have surprisingly healthy demand for products that are older or that are considered obsolete by domestic market standards. *See also* GLOBALIZATION; INTERNATIONAL MARKETING.

export-led growth An economic approach adopted by some countries who are seeking to promote economic growth by exporting to wealthier countries.

exposure The number of *consumers who have seen (or heard, or visited) a media vehicle, whether or not they paid attention to it.

extended guarantee The guarantee that the manufacturer offers at additional cost to the customer that extends beyond the timescale of the original guarantee. This can be quite lucrative for the manufacturer and plays on the customer's fear of breakdown. This is often called selling the customer 'peace of mind'. Guarantees are an integral part of *consumer goods marketing and can also be applied to leased equipment as well as purchased equipment.

external audit *See* ENVIRONMENTAL SCANNING; MARKETING AUDIT.

external stimuli *See* EXHIBIT.

extranet A company's secure site that can be accessed with a password and which can be used by third parties, often for commercial transactions. The extranet provides a link with the company customers, partners, and suppliers and enables a 'community of interest' to be formed. *See also* DIGITAL MARKETING; ONLINE MARKETING.

eye tracking A research method that determines which part of an advertisement consumers look at, by tracking the pattern of their eye movements.

e-zine An electronic magazine, whether delivered via a *website or in the form of an *e-mail newsletter. E-zines range greatly in size and scope, from irregular newsletters reaching a handful of subscribers to daily journals reaching hundreds of thousands of subscribers. Some e-zines are strictly non-profit. Some are extremely profitable. Others are for-profit but don't make any profit because they are unable to attract the necessary audience and advertisers. Additionally, companies are starting to use internal e-zines to communicate information to employees in a relative low-cost way.

e-zine directory A directory of electronic magazines, typically those that are delivered by e-mail.

Facebook The world's largest and most popular social networking website, founded in 2004 and privately owned by Facebook Inc and available to anyone over 13 with a valid e-mail address. *See* APPENDIX 2 for more details on Facebook.

face-to-face interviewing Questioning an individual in person, rather than by telephone, postal, or any other means.

face value The nominal value printed on the face of a coin or paper note; the perceived value of something.

facilitator *See* MODERATOR.

fact book A file of information and intelligence on products, countries, markets, or a range of areas of expertise. An example could be the *Economist* Intelligence Unit reports on various countries and their economies.

factor analysis A method used by researchers to make large sets of data more manageable by reducing the number of variables and by determining commonality between these variables. For example, if there is a questionnaire with 100 questions on how travellers choose which hotels they frequent, the answers can potentially be grouped together by similarity to bring the total answer set down to 20 or 30. There may be a category called service that would include things like speed and efficiency of check-ins and check-outs, or how fast room service or housekeeping respond to enquiries. Another item that might be included in the service factor could be how friendly the staff is.

factory outlet A store in which the manufacturer sells its products at a *discount including stock companies supplies, discounted lines, seconds, and lines from previous seasons.

fad A short-term obsession with a style, product, idea, or concept. Fads are characterized by high *adoption (expressed in either increased *sales or *publicity or *word of mouth) and equally fast disappearance and *obsolescence.

fairtrade movement The organization that works to ensure that producers from the Second and Third World, exporting to First World countries, achieve a fair and ethical price for their products. It also aims to promote sound social and environmental conditions for workers and their families, and prohibits the trading of items produced by child and slave labour. Fairtrade products are now widely available through many major retailers. *See also* ETHICAL MARKETING.

family The basic unit of social organization in most countries in the world and also the main focus of consumption; as such it is very important to *consumer marketers. In recent years the home has become increasingly the focus of *direct marketing. The combination of the home as a *purchasing unit as well as rising family income make the family a powerful economic force, and also one with a tremendous influence on buying behaviour. There is market influence from both parents and children. Demographic changes as well as changing social habits (such as the rise of extended 'second' families, divorce, single-sex marriage, and cohabitation) mean that marketers can no longer assume the classic nuclear family as the basic unit of social organization when preparing their marketing messages and products. *See also* FAMILY LIFE CYCLE; LIFESTYLE MARKETING.

family brands Those products that are specifically targeted at family use and family values.

family life cycle

A way of *segmenting the family market at different stages of the life cycle to determine what products and services members buy at each stage and also their levels of *disposable income. This segmentation charts the stages through which families pass as they age.

The main variables are age, marital status, career, and disposable income as well as presence and absence of children in the family home. Stages of the family life cycle are as follows.

1 *Single young people not living at home*. Typically they would have few financial burdens and marketers would focus upon their interests in fashion, leisure, basic household items, cars, equipment, and holidays. Financial services marketers increasingly target this group at the student level and as they gain their first jobs, hoping to build a lifelong relationship with them as their financial needs grow.

2 *Newly married couples that have no children*. Typically these couples are wealthier than the singles group. The main focus of the marketer is their initial purchase of starter homes, household and consumer durable goods, holidays, and financial services.

3 *Full nesters stage I*. Couples with children under six. This group is very focused on home purchase but tend to have low levels of disposable income and savings, usually because of mortgage commitments, or the wife having taken time off to have children. This group is a target for marketers selling financial services, typically

credit products, such as cards, loans, and overdrafts. The main focus of disposable income is the children and this group is therefore the main target for baby products and clothes, as well as children's toys and books.

4 *Full nesters stage II*. Couples with youngest child, six or over. Usually, if the job market is good, this couple's financial position is better, perhaps through pay rises, perhaps because of the wife's return to work. Children continue to dominate the decisions of the household. Marketers focus on this group for consumer goods, clothes, bicycles, sports gear, musical instruments and lessons, and activity holidays.

5 *Full nesters stage III*. Older married couples with dependent children, perhaps in full-time higher education or first jobs. The financial position of this group continues to improve, but could also be offset by rising financial demands of children's education. Wives are working. The main focus is on schooling, educational attainment, and educational costs. The marketer focuses on this group buying new, more tasteful furniture, luxury goods, boats, timeshares, and exotic holidays.

6 *Empty nesters stage I*. These are older married couples, no children living with them but with the parent(s) still working. Their mortgage payments are less onerous and they may be thinking of trading down their house. They have a high degree of savings and disposable income. They are interested in unique travel experiences, possibly a second home in a foreign country, sophisticated leisure, and self-education. They observe their children gain qualifications and move to the first stage of the family cycle. The marketer targets this group as perhaps the wealthiest of all, buying luxury goods, expensive home improvements, specialist holidays, and possibly top end of the range cars.

7 *Empty nesters stage II*. These are older married couples, with no children living at home, but with the main breadwinner retired. This group experiences a significant cut in income and is heavily dependent upon the pension provision that they have made. They tend to spend less on leisure and buy more medical appliances or medical care products. They cease to help their children financially and are constantly concerned with levels of savings and pension. This group is no longer a main focus of the marketer except in financial services (such as annuities, income-generating plans) and providers of hobbies and pastime products.

8 *Solitary survivor stage I*. Still working, but may have divorce and maintenance costs to bear. Income is still adequate but is likely to sell family home and purchase smaller accommodation. Is worried about security and increasing dependency. Some expenditure is made on hobbies and pastimes and specialist holidays catering for singles. This group is not a top target for the marketer.

9 *Solitary survivor stage II (retired)*. Has a significant cut in income and requires increasing amounts of care, particularly medical, and special attention and security. Possible dependence on other family members for personal financial assistance, in the same way as children were dependent on them for assistance. This group is no longer a target of marketers, but their relatives may be, particularly for financial services, such as insurance, and also for medical care services.

farmer A *sales representative who is responsible for increasing sales from current customers. In sales, the farmer will 'grow' sales as in agriculture the farmer will grow crops.

fashion A currently accepted or popular style in a given field. Fashion, that is, apparel, accessories, and jewellery, is a huge industry in its own right. Marketing the fashion apparel of a *haute couturier*—such as Dior, Lagerfeld, or Yves Saint Laurent—is more to promote the *brand than to promote the clothes. Usually, the couturier part of the fashion business is unprofitable; the extensions of the brand, for example to perfume or accessories, are where the profits are made.

fast food A type of edible product that is cooked and delivered to the customer very quickly and can be eaten either on the premises or taken away. Originating in the US in the 1960s, the fast-food market revolutionized food retailing and eating habits and is associated with global brands like McDonald's, Pizza Hut, or KFC.

fast-moving consumer goods (FMCG) Frequently purchased products that usually sell in retail outlets and which, literally, sell quickly because they are highly consumable. *See also* CONSUMERS; CONSUMER MARKETING.

favicon A compound word meaning favourite icon with 16 pixels square and associated with a particular *website, usually displayed in the *browser address bar.

favourite *See* BOOKMARK.

feeds *See* RSS.

feel-bad factor Depressed *consumer and business confidence that results in a psychological withdrawal of consumers into a pessimistic state, resulting in flat or falling spending on *products and investment goods. Because consumer confidence is so vital to a modern economy, the contrary condition causes much concern to politicians and businessmen. *See also* CONSUMER MARKETING.

feel-buy-learn model A concept that shows how in certain situations consumers do not follow the traditional learn-feel-buy model, but instead use feelings and impressions to make their purchase, and then learn about the product afterwards. *See also* BUYER AND BUYING BEHAVIOUR; CONSUMERISM.

feel-good factor Buoyant consumer and business confidence, which results in high spending and confidence about taking on extra credit facilities. For example, it is a well-known factor in the UK that if homeowners feel that property prices are rising, and therefore their net wealth, they will spend much more freely on consumer goods, household furnishings, and leisure services.

field marketing The marketing of a product or service in the location where customers are most likely to experience and engage with the product, involving the organization's staff meeting the customers in person.

field research The gathering of survey data on location. *See also* PRIMARY RESEARCH.

film advertising The use of advertising copy either before or, more subtly, as indirect advertising within a film, in which the sponsor pays for their product to be used in a particular film or during its screening. This type of advertising can also be adapted to the local cinema audience. *See* ADVERTISING; MEDIA CHANNELS.

finished product Completed goods that are ready to market. *See also* PRODUCT.

firewall A computer security measure which blocks unauthorized access, but allows authorized ones.

first-mover advantage The first significant company to enter a new market in a substantial way, often with a new service or product that has no previous track record. First-mover advantage was initially thought to be a crucial and necessary *marketing strategy in the *Internet economy, but experience has now shown that this has not always been the case. First-mover advantage can be instrumental in building market share, but the early years of the Internet economy have not shown conclusively that this leads to business success. eBay and Amazon.com are examples of online companies that have gained successful early-mover advantage. There is no single reward for early movers. Some industries reward first movers with near-monopoly status and higher margins. Other industries do not necessarily reward the first mover, allowing late movers the chance to compete more effectively and efficiently against early entrants.

first to market *See* MARKETING PLAN.

five forces model

Developed by Michael *Porter, this model provided a framework for an overall set of competitive rivalries within an industry structure. Marketers seeking to develop a *competitive advantage can use this model to better understand the industry context in which the firm operates.

The model is illustrated, then expanded upon:

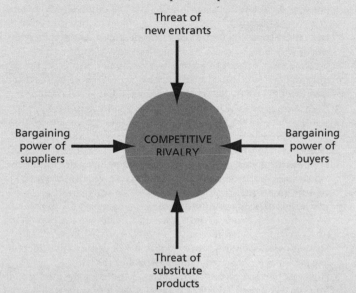

Five Forces Model

If rivalry among firms in an industry is low, the industry is considered to be disciplined. This discipline may result from the industry's history of competition, the role of a leading firm, or informal compliance with a generally understood code of conduct. When an important rival takes an action that precipitates counter-moves by other firms, rivalry intensifies. The intensity of rivalry is classified into various ranges, based on the firm's aggressiveness in attempting to gain an advantage.

In pursuing an advantage over its rivals, a firm can choose from several *competitive strategies:

- *Pricing: raising or lowering prices to gain a temporary advantage.
- Improving *product differentiation.
- Creatively using *channels of distribution: using *vertical integration or using a distribution channel that is novel to the industry.
- Exploiting its relationships with its suppliers.

Various industry characteristics that affect the intensity of rivalry:

- **A larger number of firms** increases rivalry because more firms must compete for the same customers and resources. The rivalry intensifies if the firms have similar *market share, leading to a struggle for *market leadership.
- **Slow market growth** causes firms to fight for market share. In a growing market, firms are able to improve revenues simply because of the expanding market.
- **High fixed costs** result in an economy of scale effect that increases rivalry. When total costs are mostly fixed costs, the firm must produce near capacity to attain the lowest unit costs. Since the firm must sell this large quantity of product, high levels of production lead to a fight for market share, resulting in increased rivalry.
- **High storage costs** *or* **highly perishable products** cause a producer to sell goods as soon as possible. If other producers are attempting to unload products on the market at the same time, competition for customers intensifies.
- **Low switching costs** increase rivalry. When a customer can freely switch from one product to another there is a greater struggle to capture customers.
- **Low levels of product differentiation** are associated with higher levels of rivalry. Brand identification and loyalty, on the other hand, tends to constrain rivalry.
- **Strategic stakes are high** when a firm is losing market position or has potential for great gains. This intensifies rivalry.
- **High exit barriers** place a high cost on abandoning the product. The firm must compete. High exit barriers cause a firm to remain in an industry, even when the venture is not profitable.
- **A diversity of rivals** with different cultures, histories, and philosophies make an industry unstable. There is greater possibility for mavericks and for misjudging a rival's moves. Rivalry is volatile and can be intense.
- **Industry shakeout** A growing market and the potential for high profits induces new firms to enter a market and incumbent firms to increase production. A point is reached where the industry becomes crowded with competitors, and demand cannot support the new entrants and the resulting increased supply. The industry may become crowded if its growth rate slows and the market becomes saturated, creating a situation of excess capacity with too many goods chasing too few buyers. A shakeout ensues, with intense competition, price wars, and company failures. It is clear that market stability and changes in supply and demand affect rivalry. Cyclical demand tends to create intensive competition.

Threat of substitutes

In Porter's model, a substitute product refers to products in other industries. Substitute products affect a product's price elasticity: as more substitutes become available, the *demand becomes more *elastic since customers have more alternatives. A close substitute product constrains the ability of firms in an industry to raise prices.

The *competition engendered by the threat of a substitute comes from products outside the industry. While this typically impacts an industry through price competition, there can be other concerns in assessing the threat of substitutes. For example, the transmission of television signals was once done in a single way: from local transmission stations by airwaves via an aerial to a TV receiver. Now there are substitute alternatives: transmission via cable, satellite, broadband, wireless, and even high-capacity copper telephone lines. The new technologies available and the changing structure of the entertainment media are contributing to competition among these substitute means of connecting the home to entertainment.

Buyer power

The power of buyers is the impact that customers have on a producing industry. In general, when the power of *buyers is strong, the relationship to the producing industry is characterized by a market in which there are many suppliers and one buyer. Under such market conditions, the buyer sets the price.

Buyers are strong if:

- They are concentrated in a given market: there are a few buyers with significant market share;
- They purchase a significant proportion of output, particularly standardized product which enables them to switch suppliers;
- They possess a credible backward integration threat: they can threaten to buy the producing firm or a rival.

Buyers are weak if:

- Producers threaten forward integration, i.e. producers can take over own distribution/retailing;
- There are significant buyer switching costs: for example, products not standardized and they cannot easily switch to another product;
- They are fragmented (many, different); in this case no buyer has any particular influence on products or prices;
- Producers supply critical portions of the buyers' input, for example in the distribution of purchases.

Supplier power

A producing industry requires raw materials, such as labour, components, and other material supplies. This requirement leads to buyer–supplier relationships between the industry and the firms that provide it with the raw materials used to create products. Suppliers, if powerful, can exert an influence on the producing industry, such as selling its raw materials at a high price, expropriating some of the industry's profits. An example of this is the car industry that clearly dominates its distribution channels and dealers.

The following outlines some factors that determine supplier power. Suppliers are powerful if:

- There is a credible forward integration threat by suppliers, for example car companies taking over direct selling and servicing of their vehicles;
- They are concentrated in a market;
- There is significant cost to switch suppliers—to some extent the suppliers have locked in their buyers;
- Customers are powerful.

Suppliers are weak if:

- There are any competitive suppliers—the product is standardized;
- The buyers purchase commodity products which can be found easily elsewhere;
- There is a credible backward integration threat by purchasers;
- There are concentrated purchasers;
- Customers are weak.

Barriers to entry/threat of entry

It is not only existing competitors that pose a threat to firms in an industry; the possibility that new companies may enter the industry also affects competition. In theory, any firm should be able to enter and exit a market, and if free entry and exit exists, then profits always should be nominal. In reality, however, industries possess characteristics that protect the high profit levels of firms in the market and inhibit additional rivals from entering the market. These are *barriers to entry*.

Barriers to entry are more than the normal equilibrium adjustments that markets typically make to control the entrance of new suppliers. For example, when industry profits increase, one would expect additional firms to enter the market to take advantage of the high profit levels. Over time, the entry of new competitors and suppliers would drive profits down for all firms in the industry. When profits decrease, we would expect some firms to exit the market and this would restore market equilibrium. Falling prices, or the expectation that future prices will fall, deter rivals from entering a market. Firms also may be reluctant to enter markets that are extremely uncertain, especially if entering involves high start-up costs. These are normal accommodations to market conditions. However, if firms individually (collective action would constitute illegal collusion) keep prices artificially low as a strategy to prevent potential entrants from entering the market, such *entry-deterring pricing* establishes a major barrier to market entry.

Barriers to entry are unique industry characteristics that define the industry. Barriers reduce the rate of entry of new firms, thus maintaining a level of profits for those already in the industry. From a strategic perspective, barriers can be created or exploited to enhance a firm's competitive advantage. Barriers to entry arise from several sources:

1 **Government creates barriers.** Although the principal role of the government in a market is to preserve competition through anti-trust actions, government also restricts competition through the granting of monopolies and through regulation. Illustrative of this kind of barrier to entry is the local cable company in the UK. The franchise to a cable provider may be granted by competitive bidding, but once a community awards the franchise a monopoly is created. Similarly, the government grants various types of licence that enable entry into a market, such as broadcasting and wireless telephony.

2 **Patents and proprietary knowledge serve to restrict entry into an industry.** Ideas, processes, techniques, expertise, and knowledge that provide competitive advantages are treated as private property when patented. This prevents others from using the knowledge and creating a barrier to entry.

3 **Asset specificity inhibits entry into an industry.** Asset specificity is the extent to which the firm's assets can be utilized to produce a different product. When an industry requires highly specialized technology or plant and equipment, potential entrants are reluctant to commit to acquiring specialized assets that cannot be sold or converted into other uses if the venture fails. Asset specificity provides a barrier to entry because when firms already hold specialized assets they fiercely resist efforts by others from taking their market share. New entrants can anticipate aggressive rivalry. An example is control of the 'local loop' telephone exchanges by incumbent communications companies that make the final connection to domestic customers. All competing communications companies have to use these local loops in order to serve local customers.

4 **Organizational (Internal) Economies of Scale.** The most cost efficient level of production is termed *Minimum Efficient Scale* (MES). This is the point at which unit costs for production are at minimum, i.e. the most cost-efficient level of production. If the MES for firms in an industry is known, then it is possible to determine the amount of market share necessary for low-cost entry or cost parity with rivals. The existence of an economy of scale creates a barrier to entry. The greater the difference between industry MES and entry unit costs, the greater the barrier to entry.

We can generalize about an industry's barriers to entry/exit, as follows:

EASY TO ENTER IF THERE IS:	DIFFICULT TO ENTER IF THERE IS:
Common or standardized technology	Difficulty in *brand switching, or extreme *brand loyalty
Little brand franchise	Patented or proprietary know-how
Access to *channels of distribution	High scale threshold to enter the market
Low scale threshold to enter the market	Restricted *channels of distribution

DIFFICULT TO EXIT IF THERE ARE:	EASY TO EXIT IF THERE ARE:
Specialized assets	Saleable assets
High exit costs	Independent businesses
Interrelated businesses	

Source: M. Porter *Competitive Advantage* (1980).
See also COMPETITION; COMPETITIVE POSITION.

fixed costs *See* BREAKEVEN ANALYSIS.

fixed-sum-per-unit method A method of determining an advertising budget which is based directly on the number of units sold.

flagship The pre-eminent or best-selling *product, *service, or *retail outlet of a company. For example, retailers with high-visibility retail outlets on 5th Avenue in New York, Bond Street in London, Red Square in Moscow, the Ginza in Tokyo, or the Champs Elysées in Paris could refer to these stores as flagships, because their main purpose is to display their *brand.

flanker brand A new *brand introduced into the market by a company that already has an established brand in the same *product category. The new brand is designed to compete in the category without damaging the existing item's market share by targeting a different group of *consumers. Flanker branding is important because it allows a company to attract new customers from various market segments. This technique is also known as multibranding and is used to achieve a larger total market share than one product could achieve on its own. An example is Diet Coke that extended the Coca-Cola brand for the growing weight-watcher part of the market. Companies with multiple brands in a single product category generally have a *premium brand that offers high quality at a higher price in their overall portfolio. They usually own one or more 'value' brands offering a slightly lower quality or a different set of benefits for a lower price.

The main brand of a company's portfolio should target the *market segment containing the most consumers. Another brand can then be positioned to convert users from other market segments by using a different set of benefits or product characteristics. A flanker brand should attract customers from competing brands and not from the main branded product.

There are a number of advantages to developing a flanker brand:

- In consumer goods a flanker brand can gain more shelf space for the company, which increases retailer dependence on the company's brands.
- Flanker brands can capture those consumers who like to switch brands by offering several brands.
- Creation of internal competition within the product portfolio between the different brands without harming the overall brand. Giving a product its own unique name means it will not be readily associated with the existing brand. This reduces risk to the existing brand if the product fails.
- Companies with a high-quality existing product can introduce lower-quality brands without diluting their flagship brand names.

Introducing a new brand is costly. Creating another independent brand requires name research and substantial advertising expenditures to create name recognition and preference for the new brand. One thing that has to be considered is the extent to which the new brand will have unique qualities that will appeal to a separate group of consumers and provide additional value over and above the existing brand. An assessment of the new brand's impact on existing brands has to be made and considered as well as the new brand's impact on competitors' brands.

flash A multimedia technology that allows interactive images to be created within a relatively small file. It can be used to create entire *websites or to add interactive elements to standard *HTML websites. Non-flash sites accompany some flash-only sites in an effort to cater to a wider audience. Flash technology can also be used in interactive banner advertisements.

flash pack A package upon which a sales promotion message features prominently.

flat rate A media buying rate that allows for no discounts.

flighting The overall approach and execution of *media strategy in terms of timing, seasonality, and level of repetition, particularly for commercials running on *print and *broadcast media. In broadcast media, inventory is purchased by 'day part,' that is, a certain time block during a 24-hour period. Overnight day parts (which are not even measured by ratings) are much less expensive than, say, prime-time (8 p.m. to 11 p.m.) day parts. *See also* ADVERTISING; MEDIA.

fly poster An illegal or unauthorized advert placed on a legitimately owned hoarding or advertising site, or on other private property.

focus group A method of studying behaviours or responses by having an organized group of participants discuss a given topic or product or idea. Focus groups are typically used in *consumer research where it is necessary to obtain information about an individual's reactions, behaviours, and usage patterns and to understand the reasoning behind these patterns or behaviours. It is a *qualitative market research technique and needs a skilled moderator. A good size for a focus group is about 10 people. Typically, 3–4 focus groups would be run around a specific topic. The first focus group should provide a lot of insight. The next couple of focus groups should reinforce the conclusions that have come out of the first focus group. After 3–4 focus groups, there is not as much valuable information that can be obtained and there are diminishing returns for the investment. Focus groups can be used in conjunction with interviews.

fold The section of a *website page that is visible without scrolling. The fold varies depending on the resolution settings on a visitor's monitor. At lower settings (i.e. 640 × 480 pixels) the fold is relatively high on the page. At higher setting (i.e. 1280 × 1024 pixels) the fold extends much further down the page. Decisions concerning what goes above or below the fold are often made based on a minimum targeted resolution. Advertisers often look favourably at *banner ad placements that are high on the page, assuming that their ads will be viewed and clicked more often.

footfall The number of customers visiting a shop or venue over a set period of time, used to gauge a retailer's customer reach, but not always reliably leading to higher sales.

foot-in-the-door technique A method for persuading a customer to spend a large amount or take a large risk, by first inducing him to take a smaller less risky step, but thereby predisposing him to make the next, larger commitment. Originally, a technique used by a door-to-door salesperson to gain entry into a potential customer's house by blocking the customer from closing the door in their face.

forecast A statistical synthesis of probabilities and expert opinion that attempts to define an outcome either in terms of numbers or actual courses of action. Forecasts range from the short-term (usually up to three months), the medium-term (normally covering one or two years), and the long-term (three years plus). Market forecasting is one of the most difficult arts of the marketer; no matter how well informed the underlying data. Investments in product and services launches are usually made on the basis of market forecasts.

forecasting

The identification of factors and quantification of their effect on an entity, as a basis for business planning and investment. Forecasting approaches include quantitative (objective) and qualitative (subjective) estimates of the future. Forecasting is important because, by predicting future sales, the company can estimate revenue and therefore plan production, capital, and human resources accordingly.

Sales forecasting

This is critically important to overall *marketing investment. It is a time series model that takes historical data and projects trends into the future (for example, previous sales figures, moving averages, seasonal aspects, cyclical fluctuations). It can also include causal models, for example those models that relate sales to relative prices, complementary goods sales, and promotional advertising. There are other forecasting models that are qualitative—for example, those that rely on expert opinions to predict the future. *Sales budgets are usually based on company forecasts of future sales, but may be adjusted to take a prudent or conservative view of the expected volume and value of sales.

The following factors are used to determine a sales forecast:

- Past sales patterns, often risky as in today's economy previous sales patterns are an unreliable guide to the future.
- The economic environment, particularly factors that affect investment and growth, or which affect demand, directly or indirectly, of the goods being sold.
- Results of market research, particularly research into buyer intentions over defined time periods.
- Anticipated advertising during the budget period, which could act as a fillip for sales.
- Competition, and its intensity in the defined market where the sales force will operate.
- Changing consumer tastes: these can totally wreck a sales forecast that is based upon historical patterns of consumer taste.
- New technology, which can often change the pattern of market demand or create new demand.
- Distribution and quality of sales outlets and personnel: for example, an increase in either volume or quality of direct and indirect sales can have a positive effect on total sales volume.
- Pricing policies and discounts offered: often creative pricing and discounting can increase sales volumes, if not always profits.
- Legislation either local or national.
- Environmental factors, for example the rise in organic food can increase sales to retail outlets.

Sales forecast accuracy

Sales forecasts are rarely 100% accurate. There are some factors that can help improve their accuracy:

- Good, up-to-date internal data and market intelligence are needed to make an accurate forecast, which reduces the use of 'gut feel' or approximation based upon personal hunches.
- Sales statistics should be available in a suitable format and easy to understand.

- All the factors affecting sales, including external market conditions, should be understood by the people involved in the forecasting process.
- Appropriate methods of forecasting should be used, whether quantitative or qualitative or a combination of both.
- Assumptions made in the sales forecast (such as the rate of inflation, exchange rates, rate of adoption of a product, increase in a competitor's promotional activity, etc.) ought to be clearly stated so that changes can easily be made to the forecast if the assumptions change.
- Sales forecasts should be reviewed regularly and should take into account any new information in order to keep them up to date and accurate.
- An organization's own marketing strategy must be taken into account. Increased advertising, sales promotions, or a new price list must be considered when making sales forecasts.
- Accuracy can be improved by combining a number of different methods such as quantitative methods (essentially extrapolations of past sales levels) with qualitative methods (based more on judgement and personal interpretation).

The consequences of inaccurate sales forecasting are punitive. For example, sales forecasts that are too ambitious can lead to over-stretching and unrealistic sales targets for the sales force. Inaccurate sales forecasts can also set wrong expectations not only for management but also for investors in the company. For example, if the company is quoted on the stock exchange, the effect on the investor community of overstating the forecast and having to issue a profits warning may lead to a loss of confidence that could adversely affect the share price.

Sales forecasts feed into manufacturing production plans. Over-optimistic forecasts can lead to excess inventory in the company warehouse. The excess inventory situation ties up working capital and can also increase the likelihood of damage and waste. Extra staff may have been taken on in sales or production to cope with the expected level of sales and, if this does not materialize, there may need to be redundancies that can be very demoralizing to the rest of the workforce. Additionally, relationships with suppliers of materials could be disrupted and damaged if expected forecast levels are not met.

forum An online community where visitors can read and post topics of common interest. Forums can be useful for anyone doing business online, both in terms of reading the content and actively participating in the discussions. Reading a forum's archives can be a good way to obtain a basic knowledge about a topic, as well as providing a historical perspective on trends and opinions. Participation, whether as a member, *moderator, or owner, can help one achieve recognition within an online market or business community, and may even generate highly qualified business leads. Forums differ, however, in their treatment of self-promotion; some disallow any hint of self-promotion, some are geared specifically towards self-promotion, and many fall somewhere in between, limiting *URLs to an off-the-page member profile.

frames Structures that allow the division of a *website page into two or more independent parts.

franchise A trading agreement between a supplier (franchiser) and *retail outlet (franchisee), often in the service industry, where the retail outlet is given the support of the supplier in return for use of the franchiser's brand and various marketing tools. *See also* FRANCHISING.

franchised position An ad position in a periodical publication to which an *advertiser is given a permanent or long-term right of use.

franchising A marketing and sales process in which the franchiser contracts to the franchisee to market and sell his products and service, with strict controls on supply of product, use of the franchiser's *logo, and quality control over product and services. The franchiser provides the franchisee with marketing services; in return the franchisee purchases equipment and supplies and pays the franchiser a percentage of revenues and a franchise fee. The franchisee has exclusive marketing and retail sales rights in a designated area or location. Franchising is a fast-growing and lower-risk form of business expansion. The main characteristics are: the franchiser sells the right to market a product under its name to a franchisee; the franchiser and the franchisee are separate entities but interdependent businesses. It can lead to rapid growth, especially in consumer goods retailing. It is a ready-made opportunity for an entrepreneur with capital wishing to minimize risk of a new venture and to use a tried-and-tested brand rather than create a new one. McDonald's and the Body Shop are franchised businesses. *See also* CHANNELS OF DISTRIBUTION.

free-standing insert (FSI) An advertisement or group of ads inserted (but not bound) in a print publication or pages that contain only the ads and are separate from any editorial or entertainment matter.

freeware Software that can be used, at no charge, by other users, either because it is in the public domain, or copyrighted but free to anyone who wants to download it from the source provider.

free website promotion A range of techniques where *websites work cooperatively to promote each other's sites. This acts effectively as free promotion for the various websites. Often this cooperation is based upon mutual deals that do not involve exchange of money.

Some techniques of cooperative website promotion are:

Banner exchange: a network where participating sites display banner ads in exchange for credits which are converted (using a predetermined exchange rate) into ads to be displayed on other websites.

Button exchange: a network where participating sites display button ads in exchange for credits that are converted (using a predetermined exchange rate) into ads to be displayed on other websites.

Text link exchange: a network where participating sites display text ads in exchange for credits which are converted (using a predetermined exchange rate) into ads to be displayed on other websites.

Web ring: a means for navigating a group of related sites primarily by going forward and backward.

frequency 1 The number of times that an average person or home is exposed to a media vehicle (or group of vehicles) within a given time period. *See also* ADVERTISING.

2 The position of a television or radio station's broadcast signal within the electromagnetic spectrum.

frequency curve A graphical representation of a continuous frequency distribution.

fringe time A time period directly preceding and directly following prime time on television.

fulfilment The processing and delivering of orders received from a direct campaign. This is usually contracted out to a third-party *fulfilment house. It is rare for the producer to act as its own fulfilment house. *See also* DATABASE MARKETING; DIRECT MARKETING.

fulfilment house A clearing house for companies that use coupons as an incentive; it receives coupons and manages their accounting, verification, and redemption.

full cost plus pricing *See* PRICING.

full position A position for an ad in which it is surrounded by reading matter in a newspaper, making it more likely that consumers will read the ad. This is a highly desirable location and is usually more expensive.

full service agency *See* ADVERTISING AGENCY.

funnel A sales pipeline management system that shows the sequence of sales progression, highlighting 'leads' (top of the funnel) to 'prospects' to 'qualified prospects' to 'potential customers' to 'actual customers' (bottom of the funnel).

galley proof A typeset copy of an ad or editorial material before it is made into pages for final production.

Gallup, George (1901–84) A pioneer in the methods and techniques of public opinion polling and analysis, creator of the *Gallup Poll*, Gallup was a firm believer in the concept that *consumer attitude research had to precede creative work. Gallup started in 1922 as an interviewer for D'Arcy Advertising, St Louis, and later proposed research approaches in his University of Iowa PhD thesis. At Northwestern University in 1932, his male-female copy appeal ratings (economy, efficiency, sex, vanity, quality) caught Ray Rubicam's attention and Gallup then joined Y&R. The copy research department he created and ran for 16 years also trained research leaders. On leaving Young & Rubicam in 1947 with Claude Robinson, Gallup established his Gallup Poll and 'impact' evaluations as national influences.

galvanometer test A research method that measures physiological changes in consumers when asked a question or shown some stimulus material (such as an ad). *See also* MARKET RESEARCH.

Game Theory A study of competitive strategies among rival groups with incomplete information about each other's intentions, but in which the participants' intentions are in conflict with each other and the path is determined by individual choices rather than measurable cost variables. Developed by John Von Neumann, a mathematician, in 1944, it is often used by sophisticated marketers to devise competitive strategies and to assist with decision-making.

GANTT chart A project management tool with horizontal bars showing a project schedule, including start and finish dates, timescales, task break-downs, and other variables. Based on the original model created by the American engineer Henry Gantt (1861–1919) it is often used for marketing and communications planning.

gap analysis A process for identifying gaps in the market and the methods by which those gaps might be closed. It is an integral part of *marketing strategy. Gaps in the market tend to be caused by customers not having their needs or expectations met by current market providers and suppliers. Gap analysis proposes that *customer perceptions of the quality of a product or service are determined by the degree to which they believe it meets their expectations. Gap analysis measures levels of satisfaction, identifies the source of dissatisfaction when it occurs, and then makes recommendations about how to eliminate the gap. Gap analysis often leads to the development of new products or services, or new combinations, designed to meet these unfulfilled needs. *See also* MARKETING STRATEGY.

gatefold A double or triple-size page, generally in magazines, that folds out into a large *advertisement.

gatekeepers The individuals who control access to an organization and its decision-makers and, consequently, control the flow of information in and out of an organization. Many personal *salespeople, for example, initially concentrate upon their target buyers' gatekeepers, who can range from senior management to personal secretaries, as they control direct access to the target buyer and the communications and visitors that he or she receives. *See also* BUYER AND BUYING BEHAVIOUR; SELLING.

Gates, Bill (1955–) American computer software executive and founder (in 1975) of Microsoft Corporation, the world's most powerful computer software company. Gates's central early insight was that personal computing would expand enormously and that his future would lie in creating the software to drive these PCs. This insight led to near-total dominance of the PC and operating system software market. Microsoft became a major gateway to access the *Internet with their *Internet Explorer product. The company was accused by its commercial rivals of attempting to monopolize access to the *web, which led to a long running legal trial against the company. As well as continuing to dominate operating systems, Microsoft has turned its attention to multimedia games and to mobile communications and interaction. Gates retired from full-time work at Microsoft to concentrate on giving away large amounts of his enormous personal fortune to charity, through his $24 bn Bill and Melinda Gates Foundation.

gender analysis An area of market and social research that focuses on the differences in the roles of men and women in a given context; these differences are often studied by marketers in order to *segment markets on the basis of gender to identify business opportunities and product and service development.

generational marketing Promotional activities aimed at individuals within groups who were born around the same time, with common interests, and at the same stage in the life cycle.

Generation X A term coined by author Douglas Coupland to describe the generation born in the 1960s and up to 1980, the post-*baby boom generation. This group is characterized by its political disengagement (in contrast to their parents' generation of the same age) and their lack of focus on career (in contrast to their parents in mid-life); they exhibit less social trust or confidence in government, have a weaker allegiance to their country or to political parties and are more materialistic than their parents' generation. They are also the most indebted generation of all, running up huge amounts of personal debt in an age of freer credit and higher consumption. In terms of disposable income they have less available than the baby boom generation.

Generation Y Although there is no specific year boundary, this is generally portrayed as the generation that follows *Generation X and who were born in the 1980s and 1990s. The dominant trait is their reliance on technology, particularly the *Internet, social media, and computer games and their need for constant interaction across these media.

generics Those consumer goods that are sold without major investment in their packaging or promotion. They are often referred to as 'no-frills' goods. *See also* CONSUMER MARKETING.

geocoding The process whereby addresses are segmented by county, district, road, etc., in order to compare them with information about the *demographics and *psychographics of those geographies. Geocoding is integral to demographically enhanced mailing lists and cluster analysis. *See also* GEODEMOGRAPHICS.

geodemographics The technique of classifying *consumer groups by a combination of geographic and demographic variables. This is a popular *segmentation technique, particularly for consumer marketers, in the US. It is predicated on the concept that people living in the same district or neighbourhood will have similar lifestyles and buying characteristics. *See also* CONSUMER MARKETING.

geodemographic databases Used for market research and product sampling, new retail outlet location, direct mail campaigns, and overall marketing planning, particularly for consumer marketing. Geodemographic databases have their limitations: it is not always the case that people living in the same location have the same lifestyles or buying tendencies. Often the information on the databases is outdated after two or three years and is not constantly refreshed; the information is not in-depth enough to form more sophisticated profiles. Geodemographic databases can link together data from the National Census with other information, for example for credit ratings or investor registers, to enable identification of different types of households. Using *cluster analysis, the geography can be broken down into neighbourhoods of around 150 households. The basic assumption is that two people living in the same neighbourhood are more likely to be similar than two people chosen at random. In the UK there are programs such as *ACORN (A Classification of Residential Neighbourhoods) that divides up the entire UK population in terms of the type of housing in which they live. For each of these areas, a wide range of demographic information is generated. The system allows assessment of product usage patterns, dependent upon the research conducted within national surveys. There are 54 separate groupings including for example:

- wealthy suburbs, large detached houses;
- private flats, elderly people;
- gentrified multi-ethnic areas;
- rural areas, mixed occupations;
- council areas, residents with health problems, etc.

These geodemographic categories are also classified and segmented as: Thriving, Expanding, Rising, Settling, Aspiring and Striving. *See also* MARKET RESEARCH.

Another database is CCN's *MOSAIC. This has started to build classifications within Europe. This system also analyses information from various sources including the census, which is used to give housing, socio-economic, household, and age data; the electoral roll, to give household composition and population movement data; postcode address files to give information on post-1991 housing and special address types such as farms and flats, as well as credit search information and bad debt risk.

Another is PINPOINT. Pinpoint Identified Neighbourhoods utilizes information from disparate sources and overlays this with Ordnance Survey data to target individuals.

FiNPiN, Financial PIN, uses data not only from the census, but data from the Financial Research Survey which comprises 30,000 respondents. It was intended to segment the financial services buyers' market. Information concentrates upon details of financial holdings and usage patterns, so that FiNPiN neighbourhoods are able to describe financial activity as well as demographics. Data sources include: the number of company directors, the level and value of share ownership, the demand for various types of financial service, such as household insurance, home ownership, mortgage holding, and county court judgements.

geodemographic segmentation A system in market research. A multivariate statistical classification technique for discovering whether the individuals of a population fall into different groups by making quantitative comparisons of multiple characteristics. The differences within any group should be less than the differences between groups. Often used for consumer segmentation and brand positioning. Often known as *cluster analysis. *See also* ACORN; GEODEMOGRAPHICS.

geographical segmentation *See* MARKET SEGMENTATION.

geographic encoding *See* GEOCODING.

gestation period The time period between initial interest in a purchase and the placing of the actual order for the purchase.

GIF (graphic interchange format) Developed in 1987 and widely used on the *World Wide Web, particularly for the exchange of photographs and images with up to 256 colours.

gimmick An *advertising or promotional device used to create and retain the *attention of the *target audience with the purpose of drawing interest in the product or service, particularly by doing something incongruous or memorable. Devices that work best are usually those which involve the target audience getting something (that they probably don't really need or want) for free, and being well disposed to the product as a result. *See also* GIVEAWAYS.

giveaways Free, low-cost promotional items, often in the form of a sample, given to potential customers as an inducement to buy the product. Food, drinks, and perfumes are good examples.

GLAMS Acronym for *target market group: Greying, Leisured, Affluent, Middle-Aged.

global focus groups A market research technique conducted using satellite video technology in which participants are located in different places, normally in different countries.

globalization

A trend that has been revolutionizing the practice of marketing since the mid-1980s. Technological and economic forces that reduce the costs and mobility of products, services, people, knowledge, and money across geographical borders drive globalization. However, world markets have not been entirely globalized and some economists argue that the world trading system was more openly globalized in the late 19th century than at any other time. There are some barriers to globalization (both tariff and non-tariff) which are increasingly exercised by regional trading blocs such as NAFTA, the EU, and ASEAN rather than individual nation states which are no longer powerful enough to resist globalization.

Since the 1990s marketing agencies and marketing teams within large companies have stressed the global nature of their marketing programmes and capabilities. In one dimension, global marketing is the next evolutionary stage and extension of *international marketing: thinking of, and treating, the world as a single market rather than as confederations of separate national markets. This has proved less difficult for products and brands than it has for services. There has been a consequent rise in placing production facilities in low-cost countries but making *distribution global; the trend has also been accelerated by the globalization of capital markets and investment, the increased numbers of cross-border mergers, acquisitions, joint ventures, licensing agreements, the global superhighways, deregulation of industries, reduction of trade barriers, digitization, and a marketing and executive management cadre that thinks and acts increasingly globally.

Concurrently, there has been the rise of global *brands. This has been led by consumer goods such as Coca-Cola, Nike, McDonald's, and Kodak film. Increasingly, branding has become the most visible global marketing programme, whilst other aspects of marketing remain stubbornly local. There has been a globalization of certain media broadcasting channels, such as CNN and the BBC, but print media remains at best regional. Most of the top titles (e.g. *The Financial Times, The Wall Street Journal, The Economist,* and *The New York Times*) have developed excellent websites which give them greater global reach access than their print titles. Within companies, there has developed a huge tension between globalization and localization. Most companies still struggle at being global within their internal organization. There is a constant reversion to multi-domestic approaches. An international company is primarily focused on *exporting to foreign countries something that has been successful in their domestic market; a multinational company attempts to attack the market in each country with the same intensity, usually creating an infrastructure in each country to do so; a global company treats the world as a single market, irrespective of geographical boundaries and focuses on the trends and markets that are global. *See also* INTERNATIONAL MARKETING; MARKETING.

global marketing A commitment to addressing the world market as a whole with techniques in which promotional activities are fully integrated and indivisible, rather than an aggregate of different countries or internal divisions. Global marketing particularly suits those companies who have committed resources to the global market and whose position requires a global approach in many areas of marketing and communications: examples are management of a global brand, a global product or service, corporate reputation management, investor communications, the company's global *website, corporate social responsibility, environmental and ethical marketing, global client management, and information systems.

glocal market A fusion of *global and local marketing programmes and activities. This approach, designed to achieve the best of both worlds, prevents the *global marketing from becoming too detached from local realities, and ensures consistency and relevance in local marketing. Typically a company attempting such a fusion must be able to identify those marketing programmes that are better handled globally from those that benefit from local marketing management and control.

glossy A term for an upmarket monthly magazine (such as *Vogue* or *Tatler*) which is derived from the glossy paper on which it is printed.

goal A monetary amount or number of units which should be sold in a specified period of time.

Godin, Seth (1960–) A leading marketing thinker and writer, particularly focused on how the web has changed traditional marketing methods. *See also* PERMISSION MARKETING.

(((⊕))) SEE WEB LINKS
• Seth's Blog—the popular blog site of Seth Godin

Goebbels, Josef (1897–1945) A German Nazi politician and propagandist, Hitler's Minister for Enlightenment and Propaganda (1933–45), Goebbels devised many propaganda campaigns, most notably for the glorification of Hitler and the Nazi regime and, most sinisterly, against the Jews. Propaganda was one of the more powerful and successful aspects of the Nazi regime, and Goebbels was its controlling hand and master manipulator. He made use of every technique of mass psychology *propaganda, and of the available communications channels of the age, notably cinema, posters, mass rallies, and radio, to build a base of support for the Nazi regime. Goebbels is sometimes described as a malevolent advertising genius, though he himself conceded that his techniques derived in large part from the mass propaganda techniques developed in the USSR. His maxims include: 'Never lose sight of the fundamental principle of all propaganda, the constant repetition of the most effective arguments' and 'The more the movement grows, the more we must exploit technology'. He and his wife committed suicide shortly after Hitler in the ruins of the Reich's Chancellery in Berlin, having also poisoned all of their 6 children. *See also* MEDIA POWER; PROPAGANDA; RIEFENSTAHL, LENI.

goodwill The intangible value of a business over and above its net book value, based upon its reputation and customer loyalty. *Brand value represents an element of goodwill.

Google The leading *Internet search company, whose primary business mission is to organize the world's information. Google also has a robust business model, and derives its revenues from a unique form of self service, results-based advertising. Founded in 1996 by Larry Page and Sergey Brin, *Google Inc.*, was incorporated in 1998 in a garage in California. The name 'Google' originated from a misspelling of 'googol' which refers to the number represented by a 1 followed by one-hundred zeros. The verb 'to google' was added to the *Oxford English Dictionary* in 2006, meaning, 'to use the Google search engine to obtain information on the Internet'.

See APPENDIX 2 for more information on Google.

Google Adwords A service that accepts advertisements for placement on others' *websites. Advertisers pay *Google for this service, and Google shares this revenue with the other website owners who publish these ads. *See also* ADSENSE.

Google Bot Search software used by *Google to collect documents from the *Web that contribute to the searchable index for the Google *search engine.

Google Earth A virtual globe, map, and geographic information service which is accessible as part of Google's service.

Google Reader An aggregator service capable of reading *RSS feeds available since 2005.

Google Trends A graphic rendering of information on search terms used relative to total search volumes, with key news articles worldwide and in various languages. A valuable tool for marketers. *See also* SEARCH ENGINE OPTIMIZATION.

googling Verb derived from Google which is a neologism for searching the web to find specific information using the Google *search engine.

government expenditure *See* AGGREGATE DEMAND.

government market Also known as the public sector market and composed of national and local government purchasing. Typically the government is the largest individual *consumer and buyer of goods and services in almost every national market and their demands can vary from buildings, to outsourced services, to information technology, consultancy, and capital goods such as military equipment.

government marketing A combination of marketing to the government by a company and also marketing by the government to its citizens. The former involves treating government departments as discrete markets to be targeted and sold to, as well as understanding the culture and *buying process, which is typically more complex than the private sector. It can also include specific public affairs departments within companies whose primary role is to influence government and to create good relations with them. The latter definition involves the use of marketing and communications by government to promote specific policies, services, or public information to citizens.

Graham, Katherine (1917–2001) American newspaper proprietor. Following the suicide of her husband in 1963, she took control of the *Washington Post*, and was publisher of the paper 1969–79. She gave full backing to her editor Benjamin Bradlee's decision to publish the so-called 'Pentagon Papers', the Pentagon's own 'secret history' of the Vietnam War, in defiance of both legal advice and the US government, and gave full support to the journalists Woodward and Bernstein during their 1972 investigation of the

Watergate scandal, support which led to the exposure and fall of US president, Richard Nixon. Her reign at the *Washington Post* proved the power of the media to unseat even the most powerful man in the world. *See also* MEDIA POWER.

green marketing Promoting a product or service's ability to improve the environment and conserve the earth's natural resources. For example, in recent years leading petroleum companies, stung by criticism of their harmful effect on the natural environment, have begun to produce advertising promoting their environmental credentials, from environmentally sensitive packaging to sustainable products and renewable energy. The care for and quality of the environment, being one of the great issues of the day, and thereby gaining a great deal of public attention, has attracted the advertising industry.

greenwashing The practice of overemphasising a company's environmental credentials, often by misinforming the public or understating potentially harmful activities.

Gresham's Law Originally encapsulated in the 17th-century maxim 'bad money drives out good money'; applied to marketing this refers to bad practices, poor quality service, or faulty products creating an unfavourable reception for good ones from the same producer, often forcing them out of the market.

grey markets The legal but unauthorized channel for branded goods. Alternatively, the over-55 age group, which is highly targeted because it is the most affluent in society.

grid A graphic provided to *focus group participants in conceptual mapping and *attitudinal scaling exercises.

grid card A *broadcast media rate card that lists rates on a grid, according to the time periods that might be selected for the ad.

gross audience The combined audiences of all vehicles or media in a campaign. Some or much of the gross audience may actually represent duplicated audience.

gross impressions The total number of unduplicated people or households represented by a given media schedule.

gross rating points (GRPs) A measure of the advertising weight delivered by a vehicle or vehicles within a given time period, calculated by reach times average frequency.

group depth interviews *See* GROUP INTERVIEW.

group discussions *See* GROUP INTERVIEW.

group interview A qualitative research technique involving a discussion among eight to ten *respondents, led by a moderator. Also called *focus groups, *group discussions, panels,* and *group depth interviews.*

group think A tendency for groups to reach consensus at any cost, thereby filtering out any views that might conflict with the prevailing consensus. This is seen as inimical to innovative or radical thinking. Group thinking is deadly in a creative marketing environment.

Growth Share Matrix *See* BOSTON CONSULTING GROUP (BCG) MATRIX.

grudge purchases *See* PRODUCT.

guarantee (warranty in the US) An assurance, written or implied, that a product is as represented and will perform satisfactorily. This is mandatory for product sales. Guarantees are necessary for the marketing of *consumer durables. Some manufacturers have created a profitable secondary revenue stream by offering *extended guarantees.

guaranteed circulation A *media rate that comes with a guarantee that the publication will achieve a certain circulation to the *target audience.

guerrilla marketing A term coined by Jay Conrad Levinson, former advertising director and marketing professor, in 1984 broadly meaning unconventional marketing in order to get maximum results from minimal resources. It is focused on rapidly gaining attention and amplification through *word of mouth. Guerrilla marketing is contrasted with traditional marketing, as guerrilla warfare is different from traditional warfare. It has come to represent low-budget marketing in which innovation, daring, and wit are used to gain maximum exposure and attention using a targeted approach and concentrating both on new and unusual means of communication. Originally intended for small businesses which did not have access to vast corporate marketing resources, guerrilla marketing is now catching on in even the largest corporations who are seeking new ways to differentiate themselves in a noisy and cluttered market space. *See also* VIRAL MARKETING.

GUI (graphic user interface) A user interface based on graphics rather than text.

gut feeling An instinct or hunch, based on intuition and accumulated experience, rather than logic, research, and facts. Often used by experienced marketers and sales people as a substitute for detailed research and planning.

gutter The inside margins of two pages that face each other in a print publication.

habit buying The repetitious purchase of the same *brand without question, showing a high degree of brand loyalty. *See* BRAND; BUYER AND BUYING BEHAVIOUR; CONSUMER MARKETING.

halftone A black and white photograph or illustration reproduced by representing various shades of grey as a series of black dots.

hall test A research technique of assembling members of the public in a hall in order to conduct *market research, usually on new products and services, by showing a presentation video, displaying marketing materials and asking questions, often by written questionnaire.

halo effect A psychological condition in which the *perception of positive traits, qualities, or benefits of one entity influences (with a positive bias) the perception of the traits, qualities, or benefits of another entity, without the characteristics of the first entity necessarily existing in the second entity. The effect is based on the work of E L Thorndike in an article of 1920. The most common occurrence of the 'halo effect' is when the attributes of a strong *brand have a positive influence on an untried *product or *service from the same company that owns, or is, the strong brand, when the originator creates an extension to the core brand into new products or services, or when launching a related product or service. In order to use the 'halo effect' to best advantage, the marketer must have deep knowledge of the *perception of the core brand (the source of the 'halo') in order to determine how the positive effect can be used for other products, services, or initiatives. For example, the attributes of the strong Apple brand could be said to have a 'halo' effect that transfers to its new product lines and services.

handbill A small printed *advertising flyer handed out directly to prospective customers.

hard sell Anything that is interpreted by the *customer as aggressive or undue sales pressure to force them to buy. This type of *selling was characteristic of the production era but is gradually eroding in face of consumer distaste. The dividing line between hard selling and misleading selling can often be very narrow. Whilst hard-selling salesmen were often lauded and promoted by product and commodity companies, they are now discouraged, with most market-driven companies now preferring a more sophisticated approach based upon satisfying customer needs rather than trying to shift product. *See also* SALES.

harvesting The last stage of the *product life cycle, when marketing and promotional support is effectively withdrawn from the product and it is 'harvested' for profits prior to full withdrawal from the market. *See also* BOSTON CONSULTING GROUP MATRIX; PRODUCT LIFE CYCLE.

headline A large-print text at the top of an *article, *broadcast, news story, *advertisement, or *blog, concise, reductive, often in colour, designed to grab the *attention of the *reader, viewer, or listener.

Hearst, William Randolph (1863–1951) Founder of the Hearst Corporation. Hearst was born on April 29, 1863, in San Francisco, California, as the only child of George Hearst, a self-made multimillionaire miner and rancher. In 1887, at 23 he inherited the *San Francisco Examiner* which his father, George Hearst, accepted as payment for a gambling debt. Trained initially as a newspaper reporter and influenced by Joseph *Pulitzer, Hearst revolutionized popular journalism and newsprint. He was, along with Joseph Pulitzer, viewed as the pioneer of 'yellow journalism'. Much of what we take for granted nowadays as classic tabloid journalism was pioneered by Hearst: 'mass appeal' editorial content; interconnected newspaper chains; top writers as 'star' journalists (he employed Mark Twain, Jack London, and Stephen Crane); bold banner headlines, lavish illustrations such as halftone newsprint photos; colour comic strips; the use of the latest printing technology as well as heavy promotion and marketing of the newspaper itself (see his editorial guidelines). At the pinnacle of his power, he owned 28 major newspapers and 18 magazines, along with several radio stations and film companies. His worldwide publishing empire eventually would include 32 major city papers; 13 magazines; King Features Syndicate; radio and TV stations; Metrotone News; and movie and book companies. Hearst turned his newspapers into a combination of investigative reporting and sensationalism. Hearst was also a member of the United States House of Representatives (1903–07). In the 1920s Hearst built a castle on a 240,000 acre ranch at San Simeon, California. The Great Depression weakened his financial position and by 1940, he had lost personal control of his vast communications empire. He became a pro-Nazi in the 1930s and a staunch anti-Communist in the 1940s. He is generally regarded to be the basis for the character of Charles Foster Kane in Orson Welles' legendary film, *Citizen Kane* (1941), which he tried to have banned.

Hearst Newspapers Editorial Guidelines (1933)
1 Make a paper for the nicest kind of people of the great middle class. Don't print a lot of dull stuff that people are supposed to like and don't.
2 Omit things that will offend nice people. Avoid coarseness and a low tone. The most sensational news can be told if told properly.

3 Make your headlines clear and concise statements of interesting acts. They should answer the question: What is the news? Don't allow copyreaders to write headlines that are too smart or clever to be intelligible.

4 The front page is your forum. Put important items and personal news about well-known people there. Sometimes condense a big story to go on the first page rather than run it longer inside the paper.

5 Nothing is more wearisome than mere words. Have our people tell stories briefly and pointedly. Let people get the facts easily. Don't make them work at it.

6 Please instruct copyreaders to rewrite long sentences into several short ones. And please try to educate the reporters to write short sentences in the first place.

7 Photographs of interesting events with explanatory diagrams are valuable. Make every picture worth its space.

8 If you cannot show conclusively your own paper's superiority, you may be sure the public will never discover it.

heavy user The segment of the market where the main concentrations of product sales are made.

hedonic scale A scale for measuring general overall opinion of a product.

Herbert, Ira C 'Ike' (1927–95) Coca-Cola. Initially a brilliant account supervisor with McCann-Erickson on the Coca-Cola account, Herbert was recruited to Coca-Cola in 1965. During his 27-year career there, he served as brand manager, marketing director, president of Coca-Cola Foods, president of North America soft-drinks operations, and president of Coca-Cola USA. Herbert played a key role in the launching of 'Things go better with Coke,' the brand's first global campaign; the follow-up classic, 'It's the real thing'; and the widely honoured offshoot spot, 'I'd like to teach the world to sing'. Herbert, who retired in 1991 as Coca-Cola's deputy to the president, started his career in 1951 at Chicago's MacFarland Aveyard and was at Edward H. Weiss & Co. from 1956 to 1963.

Hidden Persuaders, The (1957) A book by Vance Packard which explores the use of *advertising, and ethically controversial techniques such as *subliminal advertising to manipulate the buying behaviour of individuals. *See also* ADVERTISING.

hierarchy of effects

A communications model developed by Lavidge and Steiner and published in 1961 as 'A Model for Predictive Measurements of Advertising Effectiveness' in the *Journal of Marketing*. This model builds on earlier work such as the *AIDA and *DAGMAR models and describes the stages that a customer passes through, from *awareness to *purchase. Lavidge and Steiner suggested that advertising effectiveness should be measured in terms of progression through the hierarchy rather than just on its ability to cause purchasing action in the *consumer. Additionally, the new model of the hierarchy took into account theories and models from the field of psychology that attempted to describe learning itself as a process. These stages are broadly described as: *cognitive*, in which the customer becomes aware of the product and gathers knowledge about it; *affective*, where the customer starts to react emotionally with the product or service; *conviction*, where the customer develops a preference for the product; and *conative*, where the customer finally purchases the product. Lavidge and Steiner divided each category into two corresponding mini-stages and presented a model of the hierarchy with the following ordered phases: *Awareness, Knowledge, Liking, Preference, Conviction,* and *Purchase.*

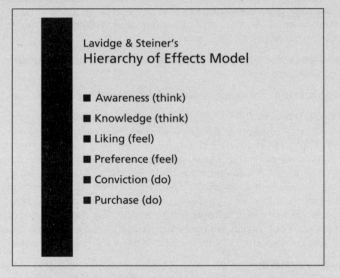

Lavidge & Steiner's
Hierarchy of Effects Model

■ Awareness (think)

■ Knowledge (think)

■ Liking (feel)

■ Preference (feel)

■ Conviction (do)

■ Purchase (do)

Hierarchy of Effects Model. Reproduced courtesy of marketingteacher.com

The developed model required the consumer to pass through all six of the stages, in the given order, before reaching the final stage (action). They did, however, address some possible criticism of sequential models by stating that stages are not necessarily equidistant, that it is possible to move up several steps simultaneously, and the greater the psychological and economic commitment, the longer it takes to move upward on the hierarchy. *See also* ADVERTISING; AIDA; CONSUMER MARKETING; DAGMAR; THREE ORDERS MODEL.

hierarchy of needs A layered and categorical view of human need developed by Abraham Maslow, often used as the starting point or background to understanding basic *consumer motivation. In this model, only a few people get to satisfy their higher level needs. The most basic need is to fulfil survival necessities such as food, air, water, and heat. Once a level of safety and survival has been attained, we need to fulfil our social needs: to belong to a community, to marry, or join groups of friends and like-minded associates. The final two levels are esteem and self-actualization. Fewer people satisfy the higher level needs. Esteem means that you achieve something that makes you recognized within and even beyond your community and gives personal satisfaction. Few achieve self-actualization, regarded as the highest need of all. Although a venerable model for generations of psychology and marketing students alike, Maslow's hierarchy is now seen to be overly simplistic for marketing analysis.

Abraham Maslow's Hierarchy of Needs. Reproduced courtesy of marketingteacher.com

high involvement model Media advertising that requires active rather than passive participation from the target audience: this is a hallmark of Internet-based advertising that requires *click through to gain further information.

high involvement products Typically products about which consumers deliberate for a long time prior to purchase. They tend to be expensive *products that directly affect their *image or *lifestyles, such as houses, cars, holidays, major household improvements. *See also* BUYER AND BUYING BEHAVIOUR; CONSUMER MARKETING; PRODUCTS; PRODUCT MARKETING.

high pressure selling An unethical and unsophisticated selling technique (also known as 'hard selling') in which the salesperson exerts relentless and persistent pressure upon the customer, using inducements and psychological pressure to gain a fast sale. Typically this type of activity is driven by sales people who have targets and commissions. *See also* HARD SELL; SELLING.

high street A UK term that means the concentration of shopping outlets in the centre of a town, suburb, or city. High-street *retailing has come under greater pressure as more and more major shopping centres move outside the city where they can have a larger-scale display of goods, wider choice, and better parking facilities. It also remains to be seen if *Internet and *teleshopping can displace the physical shopping habits of the majority of *consumers. *See also* DEPARTMENT STORE; RETAILING.

hire purchase A type of customer credit in which the customer effectively 'hires' the product for a given period of time, making stage payments that are divisions of the overall retail price. With the final payment the 'hired' product becomes a 'purchased' product and is owned by the customer. The extension of hire purchase terms to a mass of consumers from the 1950s onward was a massive boost to consumerism and to market development. *See also* CONSUMERISM; CONSUMER MARKETING; CREDIT.

hit A request of a file from a web server. In online marketing, the term is often mistakenly used to mean unique visitors, visits, page views, or all of these. It is often used as a measure of attractiveness of a *website or its content.

hit rate The rate at which sales calls are converted into actual sales, expressed as a percentage ratio. *See also* SALES; TELE-MARKETING.

hoarding Another word for *billboard. This is one of the oldest and most popular *media channels.

holding power The ability to hold the *attention of an *audience throughout a *broadcast, rather than having them change channels. It is represented as a percentage of the total audience. With the growing number of *media channels this is becoming an increasingly challenging element of the advertising impact.

holdover audience (inherited audience) The percentage of a programme's audience that watched or listened to the immediately preceding programme on the same station.

hologram A three-dimensional photograph or illustration, created with an optical process that uses lasers and which is increasingly used in *advertising and *promotional material.

home audit A type of *market research conducted in the respondents' home, office, or premises, so as to determine the extent of purchase and ownership of certain products and brands.

home page The first or main page of a *website.

honorarium *See* CO-OP PAYMENT.

Hopkins, Claude C (1866–1932) Lord & Thomas. An early proponent of the viewpoint that the main purpose of advertising is to sell something, his hugely successful copy (notably his Schlitz beer slogan, 'The beer that made Milwaukee famous') led Lord & Thomas's Albert Lasker to recruit him. In 1907, Hopkins insisted copywriters acquire detailed knowledge of client products and produce brief, dry, rational copy. He also promoted couponing, premiums, free samples, mail order, and *copy testing, which were innovations at the time. For Pepsodent toothpaste, he 'discovered' plaque; he then invested in the company and made another fortune. His classic work, *Scientific Advertising*, was published in 1923, after he retired from L&T, where he had served as president and chairman. *See also* ADVERTISING; BRANDING.

horizontal circulation The spread of a *publication that sells across a range of social sectors and interest groups, in contrast with vertical circulation which tends to appeal to specialist readers of specialist publications.

horizontal discount A discount on a *media purchase resulting from a promise to advertise over an extended period of time.

horizontal diversification The acquisition of *competitors, or *products and *services, that are different from the main market specialization of the acquirer.

horizontal integration The acquisition of competitors, or products and services, that are the same as those of the acquirer—for example within the same industry, or producing similar products in the same industries (in contrast to *vertical integration which means the acquisition of suppliers and retailers in the same industry). At some point, horizontal integration brings the attention of those public bodies that regulate competition in a market. *See also* MONOPOLY.

horizontal marketing system A negotiated arrangement in which two or more companies in the same channel join together to follow a new marketing opportunity. *See also* MARKETING.

horizontal publications Business publications designed to appeal to people of similar interests or responsibilities in a variety of companies or industries, for example purchasing or financial officers.

host/hostess The individual responsible for greeting the focus participants as they arrive at the facility and for preparing the room. Their responsibilities include providing food for the participants and the client observers, screening respondents when they arrive, preparing name tags, etc.

host/hostess gift A gift from a producer to a *consumer who sponsors a sales demonstration party in a domestic or neighbourhood setting with the intention of selling to neighbours, for example household goods, or health and personal care items.

house ad A self-promotional ad that a company runs on its *media outlets with the objective of putting unsold inventory to use. Many ad spaces are relatively fixed, and house ads are often the logical solution to fill the space. House ads are often used to promote new features, other in-house revenue generators, and other media properties. *See also* ADVERTISING.

household All the people who live in the same house, the fundamental unit of consumer market research. In marketing the term is often used to measure the greater parts of goods that are bought more for consumption by a household than for an individual within that household. *See also* CONSUMER MARKETING.

household brand A product that is so universally popular that it is recognized virtually everywhere. *See also* BRAND.

households using television (HUT) The number of households in a given market watching television at a certain time.

house magazine A periodic journal published by a company and whose principal audiences are the staff and shareholders of the company. Increasingly these publications are electronic and in *multimedia format.

house organ A publication owned and operated by an advertiser, and used to promote the advertiser's products or services. Services companies, such as those offering financial services, will often promote their own services under the guise of analysing the market or economy.

house style The standards for an organization covering grammar, typography, writing style, format, graphics, and spelling in its formal communications internally and externally.

HTML (hypertext mark-up language) A coding language for web-based text. The *World Wide Web Consortium governs HTML language and standards. HTML was crucial to the commercialization of the *Internet in the period after 1994. This language made the Internet user-friendly for a mass audience.

HTML banner A banner ad using HTML elements, often including interactive forms instead of (or in addition to) standard graphical elements. They are often used for pull-down menus and search boxes, allowing interaction before the visitor even reaches the destination site. This interactivity often results in higher response rates than purely graphical banners.

HTML e-mail An e-mail that is formatted using hypertext mark-up language, as opposed to plain text e-mail.

HTTP (hypertext transfer protocol) The enabling protocol of the *World Wide Web, defining how messages are formatted, transmitted and what actions web servers and *browsers should take in response to various commands. *See also* INTERNET; WORLD WIDE WEB.

hunter A salesperson who is responsible for locating and bringing in new *sales (often contrasted with the *farmer).

hybrid model A combination of two or more online marketing payment models. A hybrid campaign might be a mix of impression-based (CPM) and performance-based (CPC or CPA), or a mix of two performance-based models. Hybrid deals are sometimes seen as a way to split the risk between publishers and advertisers. *Advertising campaigns sometimes bundle CPM and CPC in a hybrid buy, and sometimes even CPA. *Affiliate programmes have been known to offer a few cents per-click in addition to paying for a *sale, *lead, *download, or other conversion activity. *See also* ADVERTISING; COST PER ACTION (CPA); COST PER CLICK (CPC); PAY PER CLICK; PAY PER LEAD; PAY PER SALE.

hypermarket A large retail outlet combining a supermarket and a *department store, typically in the range of 2,500 square metres, offering a vast range of *merchandise under one roof and typically built away from the main town or city thoroughfare to enable easy access and parking.

IAA The International Advertising Association, founded in 1938, with the aim of promoting freedom of commercial speech, to defend the *advertising industry against restrictions and legal constraints, and to develop educational and professional initiatives that serve the advertising industry. *See also* ADVERTISING.

Icarus paradox A term coined by the business writer, Danny Miller, in a 1990 book by the same name, from the myth of Icarus in Greek mythology; Dedalus was an artificer who, with his son Icarus, created waxen wings to escape from danger, and then Icarus flew too close to the sun, causing his demise after his artificial wings melted. Miller used this myth to describe the business failings of those who had known phenomenal success in a short period of time, and then crashed abruptly, possibly caused by complacency, or market blunders, or a rapidly changing environment.

iceberg principle A psychological concept that holds that, similar to the iceberg being 90% beneath the surface of the water, innate human *desire is similarly hidden in the subconscious. These desires are not normally yielded by traditional marketing surveys and research, or even observation of current patterns. Therefore, marketers are always alert to the latent desires of *consumers, whose deepest desires are unfulfilled.

ID A station identification during a commercial break in a television or radio programme.

illustration Any visual or graphic artwork used in an *advert or *marketing publication to enhance or to explain a concept. In writing, it is the use of a case study or example to make clear an idea or a generalization.

image The way in which the *customer or public perceives a company, *product, *service, individual, or *brand. It is the place that they occupy in the mind of the target audience. Image can be communicated through a number of marketing tools, including *public relations, *sponsorships, *advertising, *web marketing, the performance of *products, the performance of *customer service, the behaviour and culture of staff, and the 'history' of a company. While much work has been done on the development and management of image overall, and how the attributes that compose an image are projected, it is, however, essentially of value in the mind of the beholder. Image, therefore, should not be confused with identity or brand that is within the power of the individual or company to change and *reposition. Image which leads to a powerful and sustainable *reputation is indispensable in *services marketing. *See also* ADVERTISING; BRAND.

image repositioning *See* POSITIONING.

imitation effect A study of the influence on non-adopters created through connection and interaction with early *adopters of innovation, which has the effect of spreading the uptake and *diffusion of the innovation through society. For example, in the early days of marketing televisions in America, the television manufacturers would seek out influential persons in a given neighbourhood, and provide them with a free television, on the basis that they would invite their neighbours around to watch popular television shows. The intention was to spread the word on innovation and to encourage others to imitate and purchase television sets. *See also* DIFFUSION OF INNOVATION; WORD OF MOUTH.

impact An estimate of the number of exposures to *advertising. *See also* ADVERTISING.

imperfect competition Any form of *competition where the requirements of perfect competition are not met. Forms of perfect competition include: *monopoly (single supplier in the market); *oligopoly (few suppliers in the market); monopolistic competition (one supplier selling many different types of goods); monopsony (in which there is only one buyer of goods and services); oligopsony (in which there are only a small number of buyers of goods); and information asymmetry (where one competitor has access to better information than other competitors). *See also* COMPETITION.

import quota A trade restriction setting a limit on the amount of commodities allowed to be imported during a specific period of time, and often levelled against specific exporting countries.

import substitution An approach adopted by developing countries whereby local production facilities are set up to avoid imports that can lead to *inflation. As a means of ensuring development and growth it has been a less successful technique than *export-led growth. Import substitution characterizes many Third World economies. Local producers may not be large enough to produce efficiently, and are not subject to competitive discipline. *See also* EXPORTING.

imprinted product A promotional product carrying a company *logo or *advertising message printed on it.

impulse buying The decision to buy goods without much deliberation or research. These tend to be low-cost *consumer goods that are used regularly. Many *supermarkets surround their *point of sale with impulse purchase goods that catch the customer's *attention whilst queuing. This contrasts with *high involvement purchases. *See also* BUYER AND BUYING BEHAVIOUR; CONSUMER MARKETING; PRODUCTS.

impression A single instance of an *online advertisement being displayed.

impulse goods *See* PRODUCTS.

inbound link A link into one *website from another. *See* LINKING STRATEGY.

inbound enquiry An unsolicited question about the product placed by a potential customer.

inbound marketing A range of responses from potential customers following a direct solicitation through advertising in various *media or by *telephone, *e-mail, *website, or *direct mail. The number of these inbound communications is often used as a measure of the success of the overall marketing campaign. *See* ADVERTISING; COMMUNICATIONS; CONSUMER MARKETING; DATABASE MARKETING; DIRECT MARKETING.

incentives 1 techniques that encourage *consumers to buy more, including *price discounts, special offers, *coupons, free samples, etc. They can also refer to compensation plans for *salespeople, management, and distributors to achieve higher sales goals. *See also* SALES.

2 (market research) A fee that is paid to *respondents to a *questionnaire or a *focus group or an interview. Incentives will protect against non-response rates for surveys or focus groups. Often, the people who choose not to respond are very different from the people who choose to respond, so increasing the response rate will allow for a less biased result.

incentivized traffic Those visitors who have received some form of compensation for visiting a *website. The danger of incentivized traffic is when third-party promoters compensate people for visiting a website without disclosing that information to the visitor. Incentivized traffic is widely regarded as of a much lower quality than unincentivized traffic. Incentivized visitors typically do only what is necessary to gain the incentive and nothing more. Incentives may come in the form of cash, points, or other benefits such as software. While incentivized clicks/traffic is the most notable incentive-based action, other forms exist such as incentivized registrations. *See also* INTERACTIVE MARKETING.

independent station A broadcast station that is not affiliated with a national network of stations.

in-depth interviews A research method using *face-to-face interviews, usually carefully prepared to probe the *respondent at a level of detail beyond the normal *marketing survey, and allowing full response and follow-up questions.

indirect communications Types of communications that are not personal, face-to-face, and direct, such as *mass media advertising, *radio, *newspapers, *sales promotion or *packaging.

indirect exporting See EXPORTING.

industrial marketing See BUSINESS-TO-BUSINESS MARKETING.

inertia selling (negative option selling) A form of *selling in which unsolicited goods are sent to potential customers on a sale-or-return basis, without their prior consent or knowledge. This method is especially prevalent with book, record, and video clubs or, often, insurance products. Usually, following a 'special offer' the customer agrees to buy at least four products (typically books or CDs) a year from a wide range of choice that will be offered each month. Each month the customer receives a recommended choice from a selection. In the event that he or she does nothing (i.e. does not inform the company that the recommended choice is not wanted) then the product is sent and assumed to be sold, unless returned at the customer's expense within a defined time period. Certain types of inertia selling have been prohibited in the European Union.

inferior goods Commercial items for which demand decreases as income in the economy increases, as a result of *consumer perception that the items are no longer up to the standard required, either because of poor quality, obsolescence, or being behind competing items.

inflation The economic circumstances in which constant and often sharp increases in prices cause a decline in the *purchasing power of the currency. *See also* PRICING.

influencers Those who influence, but do not make, the final purchase in an organization or a family. Influencers can also be those people in a buying system in a large company who have major influence over the buying group. *See also* BUYER AND BUYING BEHAVIOUR; CONSUMER MARKETING.

infomercial A *television commercial, typically presented in a casual talk show format, that is designed to look like an ordinary programme but is actually a strong promotion of a product or service. Infomercials must carry a label identifying them as paid advertising. *See also* ADVERTISING; ADVERTORIAL; MEDIA.

inherited audience See HOLDOVER AUDIENCE.

initiator individual The person who first recognizes a need and initiates the *buying process.

innovation The process through which new *products, *concepts, *services, methods, or techniques are developed. Innovation, particularly technological innovation, can cause 'discontinuities' in a market that may lead the market to be radically different from one responding to a classic *product life cycle. The major variables with innovations are the speed and scale of their *adoption in the marketplace. The rate of early adoption of, say, the *Internet was much faster than with electricity or the telephone, but had much more market to penetrate to catch up with these innovations.

The diffusion of innovations in communications and media has been much more accelerated than of those that drove the industrial economy of the 20th century. For example, it took almost 50 years for electricity to be widely used in households and factories; it took 40 years for radio to gain 50 million listeners; television took 15 years to reach 50 million viewers. In contrast, the Internet reached 50 million users in four years once it had been opened to the general public (1994). Usage of the Internet has been doubling every 100 days. If the current growth of 'Internet Population' continues, there will be 5 billion people connected to the Internet in 2015. The other interactive network—the global telephone network—is also growing. Usage grew from 4 billion minutes in 1975 to 100 billion minutes in 2001. Communications costs are collapsing; a transatlantic telephone call now costs 1.5% of what it would have cost 60 years ago. This trend, combined with increasing computing power available for lower prices, is a powerful dynamic. Personalization of communications is another important trend: there are more than 200 digital mobile communications networks, operating in 100 countries, with over 55 million users. As well as the Internet and the global fixed and mobile communications networks, there are now a plethora of satellite-based systems impacting the global communications market. Broadband multimedia services delivered by satellite were expected to reach 16% (50 million) of total users by 2010. *See also* DIFFUSION OF INNOVATION; IMITATION EFFECT.

innovator *See* DIFFUSION OF INNOVATION.

insert A detailed promotional copy or material inserted into a newspaper, magazine, or journal. *See also* ADVERTISING.

insertion An ad in a print publication.

insertion order An agency or advertiser's authorization for a publisher to run a specific ad in a specific print publication on a certain date at a specified price.

instalments A credit arrangement in which the seller allows the buyer to pay for goods in instalments over an agreed period of time, either with or without interest payments. Instalment-based payments fuel consumer demand by making it easier for consumers to buy more. *See also* CONSUMERISM; CREDIT; HIRE PURCHASE.

instant gratification The inability to wait in order to obtain what one wants and desires—and those consumers most susceptible to the 'buy now,

pay later' proposition from selling organizations. *See also* DELAYED
GRATIFICATION.

instant messaging A real-time, two-way communication over the
*Internet, usually in a private chat room using text-based communications.
Instant messaging is at the heart of the social networking phenomenon
because it allows instantaneous interaction at no cost between individuals and
groups. Popular instant messaging services are Microsoft Messenger and
Yahoo messenger.

intangible repositioning *See* POSITIONING.

integrated marketing An approach that influences transactions between
an organization and its existing and potential customers, clients, and
consumers by connecting all *marketing channels. Integrated marketing is
more of a *marketing management approach than a different type of
marketing. The primary focus of integrated marketing is to ensure that all
*communications, the *brand positioning, propositions, *reputation
development, *brand personality, and messages are delivered coherently and
with impact across every *channel and are derived from a single brand
positioning and *message platform. This holistic approach to *marketing
communication includes well-managed coordination between *advertising,
*public relations, *media, *interactive marketing, *internal marketing, and
communications, *sales promotions, events, and sponsorships. This is very
necessary because of the simultaneous fragmentation and *globalization of
*media channels and the growth of the *Web as a major communications
channel. As clients become more sophisticated and media costs spiral, many
companies feel a need to move away from mass advertising to a more targeted
approach to selected media but where a similar message would repeat across
all the channels. *See also* INTERNAL MARKETING; MARKETING MIX.

intellectual capital The intangible knowledge assets of a company, rather
than physical and financial assets.

intellectual property Ownership rights to intangible assets such as
technical expertise, methodologies, research and development, patents,
trademarks, brands, product designs, marketing and licensing rights,
inventions, artistic, musical, or literary works, copyright, performance rights,
and non-public information.

intentions The choices that people make when they decide to buy different
things at different times in their lives. Also, *direct market research in which
respondents are asked about their intention to buy something and the timing of
that intention. For example, at different stages of the *family life cycle *consumers
buy different financial products: at the earliest stage, children may have a
personal savings account and perhaps a simple current account; students start to
have credit cards and various loan products; young adults start to buy mortgages,

insurance pensions; adults at the peak of their earning power will buy investment products, bonds, stocks and shares as well as more advanced insurance and additional pensions; older people buy annuities and short-term investment products that return cash, as well as medical insurance, etc. Marketing to consumers can increasingly be focused on different intention stages. *See also* BUYER AND BUYING BEHAVIOUR; CONSUMERISM; CONSUMER MARKETING.

interactive agency An organization typically offering *Internet technology consulting, *online advertising, *interactive marketing, and e-business consulting. Interactive agencies rose to prominence during the first wave of the commercial Internet, which has become known as the dot.com boom. Initially they exploited the slowness of traditional marketing and advertising agencies to harness the marketing potential of the Internet. Most companies and businesses as well as institutions now have their own *websites. Later, the traditional agencies absorbed interactive marketing into their own portfolio of services. This, combined with the *e-commerce market crash, led to the demise of many of the pioneering agencies. *See also* ADVERTISING; INTERACTIVE MARKETING.

interactive marketing A range of techniques focused on serving customers using the *Internet as the main two-way, *direct marketing channel. Customers are showing an increased preference for dealing with suppliers interactively and remotely, partly because it is efficient, depersonalized, convenient, and saves time. They also have the opportunity to gain a good deal of information and to look at alternatives in a low-pressure environment (i.e. their home or office) before buying. They can interact with the supplier and obtain advice. Interactive marketing has become most popular for banking where the customer can become his own transaction manager 24 hours a day, transferring funds between accounts, checking balances, paying bills, buying and selling shares, and arranging other financial services without entering a bank's premises. Interactive marketing can also be used to create online, networked communities of interest around specific subjects.

Marketers using interactive techniques are also able to customize their services to suit the customer as well as gather unprecedented information about the customer over a relatively low-cost channel. Specialist groups can be targeted and all interactions are only with the permission of the customer. New products and services can be tested far faster over the Internet. This helps with the development of *customer relationships without the impediments of geographic separation. The main problem is the lack of personal contact that may limit the range of services to the transactional and the 'low touch' products. *See also* DATABASE MARKETING; DIRECT MARKETING; E-MAIL MARKETING; PERMISSION MARKETING; VIRAL MARKETING.

interactive television Digital television broadcast over cable, satellite, and transmitter and received via set-top box or digital television. It moves television from being a passive experience to an active one, in which broadcasters of programmes and associated advertising can interact with their audience. One aspect of such interaction is consumers' direct purchasing of products displayed on the television, making the television a major marketing tool, rather than just a medium to *broadcast advertising and entertainment. There has been a rise in *infomercials that run much longer than traditional adverts and whose punchlines always involve a heavy sales pitch and inducement to buy immediately. The cross-leverage of TV advertising and interactive purchase will be a fertile area for future marketers. Interactive television also enables *Internet access, the ability to pause live television shows, sending and receiving e-mail, instant messaging, ordering videos on demand, playing video games online, conducting *webcasts, video chats, participation in chat lines and also normal telephone calls. As TV penetration is far greater worldwide than that of PCs, it is possible that the television could acquire all the functions of the PC, whilst remaining more familiar to the bulk of the population. *See* MEDIA CHANNELS.

intercept interview A type of *market research where people are approached in busy public places without warning, for example in airports or shopping malls. Unsuitable respondents are eliminated by initial screening questions.

interest An indicator of the potential customer's disposition towards the product or service. It is a prerequisite stage prior to eventual purchase. Without interest there is little possibility of advancing the *purchasing cycle.

internal audit Part of the *marketing audit which examines the internal strengths and weaknesses of an organization. This is linked closely to the identification of the organization's principal competencies. *See also* MARKETING PLAN.

internal link A hyperlink that is a reference or navigation device in a document linking to another section of the same document or to another document that may be on the same *website or *domain.

internal marketing The advanced uses of communications to inform, persuade, motivate, and often change staff behaviour within a company. Previously confined to employees' internal newsletters, internal marketing is now seen as an agent of change in an organization. The rising importance of internal marketing is recognition that people are the main assets of most companies and that they are the main channel of customer communication and the service agents who deliver the final customer experience. It is very difficult to achieve excellence in customer marketing with demotivated employees. Many believe that there is an equation between satisfied internal customers and satisfied external customers. Internal marketing has similar processes and structures to external marketing. The main differences are that

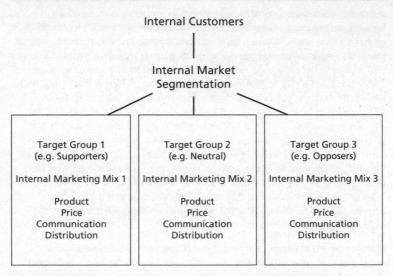

Internal Marketing based on Jobber (1995). Reproduced courtesy of marketingteacher.com

'the market' is the staff and colleagues from within the organization. In the diagram, David Jobber (1995) describes a structure for the implementation of internal marketing. The process is straightforward.

- Set objectives for internal marketing: for example it may be to persuade employees of an intended course of action and to gain their consent and support.
- Tactics would include an internal application of the marketing mix, and could include staff forums, presentations, an *intranet, away days, videos, *webcasts, personal visits by company directors, or newsletters.
- Evaluation would use an employees' survey to determine the results of the internal marketing campaign.

The next stage of development in internal marketing is for marketing to be a force of integration within the organization: to link together business, financial, investment, human resources, marketing, and marketing communication objectives against common, market, or customer-centric objectives. For this purpose, internal marketing serves as an agent of change management. Key audiences should be identified and segmented. As with external customers, these internal constituencies will have their own buyer behaviour, or way of 'buying into' the changes the organization is trying to implement. The similarity in differing groups of internal customers allows segmentation. As Jobber (1995) explains, you can target three different segments, namely 'supporters', 'neutral', and finally 'opposers'. Each group requires a slightly different internal marketing mix in order that internal marketing objectives can be achieved. Internal marketing can also play a role in employee retention, which is more important than ever, given the high costs of recruiting and replacing a lost member of staff.

international marketing A combination of multiple disciplines focused upon marketing goods and services across geographical boundaries, also entering foreign markets, sustaining marketing and sales efforts within foreign countries, and co-ordinating marketing activities in multiple countries and regions. Each practitioner faces a hierarchy: global, international, regional, and local and the intriguing interplay between them. International marketing is one of the more problematic areas: striving for global, regional, and local relevance and balance as well as economies of scale and brand. *Segmentation is particularly difficult: are customers to be segmented on a country-by-country basis? Products—can they be standardized for international markets or customized and adapted to each geographical market? The nature and methods of international marketing will also vary greatly depending on whether the company is addressing industrial or consumer products or services. Often international marketing moves by degrees to become global marketing, by tracking the space of international expansion of the overall company and its activities: this can begin with small-scale exporting and develop into full overseas acquisitions. Indeed, the task of the marketer relative to international expansion has become even more complex, because, as the level and scale of overseas expansion grows, the marketing becomes increasingly dependent upon a network of agents, alliances, collaborations, suppliers, sometimes joint venture partners, sometimes full acquisitions.

international marketing planning A process that begins with an assessment of market attractiveness: growth, size, GNP, and general economic situation, strategic location, accessibility, experience in similar markets, social, legal, language and cultural understanding, risks of entering such as political volatility, friendliness of government (national or pan-regional) to business, business risk, and competitive and currency risks. The next stage is the evaluation of the costs of entry into these markets: investment, control, risk, and return. Then the whole range of marketing planning begins in each country, with the appropriate level of marketing mix selected for each marketplace. Key decisions that relate to adapting the right mix for the right country are:

Product: can it be used in standard form or does it need to be customized?
Distribution: what level of coverage and density, and type of channel for the specific country and the distribution logistics?
Prices: how are these to be determined for the local market and in what currency?
Promotion: what is the most appropriate media channel and type of direct promotion in the given culture?

It is also important for the marketing team to have a culturally diverse group with experience of international marketing rather than taking a team that have been successful in one geography and moving it to another.

International market entry

Market entry is a prelude to full establishment and penetration of the overseas market. There are various ways in which a company can enter a foreign market: these can be divided into direct entry methods and indirect entry methods:

Direct entry methods

- Formation of an International Division to control exports.
- Establishment of foreign sales offices, sales force, and branch offices.
- Public trading agencies.
- Investment in production and distribution facilities in foreign countries.
- Joint ventures, particularly with companies with a strong presence in the target domestic market.
- Creating a wholly-owned subsidiary located in the target overseas market.
- Direct foreign acquisition of a local company in the target overseas market.

Indirect entry methods

- Exporting directly to the target overseas market.
- Use of export houses to market and sell product in the target market.
- Franchising: creating a franchise for a domestic local franchisee with local market knowledge and experience.
- Licensing: for example licensing product rights to a local manufacturer or distributor.
- Management contracts (whereby the client manufactures or assembles a product on behalf of the contractor).
- Mail order or other forms of direct marketing from the domestic country to consumers in the target overseas market.

Planning international sales structures

There are several types of international marketing and sales structures.

1 The International Division of a company that handles exporting, relationships with intermediaries and alliance partners, foreign currency operations, documentation and marketing programmes, foreign governments.
2 The International Product Division which handles the full panoply of non-standardized products and is filled with people knowledgeable in about each market in which they operate and who are able to work directly with local sales forces to customize products to local markets.
3 The regional structure which is a way of dividing the world into regions: typically North America, Asia Pacific, and EMEAI. The concept is based on the view that trans-border marketing and sales forces are not practically

effective and that people of a particular culture and with local knowledge must carry out these operations within the country.

4 The functional organization that is set up around various international functions, such as capital markets, exploration, and mining.

5 The matrix organization which is an attempt to be more flexible and to combine geographical, expert functions with global management functions. The main drawback of this organizational form is factionalism over resource allocation and complexity of reporting and decision-making. *See also* EXPORTING.

Internet, the

The Internet is the network of networks, linking by protocol component networks that are two-way, interactive, point-to-point, and electronically enabled. Often referred to as the Information Superhighway, the Internet was initially developed as ARPANET in the 1970s, a technique for maintaining communications networks in the event of a nuclear attack on the US. It is underpinned by a technique called *packet switching* that enables data to be broken up, distributed down multiple networks, and reassembled in a single place. The Internet was made available first to high-ranking academics and then to educational establishments. With the development of the *World Wide Web and easy-to-use browser technology the Internet was fully commercialized in the mid-1990s. Since then its growth has been explosive across the world. It continues to develop today and it has had a dramatic impact on marketing and commerce.

The World Wide Web and the Internet brought many benefits that are in the process of extending the marketing and communications technique. It has enabled marketing, previously dominated by the technique of 'pushing messages and products at customers', to become much more interactive with target customers, as the Internet provides instantaneous and high-speed interactivity. Additionally, customers have greater choice and greater control over how they engage and interact with sellers and merchants. Beyond that, it enables marketers to customize products, messages, and services to small audiences of common interest, and, usually, with the complicity and permission of the customer. The Internet also enables a much lower-cost marketing channel to sell directly to customers, often allowing the complete elimination of expensive channels. Smaller enterprises have benefited, because the Internet gives them global reach and wide search facilities at much lower cost than traditional international marketing. Marketers can have instant dialogue with each other and their customers. They have a whole new range of communications media: *webcasts, multi-directional e-mail communications, *websites. There are also new channels that combine with older ones through which to market to customers: *interactive TV, online shopping. Wider database access and search facilities have also improved market research techniques and speed of intelligence gathering. The Internet has also brought a whole new, but radically different, dimension to marketing's most classic discipline: *advertising. The target audience is younger on the Internet (it was becoming difficult to appeal to the 15–30 group through traditional advertising). Advertising can be tailored to each site, and can be quickly changed and updated without major cost. Information transmission and follow-up from adverts to customers can be instantaneous. Advertisers can give away clever screensavers to promote their brand. Advertising can be better linked to an entertainment experience and it can run globally around the world clock. Another two derivatives of the Internet (which is public) that have impacted marketing are *extranets and *intranets. *See also* INTERACTIVE MARKETING; SEARCH ENGINE OPTIMIZATION; WEB 2.0.

Internet Explorer The most popular *Internet *browser, provided by Microsoft.

Internet Protocol (IP) (TCP/IP) A way of communicating data across a packet switched network. It is the main enabler of Internet communications.

interview The gathering of information by asking participants questions. Interviews are one of the most widely used techniques in *primary research. They can be used to gather both quantitative as well as qualitative information depending upon how open-ended the *questions are. Interviews can be conducted in a variety of ways: in person, over the telephone, online, or via the mail.

intranet A secure site, belonging to an organization, designed to be accessible only to the organization's members, employees, or others with authorization. An intranet's *website looks and acts just like other websites, but has a *firewall surrounding it to fend off unauthorized users. Intranets are used to share information. Secure intranets are much less expensive to build and manage than private, proprietary-standard networks. The development of intranets within companies has brought many new dimensions to internal communications.

intrusive marketing The techniques of targeting and communicating with potential customers using marketing materials without their consent, such as 'junk' or 'push' *e-mail and *telemarketing. *See also* PERMISSION MARKETING.

inverse demand pattern The situation in which the expected pattern of supply, *pricing, and demand does not operate according to normal trends, for example demand increases when supply is plentiful and prices are increasing. *See also* DEMAND.

investment expenditure *See* AGGREGATE DEMAND.

investor relations An art of the *public relations function dealing specifically with communications to the financial community, particularly equity analysts, researchers, and investors. It is a form of marketing that seeks to influence those investors to recommend or buy the stock of a company and to comment favourably on it to other potential investors. *See also* PUBLIC RELATIONS.

invisible trade The exporting and importing of services, as distinct from physically visible goods. This is increasingly important as greater percentages of the world's gross national products come from trade in services. In the advanced economies, services now constitute a greater part of the total economy than manufactured goods. Consequently, in the past decade the marketing of services has also gained in strength and sophistication. *See also* EXPORTING; INTERNATIONAL MARKETING.

invisible web The portion of the *World Wide Web not accessible through *search engines.

IP address *Internet Protocol address. A unique number which identifies a computer and its location on the *Internet; a logical address assigned to every workstation, server, printer, and router on a connected network.

iPod A media player manufactured by Apple, which can store all types of multimedia applications, and, with iTunes, has transformed the music industry. Recently the range has been extended with the iPad.

island position The placement of an ad in which it is completely surrounded by editorial material, or, for a broadcast ad, surrounded by programme content, with no adjoining advertisements to compete for audience attention.

ISP (Internet service provider) A company that sells *Internet access and other related services to customers, including a software package and support services.

issue life The total amount of time that a publication may be looked at, which often goes beyond the next edition. *See also* MEDIA.

issues analysis *See* MARKETING PLAN.

issues management *See* PUBLIC RELATIONS.

jingle A short and memorable piece of music or song that accompanies an advert. Jingles began life in radio advertising and in the earlier days of television. Jingles are now considered too old-fashioned for broadcast advertising and have been largely replaced by full songs and scores. They continue to be popular for short adverts (for example Direct Line's 'car horn') and radio advertising.

Jobs, Steve (1955–) Co-founder of Apple. A pioneer of designing and marketing consumer technology, particularly the personal computer and mobile devices. Jobs founded Apple Computer in 1976, an innovative company with a central idea: that they would make PCs accessible to all which would improve creativity and productivity. Jobs, from the outset, understood marketing's role and, with Chiat/Day, created the seminal 1984 ad and promoted the idea of Apple as a cool and casual company for the new generation. Following disputes with the CEO John Scully and the Apple board, over the future direction of Apple, Jobs left in 1985 to create new companies, including the successful Pixar Animation Studios. Pixar created three of the greatest revenue-generating animated films to date: *Toy Story* (1995), *A Bug's Life* (1998), and *Toy Story 2* (1999). Jobs returned to a failing Apple in 1996 and directed a turnaround marketing effort that led to the advanced design of the ergonomic new iMac computer. He employed advertising heavily (again via Chiat/Day), to project Apple's spirit, with the new campaign 'Think different'. Having revolutionized the PC and digital animation, Jobs then revolutionized how we listen to digital music, with the development of the music player iPod and the music downloading service iTunes, and how we communicate, view movies, and read books in the digital world with the iPhone and the iPad. So important is Jobs to the future of Apple, when he was reported to have cancer, Apple's share price declined. *See also* APPENDIX 2 (section on Apple).

judgemental sampling *See* SAMPLING.

junk mail Unsolicited promotional and advertising material that is received through normal physical postal services. *See also* DIRECT MARKETING; E-MAIL MARKETING; E-MAIL SPAM.

juxtaposition An advertising term, where competitors' posters deliberately appear next to one another. *See also* ADVERTISING.

Keiretsu An interrelated Japanese family of companies with mutual obligations and trading arrangements, shareholding, and relationships. Marketing successfully in Japan requires knowledge of these complex networks of institutional relationships.

key account The most important customers to a supplier, usually meriting a dedicated key account manager to ensure customer satisfaction. There is a range of reasons as to what makes an account 'key', the main one being the volume of revenues generated by the account. Certain companies offer preferential terms to their key accounts and dedicate entire service teams directly to them.

key code A code that is placed on direct mail shots so that responses can be analysed quickly. *See also* DIRECT MARKETING; E-MAIL MARKETING.

keyword A word used in performing an *Internet search.

keyword density The number of keywords expressed as a percentage of indexable text words.

keyword marketing An online technique of putting the desired message in front of people who are searching using particular keywords and key phrases. The advantage of this activity is the potential to reach the right people at the right time. *See* INTERNET MARKETING.

keyword research The search for keywords related to a *website, and the analysis of which ones yield the highest return on investment.

keyword tag A *meta tag used to emphasize relevant *keywords on a web page.

kiosk A free-standing booth, usually in a shopping centre, or area of high shopping density, or travel area, with public access to the *Web and *Internet services.

KISS principle 'Keep it Simple, Stupid'. The idea that most systems work better if kept simple rather than being made complex.

Kotler, Philip (1931–) One of the foremost thinkers on the profession and the techniques of marketing in the modern age. A professor of marketing at the Kellog Graduate School of Management, Northwestern University, he has written many books including the much-referred-to *Marketing Management: Analysis, Planning, Implementation, and Control.* Kotler's works have examined the importance of marketing as a managed business function, and stressed the need to focus on the customer rather than the *product, the *price, and the *channel. Kotler has also charted the inexorable march of marketing into not-for-profit organizations as well as in the more traditional commercial sector.

KPI (key performance indicator) A quantifiable metric of performance, usually against a predetermined target for an individual, a team, or a campaign. These metrics can be both financial and non-financial and are used to track progress towards goals.

Kroc, Ray (1902–84) McDonald's Corp. A consumer marketing genius who fundamentally altered the eating habits of America and the world, as well as being the brain behind the global expansion of McDonald's. The company became a global icon of fast-food consumerism and a quintessentially American approach to eating. He successfully promoted, advertised, and championed the McDonald's winning formula of 'quality, value, cleanliness, and convenience' within a global branded franchise. A former salesman of milk-shake mixers, Kroc was so impressed in 1954 by the original McDonald's in San Bernardino, California that he made a franchise deal. By 1961, when he bought out the McDonald brothers, he was operating hundreds of McDonald's retail franchises. Kroc instituted new methods of food preparation, service, teamwork, standardized menus, and franchisee training schools. He also targeted the expanding US suburban market, employed teens and seniors, offered popular premiums, founded Ronald McDonald House, and remained committed to heavy advertising and promotional support of the McDonald's brand. *See also* FRANCHISING; FAST FOOD; GLOBALIZATION. *See* APPENDIX 2 (section on McDonald's).

Krone, Helmut (1925–97) Creative Director, Doyle Dane Bernbach Agency. An outstanding art director, he was also involved in the legendary Volkswagen campaign. Krone pursued perfection in all his work. He introduced a new minimalist approach that revolutionized advertising's look and appeal. *See* APPENDIX 2 (section on Volkswagen).

KSF (key success factor) Quantifiable metrics that are key to success in a competitive *marketplace.

label A visible composition of all written, printed, or graphic display on the container or box around an article. A label is usually composed of principal and secondary display panels—those most likely to be seen by the *consumer in a *retail outlet. It will have the identity of the *product and will also include a description of contents, such as weights, composition, and ingredients. Additional information will include the name of the manufacturer and the place of manufacture. Good labelling is often taken for granted but is a hugely important part of marketing.

laddering A probing technique, used in one-to-one interviews and *focus groups, designed to delve into the real reasons for participants' *attitudes and behaviour toward the topic. It is generally considered to be an intensive technique. The moderator seeks the reason behind each answer until he or she arrives at a basic human need such as ego or status.

laggard *See* DIFFUSION OF INNOVATION.

laissez-faire A concept of economic liberalism that holds that markets should be free and unfettered and that government intervention in the economy should be limited to the most basic levels of legal protection and light regulation on matters such as health and safety, and *fairtrade practices.

landing page The *web page a visitor is directed to when they click on an online advertising link, and which is, consequently, important for online marketing tactics.

late majority *See* DIFFUSION OF INNOVATION.

latent demand A *consumer need for a *product or *service that is not yet apparent or measured because it cannot be fulfilled owing to a lack of supply or availability of that product or service.

lateral diversification *See* HORIZONTAL DIVERSIFICATION.

launch The introduction of something new into the marketplace. Launches are the staple of new *campaigns and can involve new *products and *services, *concepts, public relations stunts, promotional materials, and *advertising campaigns. *See also* ADVERTISING; MARKETING COMMUNICATIONS.

Lawrence, Mary Wells (1928–) Wells, Rich, Greene. The first woman in advertising to attain superstar status. She also became the world's highest-paid female executive. Born in Ohio, Mary Wells Lawrence generated Hollywood-scale media buzz for years. Her glamour, lifestyle, taste, and advertising legend status stemmed from her achievements during the 1960s and 1970s at McCann-Erickson, Doyle Dane Bernbach, and Interpublic's Jack Tinker & Partners. Her TV breakthroughs for Alka-Seltzer and Braniff Airways led to the April 1966 creation of Wells, Rich, Greene. Mary Wells Lawrence took WRG public and added to their portfolio with the highly successful 'I love New York' and Benson & Hedges 100s cigarette campaigns. *See* APPENDIX 2 (section on 'I Love New York Campaign').

layout The draft of a finished *advert indicating the relative positions of the elements (e.g. headline, photo, *logo, *body copy, etc.) of an ad. *See also* ADVERTISING.

lead A potential *customer who has been identified as being interested in a product or service. Leads will typically be converted into actual *sales.

lead generation The use of marketing technique to attract prospective customers' *interest or to obtain their details.

lead time The time between the concept and the completion of an *advertisement. *See also* ADVERTISING.

leapfrogging The practice of overtaking *competition through by-passing a whole generation of technology developments and 'leapfrogging' to the next stage. For example, it is often suggested that developing economies will 'leapfrog' past a whole generation of fixed-line communications and go straight for the more advanced Internet-enabled mobile communications, thereby avoiding the cost of laying millions of miles of communications cable and supporting infrastructure. Other successful examples of technological leapfrogging are the development of the semiconductor industry in South Korea, consumer electronics and photography in Japan, Dutch micro-lithography, and the technological development of missiles and artificial satellites in China.

learn-feel-buy model A traditional model of *consumer buying behaviour that is based on the principle that consumers learn about a product or service before testing it out then actually buying it. *See* AIDA; CONSUMERS; FEEL-BUY-LEARN MODEL.

leasing The acquisition of fixed assets without incurring capital expenditure. Leasing is a popular method of obtaining large capital goods items such as ships and aeroplanes, and among consumers increasing numbers of cars are bought through leasing arrangements.

Lelly triads (repertory grids) Used especially by *advertising agencies to elicit consumer language for the *products in question. Products (or whatever) are written or pictured on cards that are dealt three at a time. The *respondent is invited to pick the odd one out and explain why it is odd. The language and key discriminators are noted. *See also* ADVERTISING, MARKET RESEARCH.

leverage (gearing) In financial investing, the use of debt financing to boost investment returns. It has also become a general term for ability of one side to create greater influence over another side by increasing their capacity.

Levitt, Theodore (1925–2006) A leading marketing thinker, economist, and researcher, professor at Harvard Business School, credited with inventing the term *globalization and approaches to marketing in global markets. His classic article, '*Marketing Myopia'(1960) taught a generation of marketers to better understand and articulate what business they are really in and what market they actually serve and to avoid an over-narrow definition of their marketplace. *See also* MARKETING STRATEGY.

licensing A commercial contract whereby the licensor gives something of value to the licensee in exchange for certain performances and payments. It may involve the transfer of *intellectual property, designs, rights to produce a patented product or use a patented production process, manufacturing processes, or expertise, technical assistance including the supply of essential materials, components, industrial plant, and machinery, marketing or commercial assistance, or rights to use a *trademark or *brand. Typically, the owner of the product or intellectual property (the licensor) permits the licensee in a foreign country to make use of the intellectual property or technology in exchange for access to the *local market and a share of the profits from *sales. Often the licensee will set up production facilities in the market and sell the product locally; the licensor may or may not give exclusive rights to the licensee, and will receive a royalty payment for sales over a defined time period. Often the licensor will provide training and support for the licensee. This is a frequently used method of technology transfer from wealthy countries to less advanced countries. There are several types of licence agreement, such as the joint venture or the *franchise*. Licensing is also a tried and tested, relatively low-risk, way of entering foreign markets. There are many mutual advantages in licensing. For the licensor the most tried and tested reason is that it is a relatively low-risk, low-cost, fairly fast and uncomplicated way of entering foreign markets that may otherwise be either closed or very difficult to enter. It is a ready-made set of technologies, products, or know-how for the licensor. There may be a government commitment to a certain market that facilitates the transfer of technology, particularly military technology. There may be a need to find a new market for a product that is declining in a more advanced market. New *products can be introduced to many countries quickly because of low investment requirements. It can provide all the usual benefits of overseas production without major investment. It can be a source of competitive advantage, giving the licensor greater market access and return on investment. There are disadvantages, however. Licensing usually does not generate high revenues from royalty payments. There is some risk that the licensee may eventually become the licensor's competitor in the foreign market. The licensee may not have the sales and distribution capability to fully exploit the product. There are potential risks that the product quality may deteriorate if the licensee has lower quality control standards. There could be government restrictions or conditions on payment of royalties to the licensor or on the supply of components. Policing and controlling a license agreement is notoriously difficult no matter how well the original contract is specified. *See also* COMPETITIVE ADVANTAGE; EXPORTING; FRANCHISING; INTERNATIONAL MARKETING.

life cycles *See* FAMILY LIFE CYCLE; PRODUCT LIFE CYCLE.

lifestyle The consumer's pattern and mode of living that is reflected in their *consumer behaviour. It is manifest in the consumer's home, interests, tastes, leisure pursuits, opinions, and use of time at home, at work, at play, on holiday and in pastimes, hobbies, and sports. *See also* CONSUMER MARKETING; GEODEMOGRAPHICS.

lifestyle marketing The *segmentation and *targeting of *consumer markets based on behaviour, *values, leisure time patterns and expenditure, individual preferences and tastes, attitudes and aspirations.

lifestyle research A study of *consumer behaviour, *attitudes, hobbies, activities, and opinions.

linage The size of an ad, based on the number of lines of type taken up.

line extension The practice of extending a successful *brand to other closely related products or services. For example, Nike's brand has been extended to golf clubs and golf balls. Virgin's brand was extended to mobile communications, broadband, financial services, and trains. Nivea hand lotion was extended to suntan lotion, etc. *See also* BRAND.

line filling The practice of filling the entire range out with products to ensure that there are no gaps in the market left for the competitors to fill. *See also* PRODUCT.

link building The process of obtaining hyperlinks from one *website to another. The greater the number of relevant and highly rated websites linked to a website, the better it is optimized for *web crawler which improves its overall *search engine optimization.

Linkedin A business focused social networking site mainly used by professionals, started in 2003.

linking strategy A method of connecting various *websites. It exploits one of the Web's fundamental strengths, that is the ability for any public document to connect to any other public document. For example, deep linking (linking to a web page other than a site's *home page) has started to cause some controversies. Proponents of deep linking contend that the ability to link freely is central to the philosophy behind the public *Internet. However, the legality of deep linking has been called into question in several lawsuits involving well-known corporations. Opponents of deep links, typically large corporations, argue that deep linking unfairly eliminates the ability of the home page to contribute to *brand building and advertising functions.

Other forms of link are: inbound link, which is a link from a site outside of a site; outbound link, which is a link to a site outside of a site; and reciprocal links, which are outbound links exchanged for inbound links.

link popularity A measure of the quantity and quality of sites that link to a *website.

linkrot The disappearance of *web pages previously accessible at a particular *URL, caused by movement or deletion of the pages.

link text The text contained in (and sometimes near) a hyperlink.

list broker An *aggregator who collates and sells names and addresses for direct mailing purposes to other companies. This has now expanded from just household addresses to also include e-mail addresses. *See also* DIRECT MARKETING; E-MAIL MARKETING.

list exchange The agreed access to each other's mailing lists by two companies that are not in direct competition.

list price (Manufacturer's Suggested Retail Price, MSRP) The price at which it is suggested that an item should be sold to the end-*buyer or *consumer. The list price acts as a baseline from which various sales and discount promotions can be measured ($\times$ % off list price, for example).

lobbying The remunerated practice of creating influence with legislators and politicians for a defined purpose, such as amending, introducing, or getting rid of a particular law, or to gain political support for a cause or issue. This activity is usually carried out by a specialized firm, or lobbyist, on behalf of clients, although an increasing number of large companies have their own internal departments. *See also* GOVERNMENT MARKETING; PUBLIC RELATIONS.

local advertising 1 *Advertising to a local merchant or business as opposed to regional or national advertising.
  2 Advertising placed at rates available to local merchants.

localization 1 The process by which globally launched *campaigns, *products, and *services can be customized and made relevant to the local market. In some cases this could be as simple as translation into the local language; otherwise it could mean a complete redesign of the global product or service to meet the needs and customs of the local market. An example is CNN, a global broadcasting network that has developed local language news reporting. This latter type of marketing often acts as a counterpoint to the globalizing trends in marketing that have been dominant in the past 20 years. Most global companies are now more highly sensitized to localization than they used to be. *See also* GLOBALIZATION.

2 Marketing exclusively to local markets, with in-depth knowledge of the local market's demographics, tastes, wants, and needs.

local media Newspapers and radio aimed at a local audience and carrying local *advertising.

local rate An advertising rate charged to a local advertiser, typically a retailer, by local media and publications, as distinguished from a national rate that is charged to a national advertiser, typically a manufacturer.

location advertising *See* ADVERTISING.

location marketing (destination marketing) The use of marketing techniques to promote a specific place, such as a resort, a district, a city, a country, or a region. This can be to attract tourists, inward investment, sporting or business events, or even to change the image of a location. Given that tourism is among the world's largest industries, this is a very important type of marketing. *See* APPENDIX 2 (case study of New York).

lock-out revenue The money generated from a customer who perceives it would be too much trouble to switch to a competing product.

log file A file that records the activity on a web server.

logo A sign, letter, or symbol, or a combination of all of these, that represents and illustrates a company's approved trademark. A logo is often a trigger of memory for the company's total *brand. *See also* TRADEMARK.

long domain name A *domain name that is longer than the original 26 characters, up to a theoretical limit of 67 characters (including the extension, such as .com).

longitudinal study *See* PANEL.

long-range planning The development actions for a longer duration that cannot be planned specifically like the short term. Usually linked to long-term strategy of the company or organization.

long tail The collective power of the small *websites that make up the bulk of the *World Wide Web's content.

long tail keywords Words that are longer and more detailed than general keywords; this is usually more effective for *search engine optimization because these more detailed longer words are easier to rank.

loss leader A product which is sold for very little profit or a negative profit in the hopes of improving business and leading to the sale of more expensive products which would more than make up for the negative product sale. This *pricing strategy is used to bring people into *retail stores and can also help to clear out items that are not selling well. It works well for retailers who are selling items which are not unique and where there is little brand or store loyalty, such as consumer electronics or domestic appliances. In many instances, consumers are searching for the best price. *See also* CONSUMER MARKETING; PRICING.

lottery An organized gambling competition, normally by random number draws, with very long odds against winning, often run by the state as a way of raising revenues, and involving heavy marketing to *consumers.

low involvement hierarchy *See* THREE ORDERS MODEL.

low involvement product A *product which does not demand any research, deliberation or thought in selection and purchase. It also carries little risk if the wrong purchasing decision is made, as these are usually low-cost and consumable items. *See also* HIGH INVOLVEMENT PRODUCTS; IMPULSE BUYING.

loyalty Faithfulness to a *brand or company and the making of *repeat purchases. *See also* BRAND LOYALTY.

loyalty card A marketing instrument used by the *consumer to gain loyalty points that can be used for a variety of purchases, usually controlled by the supplier. Loyalty cards have become a prerequisite of both *retailing and *services marketing. Most major food retailers or airlines have some sort of loyalty card scheme to encourage repeat purchase and to retain customer loyalty.

loyalty effect A technique that measures the impact of loyal *customers on profitability. The reason for increased profitability is that the costs of serving existing loyal customers are generally lower than the cost of *marketing to new customers. The work of the American management consultant Frederich Reichheld, *The Loyalty Effect* (1996), quantified the cost differential in certain industries (automotive, life insurance, and credit cards) as 5 times higher to win new customers than the cost to serve existing, loyal customers. Reichheld also identified several other contributions from loyal customers: the accumulation of total lifetime profits from a loyal customer; lower marketing costs, given the loyal customers' familiarity with existing products and services; higher revenues, as loyal customers tend to spend more over a longer period of time and they tend to recommend to others the products and services that they trust, and diminishing sensitivity to *price increases.

loyalty marketing A technique for growing and retaining existing *customers and encouraging repurchase through incentive schemes. Loyalty marketing is also focused on persuading customers not to switch to a *competitor. Most companies lose 50% of their customers every five years. Loyalty can be both emotional and practical. The role of the marketer is to bind in customers with compelling programmes that dissuade them from moving to a *competitor. The strongest contemporary manifestations of manufactured loyalty marketing are frequent flyer miles from airlines, loyalty points in stores and credit cards, and hotel reward programmes. The original loyalty marketing programme attached *coupons to *consumer products giving a discount on a repurchase of the same product. The next advance in loyalty marketing was the issue of stamps (from the likes of the Co-op, or the Green Shield Stamp programme) that accumulated in personal books and could be surrendered in exchange for other goods, either made by the company making the incentive or by another company. More advanced uses of loyalty marketing go beyond individual repurchase, and focus on the loyal customer becoming an advocate for the product and service to other potential buyers through *referral and recommendation.

loyalty points The points earned by a purchase in a company's loyalty programme. Points can then be redeemed for free or discounted *merchandise or travel. Some programmes offer more points per purchase once a threshold has been reached.

loyalty scheme A programme to entice *consumers to be frequent purchasers. Typically discounts and other benefits are given, depending upon the total amount or quantity purchased. A loyalty scheme is used when there is not very much differentiation between various brands. Travel companies are some of the biggest users of the loyalty scheme with frequent flier points, free upgrades, free hotel nights, and suite upgrades.

luxury brand A high quality *marque or name that produces prestige products and goods, and whose ownership is linked to success and affluence, *demand for which increases typically as income rises. These goods are generally *premium priced. In the West their measure of success is their consumer rarity value (few people have them); in the East their success is based on their ubiquity (many people have them). *See* APPENDIX 2 for examples of luxury brands.

McCann, Harrison King (1880–1962) McCann-Erickson. McCann introduced the 'total marketing' agency concept in 1912. This has led to the marketing services conglomerates that we know today. Enthusiastic about motivational research studies, he took *advertising beyond its creative focus and introduced *public relations, *research library, *sales promotion, and production survey services. The US ordered Standard Oil Co.'s break-up, soon after McCann became its ad manager in 1911, so he formed HK McCann the next year to provide ad continuity, and opened overseas offices. In 1930, the Depression led him to merge with Albert Erickson's smaller 17-year-old agency to become McCann-Erickson.

McCarthy, E Jerome Marketing professor at Michigan State University, and a pivotal figure in the development of marketing thinking, particularly what has come to be known as the 'managerial approach'. Co-author of the influential *Basic Marketing: a managerial approach* (with W Perrault Jr and JP McCann) in 1960, he developed the concept of the 4 Ps (product, price, place, promotion) within the *marketing mix.

McGraw, James H. Sr (1860–1948) Founder of McGraw-Hill Publishing Co. McGraw was a pioneer in the creation of publications for *market niches. While selling space as a college student, McGraw saw a need for specialized publications to serve the machinery, equipment, and systems fields, which were undergoing spectacular growth at the time. In 1885, McGraw borrowed money to acquire an electrical industry publication. His prospering McGraw Publishing Co. then acquired Hill Publishing to create McGraw-Hill. When McGraw retired in 1936 as chairman, McGraw-Hill had 24 national trade publications, plus *Business Week* and McGraw-Hill Book Co., the largest technical book company. Known for high editorial and advertising standards, McGraw became the first to publish circulation figures and was known as the dean of industrial publishing.

Machiavellianism The use of methods based on those of the Italian Renaissance diplomat and advisor Niccolo Machiavelli (1469–1527) and particularly his work *The Prince* (*il Principe*, 1513) and its advocacy of politica' manipulation, cunning, subterfuge, misinformation, coercion, and ruthlessness to defeat opponents and to gain power.

Machiavellian marketing A term coined by Phil Harris, Andrew Lock, and Patricia Rees to describe the influence of political *lobbying on decision and policy-making in government for professional and personal gain.

McLuhan, Marshall Herbert (1911–80) A Canadian visionary, polemicist, and educator on the power of mass media. In media, he studied both its overriding effects on society and its character as an extension of the senses of the individual. He offered critiques of the fragmentation, commercialization, and mechanization being caused by the mass media phenomenon of the 20th century. His major works are: *The Mechanical Bride* (1951) on mass media and popular culture, *The Gutenberg Galaxy* (1962), and *Understanding Media* (1964) in which he proposed a media-centred view of history. In this work, McLuhan divided history into 4 Phases characterized by prevailing media of communication: Phase I—orality; Phase II—emergence of the phonetic alphabet and the scribal tradition; Phase III—the Gutenberg publishing revolution; Phase IV—the electronic age. Communication media, for him, constituted a pervasive environment that saturates us with a whole series of perceptions of which we are largely unaware. Environments are invisible to their inhabitants and it takes a shock to discover and understand them. Well known for his semi-poetic and gnomic writing style, he is better known for his one-liners than his overall work: 'The medium is the message' (perhaps his most often quoted phrase), 'art is anything you can get away with', 'electric light is pure information.' McLuhan also predicted the future global role of media in creating the 'Global Village'. *See also* MEDIA.

macroenvironment The larger, wider forces that have influence over companies and the economies. It is usually the first element to consider in *marketing planning. These forces are usually beyond the control of the individual, the company, and often the country and typically include: political, social, and economic forces; demography; cultural forces, and environment.

macromarketing An approach to the aggregate of all the producers and *consumers within the population. Macromarketing tries to balance producer supply and *consumer demand to produce a stable economy. Macromarketing differs from micromarketing in that micromarketing is looking at the economy from the consumer's perspective. *See also* MACROENVIRONMENT; MICROMARKETING.

macrosegmentation A term to describe the division of business markets according to common and broad trends and characteristics: for example a single industry; type of *customer group; or geographical location. *Segments should be easily identifiable, measurable, and large enough to be relevant. *See also* MARKETING STRATEGY; MICROSEGMENTATION; SEGMENTATION.

Madison Avenue The generic name for the advertising industry in the US after the 1920s. Originally the avenue location of the entire New York based *advertising industry, its name is synonymous with an industry and its culture in the same way that Wall Street is synonymous with the finance industry. *See also* ADVERTISING.

magazine A physical print publication that appeals to a specific lifestyle or specific interests of its readers. The range of magazines has increased dramatically in the past 20 years as computer-aided publishing and printing has reduced costs, from very narrow specific interest magazines (e.g. *The Embalmer's Weekly*) to *mass audience magazines (the *Radio Times*). Magazines are major sellers of *advertising space and can often deliver a tailored audience for very specific products or a mass audience for products and services seeking a wider audience. *See also* MEDIA; ADVERTISING.

mailing list A database of names, addresses, postcodes used by an organization to send communications such as promotional materials. These can be created by the individual company or purchased from a specialist list company.

mail-order advertising Promotional copy for the purpose of soliciting a purchase, made through the mail. *See also* DIRECT MARKETING.

mail shot Promotional material sent out to potential customers as part of a *direct mail campaign. *See also* DIRECT MARKETING.

make good 1 To present a commercial announcement after its scheduled time because of an error.

2 To return a commercial announcement because of technical difficulties the previous time it was run.

3 To return a *print advertisement due to similar circumstances.

manual submission A way of adding a *URL to a *search engine individually by hand.

manufacturer brand Any brand that carries the name of the original manufacturer (e.g. Johnson and Johnson, Hoover, Ford, Microsoft, Hewlett-Packard, IBM). *See also* BRAND.

Manufacturer's Suggested Retail Price (MSRP) *See* LIST PRICE.

many-to-many communication *See* COMMUNICATIONS.

many-to-one communication *See* COMMUNICATIONS.

mapping The process by which a computer generates thematic maps that combine geography with demographic information and a company's sales data or other proprietary information.

marginal analysis A technique of setting the *advertising budget by assuming the point at which an additional dollar spent on advertising equals additional profit.

marginal cost pricing The point at which the product's unit price equals the additional cost of producing an additional unit rather than the actual average cost per unit. *See also* PRICING.

marginal propensity to consume The percentage of *disposable income that is spent on *consumption rather than on saving.

market An identifiable grouping of like-minded, potential customers, with similar needs and wants, with a defined location, lifestyle, or income type, or industry category, who are likely to buy products and services to satisfy those needs and wants and who have the means and inclination to do so. The defining characteristic is an *exchange* between a *buyer and a *seller. The exchange is made possible by the exchange of money for goods and services and is made more efficient by the two-way flow of information and communications between the sellers and the buyers. Originally, a market meant the physical location where sellers and buyers came together to exchange products for money or for other products. As the definition evolved, sellers became known as an *industry, the buyers as a *market. Market can also be used as a term of *aggregate demand for a *product or *service. Just as the sellers and providers have multiple *segments based upon the division of labour and expertise, so the market has spawned multiple segments and classifications, including geographical markets, industry markets, channel markets, psychographic markets, gender markets, lifestyle markets, customer function markets, mass markets, niche markets, capital markets, business markets, product markets, service markets. *See also* CONSUMERISM; MARKETING SPECIALIZATIONS.

market acceptance A level of satisfaction with a *product or *service in a *target market that merits continued or increased supply of the product or service.

market aggregation A form of *undifferentiated marketing in which all *customers are treated as a single group and are handled in the same manner.

market atomization A way to implement a *segmentation plan that focuses on very small *market segments, down to the level of the individual. This type of implementation is for *targeting those who buy highly customized and possibly expensive *products and *services. In some cases, each individual is treated as a market segment in their own right. The *web and *online marketing techniques make *direct communications with smaller and smaller segments and sub-segments of markets possible. *See also* MARKET AGGREGATION.

market attractiveness An assessment based upon the following elements: the overall size of the *target market; the *market growth rate; competitive intensity with the defined market; the cost of entering and of serving that market; and its profit potential. The determination of market attractiveness is an early part of *marketing strategy and the *marketing plan.

market connection The degree to which a brand, product, service, or organization is recognized and accepted in the market place.

market coverage The degree to which a product or service is accessible and available to its *target market or *customer groups through its *channels of distribution and *communications.

market demand

The total demand for a specific product or service over a defined time period as demanded or likely to be demanded by the total number of *customers (existing and potential) in a defined geographical area. Key determinants of market demand are: market size, *value, and profitability and *growth rate. There are three types of market demand: historical, current, and future. The first is manifestly the easier to determine, the latter the hardest. The determination of market demand is one of the more difficult tasks confronting the marketer charged with launching a new product or service. The history of marketing campaigns is littered with cases of companies that either over- or underestimated market demand. A key variable is the extent to which marketing programmes—elements of the *marketing mix—can manifestly alter normal market demand. Although all markets are susceptible to stimulation, the main determinant of market demand is the condition of the economy. Current market demand is measured by taking the total number of *buyers in a defined market and multiplying by the average quantity or value of the average amount purchased by each buyer. This is different from total market size, which also measures potential purchase and focuses on the total available or discretionary budget. The most difficult part of the calculation is to determine the number of buyers in any given market segment. Often this is broken down into defined geographical territories or *market segments and demand is estimated for each cluster. This will also involve identifying *competitors and estimating their sales volumes. This is also a good way of working out the relative *market share and relative growth rate for the company in question.

Future market demand is altogether more difficult to estimate, particularly in today's volatile world where very few markets show a level of stability and predictability that permits extrapolation of future demand based upon historical demand. Forecasts are often composed of an aggregate vision of macroeconomic forecasts (such as *inflation, GNP, interest rates, employment, investment, saving, spending, and government economic policy), industry-specific forecasts (industry analysts' forecasts of the future or, in some cases, what *customer research tells the company about customers' future *buying intentions), and company-specific *sales forecasts, including those of competitors that are externally reported. Scenarios for future demand are being increasingly used to give a range of potential market demand projections, rather than just one, as history has shown that a completely repeatable, accurate market demand forecast is impossible.

A *market demand forecast* is a calculation of expected market demand. There are three elements of market demand forecasts:

- the economy, including a review of Politics, Economics, Social, Technological, Legal, Environmental (*PESTLE);
- *market research, which is designed to acquire information on specific markets and estimate total demand for a product;
- an evaluation of market demand for both the firm and *competitor products that are regarded as substitutes. *See also* ANSOFF MATRIX; DEMAND.

m

market development The various processes through which an existing *market share is expanded, controlled, or dominated; or where new *customer groups within an existing, well-defined market are accessed; or finding new markets for existing *products and *services.

market dynamics The changes that occur within the *market, but external to a company, which influence its decision-making and impact upon its performance.

market ecology A study of the connections between culture, politics, the economy, and the social environment and the effect that these have on business methods and trading.

market entry A planned marketing campaign to start to sell goods and/or services, new or existing, to those markets not previously targeted.

market growth rate A measure of expansion commonly expressed as a percentage per annum at which a market is increasing in size relative to the previous year. This is often unreliable, because markets are seldom static and often change in form and the basis of measurement is constantly changing. *See also* MARKET DEMAND.

market indicators Several indices that show the direction and strength of market activity and dynamics.

marketing

A formal business discipline that originated in the USA. It was first taught
as a separate business subject at the turn of the 20th century in several
Midwestern universities. As a business discipline, it is seen to have passed
through three phases: the *era of production* in which marketing was
constrained only by limitation on production (up to the 1930s); the *era of
sales* in which the marketing pushed whatever the company produced
(up to the 1950s); and the *era of the customer* in which the customer was
placed at the centre of all marketing activities. In the 21st century
marketing is entering the *interactive age.*

The fundamental change in the definition and purpose of marketing in
the 21st century is that, as a business discipline, it has developed far
beyond the simple facilitation of commercial exchanges and transactions
between the producer and the consumers. Initially, marketing was very
much focused on the producer's interest—of getting the right products to
the customer at the right time, at the right price, and in the right place.
The underlying assumption of early marketers was that the producers
controlled the market. Management, functions, roles, and processes
aligned around this model of producer-centric marketing management.
This is no longer a valid assumption in the Information Age of the 21st
century.

So what is marketing in the early 21st century? A successful or accepted
new model, one that takes account of the dynamism (and often
irrationality) of global markets, capricious and unpredictable customers
that defy classic analysis, purchasing patterns, and market forecasts, the
rise of services and intangibles, the fragmentation and new combinations
of markets beyond the old industrial classifications, the increasing power
of customers, and the new tools and techniques of interactive marketing,
has not yet come into being on a grand scale or started to translate into
company marketing organizations and processes.

There are so many definitions and all-encompassing 'definitive'
pronouncements about what marketing is (I counted at least 50 in
compiling this dictionary) that it would be valueless to add yet another to
the academic pile. It is, however, worth drawing attention to the different
interpretations of the practice of marketing and the functions and skills
that actually constitute it. In the 21st century markets have become more
complex and more global, and so has marketing as a professional
discipline. As a newer profession it lacks universal clarity, classification,
and delineation of role. Different companies and organizations tend to
define marketing after their own fashion.

Some companies continue to confuse marketing with selling; some
even see marketing as a subset of sales. Others, more correctly, see selling
as a subset of marketing. There are a few, more practically, who see

selling and marketing as separate management disciplines. In some
countries, such as the US, there is a tendency to separate marketing and
communications professionals: public relations, speechwriting, and
internal communications are often separated out from marketing, which
is more focused on taking products and services direct to customers.
Other companies adopt an integrated approach in which all
communications, sales, and direct and indirect marketing are managed
holistically.

There is another strong argument that marketing is everyone's role, not
just that of a marketing department ('marketing is too important to be left
to the marketing department', said David Packard, the co-founder of
Hewlett-Packard). A modern view is that those who bear the title of
marketing managers are really expert consultants and integrators who
galvanize and inspire the entire organization towards a market-centric, or
customer-centric, frame of mind, approach, and mode of operation. They
apply their individual expertise to certain aspects of marketing. *See also*
APPENDIX 1 (MARKETING TIMELINE).

marketing audit A systematic evaluation of a company's existing
marketing environment, objectives, strategies, programmes, and organization
with a view to determining effectiveness and improvement areas. All aspects of
the audit should be done relative to competitors and perceived best practice in
the industry. The components of a systematic marketing audit are:

- *marketing environment audit* which covers the external macroeconomic
  environments (demographic, social, political, technological, cultural) as
  well as microeconomic (customers, competitors, dealers, distributors,
  suppliers, and internal factors) that form the dynamic context within which
  a full evaluation of the company's marketing programmes and functions can
  be undertaken. The dimensions of the marketing environment to be
  analysed in the first part of the audit are illustrated below;
- *marketing strategy audit* is an examination of the company's mission and
  the role of the marketing objectives and strategy to achieve this. Particularly
  important in this part of the audit is the alignment of the marketing
  objectives and strategy with the business objectives and strategy. The key
  marketing components are market segmentation and articulation of desired
  positioning within those segments;
- *marketing functional audit* examines how marketing is organized, its skills,
  and how it works within the organization. Organizationally, the audit asks if
  the marketing functions are designed to meet the strategic objectives and
  if the marketing resources are deployed in the optimum way. The skills,
  effectiveness, and impact of the marketing team are also evaluated. Also,
  this part of the audit looks at how marketing operates with other company

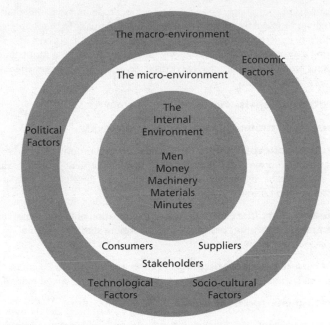

The Marketing Environment. Reproduced courtesy of marketingteacher.com.

departments, such as sales, production, purchasing, and R&D. It would then evaluate the objectives of each of the functional areas: product, service, or solutions marketing; distribution and channel marketing; promotional marketing, such as communications, advertising, new media, publicity, and sales promotions. All functions of selling would also be examined, whether a direct or an indirect sales force: objective, size, scale, coverage, skills, organization within territory, management, productivity measures, compensation schemes, morale, and processes for setting targets;

- *marketing systems audit* is an examination of marketing intelligence, planning, budgeting, measurement, and processes. Again, it is important that these are aligned to and supportive of the overall business strategy and plan;
- *marketing productivity audit* is partly a measure of the cost effectiveness of marketing and also an analysis of the profitability of the company's main marketing channels and its various segments.

marketing budget The financial means that can make the overall *marketing and *sales plan translate into high-impact programmes and results in the external market. As marketing and sales are variable budget costs, it is financially prudent to forecast, plan, and control them. Good budget forecasting and control processes are vital in uncertain and dynamic markets. Although an essential financial discipline, it is problematic in marketing given the difficulty in determining both likely demand and the likely cost of achieving a given sales target. Marketing and sales information inputs to the budgeting process could be: sales performance, revenues, *market share, and *channels of distribution.

marketing channels *See* CHANNELS OF DISTRIBUTION.

marketing communications *See* MARKETING PLAN.

marketing concept A business orientation or philosophy that holds that organizational success is dependent upon the efficient identification of the needs and wants of target markets and customers and the effective satisfaction of them. *See also* CONCEPT TESTING.

marketing costs The expenses related to execution of external marketing programmes and also the cost of internal marketing staff and external agencies.

marketing-driven organization A company in which work focus and production is entirely driven by the needs of the *target or served market.

marketing environment audit *See* MARKETING AUDIT.

marketing ethics The basis and standards upon which the practice of marketing is conducted. Waves of business scandals and malpractice have shown the damage that can be caused to the reputation of a company that has acted unethically. Treatment of customers, competitors, and employees is another area of focus. Examples of unethical marketing that an ethical marketing code can combat include:

- deceptive advertising, for example promising the audience of potential customers something that cannot really be delivered or is heavily qualified in 'small print';
- misleading *sales literature or *sales tactics, particularly high-pressure selling that forces people to buy without a 'cooling off' period;
- *price fixing or *cartel-like collusion, for example in airline fares, mobile phone charges, or oil prices;
- attacking *competitors unfairly, for example making misleading accusations about their product quality or performance;
- solicitation of competitor information by deception, for example setting up interviews for fake jobs with a competitor's employees with the sole intention of extracting information about the competitor from them.

Positive elements of ethical marketing include:

- *public relations: corporate reputation should always be founded upon a strong ethical base. Companies with weak or equivocal ethical standards will, over the longer term, decline in *reputation overall. Mistakes should be admitted; cover-ups should not be promoted. A cover-up creates a '*double jeopardy' in the event that it is later discovered. A violation of integrity and honesty, however small, dilutes the company's overall ethical strength. It is important for ethics to be manifest in actions rather than words. As the US presidential candidate and politician Adlai Stevenson said: 'It is often easier to fight for principles than to live up to them';

- the *sponsorship and active support of good causes; contributing to the local communities and charities without immediate or manifest commercial gain;
- marketing 'ethical' products, such as those mutual/unit trust funds that invest in companies that help the environment or which have programmes for the underprivileged. Many marketers refuse to market tobacco, nuclear power, arms, or personal care products that have used animal testing;
- communicating with employees frankly, openly, and honestly. A reputation for integrity begins within the company itself: it is very difficult for a company to have a reputation for honesty and integrity if its own employees do not trust it.

marketing functional audit *See* MARKETING AUDIT.

marketing history *See* APPENDIX 1 (TIMELINE OF MARKETING).

marketing information system An organizational section or piece of infrastructure whose purpose is to gather, organize, store, retrieve, and analyse *data relevant to a firm's past, present, and future operations. Information and data gathering are the lifeblood of marketing. Good information supports and informs management's marketing decisions and has four major components: an internal library of marketing information; a *market intelligence library (information from external sources); an analytical section that adds value to the information and data and turns it into actionable recommendations (for example statistical techniques, business and market modelling, and even mathematical models); and a special purpose group that leads research into non-recurring problems and areas of the market. *See also* MARKET RESEARCH.

marketing intelligence The information gathered from sources external to the firm for use in decision-making. *See* MARKETING INFORMATION SYSTEM; MARKET RESEARCH.

marketing laws Those broad generalizations and formulas used to define successful marketing. There are very few undisputed marketing laws.

marketing management The practice and operation of running a marketing team or department, marketing programmes, and developing a marketing strategy and plan.

marketing mix A term first used by Neil Borden of Harvard Business School in 1964 to describe the key ingredients, tools, and programme variables that marketers use to control the market. The image was one of a recipe to make a cake that was better than the individual ingredients themselves. The idea of a 'marketing mix' was introduced in the belief that a company ought to coordinate and integrate its various marketing programmes in order to maximize their impact and effectiveness. Different mixes are required for different objectives. There are multiple marketing mix models, each with different ingredients. The most famous and popular mix of all has become known as the **4 Ps** model, the key ingredients being *product, *price, *promotion, and *place (or distribution), which was developed by E Jerome *McCarthy. Since its inception this model has been much debated and much contributed to. There are alternatives that talk of 6 Ps (to include politics and public relations). Various academics have proffered an alternative: the 4 Cs, which takes a buyer's view of the market (in contrast to the 4 Ps that takes a seller's view of the market). These 4 Cs are: *customer value (rather than the features and benefits of a product alone), cost (to customer), *convenience (to consumer), and *communication with customers (preferred to products being promoted to them).

The 4 Ps model is now regarded as too simplistic for current marketing conditions, as well as being too focused on traditional *consumer product marketing. For generations of new marketers, however, it has served as a useful mnemonic of basic *marketing planning and programming and has encouraged the idea of mixed programmes rather than discrete functional silos.

An illustration of the 4 Ps model of the marketing mix is shown above:

- *price* can include list pricing, discount pricing, special offer pricing, credit payments, or credit terms;
- *product* can include the quality, features, benefits, style, design, branding, packaging, services, warranties, guarantees, life cycles, investments, and returns;
- *place* can include direct or indirect channels to market, geographical distribution, territorial coverage, retail outlet, market location, catalogues, inventory, logistics, and order fulfilment;
- *promotion* can include advertising, external communications with the media, direct selling, and sales promotions.

Whatever mix is chosen, the important part of the process is to allocate the right level of resources and to find the balance appropriate to the *target market.

PRICE

PLACE

The
Marketing
Mix

PROMOTION

PRODUCT

The 4 Ps Model. Reproduced courtesy of marketingteacher.com

marketing models Those theorized conceptual renderings of key elements of marketing *structure, *programmes, or laws.

marketing myopia This was identified in a seminal article written in 1960 by Theodore *Levitt, who argued against an over-narrow definition of markets. Levitt later described the article as a manifesto rather than a prescription. He said that companies that do not define their markets in terms of their customers' broader needs would inevitably decline. The famous example he used was the American railroads that defined themselves as being in the railroad business rather than the transportation business and focusing on the customer need for transportation. As transport grew exponentially across the 20th century, transport of freight and passengers was taken over by cars, trucks, aeroplanes, and ships, and train travel in North America inevitably declined except for suburban commuting. Marketing myopia has now become a general phrase in the marketer's lexicon meaning a failure by a company to define its mission broadly enough, resulting in over-emphasis on products and under-emphasis of customer needs and wants.

marketing organization A company that is focused on marketing functions, products and services, geographical territories, and customer groupings or a combination of all four. For example, a brand manager for Company X's consumer electronic equipment selling through retail outlets in the UK is a combination that takes in all the major functions. Alternatively, there could be individual functions: the *brand marketing manager, the consumer electronic *product marketing manager, the consumer electronics *services marketing manager, the *retail channel marketing manager, or the UK general marketing manager. The classic marketing organization is divided into specialist functions within geographical regions and territories, for example the media relations manager for France or the market researcher for Western Europe. This has made team working notoriously difficult, especially when faced with growing market complexity, particularly a market being increasingly defined by *customer power and *global markets. The product or *brand manager system was set up to cut across functional specialization—such as *advertising, *public relations, *brand communications, *channel marketing, sales etc.—and to integrate and to coordinate all functions behind the brand or product category. The shortcoming of this organizational model is that it perpetuates the mindset of focusing on the product and brand rather than the customer. An organizational marketing model focused on customers rather than products or brands is the least well-developed of the marketing models. This would better enable customers to define not only the products and services, but also the way they wished to deal with the producer or supplier. This model emphasizes *customer knowledge and *segmentation over product knowledge and segmentation. This model drives newer marketing functions such as *relationship marketing, *interactive marketing, and *customer care marketing, etc.

A new marketing model emerges in which the dominant figure is the *marketing manager who is able to integrate and harmonize the specialist functions, the geographical or territory marketers with the customer-centric marketers against defined objectives and metrics. Another growing strength in the *marketing portfolio is its management of customer and market intelligence functions and making these available to business and operating units.

One of the more vexed questions is the lack of marketing representation at the organizational board level. Although this varies from country to country, it is reasonable to assert that marketing's rising power is not represented in the major decision-making bodies of the major corporations.

The multiple varieties of marketing organization are symptoms of the ambiguity surrounding marketing itself—an indispensable business discipline, yet not yet quite invited to the top table of corporate organization except in a few cases.

marketing plan

The systematic approach to the achievement of marketing strategies and goals. Steps in the process include SWOT (Strengths, Weaknesses, Opportunities, Threats) analysis; *environmental scanning; *segmentation and *targets; setting of objectives; *marketing strategy formulation; development of action programmes; implementation; and control, review, and evaluation.

The plan helps to establish, direct, and coordinate all marketing programmes and activities. Preparing a marketing plan forces an assessment of the marketplace and how it affects the overall business or organization. It also provides a benchmark for later measurement. A marketing plan is also a statement of how the company intends to achieve its business goals. A good marketing plan is also important in attracting investment. Representatives from organizations that plan to lend money or invest in the business require a marketing plan as a critical component of that business plan. A marketing plan contains information about your company and its products and services, marketing objectives and strategies, as well as how to measure the success of marketing activities. The plan describes all the marketing activities that will be executed over a specified time period.

A marketing plan will also describe a company's interpretation of its addressable market and include any background information and research results used to select the *target markets and to define the marketing programmes. The marketing plan will indicate the overall investment required to achieve the planned marketing activities as well as the measurements used to determine return on investment.

Most often, a marketing plan is a component of a *business plan. Marketing plans can be presented in isolation, but should always support and be closely linked to a company's business objectives.

Basic elements of a marketing plan

- An Executive Summary introduces the proposition and explains the major features and recommendations of the plan to executives.
- An Introduction: briefly describes the nature of the business and the products or services on offer. As well as a high-level description of the context and objectives of the plan, the introduction should also contain a description of business activities including revenues and customers and current market position. Accomplishments and successes to date should also be mentioned. For new markets or new market entry, the introduction should also describe the experience, training and competencies that would enable the company to achieve the objectives as set out.

Vision, Mission Statement, and Objectives

- *mission statements should focus on the longer-range, more enduring purpose and meaning of what the marketing plan is trying to achieve (for example, 'Our success is making our customers successful' or 'To educate, entertain and enlighten').
- Company objectives are more specific and action-orientated: such as 'we will deliver consultancy services in the UK to the top 100 companies and will seek billable revenues of at least £20 m from each' or 'We will deliver a balanced range of broadcasting services to the population of the UK through two terrestrial channels'.

Team description

- It is important to describe the organizational resources and structure of the team who will deliver the plan.
- Describe the skills and capabilities of the management involved in the execution of the marketing plan.
- Close with a brief statement of the main marketing objectives and strategies contained in the plan.

Current market conditions

In the Current Situation section of the marketing plan, one should provide information about market trends and dynamics as well as the target market and the competitive environment.

Market trends and dynamics

This section should highlight those macroeconomic trends and forces that will directly affect the target market that the plan will address. For example, relaxation of import duties may cause an influx of foreign goods that will increase competition in a national marketplace; or, new developments in technology may render a current product range liable to obsolescence; or, a rise in unemployment will diminish purchasing power for goods and services in a given marketplace; or, a decline in interest rates combined with easy availability of credit will cause the market for certain goods and services to rise; or, government regulation and intervention, for example through price regulation, could cause changes in market dynamics.

Target market description

Critical to success in marketing any product is aiming all marketing efforts programmes precisely at a target market. Planning your marketing strategy without knowing the target market and target customers is to court disaster. Therefore all good marketing planning should be preceded by very detailed *market segmentation.

- It is important to describe the size of the target market. This should be specific and include statistics about the size of your target market. Also included will be information on whether the size of your target market is growing, shrinking, or staying the same. Causes for change should be indicated and explained.

The description of the target market ought to contain the following elements which will help develop an understanding of the consumers in the target market sector:

- *Characteristics* of the customers in the target segment, such as age, income level, sex, race, number of children, marital status, location, disposable income, etc.
- *Habits and patterns* that the target customers exhibit. For example, the target audience may tend to purchase in a certain way, may have some shared values, may have certain preferences and dislikes.
- *Description of their wants, needs and desires* and how the product or service fulfils them.

Description of the target customers' buying habits. For example, how do they spend their disposable income? When do they buy? How much? How often? By what means?

When the marketing plan is addressing multiple market segments, it is important to identify the primary market, which tends to be those customers who buy the products or services most often and who display the greatest brand loyalty or who can be served most profitably.

Competitive analysis and issues analysis
A deep understanding of competition, both existing and potential, will be necessary to a successful marketing plan. This section of the marketing plan should include a brief description of competitors together with a brief description of external issues that are relevant to the market. Competitors will be described in detail in the competitor and issues analysis of the marketing plan.

A competitive analysis includes information about those competitors whose products and services compete in the target market. This section should also look to develop actions to counteract or defeat competitors in the given marketplace.

An issues analysis briefly lists key external issues (such as new legislation or the impact of a technological advancement) that present potential challenges or opportunities for your business.

SWOT analysis

SWOT stands for Strengths, Weaknesses, Opportunities, and Threats and is critical to the marketing plan. Strengths and weaknesses are determined by internal elements, while external forces dictate opportunities and threats. Opportunities and threats (OTs) ought to be identified first in order to more quickly highlight the product's strengths or weaknesses. For example, if it is discovered that a competitor is losing certain licensing rights to a product in the next year, this information could be used to quickly fill that gap in the market.

Strengths and weaknesses should focus upon the following:

- Company's philosophy or mission.
- Product features, benefits, or quality.
- Product's competitive advantage. (Is there a competitive advantage?)
- Distribution methods or distributor satisfaction.
- Pricing structures. Is it priced much higher or lower than the competition?
- Target market's awareness of the product.
- Target market's attitudes toward the product (or its category).
- Target market's brand loyalty.
- Competition's activities (for example, new product launches, price changes, new companies, etc.).
- Overall market trends (shifts in needs, trends, behaviours, etc.).

Opportunities analysis could, for example, focus on the following questions:

- What problems do customers currently have with the product that could be addressed by improvement? These improvement areas may not be immediately obvious or explicitly stated.
- What steps does the buyer go through to purchase, use, and dispose of the product? This method might bring to light new product ideas (or just enhancements or packaging), services, or other value options.
- What are the customers' desires? These can often yield new opportunities: for example, customers who say that they would love

to be able to communicate to anyone from anywhere in the world yield a huge range of opportunities for mobile device and service providers.

Other areas may also need to be addressed depending on the company, product, or market.

STRENGTHS, WEAKNESSES, OPPORTUNITIES, AND THREATS TEMPLATE

EXTERNAL	STRENGTHS	WEAKNESSES	OPPORTUNITIES	THREATS
1 Company/product reputation				
2 Market share				
3 Product's ability to meet market needs				
4 Product's ability to meet market trends				
5 Value product brings to the market				
6 Product quality				
7 Customer service and support quality				
8 Quality/effectiveness of past marketing				
9 Pricing				
10 Distribution				
11 Geographic location				

INTERNAL	STRENGTHS	WEAKNESSES	OPPORTUNITIES	THREATS
1 Operational leadership				
2 Financial strength				
3 Manufacturing capabilities				
4 Responsiveness of workforce				

Strengths can be defined as any available company resource that can be used to improve market share or financial performance. Weaknesses are any company resources that may cause you to lose a competitive advantage, position, or financial state. There will be a strong correlation of threat (previously identified) and company weakness.

A threat can also be an opportunity, and a strength can also be viewed as a weakness, all depending upon who is looking at it. For example, you may see your large selection of products as a strength, while customers may consider it confusing and difficult to find what they need.

The introductory analytical part of the marketing planning process should also include a list of assumptions that underpin the plan. This may, for example, include an assumption about the future market growth rate, or currency exchange, or price competition, or the inflation rate, or the actions of competitors.

Marketing strategies and objectives

A marketing objective is that which the marketer on behalf of the company management wishes to achieve; a marketing strategy is the plan and means to achieve the objective. Marketing objectives should be:

- clear
- measurable, and
- timetabled.

Some examples of these types of marketing objectives are:

- Increase product sales in the target customer base by 30% in one year.
- Inform target audience about features and benefits of the product and its competitive advantages, leading to a 10% increase in sales in one year.
- Decrease or remove potential customers' resistance to buying our product, leading to a 20% increase in sales that are closed in six months or less.
- Increase market share in the target market by 5% in one year relative to the competitors.

There can be multiple objectives. It is important to ensure that these are mutually reinforcing and do not conflict with each other. Also, the various marketing plan components—the marketing strategy, budget, action programmes, controls and measures, people resources—must support the overall marketing objectives.

The marketing mix

Before considering the individual ingredients of the marketing mix, an overall positioning has to be established. Positioning is the perception that the target audience has of the products and services or of the company itself. Planning the positioning of the product or service must involve taking into consideration such issues as the competition and how their products are perceived, the needs and desires of your target audience, and the element of personality and emotion that the product or service evokes in the minds of the audience.

In crowded markets it is very important to position the product or service appropriately. In order to be differentiated, the product or service has to have very clear positioning in the audience's minds.

First, it is necessary to develop a general positioning strategy. This means determining if the product or service should be targeted on a market niche, should be a low-cost-leader, or should be highly differentiated (*see* COMPETITIVE ADVANTAGE). The chosen path will then lead to specific messages that reinforce the positioning. Think of the qualities of your product, its strengths and weaknesses, the opportunities you've uncovered, the pricing you've considered, and your target market to determine which broad position you will be taking.

Next, it is necessary to develop specific positioning. This could be based on a certain quality or benefit of your product or service (such as ease of use, durability, reliability, safety, convenience, delivery).

The marketing strategy section of the plan has outlined the overall approach to achieve the marketing objectives. This section will contain the mix of programmes necessary to achieve the objectives, classically known as the 4 Ps. *See* MARKETING MIX.

Product or service features and benefits

Products and/or services can be described in terms of their features and benefits.

Features are product characteristics that deliver benefits; products are mainly purchased for their benefits. Features are product characteristics such as size, colour, capability, utility, functionality, design, hours of business, content, expertise, etc.

Benefits describe the value to the buyer of the product that they would not have in the absence of the product.

Product features, being mainly tangible, are usually easier to describe than product benefits, which are often intangible. Emotional benefits run the gamut of human emotions and experience but basically allow the buyer to feel better in some way. For example, buying products made from recycled materials offers the buyer the sense of being environmentally responsible. Buying a package holiday can often make the buyer more fulfilled or relaxed. Other products and services focus on bringing the buyer financial reward, for example to:

- save money (a discount on a holiday package deal or an airfare);
- make money (savings plans or premium bonds);
- gain convenience and time (fast foods, supermarket shopping).

Identification of product or service benefits

It is necessary to articulate the product or service's benefits from the viewpoint of the buyer or customer rather than from the point of view of the supplier. To do this, it is important to have a continuous dialogue with target customers, either through regular surveys or by panels to get their views on the product's benefits. It is important also to start to profile the typical customer who has bought the products and services in the past. The profiling exercise will yield direct information on what customers value from the product and service features.

Product and service differentiation

Certain products and services may be either unique or virtually indistinguishable from competitors' products and services. Highly differentiated products and services require different marketing strategies from undifferentiated or commodity products and services. Differentiated products and services must be clearly set apart from the competitors' products and services in the minds of existing and potential customers. Having a thorough understanding of how the product and services' benefits compare to your competitors' will enable and inform competition based upon differentiation.

Strategies based upon product or service features

- One strategy could be the 'first to market'.
- Another strategy could be that of the Improver or Modifier. Instead of being the originator of totally new features, one could be known as an improver. This has tended to be the position of Microsoft's products.
- Another strategy is to combine, or group, or 'bundle' features, such as 'end to end' IT services, or building services: these would combine consultation, design, creation, building, and maintenance. Combined financial services may be 'one-stop shops' that offer pensions, savings, lending, investing, and insurance services. *See also* PRODUCT MARKETING; SERVICES MARKETS.

Strategies based on pricing

Pricing the product or service is an integral element of marketing strategy. Central to pricing is to ensure that the target market is willing to pay the prices proposed and that they generate profit for the company. Without these factors, there will be little possibility of a successful outcome. There are many approaches to pricing, some scientific, some not. Price is the selling price per unit customers pay for the product or service.

Price floors and ceilings

The cost of producing the product or service is the 'floor': prices must be set above the floor in order to cover costs. Occasionally, for marketing purposes, such as rapid market entry or a price war against competitors, prices can be set at or below cost.

The 'ceiling' is the price at which customers are willing to pay for a perception of value from the product or service, based upon what the product or service is worth to them. This is sometimes described as 'what the market will bear'. Perceived value is created by an established reputation, marketing messages, packaging, sales environments, and results delivered relative to customer needs. An obvious and important component of perceived value is the comparison that customers and prospects make between the company and its competitors.

Somewhere between the floor and the ceiling is probably the right price for your product or service; a price that allows the company to make a fair profit and that seems reasonable to customers. Consequently, once there is an understanding of the cost floor and the value price ceiling, an informed decision about how to price the product or service can be made.

In summary, if the customer doesn't perceive value worth paying for at a price that offers you a fair profit, then the marketing strategy and plan must be reworked. *See also* BREAKEVEN ANALYSIS; PRICING.

There are several pricing strategies that can be followed once the fundamentals of cost floors, price ceilings, and breakeven have been established.

Pricing for profit: cost-based pricing

- Establishing a high price to make high profits initially. This strategy is used to recover high research and development costs or to maximize profits before competitors enter the market. (Pharmaceutical companies often use this strategy when introducing new drugs or very innovative high-technology consumer goods.)
- Setting a low price on one or more products to make quick sales to support another product in development. (Some companies also employ this strategy when they need to increase cash flow.)

- Setting prices to meet a desired profit goal. For example, if the desired profit per unit is 20% and unit costs are £10 (taking into account your fixed and variable costs), then the price can be set at £12.

Pricing for profit: value-based pricing

How high can a price be before the product or service is priced out of the market?

To understand the customer's perception of the value of a product or service, the more subjective criteria such as customer preferences, product benefits, convenience, product quality, company image, and alternative products offered by the competition have to be taken into consideration.

A few value-based pricing strategies are listed below that take into account the breakeven point, but are heavily weighted with subjective judgements rather than just empirical data:

- Price the same as competitors. This strategy is used when offering a commodity product, when prices are relatively well established or when there are no other means to set prices. The marketer's challenge then becomes to determine how to lower costs so you can produce a higher profit than your competitors.
- Establish a low price (compared to the competition) on a product in order to capture a large number of customers in that market. This strategy may also be used to achieve non-financial objectives such as product awareness, meeting the competition, or establishing an image of being low-cost. It works if one can maintain profitability at the low price, or to maintain an acceptable level of sales should prices be raised later.
- If the product or service has a history, a uniqueness that is valuable to customers, then one may be able to charge a very high price relative to cost. Also, if the target market had high disposable income and the intention is to position the product as a 'prestige' product that confers status upon the buyer, an especially high price could be in order. (For example, Rolex and Cartier watches, Ferraris and Rolls-Royces.) This strategy of charging 'what customers are willing to pay' requires close attention to brand building and also to the customers' mindset. To go 'out of fashion' can lead to drastic losses and the entry of competitors.

Discounts

The pricing strategy within the marketing plan can also include discounts to customers to whom a business benefit is offered:

- Cash discounts can be offered to customers who pay promptly. This rewards those who help the company maintain a steady, positive cash flow and reduce credit-collection costs.
- Offering quantity discounts for large orders often makes economic sense when the cost-per-unit to sell or deliver a product declines as the quantity increases.
- Seasonal discounts given to buyers who purchase during a product's slow season reward customers who essentially assist a company in balancing its cash flow and in meeting production demands. For example a hotel that offers special packages for weekends of winter seasons which enables the hotel to smooth its cash flows over high and low seasons.
- Trade-in allowances for returned old products for either re-use or re-sale for a profit may benefit both a company and customers. An example would be part-exchange deals on used cars.
- Promotional allowances often make economic sense. For example, if a retail chain that includes the company's product in its ads, or in promotional activities sells a product, those activities amplify the producing company's marketing efforts. Price discounts may be offered to these retail chains.

Promotion plan

The promotion plan element within the marketing plan details the activities necessary to promote or create awareness of the product or service in the target marketplace. It is alternatively known as marketing communications. Promotion follows when all the analytical work has been done on the market, the market properly segmented, the customers targeted, and the product and prices established for those markets. A promotion plan outlines the promotional tools or tactics to accomplish the marketing objectives laid out in the overall plan. To the new or inexperienced marketer, the promotion plan might be mistaken for the entire marketing plan because it outlines where the majority of the marketing budget will be spent. It is, however, just one component of the marketing plan—there are additional strategy and planning components described in a marketing plan.

The following components can be included in a promotion plan:

- Description of the promotional programme and tactics.
- Projected costs of the promotional programmes for the year.

- Explanation of how your promotion tactics will support marketing objectives.
- Measures of success for the promotional programmes.

Preparation of promotional tactical plan

Research: a good promotional plan relies heavily on research. It includes activities such as gaining insight into the target market and finding out what competitors in the target market are doing.

A customer-centric approach: all of the promotional activities need to be grounded in media areas that will directly touch the target customers. Therefore, all the promotional activities need to be directly linked to the customers, what they read, what they listen to, what they attend, where they meet, etc.

Description of promotional tactics: the major component of the promotion plan is the description of the planned promotional tactics and how they are budgeted and the likely outcomes. The promotional plan is what brings the marketing activity to bear on sales activity: all sales promotions should dovetail with and support the selling strategies and the company image.

It is important not only to measure costs incurred against budget, but also to have specific objectives by which one can measure success or failure in each specific area of the promotional mix:

- Advertising.
- Sales promotion.
- Collateral materials, such a brochures and product descriptions.
- Public relations.
- Personal selling.
- Direct marketing.
- Interactive tools.
- Trade shows and conferences.
- Publishing articles and ideas.
- Seminars. *See also* DISTRIBUTION.

Business presentation: a regular and often overlooked dimension of business image and promotion. There are many occasions when the individual or the company will be called upon to explain its business. These business presentations will be given to many diverse audiences including potential customers, bankers, suppliers, and investors. Each group requires different information about your business and it should be presented in a format appropriate to the situation.

Creating a successful promotional strategy begins with knowing which aspects of the business to promote and why. It also involves knowing which promotional activities are most effective. Knowing these things help identify promotional goals, an important element in developing a winning promotional campaign.

Promotional programmes in a national market could include the following executive actions:

- Advertise in the classified advertising section of your community newspaper.
- Advertise in the Yellow Pages.
- Advertise in retail stores.
- Approach your prospective customers over the phone.
- Approach your prospective customers in person.
- Approach your prospective customers through the mail.
- Be a guest speaker at seminars and presentations on your area of expertise.
- Be a guest speaker on radio shows.
- Build and maintain a customer mailing and contact list on database software.
- Build your image with a well-designed letterhead and business cards.
- Design a *brochure that best explains the benefits of your services.
- Design a mail order campaign.
- Design a point of purchase display for your product.
- Design a *telemarketing campaign.
- Design an image-building *logo for your company.
- Design and distribute a quarterly newsletter or an industry update announcement.
- Design and distribute company calendars, mugs, T-shirts, caps, pens, notepads, or other advertising specialities displaying your company name and logo.
- Design and distribute a free instructional manual related to your industry.
- Design bumper stickers or balloons with your company name, logo, or slogan.
- Design T-shirts displaying your company name and logo.
- Explore cross-promotion with a non-competing company selling to your target market.
- Explore the costs of advertising in newspapers, magazines, on radio, television, billboards, bus shelters, and benches.
- Explore ways to share your advertising costs using cooperative advertising.
- Follow up customer purchases with a thank-you letter.

- Follow up customer purchases with Christmas or birthday cards.
- Have your company profiled in a magazine or newspaper that is read by prospective customers.
- Hire an advertising agency or public relations firm.
- Hold a promotional contest.
- Hold a seminar on your service, product, or industry.
- Include promotional material with your invoices.
- Look for prospective customers at trade shows related to your industry.
- Look for prospective customers in associations related to your industry.
- Look for prospective customers at seminars related to your industry.
- Look for prospective customers in magazines and newspapers related to your industry.
- Package your brochure, price lists, and letter in a folder for your customers.
- Place a pavement sign outside your store or office.
- Place flyers on bulletin boards and car windshields.
- Place promotional notes on your envelopes, and other mailing labels.
- Place signs or paint logos on your company vehicle(s).
- Prepare a corporate video.
- Prepare a list of product features and benefits to help you plan your advertising and promotional campaigns.
- Prepare proposals offering solutions to your customers' needs.
- Provide free samples of your product or service.
- Provide public tours of your operation.
- Sponsor a charity event.
- Sponsor an amateur arts or sports team.
- Sponsor a cultural event through a community arts organization.

Distribution (Place) plan

The plan for how one sells and distributes the product or service makes the entire marketing plan a reality. It is necessary first to have a strategy for distribution: how available are the products and services to be? Will they be sold directly or indirectly? As with pricing, the places where the product is available directly reflect both the quality and 'status' of the product or service. *channels of distribution must match the image goals of your product or service. There are several key elements when planning a distribution strategy. For example, there must be alignment and consistency between the distribution channel and the customers' perception of your product and service. The distribution strategy must be closely linked to the optimum dynamics of the addressable market. Also, the product or service must get the attention it needs from the chosen channel.

marketing process management Responsibility for particular
*segments, *industry or *customer groups, *brands, *products or *services, or
specific marketing functions. Marketing managers are also responsible for the
management of marketing staff, budgets, and programmes. Marketing is a
combination of expert functions, planning, processes, and management.
Occasionally, market managers are also responsible for revenues and profits.
Philip *Kotler provides useful shorthand for the key elements of textbook
marketing management process:

$$R \longrightarrow STP \rightarrow MM \rightarrow I \rightarrow C$$

Where:

R = market research, which should be the start point of the marketing
management process. Without a deep understanding of the marketplace and
the customers within it, failure becomes more likely. While experience has
shown that it is impossible to forecast with complete accuracy the behaviour of
a market, it has also shown that failure to fully understand all the dimensions
of a market and its dynamics can lead to disaster.

S = segmentation, which is the most important part of the marketing
management process, because if the segments selected are the wrong ones, then
all the marketing programmes that follow will be jeopardized. Segmentation
eventually leads to accurate targeting. It must also take into account the
organization's abilities and resources to address the chosen market segments.

T = targeting, which involves careful selection of customers within the selected
segment(s), and emerges from the detailed segmentation.

P = positioning, the place that the company wants to occupy in the minds of
those target customers within the selected segments and, by extension, how it
wishes to compete in that target marketplace.

MM = marketing mix, the combination of product/service, distribution,
pricing, and promotional elements designed to reach those customers within
the target segment that reinforces the desired positioning.

I = implementation, how all the various marketing mix programmes are
executed with the customers in the target segments. This will be a combination
of the marketing mix with other relevant parts of the company and the
distribution channel. A key element in implementation is coordination with the
producers (of products or services), the marketing team, and the sales channels.

C = control, where the measurement and feedback on all that has been
planned and implemented takes place. Results are audited and evaluated and
improvements and corrections are made in the overall management chain.
The original segmentation can be validated, rejected, or adapted. It is most
important that the feedback comes directly from the marketplace and is not a
collection of internal opinions.

marketing productivity audit *See* MARKETING AUDIT.

marketing services The specialized activities required in order to realize marketing objectives.

marketing specializations The range of professional disciplines that have their own techniques, methods, development paths, and careers within the marketing profession. Some marketing specializations are more portable than others—for example, the functional specialists of *public relations, *advertising, *communications, and *event marketing are more portable from company to company than a specialization in, say, *fast-moving consumer goods (FMCG) branding. *See the following range of the main specializations in marketing*: ARTS MARKETING; BUSINESS-TO-BUSINESS MARKETING; CAUSE-RELATED MARKETING; CHANNEL MARKETING; CHARITY MARKETING; CONSUMER MARKETING; CUSTOMIZED MARKETING; DATABASE MARKETING; DIRECT MARKETING; DIRECT RESPONSE MARKETING; E-MAIL MARKETING; ENLIGHTENED MARKETING; ETHICAL MARKETING; EVENT MARKETING; GLOBAL MARKETING; GUERRILLA MARKETING; INTEGRATED MARKETING; INTERACTIVE MARKETING; INTERNAL MARKETING; INTERNATIONAL MARKETING; INTERNET, THE; LOCATION MARKETING; MACROMARKETING; MASS MARKETING; MICROMARKETING; MOBILE MARKETING; MULTICHANNEL MARKETING; NETWORK MARKETING; NICHE MARKETING; NON-PROFIT MARKETING; PERMISSION MARKETING; PRODUCT MARKETING; PROFESSIONAL SERVICES MARKETING; RECRUITMENT MARKETING; RELATIONSHIP MARKETING; RETRO MARKETING; SCIENTIFIC MARKETING; SERVICES MARKETING; SOCIAL MARKETING; SPORTS MARKETING; VIRAL MARKETING; WORD OF MOUTH.

marketing strategy Planned choices about which parts of the market to focus upon and how to compete within that target market. The strategy must be based upon a thorough analysis and the ways and means of addressing target markets and customers. The key decision upon which the entire marketing strategy can stand or fall is the market segmentation: which segments of the market are being targeted and how the marketing mix and the product/service offering is to be positioned for each segment. *Positioning, which is the second core element of the marketing strategy, defines, in the consumer's mind, the comparisons between one capability, service, idea, product and those of the competitor. The task is identifying weaknesses in competing products and services and strengths in your own which can be reinforced so as to gain competitive edge.

Below is one comprehensive example of a range of approaches to market strategy in a competitive environment, the Strategy Clock:

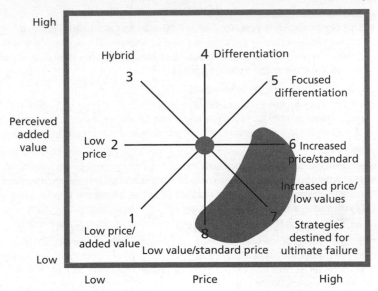

The Strategy Clock: Bowman's Strategy Options. Reproduced courtesy of marketingteacher.com

This Strategy Clock is based upon the work of Cliff Bowman from 1996. *See also* COMPETITIVE STRATEGY; PORTER, MICHAEL. Bowman considers competitive advantages in relation to cost advantage or differentiation advantage. There are eight core strategic options:

Option one—low price/low added value
- This is most probably a segment-specific approach.

Option two—low price
- This approach could lead to a price war and low margins. The necessity is to be a 'cost leader' in the defined market place.

Option three—hybrid
- This a combination of low-cost based approach combined with a reinvestment in low price and associated differentiation, such as great value at lowest cost.

Option four—differentiation
- There can be a strategy of differentiation without an added price premium, based upon perceived added value by user, which often has the benefit of yielding market share increases, or
- There is the more likely strategy of differentiation to justify a price premium, in which there is perceived added value sufficient to bear price premium.

Option five—focused differentiation

- This is when there is perceived added value to a very narrowly defined market segment (luxury holidays for wealthy widows, Harley Davidson top-quality motor cycles for the over-50s American market with high disposable income) that warrant a premium price.

Option six—increased price/standard

- This strategy involves continuously raising the bar in terms of quality and professional standards. Higher margins can be gained if one company is able to transcend competitors with lower standards and if competitors are losing market share.

Option seven—increased price/low value

- This type of strategy is only possible in the absence of free competition and is more characteristic of a very closed market with insurmountable entry barriers or else a monopoly situation.

Option eight—low value/standard price

- Such a strategy is suicidal in marketing terms and will inevitably lead to loss of market share. This can only be justified in terms of a managed withdrawal of an under-performing or loss-making product from the market. *See also* MARKET SEGMENTATION.

Arguably, marketing has now become more sophisticated than this neat division of labour and sequential approach to marketing tasks and functions. However, these are fundamentals that are rarely changed by fad or fashion and are as applicable to the new economy as the old economy.

marketing strategy audit *See* MARKETING AUDIT.

marketing systems audit *See* MARKETING AUDIT.

market intelligence A body of information that is gathered and analysed and which provides insight to understand a target market, its dynamics, shape, competitors, entry barriers, etc. *See also* MARKET RESEARCH.

market leader The company in an industry with the largest *market share relative to *competitors. It usually leads other firms in price changes, new product introductions, distribution coverage, and promotion spending. To be market leader in a defined market space is generally the goal of all marketers.

market niche *See* MARKET SEGMENTATION.

market nicher A company that serves small segments of an industry that the other firms overlook or ignore. Being a 'niche player' is often a deliberate choice, based upon evaluation of *target markets and an attempt to create *competitive advantage.

market penetration A strategy to encourage intensive growth of current products and services in current markets, measured primarily by relative market share. There are three general marketing methods to achieve greater market penetration:

- sell more to existing customers;
- win customers from competitors; or
- win new customers for existing products and services.

Market penetration also informs on consumer demand and acceptability in a given market. *See also* ANSOFF MATRIX; COMPETITION; PRICING.

marketplace The space, actual or virtual, in which a market operates; the environment in which goods and services are supplied and purchased. *See also* MARKET.

market positioning The technique by which marketers give their company, its product and services and capabilities, a distinctive position or image relative to competing products and services.

The key elements of a market positioning programme are:

- *market segmentation;
- *targeting customers within the market segments;
- well-defined and articulated *differential advantage around products, services, and propositions;
- a coherent *brand positioning strategy and an integrated *marketing plan to support it;
- an overall strategy for maintaining the desired *position relative to the *competitors;
- a *message architecture, with messages tailored to different *audiences within a given market. For example, there may be one set of *positioning messages for the *media that reports on a given market and another set for the actual *customers who compose and define the market;
- an *internal communications plan that encourages employees to 'live' the positioning in their day-to-day behaviour and in their interactions with clients;
- a fully integrated set of *communications programmes to execute the positioning. *See also* COMPETITION; MARKETING STRATEGY.

market potential The estimate of the *share of the market that can be secured over a period of time and with dedicated marketing resources and programmes.

market price A value ascribed to a product or service and determined by that which the customer is willing to pay relative to alternative products or services in order to satisfy their needs. *See also* PRICING.

market reach A potential number of customers that a company can access through its marketing staff, programmes, *channels of distribution, and capabilities.

market recognition The identity and status of an organization and its *brand within a defined *marketplace, relative to *competitors.

market research A major discipline of marketing whose main function is intelligence gathering and analysis on a particular market, industry, geography, customer group, competitors, or specific product or service area. Marketing campaigns are like war strategies: they are highly dependent upon good intelligence, before, during and after the event. In successful marketing campaigns, market research is vital to bringing a deeper understanding of the target market: its size, growth, segments, trends and dynamics, customer groupings, customer wants, needs and desires, competitors and their campaigns, demographics.

The main uses of market research are: to position a business or strategic programme; to assist in new product or service launches; to evaluate a product or service's strengths and weaknesses which will help determine how to improve a product or service; to determine consumer wants, needs, and desires; to analyse competition. Research can also help to identify new market opportunities for a product or service. Market research can help test concepts to get initial market testing and evaluation. It can research responses to marketing programmes. Market research can identify and analyse consumer attitudes and intentions and feed these back to marketing managers to test the viability of new launches.

Example: Market research and new product launches
Before a marketing campaign for a new product begins, substantial research needs to be done. Secondary research is carried out to see if there is a similar type of product or service currently in existence or in the marketplace. If such a product or service does exist, then the market researcher scans all published information and data about it in order to determine its market position and the market potential for a rival product or service. If the market is forecast to be very large, the company may choose to launch the product and compete with existing companies that are currently in the market. If the market is not supposed to grow, the company may decide to reconsider or may launch something different.

Suppose a company wants to launch a new car. Secondary market reports and forecasts for cars may provide useful information, but primary research would be more applicable. Since consumers purchase cars based upon brand name and features as well as reputation, consumer wants and needs are extremely important. Interviews or focus groups may be conducted. Consumers may be interviewed to determine which features are of the most importance. They may also be shown sketches of different versions of interiors, exteriors, or various features such as headlights or dashboard configurations to see which ones are preferred. Based upon these interviews and focus groups, the car manufacturer will know what features to include with the car based upon primary research.

While the product is being developed, primary research is again used to determine consumer reaction, or in the car example, which additional features or packages would be most popular.

Once the product is completed, marketing of the product begins. In many instances, a smaller, test market may be used to test consumer acceptance before the product is launched nationally. Again, primary market research plays an important role. A group of consumers may be asked to try the product and report their findings. Perhaps a new food product is being launched and interviewers will give consumers a taste of the new product and study their facial expressions and ask them questions about what they liked and didn't like about the food product. At this point, modifications may still be made before a national launch. Perhaps, the consumers did not like the colour of the product or maybe they did not like the smell. These are all changes that can be made before a national launch, whereas, if the product was not tested before a small group, the consumers who end up purchasing the product may never buy it again. The consumer-tasting panel can help make or break a new food product. When the product is launched nationally, consumer panels may still be used to bring about product awareness. In addition, the company will probably advertise the product heavily as well. Further research on product purchase data can then be gathered to see what areas of the country are good markets for the product. Areas where the products do not sell as well would need to be researched in order to determine why. If consumers are not aware of the product, they may not purchase it. Advertising would need to be increased in these markets to increase awareness and potential sales. Further research may show that a specific area is just not a good market for the new product.

The continued success of the product is dependent upon post-launch research. Primary research needs to be done to ensure the consumer's interests and tastes are met by the product. Potential enhancements for a new and improved version can be gained through customer panels, interviews and focus groups feedback as well as surveys of current users. Continuous research on the product and how it can be improved will always leave a good impression with the consumer, who will view the manufacturers as very customer-oriented and thereby bring product differentiation between their product and the similar product from a competitor. Competitor research also plays a crucial role in the continued success of a product. Research also needs to be done to find out the market share of the competitor, and why people are buying the competitor's products. If the company wants to increase market share, it may do additional primary research to study the buying habits of the consumers in order to determine how to get more customers. If the product is lacking a wanted feature, it can be added. All this can be determined by good research. The successful company will continuously use research to see how the product can be improved.

market segmentation

A fundamental technique of marketing strategy that was first defined by Wendell Smith in a groundbreaking article of 1956. It effectively signalled the end of the *mass marketing age. Smith was concerned at the time to separate those companies that simply offered a range of product variety (to what was viewed as a homogeneous market) from those that designed tailored products (for multiple heterogeneous market segments). Its central idea was that there were different groupings of customers with wants and needs who required different products. What resulted was the division of a totally heterogeneous market into groups or sectors with relatively homogeneous needs and wants. Good marketing, from then until the present day, would rely on increasingly sophisticated segmentation of markets, gradually weakening the entire concept of mass marketing. The minutiae, the variety, the clustering of customers against various criteria needs became central to research for marketers.

Segmentation brought three distinct advantages: it made marketers think of the customer ahead of the product; in researching customers' needs at a granular level, it brought a better dialogue with customers, and it opened up all sort of new segments of markets that were previously unexplored by the mass marketers hitherto looking to serve the producer interest. It also ushered in a new era of competition that did not always mean that the largest producer would dominate the market (because now a whole range of smaller competitors could be dominant in a number of segments) and made it unlikely that there would ever be the total domination of markets that had characterized the first half of the 20th century. The rise of the *Internet, intelligent databases, and various multimedia has made the task of the marketer easier in identifying, unifying, and selling to market segments.

The first stage of segmentation is to establish criteria for segmenting the market, then to divide the heterogeneous market into relevant, clustered subgroups. One of the first limitations of segmentation is that if the market is subdivided into very small niches, it may not have enough customers to be profitable; or it may be too costly, requiring constant changes to the marketing mix to serve segments. Market segments should be measurable, and detailed information on customer characteristics should be obtainable cost-effectively so that the marketer can size the segment; information should be accessible so that the company can communicate effectively with the chosen segment using marketing methods; it should be substantial enough to consider for separate marketing activity and meaningful—having enough customers who have different preferences that can be addressed by marketing efforts.

Following that, the characteristics of these groups are identified and analysed. Once the market is subdivided into segments it is important to evaluate market segment attractiveness: for example, the structure, size and growth rate of the market segment; the company's reputation within that segment and its ability to serve that market; the intensity of competition within that market; the costs of adapting products and services for the segment. The marketer must find the potentially profitable segments and sort these out from the unprofitable ones.

From this relatively simple idea of segmenting according to customer needs and wants, now the staple of modern marketing, were spawned multiple segmentation techniques.

Some examples are:

- *Geographical segmentation* is the most classical form of segmentation, dividing the market into regions, countries, cities, states, provinces, suburbs, or neighbourhoods. In the age of global markets geographical marketing is quite limited as a form of segmentation, but it enables predictable and transparent resource allocation and it is relatively easy to distinguish the profitable from the non-profitable territories.
- *Demographic segmentation* is the most widely used segmentation technique for consumer products. There is much census data available on age, income, sex, gender, consumer preference, neighbourhood, and ethnicity to help the marketer segment these groups in multiple ways.
- *Brand loyalty segmentation* is based upon the loyalty that consumers have for one brand over another. This can be applied to services as well as products. This is often a reflection of lifestyle disposition.

- *Usage level segmentation* clusters those groups who are light, medium, or heavy users of a service or product.
- *Product segmentation* defines the market by different types of customer who prefer different product attributes. *See also* CONJOINT ANALYSIS.
- *Benefit segmentation* is the segmentation of customers who prefer a similar type of benefit. For example, some prefer high quality and luxury; others prefer low prices and simple functionality; others prefer the newest innovations; yet others buy for security, predictability, and safety.
- *Lifestyle segmentation* is the grouping of people around how they spend their disposable income on leisure and personal taste.
- *Market niche* is when the broad industry is segmented into smaller and smaller segments until a niche of buyers with similar wants and needs that can be satisfied is identified.
- *Psychographic segmentation* is a way of segmenting the market by cultural attitude and psychological type: for example the middle-of-the-road, the fashionable, the thrill-seekers, the security-seekers, the risk-takers, the risk-averse, the aspirational, the image-conscious; the conspicuous consumers, the high achievers, the individualists, the reformers, the highly educated, the family-oriented, the self-actualizers; the strivers, the strugglers, etc.

market share The metric of total sales of a product or service in a specified market expressed as a percentage of total sales by all entities offering a similar product or service. Originally developed for the consumer market for tangible product, this metric has proven both enduring and popular. The more precise way to calculate market share is sales as a percentage of the total in the defined target market over a given time period. Market share remains one of the classic, if flawed, measures of market and marketing success. There is no generally accepted formula that links market share to profitability. It is difficult to apply to markets for services and intangibles.

market testing The stage before the launch of a new product, service, or concept, where a trial group of customers is used in order to assess the response, the problems, the advantages, and the effectiveness of various promotional *channels.

market trend The overall direction, behaviour, patterns, and dynamics of market activity repeated over time in a given market sector.

market value The price at which a good or service can be bought or sold, and determined by the interaction of buyers and sellers in a specific market at a specific point of time.

Markov model The probability that the user of each *brand in a category will switch to another brand. Mathematically sound, these probabilities are now measurable through *retail scanners and *point of sale (POS) systems.

mark-up The amount of the selling price of a product that is over and above its cost. A *retailer, for example, will add a mark-up to the product to cover expenses associated with the selling of the product that would include showroom or shelf space as well as other expenses. This practice is regarded as a more outdated way of pricing than targeting *pricing to what the market will bear. *See also* PRICING.

marque An alternative word for *brand or *trademark or *product.

Maslow's hierarchy *See* HIERARCHY OF NEEDS.

mass customization A technique of marketing in which goods and services are produced at scale but are sold at a reasonable price and are highly tailored to meet individual *customer needs. Mass customization is different from mass production where production in quantity is the goal. Mass customization typically uses mass-production techniques to complete part of the product, the rest of it then being customized based upon customer demand that will still keep costs down. Mass customized products include golf clubs that can later be adjusted to an individual player or Levi jeans, which can now be custom-made for customer's individual dimensions without much extra cost. *See also* RELATIONSHIP MARKETING.

mass marketing (unsegmented marketing, undifferentiated marketing) A philosophy in which the seller views the market as a homogeneous whole, and, therefore, has only one marketing programme. A discipline born of the Industrial Revolution and the *consumer age, mass marketing implies the same product, the same price, the same promotion and the same distribution system for everyone. Mass marketing is declining as the dominant marketing technique in the advanced economies but is still healthy in the developing economies. *See also* CONSUMER SOCIETY.

MDS *See* MULTIDIMENSIONAL SCALING.

media

The range of nonpersonal communications channels that includes print media (newspapers, magazines, direct mail), broadcast media (radio, television), and display media (billboards, signs, posters, CD, and DVD), and new interactive media (telephones, Internet, instant messaging, e-mail).

Marketers tend to speak of two classes of media channel:

Above-the-line (or 'mass') media that is: the press and magazines, radio, television, outdoor or ambient, and cinema.

These are for wide coverage and cannot have highly targeted audiences.

Below-the-line media that is: direct mail, exhibitions, shows and events, point of sale materials, and sales literature.

Below-the-line media tend to have limited coverage and are intended for highly targeted audiences.

In recent years, there has been a proliferation of types of *media channel. *See also* ADVERTISING.

Basic characteristics of major media channels:

1 **Television**
- Ability to build high awareness levels; the dominant media channel worldwide of the 20th century, particularly from the 1950s onwards.
- Large audiences. Although these are declining for single channel viewing, the BBC can still garner up to 20 million viewers for a single show.
- Visible demonstration of product in use (sound and vision).
- Compulsiveness: television has proven to be the most addictive of all media.
- Viewed at home in a relaxed manner, often at the centre of family social gathering.
- Commercial: with the onset of multiple channels, largely funded by advertising sales, public, non-commercial broadcasting funded by taxpayers is diminishing in influence. However, the downside is that the proliferation of advertising in television is irritating in its frequency and ubiquity.
- Transient medium.
- Not fully interactive: this has become the major criticism of television in the age of the Internet. Often, alternatives to television, such as entertainment delivered interactively over television or PC, is seen to be more attuned to the needs of the new generation. In the

late 1990s, the sales of PCs worldwide actually started to outstrip television sets.

2 **Magazines and journals**

- Opportunity for quality print: printed material allows greater depth of content than the broadcast media or daily tabloids.
- Appropriate, non-sensationalist editorial environment (for example in contrast to daily newspapers that need sensational headlines).
- Allows careful targeting of audiences.
- Advertisements are expected by readers, and are often seen as an integral part of the magazine.
- Longer life span than newspapers: people tend to read magazines over a longer term than newspapers, often collecting them.

3 **National print press**

- Wide coverage of the population and large circulation volumes.
- Good flexibility in terms of the timing of media buys—space can be booked at short notice.
- Poor method of reaching the target audience, given that these publications rely on mass audiences. Some of the 'quality' newspapers, such as the *Financial Times* and *Wall St. Journal*, do make claims to an elite audience.
- Advertising content is often avoided by the readership.

4 **Print posters**

- These give an opportunity for colour reproduction.
- They present an opportunity to communicate a brief message.
- They can be used at point of sale or point of consumption.

5 **Cinema**

- An effective way of reaching a young audience, given that the dominant group of cinemagoers is in the 16–24 age range.
- High production cost for cinema advertising can be reduced by the adaptation of TV creative advertising transposed to the large screen.
- Segmentation possibilities—for example by age, taste, and locale.
- Audiences tend to be smaller and highly localized.

6 **Radio**

- A medium that has established itself over the years as an 'intimate companion' with smaller audiences.

- Sound is very portable, and has taken on a whole new life in cars and portable radios.
- Segmentation possibilities—for example by time slot, by locale, by age range, and by lifestyle.
- Lack of visual demonstration can often be a hindrance in a world dominated by visual images.
- Transient medium: radio broadcasts are the least likely to be stored or taped by the audience.
- Small local audience size. Radio is in retreat as a national or international medium but has had a new lease of life over the past 30 years as a medium serving local audiences.

7 **Outdoor and transport advertising.**

- This medium has an ability to build high awareness levels, especially given traffic congestion and volumes.
- In highly congested areas a well-placed poster can have a huge audience.
- Relatively low costs.
- Campaigns are possible on billboards (the Wonderbra adverts in the UK were an example of this being done successfully).
- Segmentation possibilities—particularly around locale and traffic density.

8 **Satellite broadcasting**

- Ability to reach a large number of audience segments at different times of day and night around the world.
- Can reach a global audience.
- Ease and speed of access to medium.
- Control of message in different countries is a challenge.
- Measurement, in some cases is very difficult: satellite broadcasting has created so many channels that the broadcaster has no control of medium, with the majority of the audience having little channel loyalty and prone to continuous flicking of channels.

9 **The World Wide Web**

- Ability to interact with target audiences by use of social media.
- All traditional forms of media have a web option.
- Eventually all forms of media will converge onto the World Wide Web.

media analysis A study of the effectiveness of various media in reaching the intended audience.

media broker An agency that buys bulk media space from media owners then sells it on in parcels to clients.

media buying A function within an *advertising agency that buys time and space for advertising from television, radio, and print media owners. Buying *television media time is the most complex of the media-buying skills. It is normal now for advertisers to bundle together their media-buying requests in order to improve their purchasing power with media owners.

media-buying service The use of a company other than an ad agency to purchase media time and space.

media channels The variety of *media used to display *advertising, usually in the form of a combination or 'mix'. The most recent additions to these channels are interactive, involving a two-way exchange between the presentation of advertising and the *target audience.
   See also AMBIENT MEDIA; BILLBOARD; BROADCAST MEDIA; BROCHURES; DIRECT MAIL; DIRECTORY; DISPLAYS; FILM ADVERTISING; INTERACTIVE TELEVISION; MOVING OBJECTS ADVERTISING; POSTERS; PRINT MEDIA; WEBSITES; WORLD WIDE WEB.

media commission The amount paid by *media owners to *advertising agencies for the space and time these agencies book with the media owners on behalf of their clients.

media impact The qualitative value of an exposure through a given medium.

media kit A resource created by a publisher to help prospective ad *buyers to evaluate advertising opportunities.

media owner A person who owns any media organization, for example publishers, website owners, cinema networks, television channel owners, newspaper proprietors, radio channel owners, owners of virtual and physical advertising space, and generally anyone who owns a medium in which advertising can be purchased.

media plan An outline of the objectives of an *advertising campaign, *the target audience, and the specific *media vehicles that will be used to reach that *audience.

media planning The systematic selection of the most appropriate media to deliver messages to target audiences.

media power Media became a powerful industry in the 20th century when technological advances as well as new techniques of journalism made the media industry global. Media market leaders became more and more dominant and invested more, and this in turn attracted more *readers, which attracted more *advertising revenue which led to greater economies of scale, which made more money to invest in attracting more readers. The 20th century also created a clear distinction between the quality and popular press which continues today. The vast majority of the national papers launched in the early 20th century were popular papers operating on the 'mass circulation leads to more advertising revenue' model. However, the quality papers did not follow that business model. The quality newspapers (which all now have websites) carry a large proportion of news and current affairs material and have not followed the human interest, tabloid headlines, sensationalist or prurient stories to attract mass audiences that the tabloids have in the search for readerships of millions. The 'quality' newspapers have created fewer media barons and empires: they operate on a quality, not quantity, principle. They deliver smaller readerships to advertisers, but their readerships are affluent elites with plenty of disposable income. Advertisers will pay more for access to those groups and thus the qualities do not require such large readerships. Quality newspapers tend to generate about 70% of their income from adverts, compared to 40% for the popular tabloids that make more through sales of their papers.

Newspapers remained heavily dependent on advertising. In the 1950s and 1960s paper circulation fell while costs of production continued to rise. Then came the most significant development of the post-war period, which was the introduction of new technology to printing and publishing in the 1980s. This revolution involved the replacement of old ways of printing papers with new computerized processes. This allowed media barons like Rupert Murdoch to break the power of the print unions whose control of the printing process had given them great leverage and bargaining power. Photos are now transmitted digitally, stories are e-mailed from across the globe, and perhaps more importantly scoops are announced on websites by freelancers running their own fairly small online media agencies.

By the beginning of the 21st century, the majority of North American newspapers were local rather than national. By 2000, there were around 1500 daily local newspapers in the US. Even the well-known quality publications such as *The Washington Post* and *The New York Times* did not really circulate outside the northeastern United States. Most Americans still read a local daily paper, such as *LA Times, Boston Globe*, or *Atlanta Constitution and Journal*. Virtually all the national and international news carried by local papers in the US was supplied by news agencies, especially Associated Press and United Press International. This has led to a lower diversity of reporting in the US and a higher fulfilment of demand for news being met by the broadcast rather than print media. Local titles such as *The New York Times* and *The Washington Post* have developed national influence because they are read by politicians in

Washington. Many local papers follow their lead on stories, and some TV networks do so as well.

The early 21st century demonstrates the declining influence and weakening economics of printed newspapers, their position having been eroded by television, which itself is now being eclipsed by web-enabled media.

Overall, the 20th century was marked by the inexorable rise of media power. The great historian Carlyle predicted this in the 19th century when he coined the term 'fourth estate' to describe the rising power of the press and reporters. The 20th century began with only very few media channels, such as local newspapers, and ended with multiple channels of vastly increased range, scope, and sophistication. The power of the media and its rise created powerful media barons who have been able to influence the course of history. The media and power became closely intertwined. The media and political power, whether on a democratic or non-democratic basis, were inextricably linked. The media and political power have become closely intertwined both in democracies and non-democracies, sometimes for good and sometimes for nefarious purposes.

media relations The process of managing the flow and presentation of company or institutional information in various *media channels and outlets in order to improve, preserve, and protect the *reputation of the company or institution. While the majority of media relations focuses on individual journalists in *press, *radio, and *broadcast media, an increasing part of the work of media relations is to manage online and social media channels. Beyond the immediate audience of the individual journalist, the media relations function, and the professionals within it, targets the specific *audiences who read, view, or listen to the target medium. Media relations are also responsible for *media strategy and planning, media campaigns, developing and distributing *press releases, creation of *media kits and briefing papers, arranging and managing interviews with journalists, media training for executives, measuring *media impact, *share of voice, and, often, working on legal issues related to media exposure or risk. While the majority of the media relations function is responsible for placement of information in the *editorial of various media, a part also involves avoiding media exposure, especially if the matter is sensitive, or potentially damaging to the company's reputation. Another key element of media relations is *crisis management: the limitation of damage to a company or institution or individual's reputation likely to be caused by unmanaged, or negative, mentions in the mass media.

media release A *public relations device, in the form of a news release, or hard news, or a feature release, or human interest stories. The release is sent to various *media channels.

media representative A salesperson selling airtime, media, or online space.

media schedule An agreed publication schedule for running advertisements or television commercials between the advertising agency and the advertiser.

media strategy Using media for marketing purposes that takes the following areas into consideration:

- Costs of media buy;
- Ability to communicate the message effectively;
- Frequency of the medium (for example a single ad in a daily newspaper is unlikely to yield any result);
- Target market;
- Flexibility (*lead times);
- Temporal constraints;
- International/national/regional audiences served by the medium;
- Volume of business using the medium;
- Past results of the medium;
- Reputation of the medium.

See also MARKETING STRATEGY; MEDIA; MULTIMEDIA.

memory decay A lessening, over time, of *brand loyalty among previous loyal customers.

merchandise The goods such as pens, hats, bags, badges, apparel, and sports equipment upon which branding is displayed. *See* MEDIA CHANNELS.

merchandizing A range of advanced selling and display techniques designed to increase the sale of goods in *retail outlets. *See also* CONSUMER MARKETING; RETAIL.

message The conveyance of information about the underlying theme, vision, or idea from the transmitter to the receiver. Messages can be conveyed through all types of media in different ways. Lead and supporting messages support a *brand positioning of a company. *See also* ADVERTISING; BRAND; COMMUNICATIONS.

message management The process of ensuring that a message is communicated and brought to life with examples and points of evidence.

metasearch engine A *search engine that displays results from multiple search engines.

metatags Devices used to provide data about a website.

Metcalfe's Law Named after Bob Metcalfe, the inventor of the Ethernet computer-networking technology, it states that the value of a network grows in proportion to the square of the number of users. Once a network achieves a certain size, it becomes almost irresistibly attractive. Metcalfe reasoned that 1,000 people on a network could have roughly one million different conversations, so the value of a network grows in proportion to the square of the number of users. This is an important law for marketers, because as far as potential consumers are concerned, given the choice of joining a large existing network with many users or a new one with few users, they will almost always decide that the bigger one is far more valuable. The result is often explosive, accelerating growth once a network establishes dominance. This law is most demonstrably felt in the world's two great interactive networks—the Internet and the global telephone network.

me-too A product modelled consciously on a successful competitor: the type of product that appears on a market with no differentiating features from already-existing products.

metropolitan area Defined measurement used by the US Census Bureau to define an urban location where there is a concentration of people that can be used for statistical purposes. An MSA or Metropolitan Statistical Area is defined as a city or urbanized area with at least 50,000 inhabitants.

micromarketing The study of marketing from the perspective of micromarkets or very narrowly segmented markets right down to individual customers in very small locations. These elements include the firm's suppliers, competitors, marketing intermediaries, customers and publics. *See* MACROMARKETING; MICROSEGMENTATION; SEGMENTATION.

micromarkets Those markets in which the volumes of demand are relatively small owing to the fragmentation or splintering of *mass markets; markets in which there is great diversity in the needs and wants of customers. *See also* MASS MARKETING; NICHE MARKETING.

microsegmentation The division of a market into smaller groups of *customers on the basis of more narrowly defined *needs and wants, after having already divided or segmented it on the basis of broadly defined needs and wants. *See* MARKET SEGMENTATION.

middleman An intermediary. A middleman can be someone who is between the producer or manufacturer and the retailer or consumer. *See* DISTRIBUTION.

milking (skimming) A marketing pricing approach of charging high prices when a product is first launched and spending heavily on *advertising and sales promotion to obtain sales. Progressively, prices are lowered as the product moves into the later stages of its *life cycle. The profitable 'cream' is therefore skimmed off in stages until sales can only be sustained at lower prices. *See also* CREAMING; PRICING.

milline rate (milline) A measure of the cost effectiveness of *advertising in a newspaper, calculated by multiplying the cost per *agate line by one million, then dividing by the circulation.

mindshare The share of *perception and *attention that a *branded product, *concept, *service, company, or institution has in the minds of *buyers or principal *audiences relative to those of *competitors. The higher the level of *awareness, the more direct the *recall, the more familiar with the content, features, and *benefits of the *brand, the higher is deemed to be the mindshare. Mindshare is often the companion to the more traditional measure of *market share. Mindshare is often seen as a precursor to market share. However, mindshare, being more intangible, is more difficult to measure in practice. The usual way of measuring mindshare is by a *direct survey of the target *audience asking questions about *awareness, about how prominent the associations are ('top of mind'), and the images evoked relative to the desired *image. Mindshare can also be measured over a period of time, and particularly after a dedicated or intensive *marketing and *communications campaign. It is as relevant to those promoting an idea (such as a political party, a not-for-profit organization, or a government) as it is to a commercial organization seeking to promote a branded *product or *service. High mindshare can, but does not necessarily have to, equate to high levels of popularity or attractiveness. An eponymous name association—when a product or service gives its name to a general activity—e.g. Fedex(ing) a parcel, Xerox(ing) a document, Hoover(ing) a carpet—is often seen as a high form of mindshare.

minutage The number of minutes allowed per hour for *television advertising. The amount allowed varies from country to country. *See also* ADVERTISING.

missionary sales The education of those who will be responsible for end-user sales and bringing about an attitude of mind and technique that will lead to higher sales. *See also* SALES.

mission statement A brief description, no longer than a few sentences, that explains an organization or company's reason for existence. The mission statement should explain what the company hopes to achieve in the future. It should discuss its values and its work ethic. A mission statement should be evaluated every few years to reflect current changes. Though a company's reason for existing may not change, the methods of achieving its goals may change with the times and the mission statement should be modified to reflect these changes.

mobile marketing The promotional activities using mobile technology to convey messages directly to customers or, alternatively, marketing devices that take products and services directly to customers, such as promotional tours, roadshows, and travelling exhibitions.

mock-up A simulation of a final product for use as a promotional advertising device, or a prototype that is photographed, filmed, displayed, or published.

moderator 1 (facilitator) The person who is the leader for a *focus group or a discussion group. A moderator is necessary for open-ended discussions in order to keep the discussion on track and to make sure everything gets covered in the time allotted.

2 Someone entrusted by the online administrator to help discussions within a forum to stay productive and within the guidelines or objective. Basic moderator duties include deleting or modifying inappropriate posts, educating newcomers about forum guidelines, and possibly deleting accounts of repeat offenders. Additionally, moderators may be experts in their field who can help minimize unanswered questions. Most moderator openings are volunteer positions, although there may be substantial indirect rewards.

monopolistic competition A market structure where producers supply similar but not identical products or services.

monopoly A non-competitive market situation in which there is only one seller. Monopolies are often state-owned.

monopsony A market situation in which there is only one buyer.

MOSAIC A UK based *geodemographic segmentation system, or people classification system developed by Experian. *See also* ACORN.

mousetrapping The use of browser trickery in an effort to keep a visitor captive at a site, often by disabling the 'Back' button or generating repeated pop-up windows. Mousetrapping is one of the most extreme marketing tactics on the *Web. The goal is to extract maximum value from one-time visits, typically by bombarding visitors with a never-ending supply of traffic-exchange *banners and *pay per click links. Mousetrapping comes in many varieties.

moving objects advertising Using transport vehicles such as buses, trains, taxis (the majority of London taxis now carry advertising), aeroplanes and, to a lesser extent, airships as promotional advertising. *See* ADVERTISING; MEDIA CHANNELS.

MPEG (Moving Picture Expert Group) International group that sets the standard for the compression of digital video and audio data of files that enables their transfer and exchange across communications networks.

MSA *See* METROPOLITAN AREA.

MSRP *See* LIST PRICE.

multibranding *See* BRAND; FLANKER BRAND.

multichannel marketing The promotion of the same *product or *service across multiple *communications and *distribution channels: for example, selling *consumer goods direct to the public, over the *Web, through *retail outlets, through an *affiliate, through *mail order catalogues, via *e-mail or other form of *electronic commerce—at the same time.

multiclient survey Type of market research financed by a group of organizations with similar objectives and shared interests.

multidimensional scaling (MDS) A type of analysis used for making a *perceptual or concept map. In multidimensional scaling, each statement or concept is represented by a single point. Things that are perceived to be similar to each other are grouped together. MDS is used as an alternative to factor analysis where the comparisons must be linear. MDS is frequently used to determine a perception of how similar different brands are. MDS will allow for a visualization of product positioning. It helps answer the following questions:

• How should a product be positioned?
• How is the product positioned compared to our competitors?

multimedia A combination of *media and content such as *text, *audio, moving images, still images, *animation, video, *webcasts, and *podcasts that are delivered electronically in different forms and formats. The term was coined in 1966 by the journalist Bob Goldstein. Multimedia is normally accessed by an electronic device capable of playing multimedia formats. Multimedia is used both for display to *audiences and for interaction with users and players. It can exist in both live and recorded formats. *Advertising, *product presentations, information, entertainment, and educational services are now normally delivered in multimedia format. Most modern websites use multimedia (including *webcasts, webinars, which are seminars or educational programmes delivered to a large audience over the internet, and *podcasts) to increase their attractiveness and to increase the length of time that visitors spend on the *website.

multiple correlation A device used in *market research to measure the effect of two or more independent variables on the dependent variable.

multiple readership A publication that has more than one *reader per copy sold—for example, in a household, in a waiting room, in a club, office, etc.

multiple regression analysis A statistical method of analysis using one dependent variable and more than one independent variable. The method calculates the relationship between variables and is used to predict the outcome when one or more variables are altered.

multiple retailing A number of *retail outlets owned by one organization (for example supermarkets, chain stores) but providing central services such as personnel, administration, marketing, and purchasing departments.

multiplier effect A concept that an increase in spending has an effect that multiplies beyond the initial amount spent on a project.

multivariate statistics A method of looking at several groups of *data where there are many different variables, then studying the relationship between these variables simultaneously. By grouping the variables or people, it would be much easier to identify factors for success. Product usage as well as the relationship between *advertising and *product purchasing can also be determined. *See also* CLUSTER ANALYSIS; CONJOINT ANALYSIS; FACTOR ANALYSIS; MULTIDIMENSIONAL SCALING; REGRESSION ANALYSIS.

Murdoch, Rupert (1931–) Creator of News Corporation, formed in 1980 from diverse companies and the world's largest media-entertainment-communications empire, which controls both media content and distribution. News Corp is a vertically integrated media company. Murdoch was born in Australia into a newspaper-owning family. In the 1950s he inherited his first paper, the *Adelaide News*, from his father, Melbourne publisher Sir Keith Murdoch. He made continuous acquisitions across the planet. In the 1960s, it was Sydney (the *Mirror*), London (the *News of the World* and the *Sun*); in the 1970s, New York (the *New York Post*); in the 1980s, Hollywood (20th Century Fox and Fox TV) and again London (acquiring *The Times* and *Sunday Times*) and the satellite television service in the UK BSkyB; in the 1990s, Asia (Star Television). News Corp holdings now include the lion's share of the newspaper industry in Australia, about one-third of British newspapers and BSkyB, through which pay-per-view was introduced to the UK in 1996. In the US News Corp owns film and TV interests, newspapers, book publishers (HarperCollins), sports teams, and several other companies such as TV Guide, and the social media site *MySpace.

MySpace A social networking website with *media hosting site that includes chat room, cinema, and shopping founded by Chris de Wolf and Tom Anderson in 2003. Part of the appeal of MySpace was that it is an open site—each profile was a blank canvas for its owner and, in that sense, gives the individual the ability to do whatever he or she wants with it. It was purchased by *Rupert Murdoch's News Corp. As a site it is now eclipsed in popularity by *Facebook. *See also* FACEBOOK; WEB 2.0; APPENDIX 2.

mystery shoppers People employed by retailers to pose as consumers and shop at the competitors' and their own stores to compare *prices, displays, *merchandising, quality of customer service, and *sales offers.

NAICS *See* STANDARD INDUSTRIAL CLASSIFICATION.

naming The fundamental element in a *brand identity, whether of organization, *product, or *service, individually or in portfolio form. The name is the most important element of brand identity. The science of naming *brands, organizations, services, and products has become vastly more complex because of the *World Wide Web, and the difficulties of selecting a plain and descriptive name, because there are so few which remain available on the Web. Most companies now require a *URL and a web address for e-mail purposes. The paucity of plain, descriptive names has meant that there has been an effusion of fanciful neologisms and fusion words that have no direct description of the company's products and services. Naming has become a complex science.

NAPCS *See* STANDARD INDUSTRIAL CLASSIFICATION.

narrowcasting The use of a broadcast medium to appeal to audiences with special interests. For example in the US, cable TV stations have specialized interests such as sports, news, weather, movies, etc, and allow advertisers great selectivity; that is, advertisers can narrowcast their messages rather than broadcast them. *See also* MEDIA.

Nast, Condé (1873–1942) Condé Nast Publications. A pioneer in upmarket fashion magazines. Growing up poor in St. Louis, Nast joined *Collier's Weekly* in 1898 and there developed his idea that a market existed for magazines catering to the tastes of the affluent and fashionable. He put his ideas to the test in 1909 by purchasing *Vogue*, then a struggling New York society weekly. Editor Edna Woolman Chase and Nast turned it into an influential, stylized, photo-fashion monthly for women that attracted leading advertisers. After buying *Vanity Fair* and *House & Garden* he created Condé Nast Publications in 1922. Nast lost his fortune in the 1929 stock market crash but was able to create *Glamour* in 1939 to further extend his publishing vision.

national account A client of 'national' importance, usually with several locations throughout the country.

national advertising A type of advertising activity that is aimed at a national market, as opposed to local or global advertising.

national brand A company, product, or service which is known and advertised within a defined national marketplace.

national marketing A range of promotional activities that focuses on and is confined to national markets. Less usually, the marketing of a nation state. *See also* LOCATION MARKETING.

navigation The facilitation of movement from one web page to another.

need arousal The stimulation of the need for satisfaction from specific sources, goods, and services, often conveyed as a route to *instant gratification.

negative advertising A promotional technique used to draw attention to, and to expose, the shortcomings of a competitor's product or service. *See also* DISPARAGING ADVERTISING.

negative appeal Advertising which emphasizes the negative aspects of existing or being without the advertised product or service.

negative demand The situation where a customer does not want, and actively avoids, or sells existing versions of, a specific product or service.

negotiation The art of two sides going back and forth with their demands until some sort of compromise is reached where both sides are happy with the outcome. Usually no one will get everything that is desired. The key is to focus on the points that are the most important and arrive at a situation of mutual benefit. This is key in *personal selling*.

neon sign A sign using a tube or tubes of inert gas which provides a bright glow, used in advertising to attract maximum attention.

net cost The cost of services rendered by an advertising agency excluding the agency commission.

net export expenditure *See* AGGREGATE DEMAND.

netiquette A fusion of network and etiquette, an unwritten code of conduct regarding acceptable online behaviour. The term is commonly used in reference to popular forms of online communication, including e-mail, forums, and chat. While some netiquette issues are technical in nature, all fundamentally concern how people interact with each other in *cyberspace. Once the technical nuances are grasped and abstract concepts are understood, online etiquette is not much different from offline etiquette. Violating the code of conduct for a community (e.g. using *e-mail spam) may get you banned from the community. What does netiquette have to do with marketing? It is essential to have a good understanding of acceptable ways to communicate with potential customers. Netiquette is an early definition of the new culture of cyberspace.

net unduplicated audience The combined cumulative audience exposed to an advertisement.

network A national or regional group of affiliated broadcast stations contractually bound to distribute radio or television programmes for simultaneous transmission.

network effect The phenomenon whereby a service grows in value as more people use it. For example, services that operate over networks such as *e-mail, *text messaging, *Facebook, and mobile communication rise in value the more people are connected users. This phenomenon is spread early in the growth period through *word of mouth, and then later the market expands exponentially as the consumer believes that 'everyone' is linked to the network. *See also* METCALFE'S LAW.

network marketing A form of *direct selling in which *distributors of a product attempt to sell to *end-users and to others who will become themselves distributors. A *network effect is created.

network option time (network time) The programming time that a network controls on each of its affiliate stations.

new product launch The activities related to bringing a new product to its target market. This process is one of the most hazardous areas of marketing, where reputations can be won and lost instantly. No one has yet devised a fail-safe marketing technique to make new product launches successful. At best, the marketer can reduce the likelihood of failure. Most new product launches fail because they misinterpret or ignore some vital part of the market they are targeting. These misinterpretations can range from an over-optimistic assessment of market demand, overpricing, or making the product or service too complex for current demand to mistiming market demand as many excellent products are simply launched before the market demand is of sufficient volume to ensure success. *See also* PRODUCT LIFE CYCLE; PRODUCT MARKETING.

newsgroup An *Internet discussion group, focusing on a specific topic and sharing responses and reactions. *See also* WORLD WIDE WEB.

newspapers One of the oldest information and *advertising media of all, currently being re-invented electronically on the *Internet. Newspapers are local, regional, national, international, or electronic. Their main revenue comes from advertising. It is always difficult for advertisers to distinguish between what a newspaper's core *readership is and its published *circulation figures, which makes targeting difficult. *See also* ADVERTISING; MEDIA.

newspaper syndicate An organization that distributes material, for example news articles and features, to newspapers, for commission.

news release Written information about an event, product or service, released with the purpose of generating publicity. Also known as a *press release or media release.

niche focus *See* COMPETITIVE STRATEGY.

niche marketing A marketing *segmentation strategy designed to fill a specific or unserved need in a tightly defined part of the market. The entire company marketing efforts and resources are focused on serving one segment, or sub-segment, of the market. A concentrated marketing campaign will help to both gain deep knowledge of the specific niche and also ensure the product becomes more and more customized to meet the needs of the specific market. Niche marketing can be in the pursuit of higher profits or in an attempt to be the leader in a small market. Also known as *concentrated marketing and *competitive advantage. *See also* MICROMARKETING.

niche player A company whose main focus of business is identifying and servicing small segments and sub-segments of the market.

Nielsen, A C Sr (1898–1980) AC Nielsen Co. A pioneer of market research, Nielsen created the concept of *market share in 1923. This occurred when his new company began checking food and drugstore shelves to tally product movement. His sales audits answered client questions about their marketing efforts, and as TV arrived Nielsen adapted his audit to deliver 'the Nielsens', those influential audience totals for programmes and commercials. AC Nielsen Co is his market research company, founded in 1923 in the US, that has become the market researcher of choice for the provision of *consumer data on consumables, drugs, mass merchandise, and alcoholic beverages. AC Nielsen Co. became the world's largest *consumer marketing research organization. It conducted *retail and *consumer audits and *benchmarking services around the world. Nielsen's research continues to influence decisions related to campaigns, *media schedules, *sales promotion programmes, *distribution patterns, entertainment, and event production. Many consumer products frequently use Nielsen data and packaging companies to determine which product lines would be the most successful for each location. It regularly publishes the Nielsen Index, which describes shopping patterns. The Dutch company VNU NV acquired AC Nielsen Co. in 2001.

Nielsen rating A measurement of the percentage of US television households tuned to a network programme for a minute of its broadcast.

noise Any influence external to the sender or receiver that distorts the message in the *communication process.

noncommercial advertising Types of radio and television advertising that are designed to educate and promote ideas or institutions, e.g. public service information on healthcare.

non-probability sampling *See* SAMPLING.

non-profit marketing (non-business marketing) Promotional activities undertaken by organizations whose primary objectives are other than the traditional ones of profit, market share, and return on investment. For example, these could be charities, organizations set up to promote certain ideas, educational institutions and purposes, religious orders, performing arts, cultural institutions such as museums and galleries, military services, government campaigns for health, good and humanitarian causes, political parties, and the environment. The sources of funds and support for these types of organization are rarely the beneficiaries of their work. The purposes of non-profit marketing are to bring in a source of revenue for the organization and also to create a positive climate of consent or appreciation for their work or cause. *See also* CHARITY MARKETING.

North American Industrial Classification System *See* STANDARD INDUSTRIAL CLASSIFICATION.

North American Product Classification System *See* STANDARD INDUSTRIAL CLASSIFICATION.

Northcliffe, Viscount (1865–1922) British newspaper proprietor. Born Alfred Harmsworth in Dublin, he founded the *Daily Mail* (1896), the *Daily Mirror* (1903), and bought *The Times* in 1908. His brother, Viscount Rothermere (born Harold Harmsworth) joined him and proved gifted in garnering advertising revenue, which came to be the dominant revenue source of newspapers. Their Amalgamated Press (including *Comic Cuts*, famously labelled as 'Amusing Without Being Vulgar') became one of the world's largest media empires of its time, with a specific marketing slant towards the new reading public of literate working men and (especially) women. Northcliffe's papers were initially regarded with contempt by the British establishment. Lord Cecil's view on the *Daily Mail* was typical of the upper-class reactions of the time: 'a newspaper for office boys written by office boys'. However, Northcliffe's genius for flattering and understanding his essentially educated working-class and lower middle-class readership, resulted in massive sales. His advice to his journalists was always 'Explain, Simplify, Clarify', and his shrewd assessment of the newspaper business remains perfectly valid today: 'News is what somebody somewhere wants to suppress, all the rest is advertising.'

observation The collection of information by watching consumers' *behaviours or actions. It is the oldest *market research technique of all.

observational research The collection of *data by observing behaviours or actions. Observational research is often used in *focus groups where a two-way mirror allows people to view the reactions and behaviours of the *respondents. Though observational research only provides information on current behaviour, it is nonetheless a very inexpensive and accurate way of providing behavioural data. This type of research is also extremely useful when it is difficult to persuade the respondents to verbalize their behaviours or thoughts.

observation room *See* BACK ROOM.

obsolescence The point in the decline of a *product in its *marketplace, where the product becomes outmoded because newer, more technologically advanced, or more competitively priced products become available, or if tastes change and turn against the product.

odd pricing The pricing of a product so it ends in an odd amount such as £9.99 or £9.95 instead of £10. Consumer psychologists claim a product will sell better since consumers will have the perception that the odd-priced product is much better value than the one selling at the even price. *See also* PRICING.

OEM (Original Equipment Manufacturer) The company who makes the original product, or components of a product, which are then sold by other companies, who market it as their 'own brand' products.

off card Advertising time sold at a rate that does not appear on the *rate card.

offerings Those products or services that are designed and presented to meet a particular *segment need. *See also* MARKET SEGMENTATION.

offset deal *See* COUNTERTRADE.

off the page A marketing technique using *catalogues, where the customer makes contact in person or by telephone, their response being filed on a *database, creating a *buyer profile.

Ogilvy, David (1911–99) Co-founder of Ogilvy and Mather, Ogilvy emphasized fact-based advertising. His agency created powerful ads distinguished by graceful, sensible copy that respected the consumers' intelligence. His major campaigns were for Hathaway shirts, Shell Oil, Sears, KLM, American Express, International Paper, IBM, Schweppes tonic water, Rolls-Royce, and Pepperidge Farm. Ogilvy pioneered a fee system, as opposed to commissions, which changed the economics of the advertising industry. Ogilvy's most celebrated publication, *Confessions of an Advertising Man* (1963), contains 11 perennial points of advice on how to build great advertising campaigns:

1 What you say is more important than how you say it;
2 Unless your campaign is built around a great idea, it will flop;
3 Give the facts;
4 You cannot bore people into buying;
5 Be well mannered, but don't clown;
6 Make your advertising contemporary;
7 Committees can criticize advertisements, but they cannot write them;
8 If you are lucky enough to write a good advertisement, repeat it until it stops pulling;
9 Never write an advertisement that you wouldn't want your own family to read;
10 The image and the brand (every advertisement should contribute to the brand image);
11 Don't be a copy cat.

oligopoly *See* PRICING.

omnibus panel A study over time in which the sponsoring research company defines the *audience to be surveyed and the intervals between studies. Numerous clients participate by submitting proprietary questions. Generally clients only receive results from their proprietary questions and general demographic questions. *See also* MARKET RESEARCH.

on-air tests A way of measuring recall among viewers of a commercial or programme during a real *broadcast of the tested *communication. *See also* ADVERTISING.

on camera The act of being filmed in front of the camera, for example, an announcer, actor, or newsreader, and being visible to the viewer.

one-shot 1 A television programme that stands alone and is not part of a series, usually tailored to the *target audience.
2 A shot of one person speaking directly to the camera without any other aspect to the presentation, e.g. background or action.
3 (marketing) A one-step sale, for example buying an item of clothing, rather than a sale which involves several steps, such as a magazine subscription,

which involves the steps of paying for the original subscription, and then the repeat subscriptions.

one-sided message A marketing or advertising communication which is biased towards a point of view and usually targeted at an audience receptive to that point of view.

one-stop shopping A single place to shop without having to go to multiple locations. It has come to mean a service provider who provides a range of integrated services that were previously provided by specialist individual providers.

one-to-one marketing *See* RELATIONSHIP MARKETING.

online auctions The use of a dedicated *website to conduct the buying and selling of goods under a monitored auction, usually with a secure payment system, and a peer rating system on the integrity of the buyers and sellers. *See also* EBAY.

online catalogue An electronic listing in the form of a catalogue available on a website. An *Internet version of the more traditional printed catalogue, displaying products for sale with description, price, other relevant details, and ordering instructions.

online database A factual listing provided by an external server or organization, which a remote user can access and reach, usually by paying a subscription.

online marketing The promotional use of the full range of web tools, and *advertising techniques to promote products and services over the *Internet.

online public relations Internet-enabled way of establishing and developing relationships between companies and customers, or prospective customers, or journalists, allowing interaction worldwide and at all times. Online public relations are highly measureable on a global scale. *See also* PUBLIC RELATIONS; MEDIA.

open end 1 Time left at the end of a commercial or programme which is provided for the use of *local advertising or station identification.
    2 A *radio or *television programme with no specific time to end.

open-ended questions *See* QUESTIONS.

open source Software for which the service code is freely developed, programmed, and available.

operational excellence *See* POSITIONING.

opinion formers Groups of people, or individuals, who, through their opinions, writings, speeches, attitudes, and social, business, or political associations, are capable of initiating, influencing, and often inspiring the opinions of others, and are therefore targets for marketers and advertisers.

opinion leader A person or company that can influence or sway public sentiment on an issue. Opinion leaders are often the targets of marketing campaigns.

opinion poll A survey that is conducted to find out public sentiment on different issues usually dealing with politics or policy. *Gallup is an organization known for its opinion polls. *See also* GALLUP; MARKET RESEARCH.

opinion research A study of the general opinions of a given population, using a statistical sample of the population.

opportunity analysis An element in the SWOT analysis technique (Strengths, Weaknesses, Opportunities, Threats). *See also* MARKETING PLAN.

opticals Visual effects used to instil interest as well as portray mood and continuity to a commercial. Dissolves, cross fades, and montages are all opticals.

opt-in e-mail An e-mail that is explicitly requested by the online recipient. *See also* PERMISSION MARKETING.

optional product pricing *See* PRICING.

opt-out 1 A type of program online that assumes inclusion unless stated otherwise.
2 The action of removing oneself from an opt-out program. The term opt-out is often used in relation to ad tracking programs. By default, ad-tracking programs track everyone. In response to growing privacy concerns, some major advertising networks have offered individuals the option to be removed from tracking.

orange goods The description of a type of consumer goods, such as clothes, which the customer will replace regularly owing to, for example, wear and tear, seasonal changes, or a change in preference.

organic growth The means of developing new business growth, financed from the reserves of the company and its capabilities, rather than from mergers, acquisitions, or takeovers (inorganic growth).

original research *See* PRIMARY RESEARCH.

outbound link *See* LINKING STRATEGY.

outdoor advertising Any outdoor sign that publicly promotes a product or service, such as *billboards, movie kiosks, signs on vehicles, etc. *See* MEDIA.

outlet A *retail or trading place of business, for example a *supermarket, chain store, or *department store.

outlier An unexpectedly extreme deviation from the mean, sometimes indicating an error of measurement and sometimes a chance, genuine observation. Outliers can distort *data that is used to summarize values.

outsourcing Employing an outside company to perform functions previously done inside the company. For example, payroll, security, catering, cleaning, building maintenance, janitorial services, accounting, customer fulfilment, and information systems are functions that are frequently outsourced since costs can be quite high and they can be done more efficiently by specialized companies. Economies of scale can be achieved by using a large company with existing equipment and expert personnel that specializes in specific functions. Increasingly, companies are starting to outsource their critical business processes and functions, such as customer care and acquisition, their supply and logistics operations, and often their training and human resource functions. Outsourcing has become a major market in its own right, and is segmented into various areas of expertise.

out take A sequence, visual or audio, which is filmed or recorded, but edited out of the final production.

overlay A transparent or opaque print in a design or layout, often one of several that combine to form a finished design or graphic.

overselling Either selling a *customer more goods or services than they really need, or overemphasising the case for purchasing a specific product or service.

over-the-counter (OTC) Goods selected by individual customers which are weighed, packed, and priced (as required) by staff prior to being passed to the customer for payment at that point, or subsequently at a cash point; or in pharmaceutical products markets in which medicines and drugs can be sold by a pharmacy direct to customers, without a doctor's prescription; or any good or service available for direct sale without modification or specific work, especially where an element of such work might be expected.

own brand/label A brand or label that is produced internally. This is now frequent in retail stores, where the store's own brands compete with other brands in the same store. *See also* BRANDING.

package 1 A combination of programmes or commercials offered by a network that is available for *purchase by advertisers either singly or as a discounted *package deal.

2 A *merchandise enclosure or container.

package deal Multiple products or services are bundled together in a saleable unit, for example a holiday that includes costs of transport, accommodation, food, sightseeing tours, guiding services, and insurance in a single price.

package insert (package stuffer) An item of separate *advertising material included in merchandise packages that advertises goods or services.

packaging A means of protecting the product to be marketed (for example, the package has to be the right size to receive the product from the production line); a way of making the product highly attractive to customers; enabling easy use or *consumption of the product; helping to meet legal requirements (for example on material, on waste disposal, on *consumer information); and, occasionally, adding value to the customer experience of the *brand. The most visible form of packaging for marketing purposes is the consumer package. These packages must give high visibility to the *brand name. They must have an appropriate size relative to the product contained within. The package must be highly attractive in order to command the consumer's *attention. This attractiveness may come as a result of colour, originality or distinctiveness of design or quality of materials used in the package. An impression of good quality is always important even if the product is low price.

Packard, Vance (1914–96) Author of the best-seller *The *Hidden Persuaders* in 1957. His book played to a public perception that the advertising industry was able to persuade defenceless consumers to buy unneeded goods and services by devious means. Packard explained that ad agencies used psychiatry, motivational research, and related social sciences to create subliminal selling patterns. *See also* ADVERTISING.

Page, Larry (1973–) Co-founder of Google with Sergey *Brin in 1998. *See* APPENDIX 2 for more on Google.

pagejacking The theft of a page from the original *website and publication of a copy at another site. Pagejacking does not mean taking over a page on the original site. In fact, the original site can be completely unaware that the theft has occurred. Pagejackers siphon off traffic indirectly though the search engines.

PageRank An algorithm used by *Google to give a numeric value that represents how important a page is on the *Web. PageRank is Google's way of deciding a page's importance which itself is a major factor in determining where the *web page appears in a Google search. Under the Google system, a page acquires a higher ranking when it *links to another page. The more links that a page has, the more important the page becomes in the Google ranking system. Google interprets the number of links to a site as a vote of confidence in the site. Google also uses the quality of content to ascribe a page rank. The qualities of the pages that link to the site serve to increase the page ranking. Important, high-quality sites receive a higher PageRank, which Google remembers each time it conducts a search. Google combines PageRank with sophisticated text-matching techniques to find pages that are both important and relevant to a *web search.

page traffic The number of readers of a specific page in a *web publication, expressed as a percentage of the total *readership of that web publication.

page view A request to load a single web page. This is important to the revenue stream of the web site. If a site earns much of its revenue from *advertising, then page views are important because of their contribution to ad inventory. If a site only earns revenue on sales, then page views are not a key metric.

paid circulation The total number of a publication distributed to individuals or organizations who have paid for a subscription.

painted bulletin A freestanding steel or wooden structure, approximately 50' wide by 15' high, with moulding around the outer edges similar to a poster panel, and including a hand-painted copy message. Bulletins are generally found near highways or roofs of buildings in high traffic areas. *See also* BILLBOARD.

paired comparison A comparison between two different products or variables. Paired comparisons are frequently used to determine which product a consumer would prefer, for example Coke or Pepsi. Marketers can then use these comparisons to claim one product is superior to another in their marketing campaigns. *See also* MARKET RESEARCH.

panel 1 A type of outdoor advertising. A regular panel is only seen during the daytime, while an illuminated panel is seen also from dusk until dawn.

2 (longitudinal study) A survey where the respondents are interviewed repeatedly over a length of time. The term panel can also be used to describe the respondents in a group interview. *See also* FOCUS GROUP.

panel research A market research technique in which *consumer panels keep detailed records of their purchases and subsequent use of, and opinion of, these purchases, in order to create *data for analysis, providing information on consumer or business *purchasing habits and product service use and effectiveness.

paradigm A word derived from the Greek word παράδειγμα (paradeigma) meaning pattern: a widely accepted view, or generally accepted perspective, regarding any subject, business, political, social, linguistic model, pattern, or consensus.

paradigm shift The original phrase was coined by Thomas Kuhn in his work *The Structure of Scientific Revolutions* (1962) to describe a change in basic assumptions within the ruling theory of science. More generally, it has come to mean a radical change in the generally accepted viewpoint or structure to a new one based on a complete change in thinking, or belief system that allows the creation of a new paradigm that stands in opposition to the previous paradigm. An example might be the Japanese creation of 'Just in Time' manufacturing in the 1980s, which shifted the paradigm from viewing inventory from an asset to a liability. The *Internet and the *Web have changed the paradigm on *intellectual property and its distribution and on the value of proprietary information.

parallel pricing Those products or services which are priced the same as those of competitors. *See also* COMPETITION; PRICING.

Pareto principle A concept named after the 19th-century economist, Wilfredo Pareto, and also known as the 80–20 rule. Simply put this means that 20% becomes responsible for 80%, for example 20% of the costs are using 80% of the resources. 20% of the customers are responsible for 80% of the revenues, 80% of the profits come from 20% of the product sales. Eventually, effectiveness will go down due to diminishing returns. By using the Pareto principle, marketers can learn how to use their resources more effectively to bring about maximum results.

Parfitt-Collins model A method for predicting the ultimate *market share for new *consumer products using input data from consumer panels. The model requires actual market *data, usually from a *research panel, which includes: 1) cumulative *brand penetration (the total number trying the brand, over time) and 2) *repeat purchasing rates over time, from the time each buyer first bought the product. These form the basis for predictions of future market share. The simple formula is: Share = TxRxB where: T = projected percentage of those who use the product and will try out this product brand; R = projected percentage of those who have tried the product brand already, and who will repurchase the brand; and B = Buying-level index of repeat purchases of the new brand (compared with an index of 1.0 for the product class average).

participant *See* RESPONDENT.

participation 1 An announcement made within the context of a programme as opposed to those shown during station breaks.
   2 An announcement or amount of *broadcasting time that is shared by several advertisers.

pass-along rate The percentage of people who pass on a message or file. Pass-along rates are a measure of *word of mouth marketing. Objects typically passed include *e-mail messages, *web pages, and multimedia files. Content typically passed includes humour and entertainment, late-breaking news, and shopping specials.

pass-along reader A reader who becomes familiar with a publication without buying a copy. These readers are taken into account when calculating the total number of readers of a publication.

passing off The act of misleading customers into believing that a product or service is a different, usually more prestigious, brand than their own, for example by using a similar *trademark or *logo to 'pass off' as the prestigious brand.

passive exporting *See* EXPORTING.

payback period The time required to recover the initial cost of an investment. Normally, a good investment is one with the shortest payback period. *See also* BREAKEVEN ANALYSIS.

payment threshold The minimum accumulated commission an affiliate must earn to trigger payment from an affiliate programme at a specified time interval.

payout planning An approach to *advertising budgeting in which the money spent to advertise is represented as an investment towards sales and profits.

PayPal A *web-based application for the secure transfer of funds between member accounts. Users are not charged to join PayPal or to send money through the service, but there is a fee structure in place for those members who wish to receive money. PayPal has been a key enabler of *e-commerce on the web ensuring that credits and debits can be trusted.

pay per click (PPC) An online advertising payment model in which payment is based solely on qualifying *click-throughs. In a PPC agreement, the advertiser only pays for qualifying clicks to the destination site based on a prearranged per-click rate. *See also* ADVERTISING; E-COMMERCE.

pay per click search engine A search engine where results are ranked according to the bid amount, and advertisers are charged when a searcher clicks on the search listing.

pay per lead An online *advertising payment model in which payment is based solely on qualifying leads. In a pay per lead agreement, the advertiser only pays for leads generated at their destination site. No payment is made for visitors who don't sign up.

pay per sale An online *advertising payment model in which payment is based solely on qualifying sales. In a pay per sale agreement, the advertiser only pays for sales generated by the destination site based on an agreed commission rate.

pay TV The *television channels which can be accessed only on payment of a subscription. This has become the dominant model for television viewing in the digital age, eclipsing public service television.

Pearson's Coefficient Correlation The most frequently used method to determine the strength of the relationship between two variables. The correlation coefficient is between -1 and 1; if there is a positive relationship, the coefficient is 1 and if there is a negative relationship the coefficient is -1. For example, if the statement that the taller an individual the more he would weigh were always true, the coefficient would be 1 since as the height increased, the weight would always increase.

peer group A distinct group of people with similarities and common status, for example age, social standing, rank, education, aspiration, or income. Such groups are much used in *market research.

penetration analysis An analysis of how pervasive or widespread a particular product is in a given market. This is used to calculate *market share or *market penetration.

penetration pricing The manipulation of *pricing for new products (typically setting them lower than the market average) and promoting them widely in order to penetrate a target market position quickly and secure a desired position. *See also* MARKETING STRATEGY; PRICING.

penetration strategy *See* MARKETING STRATEGY.

perceived benefit The aspects of a product or service that will appeal to prospects and customers.

perceived value A customer's individual evaluation of the benefits to be gained from purchasing a product or service.

percent-of-sales method A method of determining the *advertising budget based on an analysis of past *sales, as well as a forecast for future sales.

perception What a customer believes to be true. Successful marketing of a product that is based upon the perception the customer has as to how good the product is. *See also* BRAND; PERCEPTUAL MAPPING.

perceptual mapping The 'mapping' of a product or service based upon its main attributes as rendered on a matrix. For example, a perceptual map of a luxury item would include how it was perceived on a number of attributes such as *price, *quality, *reputation, and *customer service and prestige. Mapping has a variety of marketing purposes including *market segmentation, identifying whether or not a product has any weaknesses as well as consumer preferences and perceptions. Perceptual mapping can also be used to determine how a company is perceived against variable perception attributed to its target audience. *See also* MARKET RESEARCH.

perfect competition The idealized, and rare, examples of completely open markets in which unrestricted free trade operates, where all goods of a specific type are homogeneous, and where buyers and sellers possess all pertinent information which they use rationally. *See also* COMPETITION; IMPERFECT COMPETITION.

perimeter advertising Type of open-air publicity displayed around the perimeter of, for example, a sports stadium, focused on the television audience as much as the spectators. *See also* ADVERTISING.

per inquiry An agreement between a *media representative and an *advertiser in which all advertising fees are paid based on a percentage of all money received from an advertiser's sales or inquiries.

periodical A print publication which appears regularly, for example daily, weekly, monthly, or quarterly.

permission marketing A school of marketing thinking popularized at the time of the *e-commerce explosion in 2000–02, the central idea of which is that marketing can only thrive by obtaining customer consent for *direct marketing, by discovering their natural affinities rather than pushing and *hard selling. Coined and popularized by Seth *Godin in a book of the same name in 1999, permission marketing is the opposite of traditional 'interruption marketing', which is based on snatching the time and *attention of customers who have not given their consent. Permission marketing is about building an ongoing relationship of increasing depth with customers or, to use Godin's own phrase, 'turning strangers into friends, and friends into customers.' Permission marketing has been hailed as a way for marketers to succeed in a world increasingly cluttered with marketing messages and the declining effectiveness of mass advertising. *See also* RELATIONSHIP MARKETING; VIRAL MARKETING.

personal marketing A highly customized approach to marketing in which products and services are tailored to meet the specific requirements of the individual customer who is studied in detail. Also known as *one-to-one marketing. *See also* RELATIONSHIP MARKETING.

personal selling A two-way, interactive form of selling which is usually conducted face to face, but which can also include telephone selling. It is a tried and tested form of oral persuasion and negotiation involving the seller and the potential *buyer. The seller attempts to build interest and rapport, while also informing, then persuading the potential buyer to purchase products and services. The *customer is able to demand greater and more detailed information, then to negotiate. Personal selling enables the formation of a personal relationship between buyer and seller, which brings another dimension to the product and service. Although this type of exchange is highly effective and informative, it is declining as a way of selling commodity goods and transactional services. In the first instance it is an expensive way of selling. The salesperson usually earns a commission, raising the overall cost of sale. Potential customers may not always react well or trust the individual salesperson and be wary of their individual persuasion techniques. Additionally, personal selling has a very limited range of coverage. *Internet-based selling, which provides the customers with information without the inducement pressure of an individual salesman, has done much to move simple products and services such as insurance, that were previously the domain of personal salespeople, to indirect selling over the phone and Internet. The future of personal selling appears to be moving toward high-value products and services. *See also* NEGOTIATION; SALES.

personalize To add a name or other personal information about the recipient to *direct mail advertising.

persons using television (PUT) A percentage of all persons in a certain viewing area that are viewing television during a specific amount of time. *See also* NEILSEN, AC.

persons viewing television (PVT) The term used by Arbitron for *persons using television.

persuasion process The process used by *advertising to influence *audiences' or *prospects' attitudes, especially purchase intent and product *perception, by appealing to reason or emotion.

PESTLE Acronym for the six areas which provide context for a market planning process: Political, Economic, Social, Technological, Legal, and Environmental. *See also* MACROENVIRONMENT; MARKETING PLAN.

phishing The action of trying to acquire valuable personal information, for example passwords and financial details, by posing as a legitimate, trustworthy *website, or, for example, simulating the users' bank website in order to obtain their details.

photoanimation A process of creating animation through the use of still photographs.

photoboard Any of a set of still photographs made from a television commercial, accompanied with a script, to be kept as records by an agency or client.

photo opportunity An event staged to bring together journalists and photo journalists, normally for politicians and celebrities in various fields, with the purpose of gaining publicity through *media exposure.

picture window An ad layout in which the picture is placed at the top of the page, and the copy is placed below.

piggyback 1 A *direct mail offer that is included free with another offer.
2 Two commercials shown back-to-back by the same sponsor.

piggybacking A low-cost *market entry tactic in which manufacturers of products arrange for manufacturers of complementary, non-competing products to represent their products in another country or region.

pilot A test of a limited number of users to test the feasibility or acceptance of a product. Pilot testing is a crucial stage before any major project launch, the feedback being used to further tailor the product to its *target audience.

PIMS (Profit Impact of Market Strategy) A database that started in the 1970s, a coming together of an internal research programme at General Electric and the Market Sciences Institute at Harvard Business School. PIMS has a database of over 4,000 participating companies, with each business profiled on 200+ factors over a five-year time horizon. This enables the profitability of actions taken in the market and relative market share to be assessed. For marketers, the most common use of the PIMS database has been the *regression model, which has nearly 40 variables grouped into seven categories:

- attractiveness of the business environment;
- strength of competitive position;
- differentiation of competitive position;
- effective use of investment;
- discretionary budget allocations;
- characteristics of the owning corporations;
- current change in position variables.

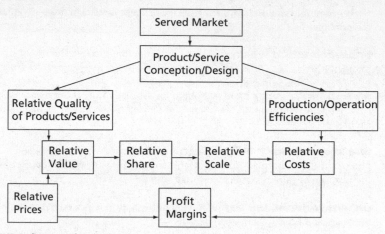

PIMS: Profit Impact of Market Strategy

pitch/pitching An attempt to sell a concept, idea, or product. *Marketing managers and *salespeople will 'pitch' a product. *See also* SALES.

place marketing The favourable promotion and presentation of a particular geographical area in order to attract tourists or investors. *See* LOCATION MARKETING.

placement test Where a *product or *service is placed in the environment in which it will ultimately be used or consumed, after which the *consumer or tester provides detailed feedback about all aspects of the product, for example performance, price, and value for money.

platform 1 The basic concept or idea behind an *advertising or *marketing campaign.
2 The hardware and operating system base on which software applications and programs may be run.

podcasting A method of preparing and publishing multimedia files to the *Internet, allowing users to subscribe to a feed and receive new files automatically on a music or multimedia device. The technique enables amateur and professional producers to create self-published, syndicated performances. The name has its origins in the name of Apple's iPod digital music player, fused with the term 'broadcasting'. However, podcasting does not require an iPod—any digital player or computer or *personal digital assistant with the appropriate software can play podcasts. Content producers are increasingly turning to podcasting as an inexpensive and simple distribution channel that has the potential to reach a large audience, particularly uploading to *YouTube. Podcasting has been likened to viewer-controlled subscription television because it allows viewers to see their selected podcasts whenever they like.

point of presence (POP) A service provider's location for connecting to users.

point of purchase The location where the item is purchased, such as an in-store display.

point-of-purchase display (POP display) Advertising display material located at the retail store, usually placed in an area where payment is made, such as a check-out counter.

point of sale The location where the item is sold, such as at an in-store check-out counter.

political advertising The paid-for *promotions in support of political parties or issues or specifically, the marketing of a political campaign.

political environment *See* PESTLE.

poll A quick survey of customers, usually for instant opinion rather than in-depth study. *See also* GALLUP.

Pollyanna effect (Pollyanna hypothesis) The tendency to accept and recall pleasant, positive information more easily than that which is unpleasant or negative.

pop-up window An ad used on the *World Wide Web that displays in a new browser window. Pop-up windows come in many different shapes and sizes, typically in a scaled-down browser window with only the 'close', 'minimize', and 'maximize' commands. There is a strong resentment by some web surfers towards pop-up ads. Marketers often do not realize the ill-will generated by pop-ups because it is easier to click the 'close' button than send an e-mail to complain. What can often be seen is an above-average *click-through rate, although some of this can come from 'false positives,' unintentional clicks when the pop-up gets in the way of the desired target. Advertisers can get a better picture of the effectiveness of pop-up advertising by paying attention to *conversion rates and return on investment (ROI).

portal A site featuring a suite of commonly used services, serving as a starting point and frequent gateway to the *Web (web portal) or a niche topic (vertical portal). It is a major element of *online marketing.

Porter, Michael (1947–) Roland Christensen Professor of Business Administration at Harvard Business School (HBS). An influential business guru in the field of how firms compete in industries and how they gain competitive advantage. Porter joined the HBS faculty in 1973 after earning his doctorate in business economics at Harvard, and he soon became one of the school's youngest tenured professors. A prolific scholar, he has written 16 books and more than 75 articles. His 1980 seminal work, *Competitive Strategy: Techniques for Analyzing Industries and Competitors*, has been translated into 19 languages and is considered the pioneering treatise on corporate competition and strategy. He has also worked on the competitive advantage of nations and why some cities, states, or nations can be more competitive or prosperous than others (*The Competitive Advantage of Nations*, 1990), and on how competitive thinking can be applied to social problems. His various models have become cornerstones of market strategy and analysis. In his own words, he has defined his groundbreaking work: 'From the start, my goal was to integrate what we knew about the economics of markets and industrial organization and what we knew about companies and business strategy. These two fields had never really intersected before. In addition to scholars, I wanted to reach practitioners, offering them a systematic framework for developing an overall strategy for competing in an industry.' *See also* COMPETITIVE ADVANTAGE; FIVE FORCES MODEL.

positioning

The way in which a company or organization and its capabilities are perceived relative to *competitors in its *marketplaces by existing and potential *customers. Positioning, therefore, indicates on what basis and with what means a company or organization wishes to compete in its marketplaces. Positioning is one of the most important elements of *strategic marketing. If it is not right for the company, or its products and services, then many of the marketing executions that flow from the positioning idea will be ineffective. Positioning is closely related to *brand equity and *market segmentation, as all good positioning must be related to external market realities, *trends and dynamics. It is most dangerous to claim a *market position for a brand which the company or organization cannot or can no longer deliver against. Also, the overall position should be relevant and compelling to a sufficient mass of potential buyers to make investment in the overall brand positioning worthwhile. In addition, the market must value the specific positioning of an attribute. *See also* MARKETING; MARKETING STRATEGY.

Theoretical models of positioning

Michael *Porter has suggested three types of positioning strategy:

- cost leader;
- product differentiation;
- niche player.

He argued that successful firms must be superior in at least one of these positions and cannot be average, or dominant, in all three positions. While Porter's framework remains valid and relevant, in marketing terms it has been further developed. Others have developed a framework of value disciplines:

- product leadership (for example Mercedes or Apple);
- operational excellence (for example IKEA, Dell, or McDonalds);
- customer intimacy (for example Virgin Atlantic Airlines or Disney).

Trout & Ries defined positioning in terms of its outcome—how it leads to perceptions in the mind of the customers, either existing or prospective. Philip *Kotler has produced a detailed taxonomy of specific types of positioning:

- **Attribute positioning** in which the company, organization, product or service promotes a prominent attribute or feature (e.g. the world's best-selling car, England's oldest hotel, the most expensive perfume).
- **Benefit positioning** is a more typical type of positioning that focuses on the benefit derived from the product or service (e.g. the fastest overnight parcel delivery, the cleanest clothes after washing, the most reliable power tools, the greatest number of software applications that run on the device, the most detailed information from a search).
- **User/application positioning** in which a product or service is positioned for a definite application or use (e.g. a first-time buyer's mortgage, golf clubs designed for low handicap golfers, the best clothes for resisting heavy rain and inclement weather).
- **User group positioning** in which a company, organization, product, or service aligns and creates affinities with a specific user group (e.g. The Gap for fashion-conscious youth, Volvo with safety-conscious drivers who also value durability, Apple for 'cool' people, Disney for families, Saga with senior citizens).
- **Competitor positioning** in which a company defines itself relative to its main competitors. Frequently companies that are challenging the market leader or dominant brand use this type of positioning (in the early days Apple did this, by implication, with IBM in which Apple promised freedom and creativity with its PC; Pepsi is constantly inviting customers to compare its drinks with those of Coca-Cola; Virgin Airlines constantly positions itself against British Airways, Avis against Hertz, etc.). *See also* COMPARATIVE ADVERTISING. This type of positioning often defines the market in terms of the top two or three brands.
- **Category positioning** in which a company or organization may describe itself as a leader in a category, rather than a specific product (for example, Hewlett Packard in colour printing, Kodak in photography, Coca-Cola in soft drinks).
- **Quality/price positioning** in which a product or service promotes its quality relative to its pricing (for example Burger King burgers being the best value for money rather than being the best burgers,

Stella Artois beer being 'reassuringly expensive' rather than the top lager, Best Buy being the best products at the lowest prices).

- **Re-positioning** is the set of marketing activities that changes the target market and buyers' perceptions of a given product, service, or company. This can cover a number of types of repositioning (*See* D. Jobber, principles and practice of marketing 1995).

- **Image repositioning** in which the product is the same but with a different perception (for example the Marlboro cigarette being moved from a woman's cigarette in the 1950s to a rugged, macho man's cigarette from the 1960s onwards). *See* APPENDIX 2.

- **Product repositioning** in which a product is adapted to either meet the needs of its target market more closely (Microsoft's various versions of Windows) or to increase the size of the market (e.g. Lucozade being adapted and repositioned from a single bottled drink that people took when they were poorly, to being an energy inducing drink for sports and other active people in various forms and flavours).

- **Intangible repositioning** in which a different market segment is targeted with the same product (for example taking Disney theme parks to the very different markets of Japan and Europe).

- **Tangible repositioning** in which target markets and product/service are changed (for example the evolution of Nokia from a wood products company to a mobile phone and services company). *See* APPENDIX 2.

- **Value positioning** in which luxury goods and services command a high price premium but which confer status on the user (Ferrari, Mercedes, Rolls-Royce, Gucci, Mont Blanc, Berlutti shoes). *See* APPENDIX 2.

Wholesale, factory outlet, and discount stores can provide leading brands for less than other stores. Also, various Internet websites can provide lower prices than traditional or branded retail outlets. This is usually based upon bulk *purchasing and *retailing techniques. In this case the outlet—either physical or virtual—is the leading brand rather than the individual products that it sells (Wal-Mart, Toys 'R' Us, Best Buy, Matalan, Amazon.com).

There is now a range of 'no-frills' product and service providers that offer a basic service or product at much lower prices than competitors by eliminating some service features (e.g. IKEA requires the customers to assemble purchased furniture from flat packs; South West airlines, Easy Jet, and Ryan Air offer very low-cost air travel by eliminating certain service features such as food onboard and pre-assigned seats, using direct booking without agents and not transferring baggage to other airlines. Online banks offer more attractive interest rates but require all transactions to be carried on over the Internet, thereby obviating the need for physical locations and service personnel).

positive appeal An advertising technique of emphasizing the positive benefits a *customer will gain from purchasing a product or service, in order to remove the reservations the consumer may have before the purchase.

postal research A technique of conducting research by targeting respondents by post rather than *face-to-face, *online, or by telephone.

postcode analysis A marketing device of using the geographic information inherently provided by postcodes to determine where to target specific products and services.

poster The most popular, and one of the oldest forms of outdoor *advertising. Poster size can range from a small wall poster to a large billboard; there is no standard international poster size. Posters are targeted at the general and casual audience who happen to pass the poster, and tend to be placed near where there are lots of travelling audiences, such as at the sides of busy or congested roads, high-density pedestrian areas, at airports, or other transport centres. The benefits of posters are: they are very flexible in terms of location and can be changed quickly and they can reach a large part of the population at relatively low cost. Poster advertising is normally used to supplement other types of *communication, such as TV or *print media advertising. The drawbacks are that posters only permit very basic types of *advertising and it is very difficult to target the audience and, therefore, measurement of effectiveness is extremely difficult. *See also* BILLBOARD.

post-purchase dissonance This describes the customer's post purchase sense of anxiety that they made the wrong choice in making the purchase.

post-testing Testing the effects of an *advert after it has appeared in the media. *See also* MARKET RESEARCH.

Powers, John E (1837–1919) An independent ad writer, New York. Known as the father of modern creative advertising, Powers proclaimed, 'Fine writing is offensive.' A former publisher of *The Nation*, Powers ranked No. 1 among independent copywriters at the turn of the century, both in fees and ability. 'Powers style' meant simple, short, lively, cogent, reason-why copy that was significant, truthful, opinionated, and stubborn. Powers worked only for those he considered trustworthy. His Wanamaker ad, 'We have a lot of rotten gossamers and things we want to get rid of', sold out the lot in hours. He was called 'advertising's most influential copywriter' and his work still serves as a model for advertising campaigns.

pre-campaign research The process of testing and assessing prospective consumer attitude and awareness of a product or service in its target group before launching a campaign. *See also* MARKET RESEARCH.

predatory pricing *See* BARRIERS TO ENTRY.

pre-emptible rate A (usually) discounted rate for commercial time which is sold to an *advertiser and is not guaranteed. As time may be sold to another advertiser who is willing to pay more, the advertiser buying this rate gambles to save money on the spot. *See also* ADVERTISING.

preferred position A position in a printed *publication that is thought to attract most reader attention and is sold at a higher rate; for example, the back cover of a *magazine.

premium An item, other than the product or service itself, which is offered free or at a nominal price as an incentive to purchase the advertised product or service.

preprint A reproduction of an *advertisement which is viewed before actual publication and is created by an advertiser for special purposes, e.g. to serve as a *retail display or to gain support from retailers.

press conference A managed meeting with journalists, usually in relation to a specific event, for which *press packs of information are provided in advance, and during which the press are invited to ask questions.

press cutting An excerpt cut from a *periodical, usually assembled with other cuttings, in order to gauge the extent to which an event, individual, or product is being publicized. Nowadays this process is usually done electronically rather than manually.

press mentions References in the media to, for example, a *brand, organization, individual, or event. *See also* SHARE OF VOICE.

press pack A package of relevant information (in print, audio, and/or visual) that is provided to journalists by the originator to give up-to-date and advance and background details about, for example, a product launch, a major *news item, or a forthcoming *press conference.

press release (news release) A short statement that outlines some newsworthy event or activity and that companies send to reporters and editors with the hope of getting press coverage. Press releases for television are often done on videotape and are now also released to online news agencies and newswires. *See also* MEDIA.

pre-testing A very small sample size to determine whether or not the desired outcome is produced. In *market research, pre-tests can be developed for surveys or interviews to see if the questions are easily understood.

price ceiling The price which customers are willing to pay for a perception of value from the product or service, based upon what the product or service is worth to them. This is sometimes described as 'what the market will bear'. *See also* PRICING.

price elasticity *See* PRICING.

price floor The cost of producing the product or service: price must be set above the floor in order to cover costs. *See also* PRICING.

---

pricing

An indicator of the value that a product or service can command in a *marketplace. Pricing is the crucial dimension of the *marketing mix. Prices are usually dependent upon three major variables: cost, competition, and customer. There are various strategies for pricing, depending on the overall market strategy and cost base of the company and there are various types of pricing: for example, cost-based pricing (in which companies apply an addition or mark-up to their cost base) and value-based pricing (which is based upon an estimation of what the market or consumer will be prepared to pay relative to the perceived value delivered). Prices can be merchandized into packages; they can be bundled into special offerings; they can be broken down into individual elements.

Pricing in a free market economy is very different from pricing in a controlled economy. Pricing is directly affected by the presence of monopolies. When a company completely controls price and supply it can be deemed to be a *monopoly. An example of this could be the diamond industry. When a few large-scale producers control pricing, then that can be deemed to be an *oligopoly. An example of this could be the oil industry. Another characteristic of an oligopoly is when products are largely undifferentiated and prices are similar and there is rarely price competition. Additionally, the numbers of buyers and sellers, as well as the barriers to entry which confront a new competitor entering a market, are major elements in the macroeconomic context in which prices are determined and set.

Pricing has a larger role in the economy and plays a role in regulating *supply and *demand for goods and services. If prices (and margins) are known to be high in a specific market, this encourages new entrants and therefore new *competitors into the market, provided that the *barriers to entering the market are not prohibitive. As multiple competitors enter a market, prices tend to fall and volumes start to rise as demand is enhanced by lower prices. If supply outstrips demand then prices tend to fall; if supply cannot cope with demand then prices tend to rise. (*See* BARRIERS TO ENTRY.)

The model below illustrates the four main pricing strategies that are used as a part of the overall marketing strategy:

p

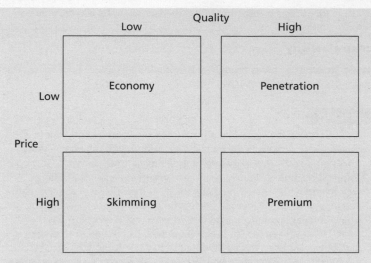

Pricing Strategies Matrix. Reproduced courtesy of marketingteacher.com

Price elasticity

Price elasticity is the determination of how sensitive *market demand is to changes in price. It is the equation between price rises and falls with concurrent market demand rises and falls. When small variations in prices have a large impact on market demand and sales volumes, these markets are called price elastic. When a change in price has little or no effect on market demand and sales volumes, these markets are called price inelastic. This leads to variations in price packages offered to different *customer segments at different times and in different places. Transport services and hotels are particularly adept at linking these prices to the market segments that are both price elastic and price inelastic. Hotels and airlines have low-demand weekend rates for pleasure travellers taking discretionary trips different from rates for peak-time weekday business travellers taking compulsory trips. The graph below gives a simple illustration of these different sensitivities of markets to pricing.

   Price elasticity of demand has many uses for individual firms. Knowledge of price elasticity allows firms to estimate the likely change in demand following a change in price. This is important for a business seeking to maximize total revenue. If demand is price elastic, a fall in price will raise total revenue. If demand is inelastic a firm may well decide to raise the price to increase total expenditure by consumers.

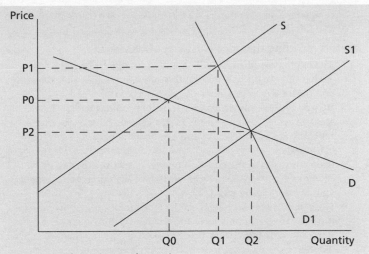

The Importance of Price Elasticity of Demand.

Factors that determine the value of price elasticity of demand

- **Number of close substitutes within the market.** The more (and closer) substitutes that are available in the market, the more elastic demand will be in response to a change in price. In this case, the substitution effect will be quite strong.
- **Luxuries and necessities.** Necessities tend to have a more inelastic demand curve, whereas luxury goods and services tend to be more elastic. For example, the demand for opera tickets is more elastic than the demand for urban rail travel. The demand for vacation air travel is more elastic than the demand for business air travel.
- **Percentage of income spent on a good.** It may be the case that the smaller the proportion of income spent taken up with purchasing the good or service the more inelastic demand will be.
- **Habit-forming goods.** Goods such as cigarettes and drugs tend to be inelastic in demand. Preferences are such that habitual consumers of certain products become desensitized to price changes.
- **Time period under consideration.** Demand tends to be more elastic in the long run rather than in the short run. For example, after the two world oil price shocks of the 1970s the response to higher oil prices was modest in the immediate period after price increases, but as time passed, people found ways to consume less petroleum and other oil products. This included measures to get better mileage from their cars; higher spending on insulation in homes, and

car-pooling for commuters. The demand for oil became more elastic in the long run.

Factors affecting the price elasticity of demand

- **Availability of substitutes.** The more possible *substitutes, the greater the elasticity. Note that the number of substitutes depends on how broadly one defines the product.
- **Degree of necessity or luxury.** *Luxury products tend to have greater elasticity. Some products that initially have a low degree of necessity are habit-forming and can become necessities to some consumers.
- **Proportion of the purchaser's budget consumed by the item.** Products that consume a large portion of the purchaser's budget tend to have greater elasticity.
- **Time period considered.** Elasticity tends to be greater over the long run because consumers have more time to adjust their behaviour.
- **Permanent or temporary price change.** A one-day sale will elicit a different response than a permanent price decrease.
- **Price points.** Decreasing the price from £2.00 to £1.99 may elicit a greater response than decreasing it from £1.99 to £1.98.

It is important to determine the basis of pricing for a service and how payments are made and collected. In services business, value is more of a *perception than a scientifically measurable entity. It is in the mind of the buyer of the service. *Value perception is where the buyer perceives greater aggregate value for a service than greater aggregate cost. For example, there are additional perceived benefits that are valued by the buyers, such as quality of expertise and advice, speed, delivery, security, convenience of payment, simplicity, and physical environment that can lead to different pricing packages. Progressively increasing benefit and simultaneously reducing costs can add value in the minds of the buyer. High perceived value gives opportunities for higher margin pricing. Therefore, services need to be priced in the context of a number of variables: the actual cost to cover the service delivered (the actual cost of the service not only includes its delivery but also its marketing and promotion), the value that the customer perceives and, therefore, the price that can be charged, and then the level of competition, which creates a variable in terms of how much the service offering price can be adjusted over and above the actual cost of delivering the service.

Other pricing methods

- **Economy** is a pricing method in which a mark-up for profit is added to the average cost of production. *See* COST PLUS PRICING.
- **Penetration** in which the price is determined by the company's *market share objectives. Lower prices are established in order to

capture or to build a larger market share than would be achievable through normal pricing. Market dynamics that enable this would include a highly price-sensitive market where the market leaders are viewed as having too comfortable a pricing position; mass volume production techniques that have reduced production cost and enable aggressive pricing relative to previous modes of production.

- **Skimming** is the opposite of penetration pricing. Skimming usually involves charging a very high price at a stage in the market where the market will bear high prices. The market conditions that enable this are usually at the early stages of a market when a new or innovative product or service has been introduced and the producer is looking to recapture his investment costs. Supply is still limited and the market is small. *See also* CREAMING.

- **Premium** is appropriate in situations of inelastic demand, in which an organization decides to keep its prices high. Reasons for such a strategy might include a growing super-premium segment of the market, overcrowding at the bottom end of the market, or the desire to create a prestige image for the product.

- **Marginal pricing** is when price is calculated to cover only variable costs (such as marketing and distribution) and little or no contribution is assumed toward fixed costs or overall net margins. It tends to be used to stimulate demand (during an economic recession), or during a reaction to competitive threat (such as a price war), or to stimulate promotional sales in a new product.

- **Full cost plus pricing** is a method of determining the sales price by calculating the full cost of the product and adding a percentage mark-up for profit.

- **Services business pricing:** services businesses use distinctive terminology to price their various service offerings: for example, fees (*professional services); tuition rates (educational services); services charges (financial services); fares (transportation services); tolls (road services); commissions (*brokers and agents); rents (housing services); admissions (museums and public buildings); ticket prices (entertainment services and sport); rates (hotels). *See also* SERVICES MARKETING.

- **Average price strategy** is a pricing strategy based on setting prices, which are average for the industry.

- **Dynamic pricing,** for example the popularity of *eBay and priceline. com, marks the beginning of an important business trend in which online prices for a growing number of consumer and business goods will change frequently according to supply and demand. For instance, some companies are using variable-pricing strategies to maximize profits, much as airlines do with ticket prices. Numerous firms are producing the necessary software.

- **Product line pricing** involves developing a product line in which each successive item in the line offers more features/higher quality for a higher price.
- **Optional product pricing** involves selling optional or accessory products along with a main product.
- **Captive product pricing** involves selling products that must be used along with a main product.
- **By-product pricing** involves accepting any price for a low value by-product that covers more than the cost of storing and delivering it.
- **Product bundle pricing** involves combining several products and offering the whole bundle at a reduced price.

Price adjustment strategies
Price adjustment strategies include the following:

- discount pricing and allowances;
- cash discount: a price reduction for buyers who pay their bills promptly;
- quantity discount: a price reduction for buyers who buy large volumes;
- trade discount (functional discount): a price reduction given to an intermediary for performing certain functions such as storage;
- seasonal discount: a price reduction for buyers who buy products or services out of season;
- psychological pricing: consideration of the psychology of prices and not simply the economies;
- promotional pricing: temporary pricing of products below list price, and sometimes below cost, to increase short-run sales;
- loss-leader pricing: used to attract customers to supermarkets and department stores in the hope that they will buy other goods at normal mark-up;
- special event pricing might be used in certain seasons.

primary data *See* DATA.

primary demand advertising Promotions designed for the generic product category, as opposed to *selective demand advertising.

primary readership The *data based on the numbers of buyers of a publication, rather than the number of readers.

primary research Techniques of original data collection or research direct from the target *respondents. Primary research is different from *secondary research in that secondary research uses data or research that has already been collected. Primary research includes qualitative and quantitative research and can include *surveys, *focus groups, *questionnaires, and *interviews. Since primary research typically takes anywhere from weeks to months to gather and is very expensive, secondary sources are typically exhausted first before any primary research is conducted.

prime time The broadcast periods viewed or listened to by the greatest number of persons and for which a *network charges the most for airtime. Weekday evening television is determined to be the time when the most people are available to watch television shows. Prime time differs by geography. It has generally come to mean in marketing terms the time of optimum exposure.

print media All forms of communication—newspapers, journals, and magazines—that are delivered by physical print. The prolific and traditional medium for *advertising, which can operate locally, nationally, regionally, or globally. *Classified advertising is found in printed media, in addition to product and service advertising. Advertising in this medium can either be directly on the page or take the form of insertions. The economics of newspapers and magazines are entirely dependent on advertising revenues, which are generally declining in the West. *See* DIRECT MAIL; MEDIA CHANNELS; MEDIA POWER.

print poster *See* POSTER.

private label A name identifying the manufacturer that is unique to the retail establishment that carries the product. A *brand name is a manufacturer whose products are widely sold across many different establishments. *See also* OWN LABEL.

probability sampling *See* SAMPLING.

problem child *See* BOSTON CONSULTING GROUP MATRIX.

product acceptance The measurement of the degree to which the launch of a product or service has been successful in its *target market.

product-based marketing organization A *marketing structure of an organization in which staff specialists have responsibility for various products (rather than for particular markets); most appropriate when customer needs are differentiated by product.

product benefits The perceived, but not necessarily real, benefits the consumer believes they will enjoy through the purchasing of a specific product or service.

product bundle pricing *See* PRICING.

product champion The person with the responsibility for the development of a new product or service, and commitment to the product or service sufficient to 'champion' it, through any resistance, to completion and to manage its *positioning in the *marketplace against *competitors.

product classification The taxonomy of products, or portfolio of products, into different types and for different purposes, linked to the external market.

product development A growth strategy in which the firm develops new products for existing markets.

product-differentiated marketing A marketing philosophy in which the seller views the market as a homogeneous whole, but produces two or more products for it. The products, differing in attributes (price, style, quality, etc), are designed to offer variety rather than to satisfy the needs and wants of different market segments. *See also* MARKET SEGMENTATION; MASS MARKETING.

product differentiation A strategy which attempts (through innovative design, packaging, positioning, etc.) to make a clear distinction between products serving the same market segment. *See also* MARKETING STRATEGY; POSITIONING.

product elimination The decision to drop a product, for example, in the decline stage of its *product life cycle, in order to use the costs associated with it to enhance profits or to release resources that could be more effectively used in other ways.

product extension The introduction of a product that is known to the company but which has features or dimensions which are new to consumers; three types of product extensions are possible: revisions, additions, and repositioning.

product failure A product that does not meet management or customer expectations in the *marketplace.

product flanking A competitive *marketing strategy in which a company produces its *brands in a variety of sizes and styles to gain shelf space and inhibit *competitors. *See also* FLANKER BRANDS.

product image The perception that the consumer has of a product or service, including value judgements and emotional responses, therefore not always an accurate assessment of the product or service's true effectiveness.

product innovation The development and introduction to the *marketplace of a product or service that is changed, improved, or new or new features added to an existing product.

product knowledge The detailed knowledge of a product's features and benefits required by a salesperson to persuade a prospect to *purchase.

product leadership *See* POSITIONING.

product liability The onus or responsibility imposed by legislation on a manufacturer to warn consumers appropriately about possible harmful effects of a product, to foresee how it might be misused, etc.

product life cycle A model which draws an analogy between the span of a human life and that of a product, suggesting that, typically, a product's life consists of four stages: introduction, growth, maturity, and decline. The concept is used as a tool to formulate marketing strategies appropriate to each of the stages. *See also* DIFFUSION OF INNOVATION; PRODUCT MARKETING.

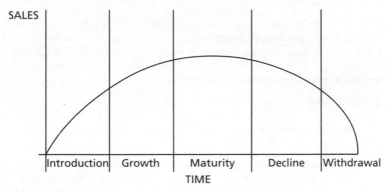

The Product Life Cycle (PLC). Reproduced courtesy of marketingteacher.com

product line A group of products manufactured or distributed by an organization which are similar in the way they are produced or marketed.

product line brand name A *brand name applied to several products within a product line.

product line extension The act of adding depth to an existing *product line by introducing new products in the same *product category. Product line extensions give customers greater choice and help to protect the firm from a flanking attack by a *competitor.

product line filling The introduction of new products into a *product line at about the same price as existing products.

product line modernization A strategy in which items in a product line are modified to suit modern styling and tastes and re-launched.

product line pricing *See* PRICING.

product line pruning The act of reducing the depth of a *product line by deleting less profitable offerings in a particular *product category.

product line retrenchment The act of reducing the width of a *product mix by decreasing the diversity of items offered across *product categories. This is common following the failure of brand leveraging to launch a brand into a related category.

product line stretching The act of adding new products into an existing *product line.

product management A system and process which ensures that total *marketing control of a *product line or *brand rests with the person who has profit responsibility for it.

product marketing A technique and discipline of marketing to determine how to develop the right product for the right set of customers at the right price and how to deliver that product to those customers at the right time and place and to ensure that they remain loyal to the product and buy more of it or the next version of it. *See also* PRODUCTS.

product mix The variety of distinct *product lines and items manufactured or distributed by an organization. Product mix consistency is the degree of closeness or relatedness between product lines in the product mix.

product modification Any substantial change made to the attributes (size, shape, colour, style, price, etc.) of a product, usually in an attempt to revitalize it in order to increase *demand.

product organization The deployment of a firm's development, marketing, and sales force so that a separate division is responsible for each of its major products or product groups.

product orientation A management philosophy, concept, focus, or state of mind which emphasizes the quality of the product rather than the needs and wants of the *target market. This assumes that *customers will favour products that offer the most quality, performance, and features and that the organization's objectives will be most readily achieved by a concentration on these.

product petrification A term used to describe the small but persistent *demand by *loyal customers for a declining product.

product portfolio The mix of products manufactured or distributed by a company relative to different *target market segments.

product position map A tool used in comparing *consumer perception of the differences between products or *brands. Consumers are asked to mark the particular location of a product or brand on a two-dimensional 'map', where the axes of the map are attributes felt by consumers to be important. *See also* PERCEPTUAL MAPPING.

product positioning research Investigative techniques used to determine how competitive *brands are perceived relative to each other on key dimensions of attractiveness and attributes.

product positioning strategy The marketing decisions and actions intended to create a particular place for a product in the market and in the minds of consumers. This strategy may attempt to *differentiate a product offer from a competitor's or make it appear similar.

product pricing research The data gathering and measurement of consumer sensitivity to different prices for a product. *See also* PRICING.

product prototype tests Research tests conducted to obtain the reactions of targeted customers to early working versions of new products.

product recall The advertised request by a company that a product be returned to it by those who have already purchased it, often deemed desirable when a product proves to be unsafe or unreliable.

product repositioning *See* POSITIONING.

products

Physical goods that cover a vast range from commodities to capital items. There are multiple ways of classifying products. Products have multiple categories and subcategories. Rather than classify the multiplicity of these products by what they actually are, it is more useful for the marketer to classify these products by how they are purchased:

Consumer products
The following are some of the major categories of consumer products based upon purchasing criteria.

- **Convenience products** are purchased without very much analysis or comparison by the purchaser, and *brand loyalty and preference play a major role in the automatic purchasing decision.
- **Staple products,** or basics, are purchased frequently and regularly, for example, milk, bread, petrol, newspapers, soft drinks, and beer.
- **Impulse products** are purchased without any prior thought or planning. These are usually purchased because of their attractiveness and *availability. They are usually playing to buyer temptation or immediate impulse. Confectionary, drinks, or magazines that are placed where buyers tend to form queues, such as at the cash till or at a sports or theatre event.
- **Emergency products** are those goods that are purchased only when there is immediate need, such as an umbrella in a rainstorm, bandages for an accident, candles in a power outage, or replacement windscreens after a car smash.

- **Shopping products** are those goods that buyers spend time searching for, and comparing and contrasting, usually from some form of *retail outlet. These can be subcategorized into homogenous and heterogeneous goods. *Homogenous* goods are perceived as largely *undifferentiated in terms of quality but *differentiated in terms of price. Therefore the buyer spends much of the time making price comparisons in the search for the lowest price within an acceptable value range. *Heterogeneous* goods are those where there are both price and quality variances. For example, home furnishings, shoes, and clothing come into this category. In these cases the buyers will constantly compare and contrast and ultimately balance the interplay between quality and price. In these cases it is important for the buyer to be provided with a wide range of options and sufficient information and guidance to be able to make a final buying decision. *See also* PRICING.

- **Speciality products** are that category of goods that require deep and intensive search, information, comparison, and often trial before a final decision is made. In these cases the purchasing decision can be very complex and time-consuming. Antiques, paintings, expensive jewellery, advanced technical equipment, and certain types of car fall into this category. The quality of the product and how it appeals to the buyer's needs and taste are usually the determinants of final purchase in these categories.

- **Grudge products:** those purchases (or unsought goods) are those goods that buyers have little interest in but which they have to buy. Examples are life assurance, funeral services, and car petrol. The availability of these goods and services is presented to the buyer in various ways, and the buyer comes to perceive that the necessity of buying them is better than the alternative consequences of not buying them.

*Consumer services are also important in relation to consumer products. Consumer goods can be rented in order to avoid the complexity, cost, and risk of buying them individually. For example, a large powered lawnmower, an industrial sander, a holiday home, an expensive car, a marquee tent, or a caravan may all be of too infrequent use and expense to consider outright purchase. Additionally, service such as maintenance contracts and insurance policies are sold relative to consumer goods, particular those with a high chance of mechanical breakdown or risk. Car sales are often of less profit value to a car dealer than the value of regular servicing and maintenance of the car that has been sold.

Product management strategies
Two fundamental issues of *product management are whether to *pioneer* or *follow*, and how to manage the product over its life cycle.

The order of market entry is very important. In fact, the forecasted *market share relative to the pioneering brand is usually greater than follower brands. The pioneering advantage is obtained from both the supply and demand side. From the supply side, there are raw material advantages, better experience effects to provide a *cost advantage, and channel pre-emption. On the demand side, there is the advantage of familiarity, the chance to set a standard, and the choice of perceptual position. Once a firm gains a pioneering advantage, it can maintain it by improving the product, creating a standard, advertising that it was the first, and introducing a new product in the market that may *cannibalize the first but deter other firms from entering. There are also disadvantages to being the pioneer. Being first allows a competitor to leapfrog the early technology. The incumbent develops inertia in its R&D and may not be as flexible as newcomers. Developing an industry has costs that the pioneer must bear alone, and the way the industry develops and its potential size are not deterministic.

There are four classic price/selling effort strategies:

SELLING EFFORT	PRICE	
	LOW	HIGH
LOW	Necessity Goods	Classic Skim Strategy *Vulnerable to new entrants*
HIGH	Classic Penetration Strategy	Luxury Goods

In general, products are clustered in the low-low or high-high categories. If a product is in a mixed category, after introduction it will tend to move to the low-low or high-high one.

Increasing the breadth of the *product line has several advantages. A firm can better serve multiple *segments, it can occupy more of the *distributors' shelf space, it offers customers a more complete selection, and it pre-empts *competition. While a wider range of products will cause a firm to cannibalize some of its own sales, it is better to do so oneself rather than let the competition do it. The drawbacks of broad product lines are reduced volume for each brand (cannibalization), greater manufacturing complexity, increased inventory, more management resources required, more advertising (or less per brand), clutter and confusion in advertising for both customers and distributors. To increase profits from existing brands, a firm can improve its production efficiency or increase the demand through more users, more uses, and more usage. A firm also can defend its existing base through line extensions (expanding on a current brand), *flanker brands (new brands in an existing product area), and *brand extensions.

The task of the marketer is to ensure product relevance (to *customer need) and *differentiation (relative to competing products). Differentiation can be on the basis of features and benefits, design, engineering quality, or services that support the products, such as warranties, installation, and maintenance or price or a combination of all of these.

product segmentation *See* MARKET SEGMENTATION.

product testing Exposing consumers to a new product, in final or *prototype form, so that they might compare it to their usual *brand and rate it. The results of product testing will indicate to the company whether further evaluation of the product in test markets is desirable.

professional advertising Promotions directed toward professionals such as doctors, dentists, and pharmacists, etc., who are in a position to recommend products to their patients or customers.

professional respondent A participant who attends many sessions by volunteering for the recruitment lists of different facilities. Most *moderators seek to eliminate professional respondents from groups, since they do not generally respond in the same objective way that fresh respondents do.

professional services marketing The promotion and development of the ideas and expertise of professional practitioners and their firms, such as lawyers, consultants, accountants, recruiters, architects, real estate surveyors and brokers, investment bankers, physicians and other medical experts, and engineers, as well as other expert professional services. The techniques of professional services marketing are very different from *consumer marketing or *product marketing and require different disciplines.

programme delivery (rate) The percentage of a sample group of people tuned in to a particular programme at a particular time.

promotion *See* ADVERTISING.

promotional product (advertising speciality) A set of *merchandise imprinted with, or otherwise carrying, a logo or promotional message.

promotion plan *See* MARKETING PLAN.

proof points Specific evidence used to substantiate the unique claims found within key *messages and *positioning statements.

propaganda A systematic effort of controlling or manipulating *public opinion or a course of action by using selected facts, ideas, or allegations through *communications media. Propaganda can help to create consent for a cause or a direction, but it can also be used maliciously in the hands of a dictatorial government.

propensity to buy The inclination in the mind of the *prospective customer to buy one product or service as opposed to another, based on a favourable opinion of the *brand, *product or *service, and enhanced by effective *advertising or *public relations. See AIDA; CONSUMER; PURCHASING.

proposal A (usually) written offer from a seller to a *buyer, detailing how the specific product or service can meet the buyer's individual needs and wants. Can be seen as prime sales and marketing document for individual organizations.

proposition The advertising or selling platform which is the basis for a specific *advertising or *product marketing campaign. *See also* VALUE PROPOSITION.

prospect A potential customer who has shown an interest in the company's products and services.

protectionism The government policy of imposing duties or quotas on imports with the purpose of protecting home industries from foreign competition. *See also* EXPORTS; TARIFF CUSTOMS.

prototypes The first version of a product, usually used as a test model for a *test market, on which decisions about its future viability and how it will be marketed will be based.

psychographics A general term to describe and measure the psychological and behavioural characteristics of *consumers. *See also* MARKET SEGMENTATION.

psychographic segmentation *See* MARKET SEGMENTATION.

psychological repositioning *See* BUYER AND BUYING BEHAVIOUR.

publication The act of making information available in the *public domain in a printed or online text or the physical or online text of specific information.

public domain Intellectual property rights available in the public space for public usage which are not owned or controlled by anyone.

publicity A type of *public relations in the form of a news item or story which conveys information about a product, service, or idea in the *media.

public relations

The practice of relating an organization to the public and those who influence the public to ensure mutual understanding and adaptation. Public relations, as a practice and as a profession, has its critics, particularly in a world of manufactured publicity events created for an ulterior purpose, of infomercials, of fictitious letter-writing campaigns, of manufactured celebrities, and political 'spin doctoring' which have disoriented people and created suspicion over what is fact and what is not. Politicians and their parties are seen to be in the grip of public relations, which has greatly increased the sense of distrust that the public has of politicians.

The earliest definitions of public relations emphasized the roles of the press agency and publicity, since these were major elements from which modern public relations grew. As it developed, public relations became a near-scientific discipline, with a strong need for research prior to initiating actions, as well as careful planning and thorough evaluation or measurement of results. Public relations became a continuing, systematic process instead of a one-time or single activity. It became an essential function of business management and public administration. Public relations defined itself through multiple audiences.

The essential elements of public relations are:

- Anticipating, analysing, and interpreting public opinion, attitudes, and issues that might impact, for good or ill, the operations and plans of the organization.
- Counselling management at all levels in the organization with regard to policy decisions, courses of action, and communications, taking into account their public ramifications and the organization's social or citizenship responsibilities.
- Research: determining attitudes and behaviours of the public and their causes in order to plan, implement, and measure activities to influence or change these attitudes and behaviours.
- Media relations: working with communications media in seeking publicity or responding to their interest in an organization.
- Publicity: disseminating planned messages through selected media without payment to further an organization's interest.
- Employee/member relations: responding to concerns and informing and motivating an organization's employees or members and their families.
- Community relations: continuing, planned, and active participation within a community to maintain and enhance its environment to the benefit of both an organization and the community.
- Public affairs: developing effective involvement in public policy, and helping an organization adapt to public expectations.

- Government affairs: communication directly with legislatures and regulatory agencies on behalf of an organization.
- Issues management: identifying and addressing issues of public concern in which an organization is, or should be, concerned.
- Investor relations: creating and maintaining investor confidence and building positive relationships with the financial community.
- Industry relations: communicating with other firms in the industry and with trade associations.
- Fundraising: demonstrating the need for this, and encouraging an organization's members, friends, supporters, and others to voluntarily contribute to support it.
- Special events and public participation: stimulating an interest in a person, product, or organization by means of activities designed to enable an organization to listen to and interact with the public.
- Marketing communications: a combination of activities designed to sell a product, service, or idea, including advertising, collateral materials, publicity, promotion, packaging, point-of-sale display, trade shows, and special events.
- Crisis management: public relations help to protect the present position when an organization is under attack.

As it develops public relations is also taking on multimedia dimensions, making greater use of the *Web to disseminate and control messages. For example, corporate websites display testimonials from satisfied customers, announce new products, services, and prices as well as responding to events. This ability to self-publish on the Web has diminished the need to have journalists write copy.

COMPARISON OF PUBLIC RELATIONS AND ADVERTISING

ADVERTISING	PUBLIC RELATIONS
Space or time in the mass media is paid for by the user.	Coverage in mass media, such as the press, is not paid for.
The advertiser shapes the central message and it is under their control.	The interpretation of the message is in the hands of the media.
The message transmitter controls the timing of the message.	The timing of the message is in the hands of those who control the media.
Tends to use the mass media.	Tends to use more focused forms of communication, such as speaking engagements, community involvement, team or programme sponsorships, lobbying, lecture tours, publicity stunts.

One-way communication—using the mass media is not interactive and does not enable direct and immediate feedback from the target audience.	Two-way communication—public relations venues and communications channels usually allow direct and immediate feedback between the message transmitter and the target audience.
Message sponsor is identified.	Message sponsor is not overtly identified.
The intention of most messages is to inform, persuade, or remind about a product or service or company or organization.	The intention of public relations efforts is often to create goodwill, to keep the company in the minds of the public, or to build or to sustain a reputation.
The public may view the message as 'commercial' because they recognize advertising as an attempt to persuade or, in some cases, 'manipulate' them.	The public often sees public relations messages that have been covered by the media as 'news' and therefore regard it as more neutral or believable.
Is a very powerful tool for creating image.	Can also create image, but not as powerfully as advertising.
Message is usually reductive and writing style is usually persuasive, can be very creative, often taking a conversational tone.	Writing style relies heavily on journalism talents—any persuasion is artfully inserted in the fact-based content such as press releases.

See also BERNAYS, EDWARD L

public relations advertising Promotions by a company that focus on public interest but maintain a relationship to the company's products or agencies. *See also* ADVERTISING; PUBLIC RELATIONS.

public relations consultant A specialist in *public relations, either an individual or part of a PR company, but usually external to the organization served, who provides expertise and programmes in the planning and implementation of public relations to those organizations who do not have relevant internal provision (for example, in a *media crisis situation).

public relations officer An employee within an organization who is designated with responsibility for *public relations with external journalists and other interested parties.

public service advertising (PSA) The use of advertising with a central focus on public welfare, generally sponsored by a *non-profit institution, civic group, religious organization, trade association, or political group.

Pulitzer, Joseph (1847-1911) Hungarian-born American newspaper proprietor. His *New York World* was notably aggressive in its campaigns, perhaps most notably for organized labour, and for war against Spain in the 1890s. He founded the annual Pulitzer Prizes in 1917, which award excellence in American journalism, literature, drama, and music. *See also* HEARST, RANDOLPH; MEDIA POWER.

pull marketing A branch of promotional activity designed to build up *consumer demand by aiming advertising strategically at the prospective target customer, who then demands the product or service from intermediaries such as *retailers and *wholesalers, who then meet the demand via supply from the original company. *See also* PUSH MARKETING.

pullout A loose, removable supplement to a publication, often for advertising or public information purposes.

pulsing The use of advertising in regular intervals, as opposed to seasonal patterns. *See also* FLIGHTING.

pupilometrics A method of advertising research in which a study is conducted on the relationship between a viewer's pupil dilation and the interest factor of visual stimuli.

purchaser (company buyer) The individual within an organization who purchases goods and services for use by that organization. Therefore, this group is often a target of marketers. *See also* BUYER AND BUYING BEHAVIOUR.

purchasing The activity of negotiating and buying goods and services for use by specific organizations. *See also* BUYER AND BUYING BEHAVIOUR.

purchasing power The ability of individuals or organizations to purchase goods or services based on their possession of funds or access to credit. *See also* DISPOSABLE INCOME.

push marketing A promotional activity designed to sell products to retailers and wholesalers, encouraging them to stock up on the products, and promote to prospective consumers anticipating demand.

pyramid selling An illegal manipulative selling programme in which the person at the top makes the most money. For every person recruited to sell items, the person recruiting them receives some portion of the revenues every recruit sells. For the recruited individual to make money, he or she must then recruit others to sell the product. As more and more people are recruited each subsequent level gets wider and wider leading to a pyramid structure in terms of how revenues are distributed.

qualified prospect A potential customer who has been subjected to various probability criteria related to eventual sales. *See also* CUSTOMER; SELLING.

qualitative research A research method based upon subjective evaluations of behaviours, attitudes, or events. Qualitative research techniques include *focus groups. Qualitative research involves a much smaller sample of *respondents and is often used to verify *quantitative research techniques. For example, if buyer statistics show a certain age group favours a particular brand of car, qualitative research will indicate why people are buying this brand. This customer understanding can help to market this brand of automobile. For example, perhaps people buy this brand because it feels more luxurious and comfortable. A marketing campaign on the comfort and the luxury may help bring about further sales. *See also* MARKET RESEARCH; QUANTITATIVE RESEARCH.

quality/price positioning *See* COMPETITION; POSITIONING; PRICING.

quantitative research A research method based upon hard data where there are definitive and absolute answers. Large groups of people can be surveyed and statistics and data can be gathered. Quantitative research is frequently used in conjunction with *qualitative research to provide hard evidence. For example, if *focus groups show that consumers buy a certain brand of automobile because of all the safety features, the researcher may want to gather accident statistics to determine how safe the automobile is. If the statistics show that owners of a certain type of automobile indeed have fewer accidents, then the safety record of the vehicle can be used in an *advertising campaign. *See also* MARKET RESEARCH; QUALITATIVE RESEARCH.

quantity discount A mark-down in price which is given to someone who purchases volumes of same item. Generally, the more someone buys, the greater the discount. This is because the *cost of selling a single unit is greatly decreased since no additional marketing needs to be done to sell the additional units.

questionnaire A set of *questions that is used in *market research to draw conclusions and to collect *data. Questionnaires can be used in both *quantitative as well as *qualitative research depending upon how open-ended the questions are.

questions The linguistic route to gathering knowledge and creation of evidence in the *market research process. Two types of questions are used in market research: open-ended questions and *closed-ended questions. Open-ended questions are used to determine attitudes or opinions. There is not a finite set of answers for open-ended questions. Closed-ended questions require a finite set of answers such as a yes or no or a multiple choice. Closed-ended questions are used to gather statistics and data that can then be used to monitor usage of a product for sales or forecasting purposes. Closed-ended questions are also called structured questions.

quota 1 A number of units or revenue which must be generated by a salesperson.
   2 (market research) A predetermined number of interviews or questionnaires that must be completed. The quota can be defined by the market researcher or by the company requesting the interviews. *See also* MARKET RESEARCH; SALES.

quota sampling *See* SAMPLING.

q

R

radio *See* MEDIA.

random sample *See* MARKET RESEARCH.

random sampling *See* SAMPLING.

rate 1 The amount charged by a *communications medium to an advertiser per unit of space or time purchased. The rate may vary from national to local campaigns, or may be a fixed rate.

  2 To estimate a particular medium's *audience size based on a research sample.

rate card An information card, provided by both *print and *broadcast media, which contains information concerning advertising costs, mechanical requirements, issue dates, closing dates, cancellation dates, and circulation data, etc. *See also* ADVERTISING.

rating point 1 In television, 1% of all TV households who are viewing a particular station at a given time.

  2 In radio, 1% of all listeners who are listening to a particular station at a given time. Both instances vary depending on time of day.

rationalization The concentration of an organization's resources on the products and services which yield the greatest return for the least effort and cost, often to the exclusion of non-profitable products and services.

reach The estimated number of individuals in the audience for a broadcast, or an outdoor ad, that is reached at least once during a specific period of time. *See also* COVERAGE.

readership 1 The total number of *readers of a publication.

  2 The percentage of people that can recall a particular *advertisement, aided or unaided.

readership survey A measurement of the number and *demographics of people who read a *publication, and their opinion of the publication, other than those who directly purchase it. For example, a publication may be bought by one person, but read by five (in a household, club, waiting room, etc.).

rebate The return or refund of part of the price paid for a product or service.

re-branding Marketing a product or service with a new *logo, name, and identity. *See also* BRAND.

recall How much people remember of a specific advertising campaign after the campaign has ended. Recall is a one-dimensional measure of the effectiveness of an ad campaign in *print and *broadcast media. Recall figures can be improved substantially by vast spending. Recall, however, does not measure whether or not the target audience has developed any preference for the *brand advertised.

recession *See* BUSINESS CYCLE.

reciprocal trading Commercial dealings between organizations for mutual benefit where each can be, at different times, both *buyer and *seller.

recognition testing The ability of research subjects to recall a particular *advert, *brand, or *campaign when they see or hear it under test conditions.

recovery *See* BUSINESS CYCLE.

recruitment advertising *See also* ADVERTISING.

recruitment marketing The application of the full *marketing mix to target the recruitment of desired personnel for a company or organization. Examples may be a graduate recruitment campaign for a management consultancy firm or a campaign to attract new military recruits.

redemption The exchange of vouchers or coupons for a stated benefit or product.

red goods Those food products that are consumed quickly, replaced frequently, and which have a low profit margin. *See also* BROWN GOODS; ORANGE GOODS; PRODUCT; WHITE GOODS.

reductionism The theory that complex ideas or systems can be reduced to simpler, understandable components. *Advertising copy is an example of reductionism at work, in which complex products, services, or ideas are reduced to their key elements of value.

reference group (control group) A baseline group used for marketing or research purposes. All other groups are then compared to the reference group.

reference price The price that the consumer holds in their mind as the baseline point for the appropriate price of a product or service, based on an often indistinct memory of past purchases and prices or comparable products and services. *See also* PRICING.

referral A recommendation by a current user of a product of another potential customer. Referrals are the most effective form of *advertising since the recommendation is based upon personal experience.

regional market A population in a particular area having characteristics that are distinguishable from other areas. A region can either be part of a nation state or a cluster of nation states (for example western Europe).

registered design A piece of *intellectual property that is licensed, so that only the person who owns the licence can use the design. *See also* TRADEMARK.

registered trademark A distinctive sign or *logo officially registered with an appropriate authority by its owner in order to protect the visual identity of the product or organization, and to prevent fraud, misuse, or theft of the trademark by other organizations or individuals. *See also* BRAND; LOGO.

regression analysis A research method used to study the relationship between several independent variables and a dependent variable. For example, two individuals can have the same amount in terms of disposable income, but one individual could have a family to support while another individual may not. These variable factors can affect how much money the individual would choose to spend on new goods and services.

regulation of advertising *See* ADVERTISING.

Reilly's Law (Law of Retail Gravitation) The concept, put forward by William Reilly in 1931, suggesting that the relationship between the variables of *retail sales, population concentration, and travel distance tolerance, is determined primarily by the size of the city: the larger the city, the larger the surrounding trade area, the more willing are consumers to travel to buy from *retail outlets in a large city, than they would be to travel to retail outlets in a smaller city or town.

relationship marketing The process of meeting *customers' needs on a continuous and repeating basis by developing a long-term, *one to one relationship with individual customers. Relationship marketing is more prevalent in services businesses than in *product businesses. The philosophy of relationship marketing recognizes that keeping existing customers happy, loyal, and satisfied ensures repeat business and is much cheaper than obtaining new customers. It is an approach that takes the long-term profit potential of an existing customer relationship into account. There is maximum emphasis on customer commitment, contact, keeping promises, and building trust. Contact happens at multiple levels in the organization under a regime of customer account management.

Relationship marketing is distinguished from other types of marketing by a focus on customer outcomes and benefits rather than just selling product features. The relationship marketer must always take the long-term view of the customer relationship. It is an older style of marketing which got lost during the mass production age and which is being revived in the information age. In the past, salespeople or retail store staff accomplished much on an individual basis when confined to a physical local environment. Today, interactive technologies make it possible to perform similar functions online. The *Web allows companies to track *consumer preferences closely, both by asking the consumer directly and by auditing the consumer's actions as they surf the company *website. This information can be used as a basis for providing a product or service that is customized to the consumer's preferences. With web technologies, a consumer's preferences can be polled during visits. The polled information can instantly be used to customize the product to meet the consumer's preferences—all in the same session. However, true relationship marketing cannot rely on these techniques alone and needs to be complemented with direct human interaction. *See also* CUSTOMER LIFETIME VALUE; CUSTOMIZED MARKETING; PERMISSION MARKETING; SELLING.

relative market share *See* COMPETITIVE POSITION.

relaunch A new presentation of a product, service, organization, or individual that was previously known to the *marketplace. A product can be relaunched if the first launch was not as successful as hoped.

relevancy The degree of importance that consumers give to a specific product or service, depending on the level of *customization to their individual needs.

reliability The length of time that a product will last before it breaks down or needs repairs.

remainder Products that are in surplus because they have fallen below current demand for the product and are therefore sold off at reduced prices, for example unsold books in a bargain bookshop.

renewal rate The percentage of individuals that renew their print media subscriptions to extend beyond the previous expiration date.

repeat purchase The process of buying the same products from the same supplier for convenience, and is usually for frequent, low cost purchases. *See also* BUYING; INERTIA SELLING.

repertory grids *See* LELLY TRIADS.

repositioning A dramatic change in how something is presented to the external *marketplace. A product may be repositioned to sell to a different audience. *See also* BUYER AND BUYING BEHAVIOUR; POSITIONING.

reputation effect The behaviours and responses among interested parties, for example customers or shareholders, to the understood or perceived qualities of a *brand, product, service, individual, or organization. *See also* BRAND.

reputation management The systematic and programme-based approach to the management of the organization and individual's *image, *brand, standing among peers and *competitors, attractiveness, and other components that constitute a relevant reputation. This is a similar approach to managing a physical asset, but with different methods and techniques to compensate for this being an intangible asset. The process involves constantly monitoring reputation with the public and the customers within the *target market, analysing the issues and gaps between the existing reputation and the desired reputation, and then taking measures to fill the gaps.

research brief A short paper where *data and statistics are used to explain things. Typically research briefs are not very in-depth but only give an overall view or impression of the deeper survey. See MARKET RESEARCHS.

research design The detailed planning of the different stages of a research project, including developing the overall strategy, collecting and analysing opinion and evidence, and then publicising results. See MARKET RESEARCH.

research ethics The agreed principles and rules within which the research will be conducted. For example, researchers may guarantee non-disclosure of the *respondent's name when returning the survey results to the individual client who commissioned the research. See MARKET RESEARCH.

research proposal A document prepared by a *research agency for a prospective *customer outlining in detail the programmes of research, its objectives, its methodology, and project timescales and costs that the agency proposes to carry out on behalf of the customer. See MARKET RESEARCH.

reserve price The minimum price which a seller is prepared to accept for an item, usually at an *auction.

residuals A sum paid to a performer on a TV or radio commercial each time it is run.

respondent (experimental unit, participant, subject, unit, unit of analysis) The person being interviewed or surveyed.

response bias An error that results from the tendency of people to answer a question falsely, through deliberate misrepresentation or unconscious falsification. See MARKET RESEARCH.

response elasticity The extent to which the *consumer market can be increased by the effect of stimuli such as an *advertising campaign. See also ADVERTISING.

response handling A service to deal with the enquiries that result from a specific marketing campaign.

response rate The percentage of *respondents relative to the total number contacted who replied to a survey or questionnaire or *advertising campaign.

retail audit A critical assessment of a company's total retailing effort to establish if the customers' needs are being met and fulfilled by the current retail operation and marketing.

retailer cooperative A voluntary contractual marketing system led by a group of retailers.

retail franchise The selling rights, provided by a franchising company with a recognized *brand, *products, and *services (for example McDonald's, Starbucks, Body Shop, Costa Coffee) in return for a fee based on a percentage of the franchisee's takings.

retailing The sales activities involved in selling goods or services directly to final consumers for their personal, non-business use. Retailers are powerful intermediaries that purchase goods from wholesalers, or in some cases, directly from producers and sell directly to the end *customer. The retailer is the main executor of the overall *marketing mix. *See also* CONSUMER MARKETING; DISTRIBUTION.

retail mix The mix of variables, including *location, *merchandising, *communications, *pricing, *services, physical attributes, and personnel, which form the overall strategic marketing components of retailing.

retail outlet The physical location of a retail operation where goods are sold directly to consumers. The location, decor, *merchandise, and supply and *sales operations of the retail outlet are vital to its overall *brand.

retail price index (RPI) (Cost of Living Index) A measure of the average, month-by-month changes in the price of a notional average 'shopping basket' of standard household goods in locations around the UK.

retail pricing *See* PRICING.

retail promotion A communication from the retailer to its *target market with an enticement to the individual customers, for example a cut-price sales promotion within a given date, or a multi-purchase promotional offer. *See* BOGOFF.

retail therapy *See* CONSUMER SOCIETY.

retro marketing The targeting and marketing of *customized products to individuals who have a nostalgia for styles and products of the past, or things which evoke a bygone era, for example 1950s' style fridges, radios, and cars, with modern technology below a traditional design.

retrospective analysis A critical examination of a marketing campaign, event, publication, or product launch after the process is completed. Sometimes called a 'post mortem'.

return days The number of days in which an affiliate can still earn commission on a conversion (sale or lead) by a referred visitor.

return on investment (ROI) The benefits gained from expenditure on total marketing spend or on specific marketing programmes. Marketing is notoriously difficult to reduce to a financial ROI because so many of the benefits are intangible and qualitative. However, the *Web affords many opportunities for greater measurement of marketing effectiveness than traditional marketing.

reverse engineering The stripping down of a competitor product to see how it is made, then searching out improvements. Originally a term used in computer science where a system is analysed to understand how its parts fit into the whole. The opposite of forward engineering, where individual parts are used to make a system.

reverse pricing model The *buying process in which a buyer defines requirements and issues them to suppliers in the form of a tender and the suppliers bid competitively for the buyer's custom. *See also* DUTCH AUCTION.

RFID (Radio Frequency Identification) A device, usually in the form of a tag, attached or built into a product, or even animal, which allows tracking of its movement. Commonly used in a *supply chain operation or in *retailing for security purposes.

rich media A *multimedia format that offers an enhanced experience relative to older, mainstream formats. New formats are regularly being introduced and old formats become part of the mainstream (or disappear altogether). Standard graphic formats such as JPEG and GIF would not be considered rich media. Some popular formats commonly considered rich media include Macromedia *flash and Shockwave, along with various audio and video formats.

Riefenstahl, Leni (1902–2003) German photographer and film director. A highly controversial figure, whose involvement in the Nazi regime is still actively debated, she is particularly remembered for two films, *Olympia* (1938), a dazzling portrayal of the 1936 Olympics (notable also for showing Hitler's anger at the black US athlete Jesse Owen's gold medal-winning performance), and *The Triumph of the Will* (1934), her film about the Nazi party rally at Nuremberg, which glorifies Hitler. In the film, one of the shrewdest blends of documentary and propaganda ever made, Riefenstahl emphasizes the emotional over the rational: Hitler is not a political figure but has godlike qualities of leadership. The rally is a spectacle designed to appeal to the subjugation of the individual to that of the serried ranks of the national consciousness. Riefenstahl subsequently described the film as a blight on her life ('it casts such a shadow over my life that death will be a blessed relief'), but its influence has been long-lasting. Riefenstahl later became a distinguished documentary film maker, making films of African tribes and underwater photography. *See also* GOEBBELS, JOSEF; PROPAGANDA.

rifle shot approach A description of a *niche marketing approach where maximum impact is gained by targeting a very precise *message or offer to a very precisely defined *target market or *customer group. The opposite is called the 'blunderbuss approach'. *See also* MICROMARKETING.

rip-o-matic A very rough rendition of a proposed ad composed of images and sounds borrowed (ripped-off) from other commercials or broadcast materials.

ripple effect The gradual spread of awareness among potential customers of a product or service. *See also* VIRAL MARKETING; WORD OF MOUTH.

roll-out A phrase for the implementation of a service or product launch. Generally, a region or portion of the population is chosen so there can be more control over the supply and demand of the product or service.

Rothermere, Viscount *See* NORTHCLIFFE.

rotoscoping The process of using live and animated characters within an advertisement.

rough An unfinished layout of an ad which shows only a general conception to be presented for analysis, criticism, and approval.

rough cut A preliminary arrangement of film or tape shots that are roughly edited together without voice-over or music in the early stages of editing.

RSS (really simple syndication) (web feed) An online service that keeps the subscriber constantly updated on changes in favourite *websites usually via a newsreader, such as *Google Reader. These newsreaders allow the user to see summaries and updates of all their information feeds in a single location. Instead of visiting multiple *web pages to check for new content, the user can look at the summaries and choose which sites to visit for the full versions.

RSS has an integral part to play in the *marketing of *publications: *headlines and links to articles and updates can be communicated instantly to subscribers without having to *email links and updates. These feeds are often delivered by a *news aggregator. RSS is more automated than e-mail: the sending and receiving of content can be done automatically with minimal set up and little maintenance. Being a much more dynamic link than, say, a static *bookmark or a *link to a single *web page, RSS can help to keep awareness of a *product or *service constant and widespread and fresh. RSS has enabled the web to become more dynamic.

For the recipient of *online content, RSS is a vehicle that allows content which they have requested to be delivered to a computer, or mobile device, as soon as it is published or updated. For the producer of online content, RSS is a way to 'syndicate' content, such as news to multiple users. Many types of content can be distributed by RSS feeds: for example, *news, stock prices, product news, web publications, discussion *blogs, blog posts, and software announcements and *podcasts. These can now be delivered to mobile devices with *Internet access, which opens up wide possibilities for both *mass marketing and *targeted marketing. RSS has its own icon which is now universally recognized . *See also* WEB 2.0.

Rubicam, Raymond (1892–1978) Young & Rubicam. An NW Ayer & Son copywriter in Philadelphia, Rubicam demonstrated leadership, teaching and supervisory gifts. His Squibb, Rolls-Royce, and Steinway work fuelled Ayer's success. In 1923, denied a partnership, he and his colleague, John Orr Young, opened Young & Rubicam. Y&R embodied a 'creative revolution' by focusing on creative excellence. With radio's arrival, Y&R produced popular shows with Jack Benny and Arthur Godfrey. Rubicam resigned from George Washington Hill's $3 m Pall Mall cigarettes account rather than replace a creative team. He instituted Y&R research, a trust fund, profit-sharing and bonuses, and was recognized as 'advertising's statesman.'

run-of-network An online ad-buying option in which ad placements may appear on any pages on sites within an ad network. Run-of-network buys are similar to run-of-site buys, except the ads appear on many sites instead of an individual site. *See also* ADVERTISING; MEDIA.

run-of-paper An ad-buying option where ads can appear anywhere in a given publication. *See also* ADVERTISING; MEDIA.

run-of-press (ROP) A newspaper publisher's option to place an ad anywhere in the publication that they choose, as opposed to preferred position.

run-of-schedule (ROS) A TV station's option to place a commercial in any time slot that they choose.

run-of-site An ad-buying *Internet option in which ad placements may appear on any pages of the target site, with advertisers generally giving up authority over placement in return for low rates and broad reach. Ads may be placed randomly in unsold, less valuable portions of the target site. Run-of-site is similar to *run-of-network, except the ads appear on an individual site instead of many sites.

run-of-week spot An agreement whereby a *TV company agrees to run a specific commercial at a time during a given week but cannot specify the exact time, and as a result a discount price is offered to the media buyer.

rushes *See* DAILIES.

r

sale or return An agreement that the price will be refunded if the goods are returned in saleable condition within the pre-agreed time.

sales

Direct personal selling particularly in the sale of products, services and in *business-to-business marketing. There are two types of sales: direct and indirect sales. While transactional and commodity sales are mainly done through indirect sales channels, such as the Web, or telephone sales, larger, more complex sales are done through direct personal sales channels. Personal selling, combining the cost and training of a salesman, together with his relative lack of coverage and high compensation plans, makes direct selling the most expensive way to sell, but in some ways the most valuable. On average 80% of sales calls are made by a direct sales force, but 20% of sales are made by indirect sales. Also, the cost of an individual sales call has risen gradually. Consequently, it is important to get the most out of sales calls and this has caused greater professionalization in the selection and training of salespeople. The role of sales relative to *marketing has long been a thorny issue. Sales is actually a type of marketing done at the level of individuals or groups of customers: it is not separate from marketing.

sales aid Any item which helps in the selling of a product or service, for example leaflet, DVD, promotional video, presentation, or free sample.

sales analysis A control measure that analyses sales orders by region, product, customer, and market over a given period.

sales branch The supplier's office established to facilitate sales in a specific territory.

sales calling A part of *sales management: the number of times that a salesperson will call a customer over a given time period, either by a direct visit or by telephone. This requires a prioritization of the importance of customers, as well as good pre-planning and effective execution of the sales call. Sales calling can also be divided into calling on existing customers and calling on new prospects.

sales campaign The implementation of all the planned stages in a campaign to acquire a new customer or to sell to an existing customer.

sales concept The orientation of an organization that emphasizes aggressive selling to achieve company objectives. This orientation is often seen to be at odds with the *marketing concept, because companies that have this orientation often resort to *high pressure selling and manipulative sales techniques to win business and recruit salespeople who are very short-term and transactional results-orientated, often to the detriment of long-term relationships with customers.

sales contest A form of motivational incentive aimed at members of a company's *sales force. These are competitions designed to boost sales and lift performance by offering awards or prizes to top achievers in a sales team in a given period. They also encourage competition between salespeople. Most companies with field sales forces offer all-expenses-paid holidays to their salespeople who have reached defined *sales quotas. Such a system becomes a major incentive to salespeople to reach their quotas in order to avoid the stigma of missing the holiday with their successful sales peers.

sales conversion rate The sales percentage achieved in proportion to *customer leads followed up or visits made.

sales coverage The extent to which prospective customers are reachable by *selling agents or *retail outlets.

sales effectiveness The success of the seller at each stage of the consumer's *buying process, with the aim of selling effectively within the timescale, and profitably.

sales force The generic name given to the direct sales channel of a company. Their territories and their targets define sales forces. Sales forces can be combinations of types of salespeople: for example, account managers, who manage existing customer accounts and who are looking to constantly expand sales in that account; new account salespeople, whose main focus is winning new accounts and beating the competitors; sales support, who are experts in product or service and who act as auxiliaries to the sales force but do not carry a commission-based *sales quota; telesales, for transactional sales that do not require a *direct sales force. This is also known as the *sales force mix*.

sales force composite A simple sales forecasting method that estimates future demand for a product or service by aggregating what each member of the *sales force expects to be able to sell in his or her territory.

sales forecast An estimation of the projected volume of sales, measured in either money or units, for a future planning period. Sales forecasting is usually done on the basis of past trends, sales force estimations, surveys of consumer buying intentions, managerial judgement, or quantitative models.

sales incentive An award or bonus offered to a seller in order to encourage performance and increase sales.

sales kit A collection of sales materials, such as manuals, brochures, calendars, posters, adverts, etc., prepared to explain a particular product or service promotion to retailers or other customers.

sales lead An individual, organization, or business that might be a likely prospect for the company's product or service. A lead may, with further qualification, become a *prospect, prior to becoming a full customer.

sales literature Printed material for external use, usually prepared by marketing, consisting of *brochures, *catalogues, *price lists, presentations, and videos to be used to assist the selling process.

sales management The management of *salespeople, involving balancing objective and *target setting, allocation of *sales territory, sales performance management, overseeing sales calling patterns, accompanying salespeople on major calls, overseeing sales budgets, selection and coaching of salespeople, keeping salespeople motivated, setting and allocating compensation targets, and sharing success.

sales penetration The degree to which sales of a product or service have reached the total possible potential within the *marketplace.

sales pitch The detailed content, line of argument, and general theme or idea of a salesperson's presentation of a product or service to the prospective customer.

sales planning A detailed assessment of the current situation in a sales region, the setting of objectives, the formulation of strategies and tactics, and the establishment of control and evaluation procedures. This may also involve account planning, which is a detailed strategy and plan to enhance sales to individual customers.

sales platform The core selling proposition on which a specific campaign is based.

sales potential An organization's expected sales of a product or service in a given *market for a specified period and against installed *competition; the share of the total market that a company can expect to attain in a given time.

sales presentation The salesperson's demonstration or display of a product, service, and concept to a *prospective buyer in order to make a sale. This can either be done formally as a set-piece presentation or informally.

sales promotion A direct inducement to buy, either by offering added value or a direct incentive to the *indirect sales channel (such as *retailers and resellers), the *direct sales force itself, or from the *sales force to the consumers. The promotions are usually a range of tactical marketing techniques, within a larger strategic marketing framework, that incentivize the sale of products and services in order to achieve specific sales and marketing objectives. These wider objectives might be:

- to add appeal to the product brand and enhance its image;
- to encourage trial or repeat purchase;
- to defend the product from competition;
- to encourage customer loyalty and repeat purchase;
- to increase sales and market penetration;
- to identify and attract new customers;
- to educate customers regarding product improvements or new product introductions;
- to bring more customers into retail stores;
- to stabilize inventories or to obtain more and better retail shelf space and displays.

There are various types of sales promotion which could include *trade shows, *exhibitions, *point-of-sale retail displays, personality *endorsements (such as book signings), attractive *packaging, *sponsorships, special offers, customer demonstrations with giveaways, contests and games, gifts, free products, extra *products, *rebates and *price discounts, buy-one-get-one-free (*BOGOFF) combinations, straightforward cash incentives (such as 'cash back' on new mortgages and credit cards), *loyalty points or stamps, free services, savings schemes, buy-back guarantees, low-interest financing of the sale, and trade-in allowances on the old product. Sales promotions need to be legal; some, such as *pyramid selling, are not.

sales quotas The volume targets set for *salespeople stating the amount they should sell and how sales should be divided among the company's products and services.

sales ratio A measure used to determine whether the cost of selling in a given period was excessive. Total expenditure on sales is expressed as a percentage of total sales revenue for the same period. The ratio of promotions to sales is another measure used to determine whether the amount spent on sales promotion was excessive. Total expenditure on *sales promotion in a given period is expressed as a percentage of total sales revenue for the same period.

sales report A salesperson's detailed record of sales calls and results for a given period. Typically, a sales report will include information such as the sales volume per product or service line, the number of existing and new accounts called upon, and the expenses incurred in making the calls.

sales representative The specialist sales person who sells their company's product or service directly to the customer, usually responsible for a specific geographical area, and aiming to secure orders.

sales research The examination of methods and work practices in both the office and field environments in order to establish how to increase sales force productivity.

sales-response function The effect of *advertising on total sales. Often used as a measure of advertising return.

sales target A company's forecast of measurable number of sales.

sales technique The methods that a *salesperson uses from initial contact with a *prospect through to closing the sale and often including long-term *account management. Sales technique has attracted an enormous body of literature, which testifies to the continuing importance of personal selling in the economy. The time-honoured fundamentals of good selling technique are: being able to build rapport and relationships with customers and prospects; ability to qualify sales situations and customers very early; persuasion skills, especially in the advancement of proposition and presentation; sensitive and rational objection handling; good call planning and execution; advanced customer listening skills; being able to understand situations from the customers' point of view; negotiation skills, particularly taking the customer to a place where he feels that he has benefited from the sale; good time management and organization; being personable and easy to do business with; and very importantly, the ability to close a sale and win the order.

sales territory The allocated geographical area for which a salesperson is responsible to achieve measurable sales targets and objectives. Sales territories tend to be allocated by *sales managers and do not necessarily accord with market segments as defined by marketers. Most sales managers favour managing sales territories on a geographical basis, rather than *market segments, but some also do it on the basis of customer accounts or by product or service types. Territorial salespeople analyse their territory, work out their sales schedules, and customer-calling patterns and frequencies. They tend to represent all of the company's products and services to customers in that territory.

sales testing *See* ADVERTISING.

sales volume An organization's total sales, in terms of units or revenue, for a specified period. Sales volume (by sales region or territory, industry, customer type, etc.) is commonly used as an aid in determining the effectiveness of the selling effort.

sample A portion of the population which is used to study behaviours, attitudes, or events. Determining the proper sample size is crucial for delivering accurate research results.

sampling The method by which the sample is selected. There are two major types of sampling: probability and non-probability.

Probability sampling is where every element of the population has an equal chance of being part of the sample. Common types of probability sampling include random sampling, systematic sampling, stratified sampling, and cluster sampling.

- *Random sampling* is typically done by computer-generated random numbers. Phone calls can be made with a random number dialler. A random sample is based upon chance where each element has equal weighting. Random samples can be used for both *quantitative and *qualitative research.
- *Systematic sampling* starts with a random number and then every nth number after that becomes part of the sample population. For example, if there is a total population of 100 and the researcher decided to look at 10% of the population, there would be a random number drawn, say 45. Then the researcher would choose every 10th number until you reach your sample size. So a systematic sample would be: 45, 55, 65, 75, 85, 95, 05, 15, 25, and 35.
- *Stratified sampling* is used to ensure the sample size is representative of the larger population. For example, in a population of 100, there are 60 men and 40 women. If 10 people are needed, then it is necessary to make sure that 6 are men and 4 are women in order to have the same ratio in the sample size. A random or systematic approach is then used to choose the 6 men and 4 women.
- *Cluster sampling* is used when there are many people to be interviewed in order to save time and money. For example, if all chief purchasing officers in the Fortune 500 companies were to be interviewed, the researcher could group all the chief purchasing officers in each company into a cluster and treat each individual company as one single entity. Then companies would be chosen based upon a random or systematic approach and the researcher would then interview the purchasing officers within the selected companies. If the researcher interviewed all the purchasing officers within the company, it would be a single-stage cluster sample. If the researcher broke down the list of purchasing officers within the selected company and used a random or systematic approach to interview a subset of those individuals, this would be a two-stage sample.

Non-probability sampling is where certain elements of a population will have a greater chance of being selected than others. *Respondents are chosen with some subjectivity because the interviewer feels they are representative of the population they are trying to survey. Types of non-probability sampling include: quota sampling, convenience sampling, judgemental sampling, snowball design, as well as self-selection.

- In *quota sampling*, a quota is determined by what the population at large is composed of. For example, someone may want to interview 100 shoppers. If 10% of the shopping population is determined to be male and elderly, the interviewer must then interview 10 elderly, male shoppers.

- *Convenience sampling* is where an interviewer will talk to anyone at random who is willing to stop and be interviewed. This is sometimes mistaken as random sampling; however, it never provides a true random sample of the population since there will be a much higher probability of bias and skewed results. Convenience sampling is often used as a pre-test to a questionnaire to determine if the questions are understandable and produce the desired results.

- *Judgemental sampling* occurs when the researcher uses his expert opinion to determine what would constitute a representative sample. Judgemental sampling is typically more biased. For example, if someone chooses to interview the shoppers in the middle of a working week during the day, it is more likely that business people would not be well represented. However, sometimes it may be the intent of the interviewer to interview more housewives or retired people since they are the ones who may be doing the bulk of the shopping. In addition, if the sample size is very small and limited to a few people, a judgemental sample may deliver more representative results than a probability sample. In the shopping centre example, the interviewer may deliberately choose to question one businessperson, one student, one retiree, and one housewife. A random or probability sample of four people would most likely not produce a businessperson to be interviewed.

- *Snowball design* is a type of judgemental sampling where the respondents are then asked to identify additional candidates to be interviewed. This method is very useful for identifying very specialized groups of people to be interviewed where it would otherwise take a great deal of research to identify these individuals.

- *Self-selection* sampling occurs when the respondent makes the decision whether or not to participate in the survey.

satellite broadcasting *See* MEDIA.

saturation coverage Short-term, intensive, usually expensive but effective and far reaching advertising.

saturation point The point at which further marketing of a product or service brings no new customers.

Schwerin test A research method for observing the changes *respondents make to their ranking of products after being exposed to *advertising.

scientific marketing 1 An approach based on a systematic and fact-based method that will help to maximize profits for a product or service. This discipline of marketing relies heavily on empirical data, trend forecasting, and directly measurable results. It is the point where marketing meets mathematical modelling.
2 The process and techniques of marketing of scientific innovation, research, or services.

screening 1 The examination of a population based upon certain criteria to determine the suitability of an individual for a product or service.
2 A preliminary set of research questions that are asked to determine if the *respondents are suitable for a particular study. Screening is done at the beginning of the entire interview process.

search engine An application programme on the *World Wide Web that seeks out and indexes documents, then attempts to match documents relevant to a user's search requests. A search engine powers the search process and provides results for a search destination. A search destination can use its own engine, a third-party engine, or a combination. Knowing the difference between an engine and a destination is important when submitting URLs; a destination using its own engine can accept direct submissions, while a destination using external engines may or may not provide a submission option. *See also* BROWSER; GOOGLE; SPIDER; APPENDIX 2.

search engine marketing A set of methods using *search engines to attract and reach prospective customers. The aim is for the desired organization, product, service, or *keyword to appear as near to the top of the first page of the list of the search result.

search engine optimization The process of choosing targeted *keyword phrases related to a site, and ensuring that the site places well when those keyword phrases are part of a *Web search. Optimization involves making pages readable to search engines and emphasizing key topics related to your content. Basic optimization may involve nothing more than ensuring that a site does not unnecessarily become part of the invisible Web (the portion of the Web not accessible through web search engines). Advanced optimization may include significant research into every element of page design, content messages, site structure, and off-the-page criteria.

search engine spam The excessive manipulation to influence search engine rankings, often for pages of little or no relevant content. *See also* BLACK HAT SEO.

search engine submission The act of supplying a *URL to a *search engine in an attempt to make a search engine aware of a site or page.

search spy A perpetually refreshing page that provides a real-time view of actual *Web searches.

seasonal demand A type of *demand relevant to specific times of year, for example barbeques or parasols in summer, and snow shovels and woollen gloves in winter.

seasonal rating adjustments (broadcast media) Rating modifications that reflect changes in the season, e.g. weather and holidays.

secondary data Research data that is collected through a third party. This is different from *primary data where the data is collected specifically for the research project.

secondary research Research using information that has already been compiled and formatted. It is different from *primary research, which is also known as original research. Analysis is frequently done with research that has been provided by a third party. This is also known as *syndicated research. Other sources for secondary research include investment banks and associations or organizations. In research, it is important to assess the secondary information that exists before time and money is spent to conduct new research. Since primary research takes a much longer time to complete and is extremely expensive, decisions are often made to go with whatever secondary research is available in the interest of both time and money. A good secondary researcher will be able to suggest proxies or alternatives in lieu of performing primary research.

second generation product A product developing on from, and eventually taking over from, one already available, for example in the rapidly evolving field of electronics or technology.

segment A small distinct group within a large one, with distinctive and identifiable characteristics and behaviours. *See also* MICROSEGMENTATION; NICHE.

segmentation *See* MARKETING PLAN; MARKETING STRATEGY; MARKET SEGMENTATION.

selective demand advertising The promotion of a particular manufacturer's *brand as opposed to a *generic product. *See* PRIMARY DEMAND ADVERTISING.

selective positioning 1 The maintenance of a specific place in a given *advertising medium aimed at a specific audience.

2 The process of deciding what *market segment, and what needs and wants within it to aim for, in order to gain the desired *position in the mind of the consumer.

self image One's perception of oneself, and one's perception of how one is seen by others.

self-selection *See* SAMPLING.

self service A retail situation where customers serve themselves directly from the *merchandise and pay at a designated point, for example cafeteria, petrol station, or supermarket.

sell-by date A date printed on a perishable produce indicating the date by which it can be legally sold.

sellers' market A market where there are more people interested in buying a product and where demand outstrips supply. The seller is almost guaranteed to be able to sell the product at any price.

selling-in The process of educating the *sales force and distributors to sell a new product as part of the preparation for its *launch. This process involves presentations, the development of *sales kits, briefings on the *target market and competition, and outlining the organization's plans to create *consumer demand.

semantic differential A method of examining the strengths and weaknesses of a product or company versus the *competition by having *respondents rank it between dichotomous pairs of words or phrases that could be used to describe it; the mean of the responses is then plotted in a profile or image.

service delivery *See* SERVICES MARKETS.

service guarantee A formal written assurance that a product or service will perform according to specification for the agreed time.

service level agreement *See* SLA.

service quality The consumer's subjective, perceived impression of the standards of an organization's service to its public.

services marketing The active marketing of something that is intangible and which is usually consumed at the point of delivery. Services can cover a wide range of offerings and be delivered by the same company or organization: professional services, customer services, medical services, entertainment services, personal care services, maintenance services. Services marketing has a different range of techniques and challenges from other forms of traditional marketing. *See also* SERVICES MARKETS.

Key elements of services marketing:

1 People: in services businesses the delivered quality of many services depends on the quality of the people delivering it. *See also* INTERNAL MARKETING in this entry.

2 Physical evidence: given the intangible nature of services it is important to constantly illustrate the benefits with tangible evidence of success, for example customer reference sites where the application of the services have been successful.

3 Delivery processes: how the service is actually delivered can define the marketing programmes and the overall branding of the company.

The four core marketing management tasks for service marketers are:

1 Managing differentiation against competitors. Customers make fewer price comparisons with services than they do with products, but they do consider differentiation and unique qualities, particularly delivery and quality of the people delivering the service.

2 Managing the overall brand image. The customer's perception of the company is a critical factor when deciding to buy a service. Without a good reputation, it is impossible to have powerful services marketing programmes.

3 Managing the quality of service delivered to customers and setting their expectations. Customers view services as having variable and inconsistent quality. It is important to invest time in reducing the customer's uncertainty and only to promise what can be delivered, to avoid disappointment and loss of reputation and trustworthiness.

4 Managing communications: use clear, unambiguous messages to communicate the range, depth, quality, and level of services. Messages should emphasize the benefits of the services rather than their technical details. Build on word of mouth communication from one satisfied customer to another.

services markets

A market structure providing services which do not involve industry or manufacture, for example catering, health, travel, retailing, entertainment, or education and the delivery of which includes a human factor. Services are the fastest growing in the developed world. Two-thirds of the GNP of the advanced economies is derived from services. Services markets are characterized by their heterogeneity: services can range from plastic surgery to travel reservations to hotels to outsourcing information technology services to leading a major law suit conducted on behalf of a major corporation. Services are also integral to products; there is a huge service sector dedicated to the care and maintenance of tangible products and physical assets such as janitorial functions, cleaning, storage, and maintenance. There are multiple services—business services—that happen within organizations that are not run as external businesses. There is a growing range of services that are moved from inside a company to be handled by external contractors—outsourcing services. The worldwide expansion of *leasing, *franchising and rentals business—from cars to aircraft to domestic appliances to fast food and personal care outlets—has added further growth. Deregulation of state-owned *monopolies, utilities, and capital markets, most of which are service providers, caused a huge explosion in the competitive services market. Also, we are also seeing the early stages of globalization in services businesses, some enabled by the *World Wide Web, which were once thought to be intensely local activities. Service marketing is now a major discipline in the overall marketing range of techniques and is radically different from *product marketing. It came late to the marketing table, long after *consumer goods, and a generation after *industrial marketing. Professional services marketing was the latest entrant, following a period of restrictions, some self-imposed, upon the marketing of professional expertise. From the early 1980s onwards restrictions on *advertising accountancy and legal, medical, optometry, architectural services were removed. Also, the entire field of services marketing has been broadened by the needs of the *non-profit services, such as charities and public services, and of franchises, which are burgeoning worldwide.

Some areas of the services growth that have affected marketing are: the World Wide Web, which enables interactive marketing of services to customers; customer care centres; the greater involvement of customers in self service (such as personal banking and investment); and the massively increased ability to gather, store, and use customer information. In essence a service is a benefit that one party brings to another that is neither tangible nor separable, neither standardized nor storable. These characteristics determine the various mixes and approaches to marketing as well as setting new, non-traditional challenges. Service marketers are particularly challenged to make a service *differentiated, often by linking it to tangible evidence of its outcome, to manage fluctuations in demand and to ensure good service delivery quality.

The following are characteristics of services:

- *intangibility* Services disappear at the point of consumption and they cannot be possessed. Often the results are intangible, or at least not visible. Therefore, for services marketing the normal tools of promotion are not usable to create an abiding memory of the service brand: patenting is impossible and quality of delivery is variable because delivered mainly by people.

- *inseparability* The production and the consumption of a service are usually simultaneous and inseparable (e.g. entertainment). Services are often sold before they are produced (e.g. travel). People usually deliver services, therefore direct selling and delivery is the only channel that can be used.

- *heterogeneity* Because people largely deliver services, it is impossible to standardize them; there are multiple variances in the type and the delivery of service. Marketers can often turn this to their advantage, as there is always a price premium for customization.

- *perishability* Services cannot be stored and displayed permanently. This is a major problem for service providers who cannot get full utilization (e.g. in professional services) of their services or spaces (e.g. aircraft seats, hotel rooms, theatre seats) that they are selling. Marketing of these services, therefore, needs to constantly cope with permanence of supply, but with huge variations in demand.

- *ownership* Unlike products, services do not result in a transfer of property ownership. *See also* SERVICES MARKETING.

- *service delivery* involves the customer directly on many occasions: ordering a meal, using electronic banking, specifying a hairstyle, loading and unpacking groceries through a check-out, showing potential buyers around a house for sale, helping diagnose a medical problem. In these cases, human interaction and demonstrable expertise is paramount. In other cases, technology can be used to enhance customer service: travel booking, investment analysis, and security services. Services delivery has become a subtle interplay of technology and human interaction.

- *service distribution* Services are mainly delivered by people but in key locations, such as banks, aeroplanes, salons, travel agencies, restaurants, hotels, law offices, and hospitals. Services can be delivered remotely, such as broadcast entertainment, distance learning, financial and information services. Another way of distributing services is through a network of franchisees who have a common brand and who are trained in the same level of service delivery.

- *service encounter* A moment of direct interaction between the service provider and the customer in which service delivery is put to the test. The customer's experience of this encounter can determine the brand reputation of the service provider for a considerable time after the encounter is past.

- *service environment* The overall environment within which a service is delivered. This combines design, access and physical, emotional, and atmospheric dimensions.

- *service guarantees* are much more difficult to design and manage than unconditional product guarantees, but are becoming more prevalent as the industry expands. Holiday companies will often provide compensation for poor hotel rooms; airlines for delays; freight companies for lost packages. Service charters to customers are commonplace. The inability to offer unconditional guarantees in most of the service business has led to a higher emphasis on customer complaint handling and follow-up.

- *services marketing See* MARKETING.
- *service pricing* has as many forms as there are services: pricing of services is usually a combination of expertise, time taken, and speed of delivery. Price forms are also very different; for example entertainment services are usually priced through admission tickets with all kinds of variables; personal care services are priced based upon skill levels and time; estate agents take commission based on sale value; buses, taxis, trains, and planes take fares based upon length of travel; professional services charge fees based upon expertise by the hour or day; financial services charge interest based upon amount of debt or services; governments charge taxes for services, locally, and nationally; employees are paid salaries, wages, and bonuses for their labour and skill level.
- *service process* Very problematic particularly because of the difficulties of constantly keeping supply and demand in balance and the variability of service quality.
- *service quality* Probably the single most important factor in any service business. The company's personnel are critical to this—much more, for example, than in a product company. Customers have rising expectations of quality service delivery and can easily take their business elsewhere. Service companies have to be committed to their employees and, effectively, market to them. Marketers in service companies must be constantly working on improving service delivery programmes and quality and identifying gaps in perceived quality by customers.

s

sets in use (SIU) The percentage of television sets that are tuned into a particular *broadcast during a specific amount of time.

share-of-audience The percentage of audiences that are tuned into a particular medium at a given time, e.g. the number of people watching television between the hours of 8 p.m. and 11 p.m.

share of voice A measure of the total number of mentions that a company gets in its *target media relative to its main *competitor. It is a measure of awareness and image in the media rather than in the mind of *target audiences.

shelf life The length of time that something can stay on a store shelf. The length of time varies by product and is dictated by whether or not something will spoil or will no longer be of interest to the consumer. Perishables have a short shelf life whereas canned goods have a much longer shelf life. Generally, it has come to mean anything for which time can run out in the *market place.

shelf screamer (shelf talker) A printed advertising message which is hung over the edge of a *retail store shelf, e.g. 'On Special' or 'Sale item'.

shopping cart An online purchasing application that is used to make a site's product catalogue available for online ordering, whereby visitors may select, view, add/delete, and purchase *merchandise.

shopping mall A large indoor or outdoor collection of many individual stores with common areas for restaurants and parking.

shotgun approach An advertising or sales technique which is indiscriminate, lacking specific target customers, or means of accessing target customers. *See also* RIFLE SHOT APPROACH.

shoulder time The time immediately before or after peak-time, particularly used in the tourist industry.

showcase Literally, a cabinet for displaying items, and by extension, a setting or platform on which something can be displayed to best advantage.

shrinkage The loss of merchandise by a *retailer, usually due to theft, but sometimes due to other reasons.

SIC code *See* STANDARD INDUSTRIAL CLASSIFICATION.

signature A musical theme associated with a *television programme, radio show, or a particular *brand, product, or service.

silent commerce The use of microprocessors, sensors, and tags to make everyday objects intelligent and interactive. When combined with continuous *Internet connectivity, silent commerce provides for the collection of *data and for the delivery of services through everyday objects. This type of commerce is 'silent' because objects communicate and commerce takes place without human interaction. Silent commerce is one aspect of the emerging world of untethered, unbounded, ubiquitous computing.

simulated test marketing A forecasting method that gathers data for predicting a product's likely market performance by marketing it in artificial (for example a computer model of a market) rather than real-life test situations. *See also* CONCEPT TESTING.

simulation A test in a *virtual environment to determine if something would be successful in reality. Simulations are often used when testing in a real environment would be too expensive or dangerous. Conditions are set up to mimic reality as closely as possible.

situation analysis The gathering and evaluation of information to identify the target group and strategic direction of an *advertising campaign.

skimming *See* CREAMING; PRICING.

skyscraper ad An *online ad significantly taller than the 120×240 pixels vertical banner.

SLA (Service Level Agreement) An agreement between the buyer and seller that the seller will guarantee a specified level of service for the product.

slick A high-quality proof of an *advertisement printed on glossy paper which is suitable for reproduction.

Sloan, Alfred (1875–1966) CEO of General Motors. A pivotal figure, not just in the history of American business but also in the development of marketing. He joined General Motors in 1916 having sold his car anti-friction bearings business to them. He became president of GM in 1923 and was elected Chairman of the Board in 1937. He continued as Chief Executive Officer until 1946 and retired in 1956. His revolutionary 'standard procedures' concept, which is a market-oriented way of defining management effectiveness, is credited with enabling GM to overtake the hitherto dominant Henry Ford car company. Sloan's experiences, theories, and personal customer-based research inspired a new approach to marketing strategy. It also led to the separate Chevrolet, Buick, Oldsmobile, and Cadillac lines aimed at different consumer wallets and tastes. Through his customer-oriented management philosophy, Sloan's GM became a symbol of US industrial leadership. He understood that the automobile industry's salvation depended on changing consumers' attitudes. While Ford viewed the car as a low-cost form of transportation, Sloan at GM changed the perception of a car into a symbol of attainment, one that could induce consumers to continually upgrade. To that end, Sloan introduced the concept of planned obsolescence through constant changes to the overall product, many of them simple changes to design, colour, and model. To some extent Sloan pioneered an early approach to *market segmentation, new *channels of distribution, and *brand management: providing 'a car for every purse and purpose'. GM encouraged consumers to trade up as their circumstances improved, and provided dealers and customers with the credit tools for doing so. The car became a manifestation of conspicuous consumption. Sloan's market-centric approach triumphed over Ford's product-centric approach. GM sales overtook Ford's in 1927 and since then, Ford's sales have never been greater than those of GM. Sloan showed decisively that increased sales were not necessarily dependent upon ever-lower prices or product improvements but on more intangible factors like status, range of choice, artificial needs, and superficial change. He published *My Years with General Motors* in 1963.

slogan A phrase (from the Gaelic for 'war cry') used to advertise or market a product that is short, compelling and memorable. A successful slogan will immediately cause the consumer to make the association between the slogan and the product. For example, BMW's slogan is 'The Ultimate Driving Machine'. *See also* ADVERTISING; APPENDIX 3 for a list of memorable slogans.

snowball design *See* SAMPLING.

social marketing A concept advocated in the 1970s by Philip *Kotler and Gerald Zaltman that applies commercial marketing principles to the propagation of ideas and behaviours that should bring about social benefit and change. Among the important concepts are: that marketing can influence action; that action is undertaken whenever target audiences believe that the benefits they receive will be greater than the costs they incur; that programmes to influence action will be more effective if they are based on an understanding of the target audience's own perceptions. Examples might be to change a society's eating and drinking habits to promote better health, or campaigns to encourage people to register to vote, or to promote energy conservation. *See also* NON-PROFIT MARKETING.

social responsibility The ideology that all organizations have a responsibility to the community in which they operate, and have a social obligation to contribute to the welfare of that community. *See also* ETHICAL MARKETING.

soft sell A method of selling *merchandise where the technique is very low-pressure and undemanding of the customer. The soft-sell approach is seen as more amenable to modern customers, making them more receptive to purchasing than the *hard-sell approach, which tests have shown makes consumers feel uncomfortable and that they must purchase the item. *See also* SALES.

sole agent A sales representative who represents a single client exclusively.

sole trader An individual who owns and runs a business independently.

solus position The position of a piece of *advertising copy isolated from others, usually more expensive, for example a full-page advertisement.

Sorrell, Martin (1945–) WPP Group. At Saatchi & Saatchi (1975–86), Sorrell, as Finance Director, was the architect of the agency's massive acquisitions. He joined WPP in 1986. There he began to acquire *below-the-line advertising-related companies and in 1987 made a $566 m hostile takeover of J Walter Thompson Co. Sorrell followed this in 1989 with another dramatic hostile $825 m buy of Ogilvy & Mather. Today, WPP is one of the world's larger marketing service/advertising groups with more than 40 companies in 83 nations.

sound bite A pithy, quotable summarizing comment, often broadcast separately from its original context.

spam *See* E-MAIL SPAM.

speciality goods 1 Goods which the consumer perceives to be exclusive in some way, making efforts to afford them.
   2 Goods not easily available through the usual outlets, sold direct to the home from contact made via *advertising, for example double glazing or insurance.

speciality purchases *See* PRODUCT.

spider ('web crawler') A computer programme that 'crawls' the *World Wide Web gathering *web pages to bring them to *search engines. Understanding the operations of the spider is crucial to *search engine optimization. Spiders can read the *website links, the content of the various *tags used in the website, such as *keywords. Using the information gathered from the spider, a search engine will then classify the *website and index the information. The website is then included in the search engine's *database and its *page ranking process. Spiders can be programmed to 'crawl' through the World Wide Web periodically to determine whether there have been any significant changes to websites. Spiders are also used to locate web pages that sell a particular *product or to find *blogs that have opinions about a product. As a vast number of web pages are continually being added every day, and information is constantly changing, the spider is an important method for collecting data on, and keeping up with, the rapidly expanding Web. *See also* WEB 2.0.

spin doctor A *public relations specialist who works to present his or her client in a favourable light by pre-empting negative publicity, or by manipulating negative publicity into a more positive format.

splash The main story in a newspaper, usually on the front page.

splash page A branded, usually graphic-intensive, page that appears before the *home page of a *website. Some splash pages automatically refresh to the home page upon completion; others require the visitors to click on an entrance button or text link. While some marketers believe that splash pages are a necessary part of the brand experience, users may not view them in the same light. It is worth noting that very few of the most highly trafficked destinations on the Web use splash pages.

split run The simultaneous running of two or more different forms of an *advertisement in different copies of the same publication, used to test the effectiveness of one advertisement over another to appeal to regional or other specific markets.

sponsorship The support of a cause or beneficiary both for altruistic reasons and for reasons that help the company gain favourable attention through association. A major component of marketing communications, brand building, and image development. Sponsorship has three main advantages for the sponsor:

1 It provides them with media coverage;
2 It can have an internal benefit in terms of helping to improve employee morale;
3 It can assist in business relationships if the company personnel bring clients and customers to whatever is being sponsored. Marketing sponsorship is prevalent in sports, the arts, charities, good causes, and public institutions.

spontaneous recall The ability of a *respondent in advertising research to remember without the prompt of any audio or visual stimuli.

sports marketing Marketing via sponsorship of sporting events, teams, or equipment. *See also* SPONSORSHIP.

spot announcement A commercial or public service announcement that is placed on television or radio programmes.

spread A pair of facing pages in a *periodical, or an *advertisement which is printed across two such pages.

spyware Software that fraudulently obtains information from a computer without the user's knowledge.

stable market A market where the volume of sales shows little change when prices vary.

staggered schedule A schedule of *advertisements in a number of periodicals which have different insertion dates.

stakeholder marketing The process of winning influence with specific groups whose goodwill is vital to the organization and to whom it is important to portray an effective corporate image, for example shareholders, employees, and customers.

standard deviation (SD) The movement and variation of the spread of *data from the average. A low SD indicates that the data points tend to be very close to the mean, and a high SD indicates that the data is spread out over a large range of values.

standard industrial classification (SIC) Originally a method used by the US government's Occupational Safety and Health Administration (OSHA) to assign a four-digit number to classify all establishments in the US by category: Agriculture, Mining, Construction, Manufacturing, Transportation, Wholesale and Retail Trade, Financial Services, and Public Administration, etc. This classification system is also known as the SIC code and was last updated in 1987. It has since been replaced by the North American Industrial Classification System (NAICS) in 1997 in order to more accurately reflect the changes in the North American economy to include 350 new industries such as high technology categories dealing with computers, the Internet or wireless applications, as well as things like Health Maintenance Organizations. The NAICS was updated in 2002. In 1999, the statistical agencies of the US, Canada, and Mexico agreed upon a multi-phased approach to develop a new classification system for products to complement the industrial system. The North American Product Classification System (NAPCS) is currently under development.

Standard Rate and Data Service (SRDS) A commercial US firm that publishes reference volumes containing up-to-date information on rates, requirements, closing dates, and other information necessary for ad placement in the media.

stand out test A test where a *packaged product is placed alongside *competitors in a *retail outlet in order to decide how clearly the design of the package differentiates it from its competitors.

staple product A basic product which is constantly in demand, for example bread, milk, rice, or potatoes.

Starch rating Research method devised by Daniel Starch in 1923. By asking leaders how well they recall particular newspaper or magazine advertisements, the effectiveness of these *advertisements is assessed.

statistics The numerical *data items that represent a population. Statistics are used to determine how attractive a market is, its growth, how successful a business is, how many items are sold and produced, what types of consumers buy things as well as point out what needs to be improved.

stickiness The amount of time that visitors spend on a *website over a given time period. Stickiness is often measured in the average minutes per month visitors spend at a site or network. Sometimes stickiness is measured in terms of *page views. Stickiness has increasingly become a measure of the attractiveness and attention-holding nature of a website.

store A retail place where *merchandise is offered for sale.

store design The overall layout of *retail store displays. Proper lighting, space, *atmospherics, and store design will make shopping a pleasurable experience for the consumer and will help to sell more products. Generally, the displays in the front of the store should be interesting enough to bring people into the store. Grocery retailers tend to put fresh produce at the front of the store to give the idea that everything is fresh and natural. Basics are always at the back so that people have to walk through the store to get to them.

storyboard A series of drawings or pictures used to represent an outline of a commercial or *advertisement. This is a technique borrowed from animation film studios (Disney is expert at it) that spread to marketing.

strapline A memorable slogan associated with a specific brand, for example 'The future's bright, the future's Orange', or BT's 'It's good to talk' or L'Oreal's 'Because you're worth it'. *See also* SLOGANS; TAG LINE; APPENDIX 3 for a list of slogans.

strategic gap analysis The process of identifying and assessing gaps in the *marketplace with a view to developing appropriate products or services to suit the individualized area. *See also* MARKETING PLAN; MARKETING STRATEGY.

strategic marketing The concentration on an organization's long-term aims and objectives in considering and maintaining *market advantage. *See also* MARKETING STRATEGY.

stratification The organization of research survey questions such that interviews are informally controlled and thus produce results from which valid summaries and comparisons can be constructed.

stratified sampling *See* SAMPLING.

stringer A freelance journalist who contributes copy to *news organizations and is paid individually for each piece used.

stripping (image assembly**)** The positioning of film negatives or positives of *copy and illustrations for the purpose of creating a printing plate for an ad or page.

structured interview A formal interview with specific questions which have been predetermined. Used in *primary research. *See* MARKET RESEARCH.

subject *See* RESPONDENT.

subliminal advertising (subception**)** A visual or auditory advertising message presented below the threshold of consciousness. The message is allegedly perceived psychologically, but not consciously. It is illegal. *See* ADVERTISING; HIDDEN PERSUADERS, THE.

substitute product A product which the consumer perceives as an acceptable substitute for another product.

superimposition (super) A process in TV production where an image, words, or phrases are imposed over another image.

supermarket A medium-sized store that sells groceries and packaged goods, usually in an urban setting. *See also* DEPARTMENT STORE; HYPERMARKET; SUPERSTORE.

superstore A large store which sells everything from groceries to packaged goods to clothing, usually outside an urban setting.

supplementary media Non-mass media vehicles that are used to promote products, e.g. point-of-purchase advertising.

supply chain The sequence of processes that move a product or service from its production point to the point of availability to the consumer.

supporter A customer who is willing to speak positively on the performance of a product or service. One of the steps on the ladder of customer loyalty.

survey A structured *questionnaire that is used to gather information on attitudes or behaviours.

survey research A research technique that uses *questionnaires to gather *data. Types of survey research include:

- *Interpersonal*, when the questions are asked in person. This method allows the interviewer to study the reactions of the respondents more easily. Personal interviews generally allow for the greatest amount of flexibility and can also deliver a substantial amount of data. However, personal interviews are one of the most expensive ways to gather data. There are various interpersonal interview channels.
- Questions can be asked over the *telephone*. This method is used for shorter surveys that typically last about 10 minutes. However, there may be some issues with the accuracy of the data that is gathered via a telephone interview. Also it is difficult to observe body language and include group interaction over the telephone.
- *Online* is when the questions are asked via an e-mail or a website survey. This method is very convenient as respondents can fill out the questionnaire at their convenience. However, there may be some biases towards Internet-enabled households. Cost-wise, online surveys are the cheapest to administer and can deliver the best response rate.
- *Postal* surveys are answered via the mail. Mail surveys generally produce very good, non-biased results and are relatively inexpensive to administer. However, the amount of data that can be collected is not as good.

See also PRIMARY RESEARCH.

SWOT analysis (Strengths, Weaknesses, Opportunities, and Threats) *See* MARKETING PLAN.

S

symbiotic marketing A method in which one manufacturer sells its finished product to another for resale under the second manufacturer's label, where that manufacturer already has access to the market through a well-established *distribution system. It is a mutually beneficial and reinforcing relationship.

syndicated programme A television or radio programme that is distributed in more than one market by an organization other than a *network.

syndicated research Studies conducted by a third party based upon their definition as to who the survey *respondents would be, as well as what questions are asked. The *data, once collected, is sold to anyone willing to pay the price. Successful syndicated research firms typically specialize in specific markets. The advantage of using syndicated research is that the research is perceived by the public to be more objective than research conducted by companies trying to market their own products. A secondary researcher will look at what syndicated research is available. *See* MARKET RESEARCH; SECONDARY RESEARCH.

systematic sampling *See* SAMPLING.

tabloid A size of newspaper that is roughly half the size of a standard newspaper. The page size is normally 14 inches high by 12 inches wide. This has also become the generalized name in the UK for popular, sensationalist journalism.

tachistoscope An instrument that projects images on a screen in rapid succession in order to test memory *recall.

techistoscope testing A method used in *advertising and *packaging *recall tests to measure a viewer's recognition and perception of various elements within an ad by using the different lighting and exposure techniques of a tachistoscope, a device that projects an image at a fraction of a second. *See also* MARKET RESEARCH.

tag line A phrase that visually conveys the most important product attribute or benefit that the company wishes to convey Often a brand message that sums up the essence of a company. *See also* SLOGAN; STRAPLINE; APPENDIX 3.

tangible repositioning *See* POSITIONING.

target audience A group who have been identified as potential receivers of information or messages about a product, service, or idea.

targeting *See* SEGMENTATION.

target market A particular audience or segment that have been identified as likely customers of a product or service. *See also* SEGMENTATION.

target pricing The establishment of a selling price based on competitive *target market penetration or price points rather than building up from standard costs. In doing this, a target profit to be made on the product is set. Therefore the cost for the product is arrived at by subtracting the desired profit from the competitive market price. The formula is therefore:

$$\text{Target Market Price} - \text{Desired Profit} = \text{Target Cost}$$

See also PRICING.

tariff customs A duty imposed upon imported goods from another country. *See* EXPORTING; INTERNATIONAL MARKETING.

TATI *See* TOUCH-TONE AIDED TELEPHONE INTERVIEWING.

TDE *See* TOUCH-TONE AIDED TELEPHONE INTERVIEWING.

tear sheet A page cut from a magazine or newspaper that is sent to the advertiser as proof of the ad insertion. Also used to check colour reproduction of *advertisements.

teaser An advert designed to build up interest that does not reveal the *product, *service, or *brand that it is *advertising. It sets up the next advert and stimulates customer curiosity. Additionally, a teaser can be some gift, given, usually at no charge, to convince the user to purchase the item for future use. *See also* ADVERTISING.

tele-marketing The selling of a product or service over the telephone. Typically, a computer randomly generates phone numbers from an address *database; the individual trying to sell the product has a script to use.

telephone focus groups A technique used in *qualitative research, in which seven to ten people are connected in a telephone conference call and a trained *moderator leads them through a discussion about a particular topic. Basically a *focus group that is conducted via conference calling.

telephone research A type of *survey research that is done over the phone. This can either be *qualitative or *quantitive research, depending upon whether or not the questions asked are open-ended. *See also* QUESTIONS.

tele-shopping Television home shopping. While extremely popular as a channel in the US, it failed to take off in most other countries. However, the advent of *interactive television holds out much promise for the television as a major two-way *marketing channel.

television *See* MEDIA.

television advertising The use of various formats available on television—short commercials, long commercials, infomercials, or special shopping channels—for promotion of products and services.

television rating A system that measures how widely watched different television programmes are by viewers.

testimonial A credential for a product or service based upon successful usage. Many products use customer testimonials on product or service success in order to market and sell the product to others.

test marketing A product test prior to launch with a small representative group. Frequently, new products are released to a test market in order to determine *market potential. Feedback is gathered and the product can be improved before it is rolled out to a larger market or *audience. Samples of a proposed new product are tried out in areas that are supposed to be representative of the market as a whole. The key advantage of test marketing is that it is possible to evaluate a new product or service without launching nationally and incurring a large amount of expenditure on both promotional elements and sales training. Generally, test marketing is practised in *consumer markets rather than *industrial markets. Objectives of the test marketing should be clear. Representative areas should be chosen so that when the findings are extrapolated to the whole sales area, the results are indicative of likely activity and *market share. There are some limitations on test marketing; in particular, it can alert *competitors to the new product or service and allow them to respond. Even if the test is successful and the test area is thought to be representative, there is no way of knowing for certain that the test area is representative of the full *target market. If special plant and equipment needs to be commissioned to produce the new product, the fixed costs may make it uneconomic to launch on a limited scale and having carried out exploratory research, it may be better to launch to the full market.

text ad An advertisement using text-based hyperlinks. Their graphical-based counterparts, although common in *e-mail, have superseded text-based ads on the *Web. *Affiliate marketing is one area where text ads have flourished. However, many mainstream advertisers are only beginning to discover the power of text. While lacking some of the advantages of graphical ads, text-based ads have some powerful advantages of their own. They download almost instantly and are not affected by *ad-blocking software. *See also* ADVERTISING.

text link exchanges A network where participating sites display *text ads in exchange for credits that are converted (using a predetermined exchange rate) into ads to be displayed on other sites. *See* FREE WEBSITE PROMOTION.

text message marketing The use of text messages to conduct direct marketing to mobile phones, especially to *prospects who travel.

Thompson, James Walter (1847–1928) Born in Pittsfield, Massachusetts, a pioneer of the *advertising industry and the founder of the J Walter Thompson agency. Thompson acquired his employers' company Carlton & Smith in 1878 and renamed it the J Walter Thompson Company.

Thompson developed techniques and disciplines that defined the early history of the advertising industry, which was then dominated by *magazine advertising. As well as convincing magazine owners and editors to include advertising space in their publications (then selling that same space to the advertisers of the day), he also pioneered the concept of a 'full service agency' in which employees of his company would create content as well as acquire the space and place the adverts on behalf of their clients. As a result, Thompson became the exclusive agent for 30 noted periodicals of those times.

Thompson was also a pioneer of international advertising, opening an office in London in the 19th century having already opened offices in Chicago, Boston, and Cincinnati. In the 1880s Thompson began to publish books that expounded his advertising philosophy, showed examples of his agency's work, and provided *circulation and *rate information to prospective advertisers. 'Advertising,' he stated, 'is a non moral force, like electricity, which not only illuminates, but also electrocutes. Its worth to civilization depends upon how it is used.' Thompson also introduced the contemporary innovation of creating 'house advertisements'—which aimed at promoting the J Walter Thompson agency to companies seeking professional advertising services. The ads began appearing in both *trade and general magazines in the 1880s and increased in volume and variety with every decade through much of the 20th century.

Thompson sold his agency to a group of company officers, having expanded it over the preceding 38 years. He was succeeded by Stanley Resor who built the J Walter Thompson Company (later known as JWT) into the largest and most dominant agency in the advertising industry for the first half of the 20th century. In 1987 a British company, WPP Group plc, purchased JWT, and today it remains a prominent global advertising agency. *See also* ADVERTISING; PUBLIC RELATIONS.

three orders model A work of synthesis of previous hierarchical models such as the *hierarchy of effects, the dissonance hierarchy (which examined advertising as a method to counteract cognitive dissonance (conation-affect-cognition)), and the low-involvement hierarchy, which focused on the significant effect of repetition in advertising (cognition-conative-affect). Developed in 1973 by Michael Ray, the model states that all three hierarchies can coexist in a single multi-dimensional model. Different hierarchies would dominate in different situations and depending on different circumstances. Using the different labels: Cognition (for learning and understanding of the product or service; C); Behaviour (or action/choice of purchase; B); and Attitude (the emotional response to the product; A). Ray formulated the three types of hierarchy into a single model that was related to different hierarchies for different types of purchase. The learning hierarchy was characteristic of products in which the consumer was highly involved in the purchase and had to choose between numerous alternative products. In order to make a final, appropriate, and satisfying choice and purchase the consumer must to enter into a 'learning' or cognition process (C) then develop an emotional response to the product through the learning (A) and then move to a purchase (B). The dissonance-attribution hierarchy was the reverse of the learning model. Here the decision is made without learning and occurs first (B), then is followed by the formation of reinforcing attitude (A). Cognition (C) occurs last, and only selectively in order to legitimize the choice and the behaviour. Ray describes this hierarchy as relevant to high-involvement purchases where nearly indistinguishable alternative products are present. Finally, The low-involvement hierarchy is relevant to low-involvement products with minimal differences among alternative products. Cognition (C) takes place first, chiefly by means of frequent repetition of a message, followed by choice (B), and finally the formulation of an attitude (A) about the product. *See also* ADVERTISING; AIDA; DAGMAR; MARKETING COMMUNICATIONS; PURCHASING.

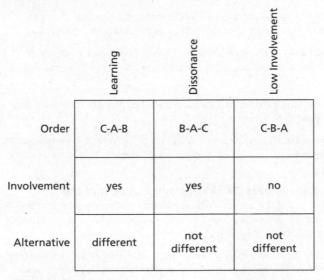

	Learning	Dissonance	Low Involvement
Order	C-A-B	B-A-C	C-B-A
Involvement	yes	yes	no
Alternative	different	not different	not different

Three Orders Model based on Michael Ray (1973). Reproduced courtesy of marketingteacher.com

threshold model A buyer-behaviour model based on the idea that consumers have a point or threshold beyond which they will not venture. *See also* BUYER AND BUYING BEHAVIOUR.

thumbnail A rough, simple, often small sketch used to show the basic layout of an ad.

time compression A technique used in broadcast production to delete time from television commercials.

time segment A slot of time in a *broadcast channel when *advertising can be booked, with variable costs relative to the popularity of the time slot with the target audience.

time series analysis (exponential smoothing) Research *data that is collected and reported in intervals of time.

time to market The average time from the initial concept of a product or service being formulated to the time when the product or service becomes available to the *marketplace.

tipping point Describes the point at which a *trend reaches a level where it becomes irreversible and it begins to gather momentum, as analysed in the book by Malcolm Gladwell, *The Tipping Point* in 2002.

title tag An *HTML tag used to define the text in the top line of a *web browser, also used by many *search engines as the title of search listings.

toll-free number A telephone number that does not cost anything to the person dialling the number. Most customer service lines have toll-free numbers.

toolbar A row of icons normally below the address bar on a *web site and used for navigation.

top level domain (TLD) The name at the top of the *Internet domain name hierarchy, displayed as the final component of the domain name, for example .com, .org, and .net.

top-of-mind awareness (TOMA) (unaided recall, unaided awareness) A technique used in *brand research where a respondent is asked which brand names come immediately to mind, without any prompting or mention of specific brand names.

top 10 The top ten search engine results for a particular search term on the *World Wide Web. The majority of browsers never get beyond the top ten search results.

touch-tone aided telephone interviewing (TATI) (touch-tone data entry, TDE) An interviewer-administered telephone survey in which the *respondent uses the touch-tone buttons of his or her phone to provide answers.

touch-tone data entry (TDE) *See* TOUCH-TONE AIDED TELEPHONE INTERVIEWING.

tracking study A quantitative technique for measuring *advertising effectiveness, usually in the minds of the *target audience. Tracking measures are primarily awareness and perception of *brand as promoted by an *advertising campaign. One of the primary measures is the respondents' ability to *recall the advertising that promoted the brand, and their interpretation of the *messages or points in the advertising campaign. Ultimately, the advertiser is attempting to create preference for the brand in the minds of the target audience—so preference and consideration relative to competing brands is also measured. *See also* ADVERTISING.

trade advertising Targeted promotional materials designed to increase sales specifically for retailers and wholesalers or a specific trade or industry.

trade cycle *See* BUSINESS CYCLE.

trade discount A reduced price that is given to members of a specific industry, trading, or practitioner group.

trade-in allowance The amount of money that represents the value of an item given in exchange for another item. This is popular for used car sales.

trade journal A magazine that focuses on a specific topic or trade or industry. Trade journals are a method by which someone can keep up with the current events and issues in their industry. The *trade associations whose members consist of the practitioners in a particular industry sponsor many magazines. *See also* MEDIA.

trademark A registered mark that gives a company the exclusive use of a name on a defined set of products and services in either a specific or a general category. For example, Kodak is owned as a general trademark by Eastman Kodak and cannot be used by another company. Other trademarks are restricted to specific categories and have exclusive right only in that category. This is important in *brand management. *See also* BRAND; LOGO.

trade press A specialist publication directed at a particular industry, trade, or profession. *See* TRADE JOURNAL.

trade show A major fair, display or event where the goods and services represented by a specific industry, topic, or interest group are displayed and discussed. *See also* EXHIBITION.

traffic A measurement of how many individuals frequent a particular area or *website. Internet traffic measures how often individuals frequent the *Internet.

transit advertising Publicity that appears on public transport or on waiting areas and bus stops.

trend 1 A new direction, habit, market dynamic, driven by the *consumer and their behaviour. Also, the prevailing direction of a market, which can be caused by macroeconomic factors, over short, medium, or longer terms.
   2 (market research) Change in a series of *data over a period of years that remains after the data have been adjusted to remove seasonal and cyclical fluctuations.

trial The testing of a product for usability and attractiveness to users.

trial offer An offer of the use of a product, for a short period of time, so that the user can decide whether or not to keep the product. The idea behind a trial offer is to let the *consumer experience or use the product with little risk attached. Often, consumers will not want to sign up for a standard length of time unless the product is something that proves to be useful. *See also* CONSUMER MARKETING.

trick banner An *Internet ad that attempts to trick people into clicking, often by imitating an operating system message, such as 'You have mail'. Trick banners seek to overcome *banner blindness and 'banner baggage' by disguising the fact that they are *advertising devices. Typically, no mention is made of the advertiser, just an imitation of an operating system or popular application. While it is common for trick banners to attract a higher-than-average *click-through rate (CTR), the quality of the clicks may be somewhat suspect, as visitors are likely to hit the 'Back' button once they realize what has happened. Aside from CTR, there is the issue of visitor satisfaction. Visitors may feel ill will towards a site that tricked them, and may decide not to return. A trick click-through is sometimes called a trick-through. *See also* BANNER ADVERTISING.

trickledown effect 1 The economic theory that wealth if created at the top of society will permeate to the poorest sections of society.
  2 (marketing) The collective *trend of *consumers to buy increasingly cheaper goods and services.

Turner, Ted (1938–) A pioneer of global media and a strong believer in the acquisition of content, after rebuilding his late father's outdoor advertising business in Atlanta, Turner acquired a failing independent TV station in 1970, successfully upgraded its programming, and bought Major League Baseball's Atlanta Braves franchise. Recognizing cable TV's potential, he rented satellite transmission time to transform WTBS into the US's first cable superstation. He next created the all-news, all-day Cable News Network (CNN) and TNT cable network. CNN, despite widespread predictions of disaster, became a global 24-hour all-news cable channel and soon proved its worth with minute-by-minute coverage of such events as the space shuttle *Challenger* disaster in 1986 and the Gulf War in 1991. Turner bought Hanna-Barbera's cartoon studio and MGM's film library, created the Cartoon Network and, in 1995, following a failure to buy CBS, merged his media company with Time Warner to create a $17 bn conglomerate. He is also widely known for his philanthropy.

TVR (Television Rating) A method for measuring television viewing and *audiences, and thus the success and impact of television programmes and *advertisements, based on the *survey research.

tweeting The act of sending a text message of up to 140 characters, known as a 'tweet' on the *Twitter micro blogging service.

Twitter A social networking and real time micro *blogging site that restricts users to messages of 140 characters in answer to the question 'what are you doing?' These short messages are called 'tweets' and were originally based on a short message service (SMS) protocol. The author's profile appears on the site and the author's subscribers are known as *followers*. The Twitter service can be used to post and receive messages to a network of contacts. A short message is sent to your Twitter account, and the service distributes it to all followers

Twitter was developed from an idea by Jack Dorsey. The name Twitter was based on its dictionary definition as a 'short burst of inconsequential information'. It was first launched in 2006 and became a separate company in 2007 founded by Dorsey, Biz Stone, and Evan Williams. In 2010, about 4 bn tweets are sent every quarter.

Twitter can be used in various aspects of *marketing. Twitter can be used as a *promotional tool to building credibility and influence. Most marketers use it to drive traffic back to their company's own *website. Others use it to monitor tweets about their *brands and what Twitter users are generally saying about a brand. Politicians have seen the value of Twitter: it was used extensively by the Barack Obama 2008 presidential campaign. Commercial organizations use it to promote special offers; *news agencies to promote their news items; *celebrities use it to develop their *personal brands and to communicate with their fan base.

See also WEB 2.0; APPENDIX 2.

( ) SEE WEB LINKS

• Main website

two-tier affiliate programme A structure whereby affiliates earn commissions on their conversions as well as conversions of webmasters whom they refer to the programme.

umbrella marketing An *advertising campaign that focuses on a family of brands, or a multi-product group. *See also* PRODUCT MARKETING.

unaided awareness *See* TOP-OF-MIND-AWARENESS.

unaided recall A research method in which a *respondent is given no assistance in answering questions regarding a specific *advertisement. *See* TOP-OF-MIND-AWARENESS.

under-delivery A situation which means fewer impressions, visitors, or conversions than contracted for a specified period of time, typically a 30-day period.

unethical SEO *See* BLACK HAT SEO.

undifferentiated market A market thought to have little *market segment differences or variation and which can be treated as a *mass market with a singular *marketing mix. *See* DIFFERENTIATION; MASS MARKET.

unfair advertising Promotional activity that is likely to harm the consumer or competitors. *See also* DISPARAGING ADVERTISING.

unique selling proposition (USP) A unique product benefit that the competition cannot claim. *See also* SALES.

unique visitor An individual who has visited a *website at least once in a fixed time frame, typically a 30-day period. Most measurements of unique visitors are estimates. Sites often calculate unique visitors based on the *IP address information found in the log files, and sometimes through *cookies.

unit pricing The price of a single item. *See also* PRICING.

unsegmented marketing *See* MASS MARKETING.

unstructured segmentation A process of *segmenting a market using *data and analysis when no prior ideas are held about the number of segments, what they are, or how and why they are different. *See also* MARKET SEGMENTATION.

up-front buy A purchase of both broadcast and print early in the buying season.

upmarket A description of a product, good, location, etc. which is seen as more expensive or wealthy and having better quality. *See also* DOWNMARKET.

URL (Universal Resource Locator) The location of a resource on the *Internet, including the protocol, the *domain name (or *IP address), and additional path information (folder/file). URLs are often important to marketers in that they are part of the phrase 'Add URL', the process of submitting a site or page to another site, usually a search engine or directory. *See also* INTERNET; ONLINE MARKETING.

usability The degree to which a product or service is easy to use and provides convenience of use.

usage level segmentation *See* MARKET SEGMENTATION.

user/application positioning *See* POSITIONING.

user friendly The degree to which products and services are easy to use, simple to understand, and relevant to the users' needs. This attribute is a key element of *differentiation.

user group positioning *See* POSITIONING.

users A vital group within the overall *purchasing process who may initiate the *buying and help to define the actual purchase. *See also* BUYER AND BUYING BEHAVIOUR.

USP *See* UNIQUE SELLING PROPOSITION.

utility The ability of a product or service to satisfy the *customer's wants or needs.

u

validation A process used to ensure that a research interview was done with the *respondent as stated. The respondent's name and contact information are verified. The interview process itself must also fall within the parameters that have been set up for all the other interviews. Validation can be done via telephone, mail, in person, or online. *See also* MARKET RESEARCH.

value The benefit that a good or a service provides, as perceived and measured by the beholder. What one customer finds of value can be different from what another finds of value. Good marketing will sell a product based upon its perceived value to a target market.

value added The additional benefit that the product or service provides over and above its component parts. When there is little to differentiate one product or service from another, products and services that are perceived to have strong value added will generally fare better than those that are perceived not to have any. The value added is often achieved through providing additional services around a core service or a product. For instance, a car dealer may have the value-added service of picking up the vehicle at someone's house whenever it needs maintenance or repairs and returning it as well as providing them with a replacement car for the duration of the repair at no extra charge.

value-added reseller (VAR) An intermediary that buys basic products from producers, adds value by modifying or expanding the products, and then resells them to final customers.

value analysis A study on how much value a product or service is providing.

value-based pricing *See* PRICING.

value chain A description of the process of manufacture from a raw product to which various values are added (extra parts or processes) resulting in a finished product to sell. More generally, it describes the relationships between an organization's value activities from input to output, modelling all of the value-adding activities in the chain. It can now be extended to any process, not just physical manufacture. As companies rid the supply chain of excess inventory, they must coordinate supply, production, and distribution to exactly match output with *demand. For example, a company's entire *supply chain can benefit from improved performance through effective use of value chain analysis to impact cycle time, quality (including predictability), and *innovation within the equipment, component, materials, and service providers.

value positioning *See* POSITIONING.

value proposition The company's core promise of benefits to clients and prospective clients. Often what the organization thinks its value proposition is, and what its customers think its value is, are different, therefore this subject needs to be constantly surveyed. *See also* USP.

variable costs *See* BREAKEVEN ANALYSIS.

vehicle A specific *channel or publication for carrying the *advertising message to a *target audience.

vertical banner A web *banner ad measuring 120 pixels wide by 240 pixels tall.

vertical discount A reduced rate offered to *advertisers who purchase airtime on a *broadcast medium for a limited amount of time, e.g. one week.

vertical integration Expansion of production capabilities to cover the spectrum of the product manufacturing process. It is also where a company merges with or takes over other companies in the same supply chain. So, if a wine maker takes over the supplier who makes wine bottles and a vineyard owner, that counts as vertical integration. A car company expanding into car tyre manufacturing is another example, or a furniture maker buying up forests and pulp mills.

vertical market A market with a *distribution channel structure in which producers, wholesalers, and retailers act as a unified system; either one channel member owns the others, or has contracts with them, or has so much power that they all cooperate.

There are three major types of vertical market system (VMS).

- *Corporate VMS*: a VMS combining successive stages of production and distribution under single ownership.
- *Administered VMS*: a VMS that coordinates successive stages of production and distribution, not through common ownership, but through the size and power of one of the parties.
- *Contractual VMS*: a VMS in which independent firms at different levels of production and distribution join together through contracts to obtain more economies or sales than they could achieve alone.

There are three types of Contractual VMS.

- *Wholesaler-Sponsored Voluntary Chain*: one in which wholesalers organize a voluntary chain of independent retailers to help them compete with large corporate chain organizations.
- *Retailer Cooperative*: one in which retailers organize a new jointly-owned business to carry on wholesaling and possibly production.
- *Franchise organization*: one in which a channel member, called a franchiser, links several stages in the production distribution process. These are yet again of three types:
  - a) manufacturer-sponsored retailer franchise system;
  - b) manufacturer-sponsored wholesaler franchise system; and
  - c) service-firm sponsored franchise system.

vertical publications Editorial content that deals with the interests of a specific industry, e.g. *National Petroleum Magazine* and *Retail Baking Today*.

video focus groups *See* GLOBAL FOCUS GROUPS.

viewing room *See* BACK ROOM.

viral marketing A marketing phenomenon that facilitates and encourages people to pass along a *marketing message, usually by *word of mouth but also using *interactive networks and forums. It depends on a high *pass-along rate from person to person. If a large percentage of recipients forward something to a large number of friends, the overall growth can multiply very quickly. If the pass-along numbers get too low, the overall growth rapidly declines. A successful example of viral marketing is Hotmail, Microsoft's free *e-mail service. Its spread helped Microsoft to dominate the *Internet. *See also* ONLINE MARKETING; WORD OF MOUTH.

virtual environment An event or situation that is not physically attended but simulated to give the illusion of physical attendance. Companies hold virtual meetings such as video- or *webcasts, to extend reach and cut time and transportation costs. Virtual meetings have also become an important marketing medium both within the company and external to it. For example, investors and analysts are regularly informed about a company's progress by means of virtual meetings; employees regularly receive communications updates through webcasts.

virtual reality A life-like artificial environment with various online applications, for example in computer games, simulations for training purposes (pilots for example), virtual tours, animation, architectural design, and advanced *advertising.

vision A perception, foresight, or strategy for future events or direction. The relationship of vision to marketing is multi-dimensional. Marketing is usually one of the elements that can make a vision happen in reality; there can be visions of future markets or combinations that create new *market demand that the current providers cannot currently see. Also, the vision itself can be marketed. This is particularly seen in 'internal' marketing where, for example, the Chief Executive will attempt to propagate his or her vision to employees and to stakeholders. Alternatively, the marketing arms of many political parties will market the vision of the leaders or the party to potential voters.

voice-over A technique used in *advertising and the entertainment industry where a narrator's voice is added to an existing video, animation, advert, movie, or television clip. As with radio, this voice is heard but not seen.

voice-pitch analysis (VOPAN) An advertising research technique of analysing a subject's voice during their responses, to test their feelings and attitudes about an ad.

volume discount A reduction in *price offered by the seller when the *buyer is purchasing a vast quantity, often staged so that the greater the amount purchased, the lower the cost.

volunteer directory A *Web directory staffed primarily by unpaid volunteer editors.

v

Wanamaker, John (1838–1922) Early pioneer of professional *advertising. Advertising's highest standards at the beginning of the 20th century were embodied by John Wanamaker, whose Philadelphia and New York *department stores pioneered *fixed prices and money-back guarantees with honest, consistent ad support. A religious man who refused to advertise on Sundays, he hired John E Powers in 1880 as the first full-time (and highly paid) department store *copywriter. Their stormy personal relationship succeeded on the professional level because Powers staunchly upheld Wanamaker's marketing philosophy. Wanamaker also reformed the US postal system while serving as Postmaster General (1889–93) in the administration of President Benjamin Harrison and was president of the YMCA from 1870–83. Wanamaker is also remembered in the advertising business for turning a phrase still talked about today: 'Half my advertising is wasted; I just don't know which half.'

warranty A guarantee that is given by the *seller that the product is free of defects. If the product breaks down or if it has defects, the provider of the warranty promises to fix or replace the product free of charge, or at a reduced cost, for a designated period of time. Warranties are usually provided for more expensive items and typically last for at least a year, depending upon the value of the item purchased. The consumer can also purchase extended warranties for an additional period of time. Such service guarantees are now a vital component of *product marketing and it is unlikely that customers would ever buy major goods from a retailer without a warranty. *See also* PRODUCT MARKETING.

waste circulation **1** *Advertising in an area where the product or service is not available or has no sales potential.
   2 Persons in an advertiser's *audience who are not potential *consumers.

wave scheduling An *advertising strategy that consists of scheduling space in the media at intermittent periods, e.g. two weeks on, two weeks off.

wealth The abundance of materials, money, or property, which has to be understood by the marketer, particularly those targets who own most of it. Wealth and, importantly, perception of wealth, is a prime conditioner of behaviour.

wear-out The point reached when an *advertising campaign loses its effectiveness due to repeated overplay of ads.

Weaver, Sylvester L 'Pat' (1908–2002) NBC. A media visionary, Weaver initiated the 'magazine format' at NBC-TV, which altered TV's content and buying patterns. His 1949–56 tenure as president and chairman led to 'Today' and 'The Tonight Show' as well as heavily promoted, star-studded specials. His bold concept of selling time in a network-controlled magazine format to a variety of advertisers was unpopular with major agencies, which would rather create and control clients' programming. But the concept revolutionized the TV industry. After his CBS Radio, Young & Rubicam, American Tobacco, and NBC-TV years, Weaver served as McCann-Erickson chairman and went on to head a pioneering subscription TV venture.

Web 2.0 (Social Media)

A term coined in 2004 which has come to represent the second generation, or second decade, of the design, development, and applications of the *World Wide Web.

The most common characteristics of Web 2.0 are community based: social networking, collaboration, harnessing of collective intelligence, personal interactions with friends and sharing of information, expertise, and personal experience.

Examples of collaboration and harnessing of collective intelligence on Web 2.0 are: software developments such as LINUX and knowledge collaborations online such as *Wikipedia. Other examples of interactive community applications are: *MySpace, *Facebook, *eBay, *Linkedin, *YouTube, Second Life, and *Twitter.

Prime activities in Web 2.0 are information searches, *online auctions, search-based advertising, *instant messaging, *podcasting, *blogging, *webcasting, uploading, and downloading *multimedia applications (such as music and video), and software development.

The application power of Web 2.0 grows in proportion to the mass of active participants who add value through providing content. The majority of successful commercial companies that use Web 2.0 applications—*Amazon.com, eBay, *Google—do not use traditional *advertising and have grown through a combination of *word of mouth, direct relationship with users, and providing *architecture and applications that enable users to generate content. They rely on mass participation to create value both for themselves and for the group.

All successful Web 2.0 applications have at their heart powerful *databases. The company that both dominates and epitomizes the world of Web 2.0 is *Google. It is the dominant *search engine on the Web. The Google product is, at its core, a web application, driven by a very advanced database, which is delivered as a service, from which revenues

w

and profits can be indirectly derived, mainly through search-based advertising. Google's advertising is less intrusive than the *pop-up banner ads of the first generation of the Web.

The rise of social networking and its various applications has diminished the traditional world of marketing and *media planning. Traditional marketing activities, characterized by the producer being able to control both the *message and the *media through which the message was pushed, either has to integrate with web applications, or else face being displaced by them. In the world of Web 2.0 *consumers are less open to 'manufactured' messages and are not influenced by traditional advertising *channels—such as *print and *television—as much as previous generations of *consumers. *Print media is diminishing in influence, and *broadcast media is fragmenting. Social networks are not a medium that can be controlled commercially, and it therefore challenges traditional marketers in traditional organizations. Users of social networks increasingly control the conversation about the image of *products and *services. Their dominant voice tends to be authentic and unrehearsed. These characteristics and behaviours will change companies' relationships with established marketing brokers, such as media buying and advertising agencies who craft messages and campaigns, print and broadcast companies. How one develops a *brand and manages an image—a staple part of the function of marketing—in the world of Web 2.0 is not yet clear to practitioners.

There have been some initial attempts to harness the commercial power of Web 2.0: for example search-based advertising (in which adverts appear alongside online search results) is beginning to catch up on traditional advertising; companies are starting to use *podcasting and *iPod applications, hosting *blogs, and taking corporate positions in social networks. Suppliers of products and services have an opportunity to have a direct conversation and continuing interaction with their customers using the Web 2.0 applications. They can listen closely to the *consumer, get an instant snapshot of sentiment about a *brand, and learn more directly rather than through *market research surveys. *Endorsement of a product or service on a social network can greatly influence its eventual *purchase. Equally, negative comment on a product or service on a social network can undermine a product.

See also WORLD WIDE WEB; APPENDIX 2 (The Rise of Online Brands).

web browser A software application that allows for the browsing of the *World Wide Web.

webcasting The use of the Web to *broadcast a video or media file over the *Internet using streaming media technology. Webcasts can be distributed to many simultaneous viewers either live or on demand. Much webcasting is done by existing *broadcasters who simultaneously broadcast their content over the web. The BBC is an excellent of example of this, both with its website and its *iPlayer* application. Webcasting is also used by companies and organizations to communicate with staff, audiences, students, and investors and is usually done at a much lower cost than in person meetings. Webcasting differs from traditional broadcasting in that it can be interactive with its online audiences.

web design The selection and coordination of available components to create the layout and structure of a web page.

web directory An organized, categorized listing of *websites. The terms 'web directory' and *search engine are often used interchangeably. Web directories are organized website listings put together by human reviewers, whereas search engine listings are put together by automated systems and lack a navigable structure. Much of the confusion stems from the various hybrid models that have developed over time, as search engines have incorporated directory features to assist with issues such as categorization and site quality. There are advantages and drawbacks to using a web directory as opposed to a search engine. One vehicle may be better suited to certain types of searches than the other. Directories place an emphasis on linking to site home pages and try to minimize deep linking. This makes directories more useful for finding sites instead of individual pages.

web ring A means for navigating a group of related *websites primarily by going forwards and backwards. *See* FREE WEBSITE PROMOTION.

---

website

A location on the *World Wide Web where specific information is grouped together in a collection of pages. A website has a main *home page and the user clicks on links from this to other pages on the site. The website is among the foremost new marketing instruments in the modern age. It can be used as an *advertising medium—which can be changed and upgraded instantly—in its own right. Most commercial organizations now have a website, giving *consumers greater information upon which to base their purchasing choices. Offline *advertising, such as posters, can increase traffic to the website. Many sites have software enabling the processing of commercial transactions and credit authorization, integrating advertising and sales. Websites can also host other companies' advertising in the form of *pop-up windows and *banner ads, enabling customers or 'surfers' to access the advertiser's site. Advertising effectiveness is measured in detail by looking at the *stickiness of the

w

website: how long the visitor remains there and the amount of *click-through that the visitor makes. Major institutions and organizations—NASA, the Library of Congress, the British Monarchy, the FBI, the CIA, the Vatican, governments, charities, tourist organizations—all have websites. Many celebrities, such as actors, authors, musicians, and models, have their own personal websites. *See also* INTERACTIVE MARKETING; MEDIA CHANNELS; ONLINE MARKETING; WEB 2.0; WORLD WIDE WEB.

website traffic The total amount of visitors that a *website receives over a given time period. This metric was initially viewed as the most important way of determining the success of a particular website or *e-commerce business. Website traffic is only partly a determinant of profitability, but it is no longer a major independent metric. It is nowadays typically combined with a visitor conversion metric to determine actual sales.

website usability A measure of how effectively visitors are able to use a *website. Usability is important in the marketing of the website and the services that it provides: 80% of website visitors abandon commercial websites before they make a purchase. *Nielsen's Law of the *Internet is that 'users spend most of their time on other people's websites'. It is vital in an age of low tolerance to delay and short attention spans to increase a website's *stickiness, to encourage multiple *click-through, and create higher *conversion rates. Ease of use is a prerequisite to all of these.

weight 1 An adjustment made in a *survey sample to correct for *demographic or geographic imbalances.
2 The number of exposures of an *advertisement.

weight-out A decrease in the weight or *package size of a *product while retaining the same *price. This will give the illusion that the price of the product has not changed, even though there is less product in the new package. This will also help to maintain the company's margin on the product since smaller packaging will make up for increased production costs.

whale Someone who will have a huge influence on sales if successfully brought in as a customer. *See also* ELEPHANT.

wheel of retailing concept A concept of retailing devised by Philip *Kotler which states that new types of retailers complete a full wheel: usually beginning as low-margin, low-price, low-status operations but later evolving into higher-priced, higher-service operations, eventually becoming like the conventional retailers they replaced.

white goods Usually utility and kitchen goods such as washing machines, dishwashers, and refrigerators. Their name is taken from their white metallic casing covers. *See also* BROWN GOODS; ORANGE GOODS; RED GOODS.

white hat SEO (white hat search engine optimization) The ethical SEO practice, approved by *search engine providers. *See also* BLACK HAT SEO.

white space Those parts of a print advertisement where nothing is printed, including between blocks of type, illustrations, headlines, etc. More generally, those parts of a market that are not yet fully defined, and, by extension, not yet fully exploited.

wholesaler A merchant who sells large quantities for *retail purposes only and does not sell to the general public. *See also* BUSINESS-TO-BUSINESS MARKETING; BUYER AND BUYING BEHAVIOUR; DISTRIBUTION.

WIIFM (What's In It For Me) The mantra that a *salesperson should always convey to the customer what benefits he would personally get from the product or service.

Wiki A software programme that enables collaboration in the creation of the contents of a *website. The term 'wiki' derives from the Hawaiian word *wiki wiki* for 'fast'. A user is able to contribute content to a website and to edit content of another user using a regular *web browser. The most famous example of the use of wiki software is the collaborative encyclopaedia known as *Wikipedia. The software is also used for community websites where collaboration is invited and for various business purposes, such as company *intranets and knowledge exchanges. *See also* WEB 2.0.

Wikipedia *See* APPENDIX 2 for details.

window dressing Making something deceptively attractive, such as with overdone sales promotions or deceptively low pricing.

window of opportunity The finite period of time in which conditions are favourable for strategic implementation of a major project.

window shopping The browsing of *retail outlets with no intention to buy.

wipe A transition of scenes in a visual production where one image appears to wipe the previous one from the screen.

word of mouth The oldest and, some would argue, the most effective way of gaining awareness. It is simply when someone finds out about something—a product, an event, a service, a place, a work—through someone else. Word of mouth is an effective method of marketing since the recommendations are coming from someone familiar—possibly who has had good experiences—and therefore gain a greater element of trust. The origins of the phrase are certainly

w

direct and verbal (hence the title), but nowadays word of mouth can also include *e-mail, chat lines, *text messages, as well as social media sites and the *telephone. The *Internet itself has been described as a 'continuous conversation'. *See also* PERMISSION MARKETING; VIRAL MARKETING; WEB 2.0.

word painting An original radio technique that uses highly descriptive words to evoke images in reading material in an attempt to place the listener into the scene.

World Wide Web

The *Internet and the World Wide Web have revolutionized not only communications, but also marketing as a technique. It covers so many of the areas that marketing in practice covered in a physical media: a worldwide broadcasting capability, a mechanism for information dissemination, and a medium for collaboration and interaction between individuals and their computers globally. Commercialization of the Internet was enabled by the creation of the World Wide Web by Tim Berners-Lee in CERN (Switzerland) in 1990. The early version of the World Wide Web included a basic *browser, along with an information server and a library implementing the essential functions for developers to build their own software. This was released in 1991 to the high-energy physics community via the CERN program library, so that a whole range of universities and research laboratories could start to use it. A little later it was made generally available via the Internet, especially to the community of people working on hypertext systems. By the beginning of 1993, there were around 50 known information servers. At this stage, there were essentially only two kinds of browser. One was the original development version, very sophisticated but only available on NeXT machines. The other was the 'line-mode' browser, which was easy to install and run on any platform but limited in power and user-friendliness. It was clear that the small team at CERN could not do all the work needed to develop the system further, so Tim Berners-Lee launched a plea via the Internet for other developers to join in. This led to the creation of browsers. For example, early in 1993, the National Center for Supercomputing Applications (NCSA) at the University of Illinois released a first version of their MOSAIC browser. The existence of reliable user-friendly browsers on these popular computers had an immediate impact on the spread of the Web to a global community. *See also* INTERNET; WEB 2.0.

Wunderman, Lester (1920–) A pioneer of direct marketing during the last half of the 20th century, Wunderman was influenced by the work of direct-marketing thinkers Victor Schwab, Harry Scherman, and Maxwell Sackheim. Hired as a copywriter by Sackheim at Maxwell Sackheim & Co. in 1947, Wunderman blossomed as a marketing strategist. Recognizing that many 'mail order' accounts were ripe for growth through broader marketing efforts, he introduced his 'direct marketing' concept. He established Wunderman, Ricotta & Kline in 1958 (acquired by Young & Rubicam in 1973) and, with his vast multimedia agency, often co-branded direct-selling 'breakthrough' campaigns, built Columbia Record Club and American Express's travel and entertainment credit card businesses.

W

Yahoo A *web portal located at yahoo.com. Yahoo was one of the more successful pioneers of the initial period of the commercialized *Internet and has now been eclipsed by *Google as a search engine. Yahoo has successfully fended off attempts by Microsoft to buy the company. *See also* BROWSER; WEB 2.0; WORLD WIDE WEB.

yellow journalism The forerunner of what we know today as sensationalist journalism. Developed at the turn of the 20th century in the US, the phrase was originally used to describe the journalism of Joseph *Pulitzer, but became synonymous with the *newspapers of William Randolph *Hearst. At this time, when newspapers were the main source of news in America, it was common practice for a newspaper to report the editor's interpretation of the news rather than objective facts. If the information reported was inaccurate or biased, the public had little means of verification. Newspapers wielded much political power and, in order to increase circulation, the publishers of these papers often exploited their powerful position by sponsoring a flamboyant approach to news reporting that became known as 'yellow journalism'. Hearst, for example, is often accused of having started the Spanish-American War of 1898 by inflaming opinion using this type of approach.

Yellow Pages *See* DIRECTORY.

YouTube A major online video sharing site, allowing individuals and organizations to broadcast themselves. Owned by *Google. *See* WEB 2.0; APPENDIX 2.

yuppie (Young Urban Professional) A term used in the 1980s and 1990s to describe someone who had a good education and made a high income in a professional service organization and tended to live in a city. Yuppies were characterized by *conspicuous consumption, unabashed materialism, the acquisition of wealth, and a hunger for luxury goods and designer clothing. For many the yuppie epitomized the changing values and economic climates of the 1980s and later became a much derided lifestyle.

zapping An *Internet term for either deleting or getting rid of something.

zero-based budgeting A method of budgeting in which past sales and previous expenditure levels are ignored. The company formulates its profit goals, determines the actions that will be required to achieve its goals, and estimates the expenditures that will be necessary to carry out the actions.

zip code analysis A *research technique in which the *market is *segmented by the socio-demographic information obtained in a zip code area. It has the assumption that a zip code neighbourhood has common patterns of *purchasing. *See also* POSTCODE ANALYSIS.

zipping The practice of fast forwarding through commercials when watching a recorded programme on advanced television sets.

zone pricing A term devised by Philip *Kotler for a geographic *pricing strategy in which the company sets up two or more zones; all customers within a zone pay the same total price, and this price is higher in the more distant zones.

Appendix 1
History of modern marketing: Timeline of key events and concepts

Date	Long-range developments in marketing (key concepts, publications, inventions, and events)
Ancient and medieval societies	Many recorded cases of advertising in ancient and medieval trade and commerce. For example early advertising (of brothels) is found in the ruins of Pompeii.
	During the Song Dynasty (960–1127 CE) in China, merchants used branding to pass-off lower grade garden tea as the higher grade hill tea by using brand names, such as 'Misty Mountain Tea', 'Garden in the Sky Tea', and 'Cloudy Mountain Tea'.
100 BC	First bound books.
105 BC	Invention of paper (China).
	Wooden printing press invented (China).
1450	Gutenberg printing press with moveable type (Germany).
	Expansion of printed communications and the rise of a literate society over the coming centuries.
1477	First known advert in England (for commemorative pies).
1650	First daily newspaper (Leipzig).
1730s	First appearance of magazines (England).
1745	*The Complete English Tradesman* by Daniel Defoe published.
19th century	Industrial Revolution —transition from agricultural to industrial economy; —mass urbanization and clusters of consumers; —opportunity for production on a scale larger than ever before; —separation of the production of goods from their distribution; —a buyers' market was replacing a sellers' market.
Early 1800s	Appearance of fly posters for advertising (England).
1831	Telegraph invented (Joseph Henry).
1836	First paid advertising in a newspaper (France).
1841	Palmer opens first advertising agency in the US.
1843	Following the invention of the telegraphic code, Samuel Morse invents long distance electronic telegraph (US).
	Alexander Bain invents first fax machine (Scotland).

(*continued*)

Appendix 1

Date	Long-range developments in marketing (key concepts, publications, inventions, and events)
1850	*The Philosophy of Advertising* by Horace Greely.
1852	First department store (France, Le Bon Marche).
1856	First full-page ad in a US newspaper, advertising the literary paper, the *New York Ledger*.
1864	Earliest recorded use of the telegraph for commercial advertising.
1867	Earliest recorded advertising billboard.
	Invention of the typewriter (US).
1870	NW Ayer and Sons advertising agency of Pennsylvania is the first agency to advertise its own services in both general and trade publications.
1876	Alexander Graham Bell patents the telephone.
1878	Thomas Edison secures basic patent for a phonograph machine.
1879	George Eastman patents a process for making dry photographic plates.
	Woolworths founded.
1880s	Earliest recorded trademark protection of brands.
1884	First usage of the term 'marketing' as an abstract business idea at Wharton University, Pennsylvania.
1886	Coca-Cola is invented in Atlanta, Georgia by Dr John S Pemberton.
	Sears, Roebuck & Company begin the first mail-order business.
1887	Gramophone invented (Emile Berliner).
1888	Eastman begins advertising the first hand-held Kodak camera.
1889	Strowger invents first telephone exchange (US) for direct dialing.
1890s	Marketing separates from economics as a business discipline.
	Era of modern mass communications begins—telephone, radio, cinema, television, within a 50-year period from the 1890s— which will revolutionize marketing as a business function.
1898	The Pepsi Cola formula is created by Caleb Bradham, a New Bern, NC druggist.
1899	J Walter Thompson opens the first overseas office (London) of any advertising agency.
	Loudspeakers invented.
1900	Early 20th century: development of basic principles of organized marketing driven by a need to understand more deeply the relationship between buyers and sellers.

Date	Long-range developments in marketing (key concepts, publications, inventions, and events)
	Marketing is viewed as a wider function than simply to increase demand for available supply and purchasing power. Demand comes to be studied as much as the ability to purchase.
	First Brownie camera sold for $1 with film at 15 c a roll. The following year the Eastman Kodak Company of New Jersey, is formed.
	Coca-Cola's advertising budget reaches $100,000.
1901	US Steel becomes the world's largest corporation.
1902	British company Philip Morris opens its New York headquarters to market cigarette brands, such as Marlboro.
	Pepsi Cola company is incorporated.
	Unilever hires the J Walter Thompson Company for advertising Lifebuoy Soap and later Lux and other products in America.
	Marconi's first transatlantic radio signal.
1903	*The Theory of Advertising* by Walter Dill Scott published in 1903.
1904	Creation of the comic book.
1905	**Period of product marketing domination begins. Early focus of marketing is on informing buyers about products and their benefits.**
	The University of Pennsylvania offers a formal business course in 'The Marketing of Products'.
1906	The First Annual Advertising Show opens in New York City, initiating the 'age of advertising'.
1908	Harvard Business School opens.
	General Motors Company is incorporated.
	The Hoover vacuum cleaner is patented.
	Airplane advertising (plane pulling a printed streamer) is used for the first time (to promote a Broadway play).
	General Electric patents the electric iron and toaster. The Ford Motor Company unveils the Model T, which initiates the age of mass car-production and ownership. Within 2 years, 200,000 cars are sold in the US.
1910	Edison demonstrates the first talking motion picture (US).
1911	Invention of air conditioning, which enables the rise of large department stores and offices as well as internal systems for homes and cars.
	Chartered Institute of Marketing founded (UK).

(continued)

Date	Long-range developments in marketing (key concepts, publications, inventions, and events)
	Beginnings of market research as formal discipline.
1912	World's first electronic bulletin board in New York's Times Square.
1913	Marketing of Camel cigarettes begins.
	Woolworths building opens in New York.
	First moving assembly line for Model T Fords opens.
1914	Hollywood becomes the centre of the American motion picture business.
	First textbook to use 'Marketing' in the title: *Marketing Methods and Salesmanship*, Ralph Butler, SH DeBower, and JG Jones (1914).
1914–18	WWI ushers in the era of marketing and public relations being used to influence mass public opinion packages and mobile civilian populations behind a total war effort. The US Committee for Public Information, for example, packages and markets the US entry into the war by a systematic 'engineering of consent' in a hitherto reluctant American public. Entry into the war was sold to the American public using the central idea of 'Making the World Safe for Democracy'. State propaganda to mobilize entire societies using all communications channels during war and revolutions. Managed public relations are used to promote entry into the war, and the transmission of public information; advertising is used for recruitment for military service and to promote the sale of war bonds.
1915	First transatlantic radio signal.
	First transcontinental (US) telephone call.
	US car ownership surpasses 3 m.
1916	First self-service retail stores (Piggly Wiggly chain of grocery stores, US).
	First radios with tuners.
1917	Lucky Strike cigarette advertising begins.
1910–1920	Development of the discipline of Public Relations.
1921	Publication of *Scientific Advertising* by Claude Hopkins.
1922	Earliest known radio advertising.
	Fred E Clark publishes *Principles of Marketing* (US).
1925	John Logie Baird demonstrates first television signals (Scotland).
1927	First advertising campaign specifically targeting women (to encourage them to smoke) in the US.
	CBS and NBC founded (US).

Date	Long-range developments in marketing (key concepts, publications, inventions, and events)
	Warner Brothers releases *The Jazz Singer* the first talking moving picture.
1930s	Development of marketing specializations, such as brand management. NH McElroy, of Proctor and Gamble, develops the concept of brand management (US).
1934	State led propaganda campaigns reach new levels of technique and mass persuasion, particularly in the USSR and in Nazi Germany.
	First tape recorder for broadcasting.
1936	Berlin Olympics uses advanced techniques of event marketing—in which a sporting event is used to market a country and its cause (Germany).
1937	Founding of the American Marketing Association.
1939–45	WWII government-inspired propaganda reaches new levels of intensity and techniques. Radio and cinema play a major role in the war efforts and public morale building of all the major combatants.
	Development of the modern computer.
1941	First recorded use of television advertising (US).
Post-war period	Period of reconstruction and consumer restrictions.
	Post-war period ushers in the **sales orientated era of marketing**—use of marketing through mass communications channels to sell more products to mass consumer markets.
1949	Launch of network television (US).
1950s	Commercial marketing begins to absorb the techniques of psychology and behavioural sciences.
	Extension of consumer credit facilities begins to enlarge the size of the market.
	Television advertising becomes the dominant and most expensive form of advertising.
	Systematic approach to direct marketing begins.
1955	*The Practice of Management* by Peter Drucker published.
	Neil Borden develops the concept of the 'Marketing Mix'.
1957	*Marketing Behavior and Executive Action* by Wroe Alderson published.
1958	Photocopier invented (Chester Carlson).
	Integrated circuit invented—enabling miniaturization of electronic devices.
	Marketing and Economic Development by Peter Drucker published.

(*continued*)

Date	Long-range developments in marketing (key concepts, publications, inventions, and events)
1960s	Gradual shift of power from the producer to the retailer then to the consumer, underpinned by legislation and pressure groups.
	As markets become saturated and competition intensifies, the era of **customer orientated marketing** begins.
	Marketing is focused on researching and analysing the needs and desires of customers and shaping product requirements to those needs.
	4 Ps of marketing concept developed.
1960	*Marketing Myopia* by Theodore Levitt published.
	Basic Marketing by E Jerome McCarthy.
1963	US Consumer Rights Bill.
	Confessions of an Advertising Man by David Ogilvie published.
1967	*Marketing Management* by Philip Kotler published.
1972	HBO invents pay-TV service for cable.
1976	*History of Marketing Thought* by Robert Bartels published.
1970s	Floppy disk and microprocessor invented.
	Development of the Internet, beginning in 1969 with the creation of its forerunner the ARPANET.
1980s	Development of PC and database marketing.
	Development of mobile phones for consumers.
	E-commerce begins.
	Emergence of **relationship marketing**.
	Emergence of computer-generated spam.
1980	Publication of Michael Porter's *Competitive Advantage*. Sony Walkman invented.
	First commercial PC goes on sale.
1982	*In Search of Excellence* by Peters and Waterman published.
	Positioning: the battle for your mind by Ries and Trout published.
1983	'Globalization of Markets' article published by Theodore Levitt.
1984	Introduction of **guerrilla marketing**.
1985	Desktop publishing revolutionizes the production of print-advertising.
1986	*The Marketing Imagination* by Theodore Levitt published.
1990s	**Integrated marketing communications model** begins: all marketing channels linked together in specific targeted

Date	Long-range developments in marketing (key concepts, publications, inventions, and events)
	campaigns becomes the dominant model of marketing management.
	Commercialization of the Internet.
	Development of the World Wide Web and web browsing. Rise of Client Relationship Marketing systems.
	[PC sales exceed TV sales]
1994	Commercialization of the Internet and the advent of web browsers.
1995	Beginnings of web search browsers.
1998	Foundation of Google.
1999	*Permission Marketing* by Seth Grodin published.
1995–2000	First wave of commercialization of the Internet leading to the dot.com bubble.
	Digital cameras.
2000–	Internet revolutionizes marketing techniques enabling: —global reach without large scale media purchasing budgets; —micro targeting of consumers with very specific needs and desires; —movement to 'pay per click' and search advertising begins to undermine the traditional model of media buying; —ability of marketing departments to control a message and campaign is undermined by user generated content and consumer interaction on social media.
	Podcasting, Search Engine Optimization, Social Media [Internet advertising].
2000	*No Logo* by Naomi Klein published.
2001	Apple iPod launched.
	Broadband Internet.
2003	*The End of Advertising as We Know It* by S Zyman published.
2004	Facebook launched.
2005	YouTube Launched.
2006	Google Adwords.
	Twitter launched.

Appendix 2
Iconic brands of the 20th and 21st centuries

The 20th century witnessed the phenomenon of brand building on a global scale. Although multiple elements of marketing were used to build and develop brands, the major instrument of the 20th century was the advertising campaign, initially in print but later in broadcast media. Towards the end of the 20th century, however, we see the phenomenon of brands being built to global scale and recognition whose primary instrument of brand building is the internet and its multi media applications.

This appendix gives a selection of some of the more iconic brands of the 20th and early 21st century. It is a representative selection rather than an exhaustive or definitive selection. Understanding the development of these brands, and the campaigns that enabled their development will assist in an understanding of modern marketing and its application. The selection is presented below in various categories:

Automotive and Petroleum Industry

Throughout the 20th century, the automotive industry has been in the vanguard of global brand building. The industry has also been one of the higher spenders on advertising, which has resulted in many memorable brand development and advertising campaigns.

Here are a few successful car brands:

BMW

(🌐) SEE WEB LINKS

BMW—Bayerische Motoren Werke—is a fine example of a powerful brand whose core value is the driving performance of its range of vehicles. Its enduring brand slogan is aligned, and in tune, with its core value of high performance engineering.

The company that led to the creation of BMW was established as an aircraft engine manufacturer in October 1913 by Karl Rapp in Munich and known as 'Rapp Motoren Werke'. In 1916, it merged with Gustav Otto's nearby company to form Bayerische Flugzeug-Werke or BFW (Bavarian Aircraft Works). In March 1916 it was then changed to Bayerische Motoren Werke and was taken over by Popp with chief engineer Max Friz. The first engines were used in biplanes and sold to the German government in the last year of the First World War. After the war, with the prohibition on military aircraft as part of the Versailles Treaty, BMW turned to other types of transport engine: tractors, trucks, boats, cars, motorbikes. By the 1930s BMW was established as a car manufacturer. Under Hitler, BMW resumed making aircraft engines, both for civilian and military use. During the Second World War, BMW stepped up its manufacture of fighter aircraft engines for the Luftwaffe and also produced military motorcycles for the Wehrmacht. During the war the company started to manufacture jet engines and rockets for military use. By the end of the war, however, the majority of BMW factories had either been bombed into ruins or dismantled by the Allies and a three-year ban on all military engine production was imposed. BMW in the post-war period was confined to motorcycles, in which it became a world leader. In 1951 the company resumed car production; by 1956, it was manufacturing sports cars in West Germany. The new director, Paul

G Hahnemann introduced a marketing strategy to segment the market for BMW products and started to restructure the company around market niches both within Germany and internationally. Under his leadership, BMW undertook a systematic expansion into markets outside Germany—increasing the range of car and motorbike models throughout the 1960s and '70s. BMW gradually started to dominate the market for luxury high performance cars. To reinforce their image, BMW also became a major sponsor of Formula 1 and started to compete which deepened their knowledge of high performance engine design. In the 1980s BMW started to make Formula 1 engines and to sponsor leading racing teams. In 1994, it bought out the Rover group and increased the number of brands under its management, notably the Mini.

Campaign
BMW's iconic campaign from which its famous strapline emerged started in 1975:
The Ultimate Driving Machine, 1975 (Puris and Ammirati)
((⊕)) SEE WEB LINKS

The campaign not only helped to define the essence of the BMW brand, but also symbolized an era of conspicuous consumption, particularly in the 1980s. BMW came to be seen as the car brand favoured by thrusting, ambitious, successful young men. The focus was on BMW's engine and handling performance and was unashamedly elitist. The ads targeted the affluent and successful professionals who responded to advertising that tapped into their sense of superiority.

The campaign and slogan that started in the 1970s spanned three decades and lasted until 2010.

Rolls-Royce
((⊕)) SEE WEB LINKS

The Rolls-Royce car brand (the company also made aircraft engines) is among the most prestigious in the history of the automotive industry. Since 1907, the name of Rolls-Royce has been synonymous with refined and distinctive motor cars that have made it one of the world's most celebrated marques. The famous Rolls-Royce badge has two interlocking letter R's and these simple initials of the founders, Sir Henry Royce and the Hon. Charles Rolls, have acquired significance as an immediately recognized symbol of quality, evoking ideals of precision, integrity, and attention to fine detail. The Spirit of Ecstasy mascot, which has adorned the motor cars since 1911, likewise identifies characteristics of Rolls-Royce with a romantic representation of elegance and craftsmanship.

Engineer Royce had focused his unquenchable enthusiasm to improve the mechanical aspects of automobiles. He had firm views on the need for quality and a Victorian fancy for expressing his aims in stirring phrases. 'Small things make perfection, but perfection is no small thing,' declared Mr Royce. 'Whatever is rightly done, however humble, is noble,' he added. And one of his memorable observations was: 'The quality remains long after the price is forgotten.' Those seeking to emphasize value over price in their marketing often use this phrase.

Campaign
As well as numerous appearances in the movies throughout the century, one landmark campaign helped reinforce the luxury marque of Rolls-Royce:
'At 60 miles an hour the loudest noise . . . comes from the electric clock' 1958
((⊕)) SEE WEB LINKS

Written by David Ogilvie, it epitomized many of Ogilvy's tenets of good advertising copy:
  Specificity: Ogilvy's copy gives an actual speed of the car.
  Quotation marks: The quotation marks around the Rolls-Royce headline indicate to the reader that this was a remark made by someone authoritative, such as the engineer.

Appendix 2

Believability: the image of driving in a car in which the electric clock is actually louder than the engine is believable—it is 'the loudest noise'—whereas the mind rejects the idea of a moving car making absolutely no noise except for that of the clock.

Emotional: noise is unwanted—but that the loudest noise in the car comes from a ticking electric clock invites the driver to experience a near silent engine and an interior which removes outside noise.

Substantiation: the full copy includes engineering and expert testimonials or quotes and provides 12 bullet points of factual copy—facts proving the extreme quality, engineering, and attention to detail that goes into making a Rolls-Royce and states the actual price of the car. This slogan saw sales of Rolls-Royce cars jump by 50% in the following year.

Volkswagen

(⊕) SEE WEB LINKS

The development of the Volkswagen brand is intertwined with the history of the 20th century. It is one of the greatest automotive brand successes in history.

The Volkswagen Company was originally operated by the German Labour Front (Deutsche Arbeitsfront), a Nazi organization specifically charged with the organization of the German workforce without trade unions. The legendary German car designer, Ferdinand Porsche, designed the original 'People's Car' during Hitler's tenure of power. Nazi propaganda heavily promoted the Volkswagen as a symbol of German technological progress and social community. World War II interrupted production of the Volkswagen and its production was shifted to armaments. Slave labourers, captured from all over Europe, were forced to work at the plant. By 1945, both the Volkswagen factory and its home city of Wolfsburg were in ruins. Volkswagen was seen through its association with the Nazi regime as having a tainted brand and, for some, an unsaleable brand. A series of famously missed opportunities occurred. The British, who administered the northern zone of Germany in the post-war period, refused to transfer the plant to the UK on the grounds it could not be successful again! The British, however, did start up production again at the Volkswagen Werks. The French tried to get the British to sell the equipment to France, but that did not happen. The machinery was also taken as payment in kind for war reparations. The British occupiers looked for a car company to manage the Wolfsburg plant. The Ford Motor Company was contacted, and Henry Ford II assessed the plant. Their opinion was that the Volkswagen was not worth their investment.

Eventually, and despairingly, the plant was turned over to German management under Heinz Nordoff. The Volkswagen Corporation that we know today was born. Exports to most parts of the world grew in strength. In 1955 the company had produced its one millionth car. However, the vast and profitable market of the US remained elusive until the 1950s. The Volkswagen car's unusual rounded appearance, its engine in the rear, together with its historical connections with Nazi Germany, originally proved a disincentive in the US, particularly in the key market of New York.

This changed in 1959, when the New York advertising agency, Doyle Dane Bernbach, began a landmark advertising campaign, dubbing the car 'the Beetle' because of its shape and pointing to its small size as an advantage to the consumer. This campaign, which used minimalist techniques ('Think Small') against all the accepted wisdom of the time to glamorize, was very successful, and for some years following, the Beetle became the leading automobile import sold in the United States. Its apex was reached when the Beetle became the 'hero' of the popular Disney 'Love Bug' movie series.

Although the German government had founded the company, in 1960 the state denationalized Volkswagen by selling 60% of its stock to the public. Volkswagen acquired the Audi auto company in 1965. In 1972 Volkswagen broke the world car production record with 15,007,034 units assembled: more Beetle models had been produced than that of the previous record holder—the Ford Motor Company's Model T Ford, between 1908 and 1927.

Volkswagen and its affiliates operated plants throughout most of the world. In addition to cars, the company produced vans and minibuses, automotive parts, and industrial engines. Volkswagen owns several other auto companies, including Audi in Germany and SEAT (Sociedad Espanola de Automoviles de Turismo) in Spain, and it also makes and markets cars with Fiat of Italy and Skoda of the Czech Republic. The Volkswagen hardly changed from its original design: by 1974 it had fallen out of fashion and, with increasing competition from other compact foreign cars, Volkswagen came near to bankruptcy. This spurred the company to develop newer, sportier car models. After a period of absence from production, in 2000 the legendary Beetle design was revived with a new engine, with great international success. Billboards in New York for the new Beetle cleverly read 'The World's Cup Is Half Full Again'.

In 1998 Volkswagen was taken over by another iconic brand—Porsche—whose founder had, ironically, been the original designer of the People's Car.

Car Petroleum
Exxon Corp.

((⊕)) SEE WEB LINKS

Notable campaign
'Put a Tiger in Your Tank'

Exxon started to use a tiger in various images from the 1950s. Esso first used the tiger in the early days of branded petrol that followed the end of rationing after World War II. The tiger image has adapted over time, to meet the changing times.

In the 1960s, the tiger assumed the aura of a cartoon, contrasting humorously with the fashion at the time for baffling scientific improvements to the performance of petrol. 'Put a tiger in your tank' became one of the most famous campaigns in advertising history, complete with merchandised 'comical' tiger tail to fix around the petrol cap along with the bumper-sticker proclaiming 'I've got a tiger in my tank': 2,500,000 tails were sold.

Esso, the UK brand for Exxon, started to use tiger images in the 1950s, but it was only in the 1960s that it became a craze. A cartoon tiger was used and a whole range of merchandise using the tiger was given away at filling stations. The campaign was also taken to France ('Mettez un tigre dans votre moteur') and to Germany ('Pack den Tiger in den Tank'). In the UK, the campaign then gave way to a real and beautiful tiger, carrying a subtler environmental message.

Cigarette Industry

The discovery of the link between lung cancer and smoking was made in the 1950s. However, it was not until half a century later that the advertising of tobacco-based products was banned in the West. During the 20th century however, the advertising of cigarettes (much of which now seems both risible, and dangerous to public health) was expansive and, given the rising public clamour against the tobacco industry, increasingly creative in its indirect advertising and brand development.

Philip Morris
The Marlboro Country campaign
Come to where the flavour is. Come to Marlboro Country, 1950s

((⊕)) SEE WEB LINKS

The 'Marlboro Country' adverts are among the most successful (and most controversial) sustained ad campaigns of all time. Created by the advertising agency Leo Burnett in 1954, they were originally intended to reposition Marlboro's filter cigarettes as a male cigarette by associating it with rugged, individual cowboys alone in the great American outdoors—as filtered cigarettes were viewed as a woman's cigarette. The 'Marlboro Man' and the 'Marlboro Country' campaigns ran through four decades and, despite the public outcry against tobacco and the banning of cigarette advertising in the West, sales increased year after year and Marlboro remains in the top ten of most valued brands into the 21st century.

In a sadly macabre counterpoint to this commercially successful advertising campaign, the three men who appeared in Marlboro advertisements—Wayne McLaren, David McLean, and Dick Hammer—all died of lung cancer.

Richard J Reynolds
Camel Cigarettes campaigns
I'd walk a mile for a Camel 1944–69

((⊕)) SEE WEB LINKS

The Richard J Reynolds company created Camel cigarettes in 1913. The cigarette pack was simple. The front panel showed one single-humped, riderless camel on a desert landscape with two pyramids and three palm trees. The brand's name in silvered blue Arabic style letters appeared across the sky. The name of the camel that modelled for the pack was 'Old Joe'.

Camel advertisements of the 1920s spoke of the quality and mildness of its tobacco. They showed smokers of good taste and breeding in evening attire, at dinner parties, on ocean liners, and at tennis or polo matches. All were urged to 'Have a Camel'. In the 1930s the company used advertisements that implied that Camel cigarettes relieved stress and tension. It became a popular belief that cigarettes were 'good for your nerves'. The RJ Reynolds Tobacco Company began to make health claims in their advertisements. They even employed practising doctors to endorse cigarette smoking! Endorsements by athletes stated, 'They [Camels] Don't Get Your Wind'. The advertisement implied that cigarettes were harmless by stating, 'So mild . . . You can smoke all you want'.

In 1942, The RJ Reynolds Tobacco Company put up a billboard in New York's Times Square. It became famous overnight. It was two storeys high. The brand name was in giant letters. The slogan read 'I'd Walk a Mile for a Camel'. The sign remained for twenty-five years and served as the prototype for smaller versions around the country. By 1988, when Camels celebrated their seventy-fifth birthday, and the world was very different and actively hostile to cigarette advertising, the company initiated the company's most effective, and infamous, advertising campaign. The RJ Reynolds Tobacco Company turned 'Old Joe' (formerly used for French advertising) into a 'smooth character'. 'Joe Camel' was suave, confident, independent, wealthy, and appealing to women. He became the quintessential party animal, in a tuxedo and sunglasses, with a cigarette dangling from his lips, surrounded by women. The company budgeted about $75 m a year to advertise and promote 'Joe Camel'. They put up a huge illuminated billboard in Times Square a block away from where the first Camel sign was. The company also promoted 'Joe Camel's' likeness in a line of merchandise. Anti-smoking advocates saw 'Joe Camel' as proof of the tobacco industry's desire to target children. The RJ Reynolds Tobacco Company denied the allegations, claiming the campaign was directed at persuading young adults to switch from other brands. In any event, the RJ Reynolds Tobacco company succeeded in gaining younger customers, mainly from the leading Marlboro brand. By 1993 Camels' market share in the 24-and-under sector had risen to 7.9% from 4.4% in 1988. However, the brand's total market share had risen only 1% to just over 4. In 1988, 67.2% of Camel smokers were under 50. By 1992 78.3% were under 50. In 1991 Camel's market share among underage smokers increased from less than 1% to 32.8%. However, its share of the adult market barely budged. In 1989 only 8.1% of adolescents preferred Camels. By 1993 this figure was up to 13.3%.

On May 28, 1997 the Federal Trade Commission charged the RJ Reynolds Tobacco Company with illegally targeting minors with its 'Joe Camel' advertising campaign. The company denied that it focused on under-age smokers. Despite their reluctance to drop the campaign, RJ Reynolds backed down in the face of overwhelming public dismay and accusations that they were encouraging children to smoke. In 1997, 'Joe Camel' died at the age of 23. 'We must put tobacco ads like 'Joe Camel' out of our children's reach forever,' said President Bill Clinton.

Clothing

Clothes are more difficult to market as individual items—therefore, clothes brands have tended to take prominence in specific campaigns.

United Colours of Benetton campaign, 1980s

(⊕) SEE WEB LINKS

Striking print advertising:

(⊕) SEE WEB LINKS

The photographic poster ads depicting the 'United Colours' of Benetton by Oliviero Toscani became increasingly shocking as they portrayed Aids victims, the clothes of dead soldiers, new babies soaked in blood from the womb, and black stallions mounting white mares. It is an excellent example of an advertising campaign that builds an image without actually mentioning the core product, which is a range of expensively priced clothing. As it generates controversy, usually through demands to ban the public display of the photographic images, then more people are drawn to the campaign, which then becomes fuelled by word of mouth and unpaid media attention.

Luciano Benetton summarized his views: 'The purpose of advertising is not to sell more. It's to do with institutional publicity, whose aim is to communicate the company's values. . . . We need to convey a single strong image, which can be shared anywhere in the world.' Oliviero Toscani the photographer who created the startling images said: 'I am not here to sell pullovers, but to promote an image . . .' Benetton's advertising draws public attention to universal themes like racial integration, the protection of the environment, and the devastating effect of Aids.

Equipment for the Masses

Mass consumer electronic goods became the symbol of rising affluence in society and economic development for countries in the 20th century. The creation of a mass market for sophisticated electronic products, previously only used by scientific experts, for people of all levels across the world (the majority of whom did not understand, or care, about the underlying technology behind the devices) became one of the more advanced disciplines in brand building and marketing.

Here are some examples of companies who excelled at bringing sophisticated equipment to mass consumers throughout the 20th and 21st centuries:

Apple

(⊕) SEE WEB LINKS

Apple, created in 1976 in his family garage by Steve Jobs with Steve Wozniak and Ronald Wayne (who sold his share for $800 only 3 months after its inception), is now an iconic, global consumer electronics brand. It has, over the course of its commercial existence, brought intuition and style to product design, which, when combined with its innovative marketing, created a worldwide following of consumer advocates. Apple is a leading example of how a company can also generate an emotional response to what is at its core a sophisticated technical product.

Apple was an early leader in the PC revolution of the early 1980s, and in the early 21st century the company has enjoyed major success with the innovative iPod (combined with the iTunes service), then the multimedia iPhone and, more recently, the iPad. Not only was this a popular product, it also provided a new dynamic of change in the music and mobile phone industries. The 'i' range (Mac, pod, tunes, phone, pad) not only enhanced Apple's brand as an innovator in consumer products, it also revolutionized the media distribution and its business model.

Apple's iPod, however, did not begin well: for the first 3 years of its existence the iPod was unsuccessful. The iPod was launched in October 2001, and between 2001 and 2004 iPod sales were between 100–200 thousand units per quarter (today 10–20 million units per quarter are sold). Then, in June–August 2004 something happened, and iPod sales began to grow strongly, quarter after quarter. It was content that made the difference. Apple launched its iTunes store in 2003, offering legal music downloads for 99 cents per song. (iTunes software had already debuted in 2001 as a music storage and organization system for Apple computers.) Apple's entry into digital music sales changed the industry. The iTunes store was significantly easier to use than its competitors' services, with a vastly greater library: in its first week, iTunes sold 1 million songs; within a year, it sold more than 50 million. The iPod + iTunes, the launch pad for Apple's recent success, was a business idea that was not conceived inside Apple but proposed to Apple by an outside source, a music lover and engineer named Tony Fadell.

In June 2007 the iPhone was released to tremendous popular acclaim and in 2010 the iPad.

Historic campaign
'1984' (Chiat/Day)

(⊕) SEE WEB LINKS

A landmark television ad heralding the high point of the first wave of the PC market, and directed by Ridley Scott, this ad cost $1.6 m to make and was inspired by George Orwell's *Nineteen Eighty-Four* (1948). The ad, where a young lady silences Big Brother with the aid of a hammer, was only ever shown once, during the US Super Bowl in January 1984, to announce the launch of the Apple Macintosh on 24th January 1984, promising 1984 would not be like 1984. Despite only being shown once, the ad had one of the highest audience recall figures in America.

This ad is often seen to be the beginning of advertising as a major event rather than just a campaign. The ad launched the Apple Macintosh without even showing the product.

The memorable line, 'Why 1984 won't be like 1984', was written for an Apple II newspaper ad, then rejected, then recycled by copywriter Steve Hayden and art director Brent Thomas in 1983.

The main purpose of the campaign was to stop customers from buying the IBM PC until there were sufficient quantities of the Apple Macintosh on the shelves. The ad was almost not shown. When Apple initially dragged its feet on approving a 60-second version of '1984' at a pre-screening for their board of directors, one board member called for the agency to be fired. Shortly before the Super Bowl, the company decided to sell off its airtime. However, the valuable time could not be unloaded, and the spot ran. Nearly 20 years later, clients spend millions to advertise during the Super Bowl.

The 1984 advert reappeared nearly 25 years after its original outing as a political parody used by Barack Obama supporters during the primary campaign against Hillary Clinton ('2008 won't be like 1984').

Eastman Kodak

【(⊕) SEE WEB LINKS】

With the slogan 'you press the button, we do the rest', George Eastman put the first simple camera into the hands of a world of non-specialized consumers in 1888. In so doing, he made a cumbersome and complicated process easy to use and accessible to nearly everyone, opening the door for photography for the masses. Eastman's goal was to make photography 'as convenient as the pencil'. The name 'Kodak' itself has no meaning. It was Eastman himself who created the brand name and he explained it thus: 'First. It is short. Second. It is not capable of mispronunciation. Third. It does not resemble anything in the art and cannot be associated with anything in the art except the Kodak.' Eastman built his Kodak business on four basic principles:

- mass production at low cost;
- international distribution;
- extensive advertising;
- a focus on the customer.

He saw all four as being closely related. Mass production could not be justified without wide distribution. Distribution, in turn, needed the support of strong advertising. From the beginning, Eastman had a strong conviction that fulfilling customer needs and desires was the only road to corporate success.

Advertising became a major factor in George Eastman's success, making Kodak a household word around the world. Eastman created an advertising department as early as 1892. A well-known icon, the Kodak Girl, began to appear in magazine and poster advertising in 1893. By the end of the 19th century, the company was spending $750,000 annually on promotion, which was an enormous sum for the time. The company carefully positioned its magazine advertising, placing it in quality titles with high circulation. Eastman Kodak commissioned noted artists to illustrate many of its magazine ads, especially from 1900 to about 1915. Snapshot-like photos of families, holidays, get-togethers, and travel became mainstay illustrations in Kodak advertising throughout the century.

Since that time, the Eastman Kodak Company has led the way with an abundance of new products and processes to make photography simpler, more useful, and more enjoyable. In fact, today's Kodak is known not only for photography, but also for images used in a variety of leisure, commercial, entertainment, and scientific applications.

The Kodak logo is probably the most recognized in the world. This is how it developed:

Early 1900s: Kodak is the first company to integrate its name and look into a symbol.

1930s: Focus moved to the Kodak name and the red and yellow 'trade dress' colour.

1960s: The corner curl was introduced.

1970s: The mark retained the red and yellow colours and the Kodak name, but a box and graphic 'K' element were added.

1980s: A more contemporary type font streamlined the Kodak name within the existing logo.

Today: The box is gone, simplifying the logo. The rounded type font and distinctive 'a' give the name a more contemporary look.

Historic Campaign
You press the button—we do the rest early 1900s

【(⊕) SEE WEB LINKS】

A phrase that ushered in the age of popular mass photography, led by the Kodak 'Brownie' camera. People for a while started to call all cameras Kodaks.

Hoover Vacuum Cleaners
Hoover beats as it sweeps as it cleans 1920s

SEE WEB LINKS

Hoover in the UK became the eponymous word for a vacuum cleaner. It even became an active verb ('hoovering the carpet'). In 1926, Hoover introduced the famous 'beats-as-it-sweeps-as-it-cleans' feature which cleverly incorporated the three established but separate methods of cleaning carpets: beating, sweeping, and suction cleaning. This innovation set the standard for the rest of the market to follow and was a feature of Hoover cleaners until the 1980s.

Although Hoover's vacuum cleaners were very expensive, they carried the royal warrant and were used on the prestigious ocean liners of the late 1930s, they were also cleverly marketed under such headlines as 'No millionaire can buy better' (1947) and 'All women are equal in this' (1933), implying that if you had scrimped and saved for the 'Hoover' you were at least equal in this respect to royalty and the well-to-do. In 1935, Hoover's success was guaranteed by the launching of a British-built, compact, upright cleaner that retained the features and quality of their larger model, but at half the price. The subsequent success of the 'Junior' model (a version of which was still selling in the mid-1980s) was indicated by a biasing of the British cleaner market towards the upright format, in contrast to the rest of Europe.

In the mid-1930s Hoover USA pioneered the use of professional industrial design in vacuum cleaners by employing Henry Dreyfuss, one of the first industrial designers, to consider the design, manufacture and ease of use of their vacuum cleaner as a whole. The result was a new generation of cleaners, starting with the model 150 (1936), and the 160 (1938), which used fewer components, new light alloys, and plastics and had more benefits for the user. This development indicated the fact that by the late 1930s, at least in America, the electric vacuum cleaner was a common-enough product and required a 'design overhaul' to stimulate the next generation of sales. The basic component layout and manufacturing approach of these new models continued until the first 'clean-fan' plastic uprights in the mid-1960s.

Intel Corp

SEE WEB LINKS

Intel Inside 1990s

A brilliant advertising technique for making the invisible memorable and valuable. It was targeted at the end consumer, who knew little of microchips, rather than the manufacturer, who had been the target up to that point. In a relatively short time, Intel Inside® has grown to be one of the world's largest, most successful cooperative brand marketing programmes in history.

Before this campaign, companies such as Intel were selling their semiconductor products directly to original equipment manufacturers (OEMs), with their primary customers being the computer design engineers responsible for building computers.

With Intel's new i386™ microprocessor, Intel had developed a product far superior to everything in the industry. Despite the benefits of the improved product, many OEMs shunned using the new technology in their mass-produced computers, fearing that their customers (primarily corporate information technology managers who purchased large numbers of computers) would not react well to higher prices. Intel realized it needed a way to break through the barrier and reach the OEM's customer directly—the IT manager—to help them understand the value of the i386 chip.

To solve this problem, a team at Intel proposed a revolutionary advertising campaign, designed to stimulate the IT manager's demand for the advanced technology. In the ads the i386 processor was touted as a better investment for the future. The campaign was successful, and it taught Intel that communicating technical information to end-consumers was not only possible, but also highly desirable. It was the first time that Intel had directed the ad campaign at PC consumers rather than at just PC makers.

The response was exactly what Intel wanted, but over time it proved to increase awareness and sales for new technology among computer companies across the board, not just for Intel. It became a new approach to advertising even the driest aspects of technology. Intel needed to build long-term awareness for their brand, creating a mindset of quality, innovation, and reliability.

Rather than just market the technology, they would market Intel technology, influencing consumers to pay attention to the Intel ingredient inside the computer. With this new thinking, Intel developed a cooperative advertising program in which OEMs would add a small Intel Inside® logo to their print ads. By attaching the logo, OEMs would add strength to their own brands by being identified with the strength of the Intel® brand.

Officially started July 1, 1991, Intel Inside has issued thousands of worldwide licences to use the Intel Inside logo, as well as TV spots, computer logos, and an e-commerce programme. Since the programme started, more than $7 bn in Intel Inside brand advertising has been generated. The Intel Inside programme manufactures more than 150 million Intel Inside logo system stickers each year for multiple Intel brands, colours, sizes, systems, and product packaging. Advertising with the Intel Inside logo runs in more than 130 countries.

Nokia

SEE WEB LINKS

Founded in 1860, Nokia Corporation, headquartered in Helsinki, became the world's leading supplier of mobile communications devices and related services. Nokia accounts for almost a quarter of Finland's exports, and 2% of its GDP.

Nokia is an outstanding example of the re-invention of the core business of a company and how brand positioning can be used in the process of re-invention. Nokia's journey also marks a transition from a 19th-century approach to 'vertical integration' in a traditional industry, to the multi-sourcing and marketing approaches of the 21st century.

In 1865 the Finnish mining engineer Fredrik Idestam established a wood-pulp mill in Southern Finland and began manufacturing paper. The company, named after the River Nokia where its lumber mills were sited, started off in forestry, and later moved into making paper, rubber, and electrical cables. The Finnish Rubber Works, initially opened in 1898, established a factory on the River Nokia after its executives passed through the area and recognized the value of the hydroelectricity available there. In the 1920s, the Finnish Rubber Works started to use Nokia as their brand name. In addition to footwear and tyres, the company later went on to manufacture rubber bands, galoshes, industrial parts, raincoats, and other rubber products. The company that later became known as the Finnish Cable Works opened in 1912 in Helsinki. The increasing need for power transmission and telegraph and telephone networks meant that the company grew quickly. After World War II, the Finnish Rubber Works bought the majority of the Finnish Cable Works' shares, and gradually the ownership of these companies consolidated. Finally, in 1967 the companies were merged to form the Nokia Group. The company evolved dramatically, growing first into a conglomerate encompassing diverse industries. However, by the 1980s it was an unfocused conglomerate that made everything from galoshes to TVs. Nokia's operations had rapidly expanded into too many business sectors, countries, and products. The strategy was to expand relentlessly on all fronts. In 1988, Nokia was Europe's third-largest television manufacturer and the largest information technology company in the Nordic countries. During the deep

Appendix 2 400

recession in Finland at the beginning of the 1990s, the telecommunications and mobile phone divisions were the supporting pillars of the company. During the depth of the recession, Jorma Ollila was appointed to head the entire Nokia Group. He made the major strategic decision to divest its non-core operations and focus on the rapidly expanding market for mobile telecommunications devices.

The groundwork for the shift to mobile communications had been laid in the 1960s, when Nokia's electronics department was researching radio transmission. Nokia started to make mobile phones for the military, which took off after the establishment of a multinational cellular network by a consortium of Scandinavian state operators. This network gave the Scandinavians an advantage when it came to setting up Europe-wide networks, based on the digital GSM standard in the early 1990s.

Nokia took a major gamble and it paid off. Under Ollila's leadership, Nokia became focused on being a mobile phone and services company with a global brand. Nokia has led the mobile industry by emphasizing its brand and its design—mobile phones are fashion statements—with easy-to-use software. The company has also positioned itself to take advantage of the coming convergence between mobile phones, multimedia, and the Internet.

Xerox

(⊕)) SEE WEB LINKS

Chester Carlson, a patent attorney and part-time inventor, made the first xerographic image in his laboratory in Astoria, Queens, in New York City, on October 22, 1938. He spent years trying to sell his invention without success. Business executives could not be persuaded that there was a market for a copier; typed carbon copies, although labour intensive, were viewed to work well. The prototype for a facsimile copier was unwieldy and messy. There was no interest from the leading companies of the time, including IBM and General Electric.

In 1944, the Battelle Memorial Institute in Columbus, Ohio, contracted with Carlson to refine his new process, which Carlson called 'electrophotography'. Three years later, the Haloid Company, a maker of photographic paper in Rochester, NY, approached Battelle and obtained a licence to develop and market a copying machine based on Carlson's technology. Haloid later obtained all rights to Carlson's invention. Carlson and Haloid agreed the word 'electrophotography' was too cumbersome. A professor of classical languages at Ohio State University suggested 'xerography', derived from the Greek words for 'dry' and 'writing'.

Haloid coined the word 'Xerox' for the new copiers. In 1948, the word Xerox was trademarked. In 1958 it became Haloid Xerox Inc. The company became Xerox Corporation in 1961 after wide acceptance of the Xerox 914, the first automatic office copier to use ordinary paper. September 1999 marked the 40th anniversary of the Xerox 914, aptly named for the size of paper it used: 9×14 inches. More than 200,000 units were made around the world between 1959 and 1976, the year the company stopped production of the 914. Xerox adopted 'The Document Company—Xerox' as their corporate signature logo in 1994 to better reflect what has always been the company's core business: document management. At the same time, Xerox launched the 'digital X' as its marketing symbol/logo. The symbol's upper right quadrant depicts the pixels of digital imaging and the movement of documents between the paper and electronic worlds. In 2008 Xerox changed its logo again to move perception of their brand away from photocopiers and physical documents—the new logo removed 'The Document Company' as the descriptor in favour of a sphere sketched with lines, called 'connectors', that link to form an 'X', representing the company's connections to its customers, employees, partners, industry, and innovation.

Food and Drink

American companies have led the way in globalizing food and drink through vast commercial empires which, over time, have created a homogenous taste for certain food and drinks.

Coca-Cola

(⊕) SEE WEB LINKS

In the history of consumer brand building, Coca-Cola stands at the apex—demonstrating how dedication, discipline, investment, and creativity have resulted in global brand power which has endured across the tastes and events of three different centuries.

In May, 1886, Coca-Cola was invented by Doctor John Pemberton a pharmacist from Atlanta, Georgia. The name Coca-Cola was a suggestion given by John Pemberton's bookkeeper Frank Robinson—who also provided the flowing signature that remains part of the brand logo. Dr Pemberton's original formula was intended to be a nerve tonic, a stimulant, and a headache remedy. Thus Coca-Cola began its long life as the world's most famous drinks brand as a 'valuable tonic and nerve stimulant with properties of the coca plant and cola nuts', and also as a 'temperance drink'—to encourage it as an alternative to alcohol. It was first sold to the public for 5 cents a glass at the soda fountain in Jacob's Pharmacy in Atlanta on May 8, 1886. Coca-Cola was incorporated as Coca-Cola Co. in 1888 with Coca-Cola as its trademark. Pemberton's successors realized the power of the product and began to build it up into a global icon. By the 1890s, under the ownership of Asa Candler, who gained the entire company for $2300, Coca-Cola was already America's favourite fountain drink. At the turn of the century it was being actively advertised, with 'delicious and refreshing' as the main advertising headline. It was also distributed by means of selling the syrup to independent bottling companies who were licensed to sell Coca-Cola. This was also complemented with promotional merchandising and incentives to retailers, such as soda fountain owners.

Patented in 1893, the recipe and formula for Coca-Cola (internally code-named Merchandise 7 X) became a famous trade secret kept in a high security bank vault in Atlanta and known only to a few employees. In 1903 the final traces of cocaine were removed from the drink formula.

In 1915 the Coca-Cola bottle with the swirling lines was created. Improvements in bottling techniques, and nationwide distribution, meant that, by the 1920s, bottled Coca-Cola was the dominant means of merchandising the drink. It was packaged in six bottle cartons, which came to be known as the six packs. In 1933 automatic drinks dispensers were invented—which gave the drink another direct distribution arm. Radio advertising of Coca-Cola started in the 1930s. During the war, Coca-Cola was provided free to the armed services. By the end of the Second World War Coca-Cola was available in 44 countries and had become one of the first global brands. In the 1950s television advertising of Coca-Cola started. In 1960 the first disposable tin can was introduced to complement the glass bottle—and in 1978 the plastic bottle was introduced.

In 1985, the Coca-Cola Company created Diet Coke but also made a controversial change to the original formula. The decision to change the original formula and withdraw the original drink from the market came about because taste tests with consumers showed a distinct preference for the new formula. Also Coca-Cola's share of the market had been reducing as a result of Pepsi's 'Taste Challenge' campaign—which indicated that in blind tests, consumers preferred Pepsi Cola. Faced with mass protest by consumers against the new formulation of the original, Coca-Cola conducted a masterful recovery campaign and reintroduced the original drink to popular acclaim, but rebranded as 'Classic Coke' and it was a commercial triumph which reversed its losses of market share.

Coca-Cola is sold in 145 countries, marketed in 80 different languages and advertised in 500 TV channels across the world and on the Internet and a billion people drink a Coke each day. It is perhaps the most heavily and most successfully advertised product in history. Its first recorded advertising budget in 1890 was $11,000. It has had many legendary campaigns, including the invention of the modern Santa Claus, with his Falstaffian appearance and red and white (the colours of Coca-Cola) robes for a Macy's store campaign in the 1930s.

Some major historic campaigns were:
Thirst knows no Season 1922
The pause that refreshes 1929–40s
(⊕) SEE WEB LINKS

Things go better with Coke 1963
(⊕) SEE WEB LINKS
The Real Thing 1970
(Being the 'Real Thing' has been a constant message in Coca-Cola advertising since the 1940s.)
(⊕) SEE WEB LINKS

I'd like to buy the world a Coke 1971
(⊕) SEE WEB LINKS

Coke Adds Life 1976
(⊕) SEE WEB LINKS

Coca-Cola in China
(⊕) SEE WEB LINKS

Coca-Cola in Russia
(⊕) SEE WEB LINKS

Pepsi
(⊕) SEE WEB LINKS

As with Coca-Cola, Pepsi began with a pharmacy in the American south in the 19th century. In 1893, Caleb Bradham, a pharmacist from New Bern, North Carolina, created a drink called 'Brad's drink' in 1893. This was later renamed Pepsi Cola after the pepsin and cola nuts used in the recipe.

The name Pepsi Cola was trademarked on June 16th, 1903. Bradham's neighbour, an artist, designed the first Pepsi logo. The Pepsi Cola company was created in 1902 and its first newspaper ads were created. Its first advertising strapline was: 'Exhilarating, Invigorating, Aids Digestion.'

In 1906, Pepsi changed its logo for the third time. The modified script logo was created with the slogan, 'The Original Pure Food Drink'.

In 1909 Pepsi used celebrity endorsement for the first time: Automobile race pioneer Barney Oldfield endorsed Pepsi Cola in newspaper ads as 'A bully drink . . . refreshing, invigorating, a fine bracer before a race'.

In 1920, Pepsi changed its slogan again to 'Drink Pepsi Cola, it will satisfy you'. Despite the rise of Pepsi Cola, Caleb Bradham went bankrupt, a victim of speculation during the First World War. In the 1920s Roy C Megargel, a Wall Street broker, bought the Pepsi trademark and business from Craven Holding Corporation for $35,000, and formed the Pepsi Cola Corporation. By 1931 the company was again bankrupt. It was bought by the Lofty Candy Company who reformulated the drink. Pepsi was offered for sale to Coca-Cola, who refused it.

Only in the mid-30s did sales of Pepsi start to pick up—based on its 12 ounce drink for 5 cents. Walter S. Mack, Jr, became CEO Pepsi Cola Company. Mack, who considered advertising the keystone of the soft drink business, turned Pepsi into a modern marketing company. In 1939 came the famous 'Twice as much for a nickel' theme. The jingle that accompanied this, and was played an estimated 6 million times on radio, was 'Nickel Nickel', an advertisement for Pepsi Cola that referred to the price of Pepsi and the quantity for that price. 'Nickel Nickel' became a hit record and was recorded into fifty-five languages.

During the Second World War, in a gesture of patriotism, Pepsi changed their corporate colours to red, white, and blue. In wartime, Pepsi again changed its slogan to: 'Bigger Drink, Better Taste.' And then changed its logo again.

In the late 1950s Pepsi was introduced to the USSR and eventually opened there in the 1970s. In the 1980s it entered China.

In the early '50s Pepsi made yet another logo change and began the 'Pepsi Generation' ad campaign. In 1964 Diet Pepsi was introduced and in 1965 the can of Pepsi made a commercial debut (having been previously used by the military). In 1970 Pepsi introduced the 2-litre plastic bottle and then 12 pack cans. In the 1990s it introduced 24 can packs.

In the 1980s Pepsi started its 'Pepsi Challenge' campaign against Coca-Cola, which caused Coke to change its flavour. Pepsi's new advertising slogan became 'the choice of a New Generation'. Then in the 1990s Pepsi became 'A Generation Ahead', and used leading singers in its advertising. In 1996 Pepsi launched itself upon the World Wide Web. Pepsi World eventually surpassed all expectations, and became one of the most landed, and copied, sites in this new media,

Key campaigns:
Twice as much for a nickel ... 1930s–40s
You've got a lot to live, Pepsi's got a lot to give 1960s
This had clear implications for the generation of Americans living through the trauma of the Vietnam War.
Come alive . . . the Pepsi Generation 1964
This slogan had problems in Germany and China where it had connotations of bringing back the dead.
Pepsi 'Evolution' commercial

(((⊕))) SEE WEB LINKS

Over all Pepsi, Coca-Cola's great rival, is drunk in as many countries as Coca-Cola, but without the huge advertising budgets. Pepsi also relies heavily on celebrity endorsements and frequently uses comparative advertising under the guise of consumer tests ('The Pepsi Challenge': Taste the Difference). The latter led Coke to change the flavour, prompting massive protest, which Coca-Cola turned brilliantly to its advantage.

McDonald's

(((⊕))) SEE WEB LINKS

The McDonald's story is one of globalization of a brand, then the gradual decline of its brand in the face of public criticism and attack, then its overall reinvention in order to adapt to new tastes, lifestyles, and values.

Established in California during the 1940s by two brothers, the McDonald's restaurant became a popular with teenagers. In 1955, entrepreneur Ray Kroc bought the right to franchise the McDonald's System. The company became the McDonald's Corporation in 1960.

From the inception, Kroc focused the McDonald's brand on the family and children, spending heavily on television advertising and using the clown character 'Ronald McDonald'. The McDonald's franchise was extended to 30,000 well-located restaurants globally and a clientele of over 50 million people in more than 100 countries,

Between 1969 and 2002 McDonald's brand and marketing strategy were celebrated. It was a quintessentially global brand, epitomized by its instantly recognizable golden arches logo, with its clear and simple values and its well-understood food products. It had conquered the world by using a repeatable formula of selecting good locations and franchising them with strict marketing controls.

In the new century, the strengths that had made McDonald's a successful global brand, began to be weaknesses. Repeated public criticism and attacks combined with changing consumer lifestyle and attitudes contributed to a decline of McDonald's reputation and franchise. For a while McDonald's seemed caught in a time warp at best, and innately dangerous at worst. It was criticized for its quality and treatment of staff, for the despoliation of the environment (land purchase for grazing cattle in the Amazonian rainforests, use of Styrofoam packing contributing to CFCs), for cruelty to animals, for contributing to a burgeoning problem of obesity, and for its insidious manipulation of children from an early age. Less tangibly, it was seen as a flag bearer of globalization, of American values and lifestyle, which themselves were becoming increasingly attacked in the new century. The phrase 'McJobs', clearly focused on McDonald's workers, came to mean low-paid, low-prospect, menial work.

Between 1998 and 2002, McDonald's, whose growth had been hitherto inexorable, started to experience decline: its actual share of the fast-food market fell more than three per cent. Sales were stagnant since 2000 and plummeted 2.8% in 2002, representing the first ever decline in the corporation's history. In Europe too, competition from other fast food chains and anti-McDonald's sentiments began to affect the company profitability. McDonald's stock lost about 70% of its value. The World Health Organization's (WHO) made public warnings about an impending obesity crisis; this led to attacks on fast food outlets in general and on McDonald's in particular.

For example, in 2001, investigative journalist Eric Schlosser made a sustained attack on the fast food industry with his book *Fast Food Nation*. In this book, Schlosser attacked McDonald's for supplying unhealthy food and for its contribution to making America the most obese nation on earth. He also decried the globalization of a homogenized culture to the entire world. He highlighted the conditions under which unskilled immigrants worked in McDonald's restaurants and the anti-union practices of McDonald's. A few years after Schlosser's *Fast Food Nation*, McDonald's reputation suffered another blow with *Super Size Me*, a documentary by Morgan Spurlock meant to highlight the dangerous health effects of eating an excess of McDonald's food. Spurlock used himself as a guinea pig as he set out on a 30-day experiment in which he ate nothing but McDonald's food. The audience watched as he gained weight and doctors observed his health decline.

In the face of its relative decline, McDonald's set about revitalizing its brand for a changing world, and in responding directly to the public criticisms it faced. The brand revitalization had to be more than cosmetic (although there was a new tag line and modified logo). The changes had to go deeply into its core supply, in store operations, staff operations, food production, and its corporate social responsibility.

McDonald's first of all set about correcting the environmental charges (its packaging contributed to CFC emissions) by establishing a $16 m national recycling programme for its packaging and became a major purchaser of recycled materials. In 1990, McDonald's outlined a 40-point plan to reduce its waste by 80%. Foam packaging (the main contributor to CFCs) was eliminated from its 8,500 US outlets and paper wrappings were brought back.

The company contributed heavily to charitable causes—particularly those involving children and families. It began a programme of animal welfare. For example, McDonald's meat suppliers must ensure humane methods for handling livestock—such as phasing out the previous practice of removing chickens' beaks. It also forbids suppliers from using growth hormones on livestock. In 2007, McDonald's announced that it would buy coffee only from growers who are certified by the Rainforest Alliance.

McDonald's restaurants were given a facelift—staff were given new uniforms and there was a modernization of décor. Menus were updated to include healthier foods, such as salads. Modifications were made to accommodate local tastes (for example in India which does not eat beef). The new target market was teenagers rather than children. Their first ad in their teenage magazine featured pop star Justin Timberlake singing its new 'I'm Lovin' It' strapline.

The Great Recession of 2007-09 also helped McDonald's as many hard-strapped people returned to the fast food world and its original core value proposition—low cost food—became a necessity rather than a lifestyle choice.

In recent brand valuation surveys, McDonald's brand is once again back in the top 20.

Kellogg's

( ) SEE WEB LINKS

Kellogg changed the eating habits of the western world at breakfast time. Although there are a huge variety of breakfast cereals around the world, Kellogg's, the 'original' creator of the cereal, remains the most well-known brand. Their brand proposition is the concept of 'healthy eating'—their marketing mix is mainly continuous product development and innovative product packaging and promotions.

Will Keith (WK) Kellogg (1860–1951), along with his brother, Dr John Harvey Kellogg, was the co-inventor of flaked corn based cereal. In 1906, WK Kellogg had entered the cereal business, using only the corn grit as the basis of the food. To help consumers distinguish Kellogg's Corn Flakes® cereal from other cereal companies, WK put his signature on each package, saying that his Corn Flakes were 'The Original'. The ready-to-eat cereal market grew with the advent of pasteurized milk.

In 1914, Kellogg Company created Waxtite® wrappers, a new concept in packaging technology. They distributed free samples of Corn Flakes, and then followed up with advertising in magazines and on billboards. Kellogg's® Bran Flakes and All Bran® cereals were introduced in 1915 and 1916. Kellogg's® Rice Krispies® were introduced in 1927. After having success in the US market, Kellogg expanded internationally—with Corn Flakes reaching the UK and Australia in the 1920s. Also in the 1920s Kellogg started to use the cereal box for marketing promotions, particularly focusing on children, who were encouraged to fill in and return coupons from the boxes in order to win competitions and various gifts—which was an incentive to continuous purchase. Kellogg also sponsored radio shows for children. During the Second World War Kellogg's provided Corn Flakes as rations to US service personnel. In 1942 it extended its product line into whole-wheat cereal such as Raisin Bran®.

Throughout the 1950s the company extended its cereals product line and started to create more powerful and enduring brands such as: Kellogg's® Corn Pops®, Kellogg's Frosted Flakes®, Kellogg's® Honey Smacks™, Kellogg's® Cocoa Krispies™ and Kellogg's® Special K®, (which was the first high-protein breakfast cereal ever offered to consumers). Sales of Kellogg's Frosted Flakes were boosted by the introduction of its 'spokesperson' Tony the Tiger® who made his first appearance in the 1950s. In the 1960s Kelloggs strengthened its position with the introduction of even more new consumer products: Froot Loops®, Kellogg's Apple Jacks®, Kellogg's Frosted Mini-Wheats®, Kellogg's Bran Buds®, Kellogg's Product 19®, Kellogg's Pop-Tarts®, and Kellogg's® Croutettes™ croutons.

Kellogg became a global brand, expanding in South America, Canada, Scandinavia, Europe, and Asia. The apex of their product placement in the 1960s was when the crew of Apollo 11 had Kellogg cereal for breakfast during their lunar landing mission in 1969.

Throughout the 1970s and 1980s Kellogg continued to develop new cereal products, particularly in response to the rising demand for healthy eating in the western world. Various scientific reports affirmed the importance of fibre and grain in the regular diet, which was a major fillip to Kellogg's product marketing efforts.

In the 1990s Kellogg satisfied a generation needing fast convenience foods with snack bars such as Kellogg's® Rice Krispies Treats® squares, and Kellogg's® Nutri-Grain® bars. By the turn of the century, cereal, the company's original product, was only half its product line: following acquisition, it also produced convenience snacks and grain based foods.

Notable Advertising Campaign
Snap! Crackle! Pop! 1940s

(⊕) **SEE WEB LINKS**

Coined in the US in the late 1920s, this simple and enduring slogan was accompanied by a hummable ditty. The advent of commercial television in the late 1940 and 1950s gave this slogan and campaign a vast audience and enduring brand recognition for this Kellogg's cereal over the years. While the look and appearance of the characters has changed over the years, the slogan is etched in the mass memory of consumers. It is a fine example of 'humanizing' an otherwise humdrum foodstuff.

Maxwell House

(⊕) **SEE WEB LINKS**

Maxwell House Coffee is actually named after a hotel, the Maxwell House, in Nashville, Tennessee. Completed after the US Civil War, the Maxwell House became one of the best-known hotels in the United States for 100 years. Presidents who stayed there included Rutherford B Hayes, William Henry Harrison, Grover Cleveland, William McKinley, Theodore Roosevelt, William Howard Taft, and Woodrow Wilson.

While staying at the Maxwell House Hotel, President Theodore Roosevelt enjoyed the 'house blend' of coffee so much that he raved about it being 'good to the last drop'. The Check-Neal Company, which supplied the hotel's coffee, wisely saw a good marketing opportunity. They began packaging and selling the hotel's house blend as Maxwell House Coffee, using President Roosevelt's remark in its advertising. Both the coffee and the slogan caught on with the American public.

The hotel was destroyed by fire in 1961, but its name lives on in the Regal Maxwell House Hotel at a different location in Nashville. And, of course, the name lives on in Maxwell House Coffee, which is still advertised as 'Good to the Last Drop'.

Schlitz Beer

Milwaukee is actually famous for brewing and is known in America as the 'beer capital of the world'. Cheap, abundant ice from Lake Michigan favoured brewing before the advent of artificial refrigeration. Ice also stimulated long-distance shipping of beer, since rail cars needed to be packed with enormous quantities of ice to prevent spoilage of the beer en route. Compared to other major brewing cities, such as Chicago, Milwaukee's population (and that of its outlying regions) was relatively small. Milwaukee brewers were forced to turn to outside markets to expand sales. This unique problem ultimately transformed Milwaukee's breweries into export-minded organizations. The strategy of long-distance distribution did not cease for Milwaukee's brewers until they had covered the American market.

The large beer-consuming population of Chicago and the easy and inexpensive lake transportation acted as an early stimulant to Milwaukee's brewing industry. The Great Chicago Fire of 1871 boosted sales of Milwaukee breweries enormously. Schlitz's frequent shipments of beer to the devastated city earned it the slogan, 'The Beer that Made Milwaukee Famous'. And Schlitz enjoyed a 100% jump in sales.

Grateful Chicago was instantly bonded with Schlitz and before local breweries could rebuild, Schlitz captured the city's beer market. Within a year the company adopted the slogan, 'The Beer that Made Milwaukee Famous' for all aspects of its enduring brand marketing.

Notable Iconic Advertising Campaign
The Beer that Made Milwaukee Famous 1895 onwards

(⊕) SEE WEB LINKS

Guinness

(⊕) SEE WEB LINKS

The Guinness stout is a distinctive black drink with its equally distinctive Irish harp logo, which first appeared on Guinness in 1862. The innate distinctiveness of the drink itself has been raised to new levels by a century of outstanding quality advertising campaigns around some memorable straplines. Since its first advert in 1928, Guinness has been handled by five agencies—SH Benson, J Walter Thompson, Allen Brady, Marsh, Ogilvy & Mather, and currently Abbott Mead Vickers.

Guinness's advertising agency (SH Benson) did some market research during the 1920s to find our what people liked about Guinness. People responded that they felt good when they had their pint and the slogan 'Guinness Is Good For You' was born. The slogan is still used in some countries (Africa) that do not regulate advertising claims. Some advertising even features athletes implying that their athleticism can be attributed to Guinness. In the UK, post-operative patients used to be given Guinness, as were blood donors. In Ireland, Guinness is still made available to blood donors and stomach and intestinal post-operative patients. Guinness is known to be high in iron content.

Guinness used the talented artist John Gilroy to craft a memorable and enduring set of images to develop the idea that Guinness was good for you. Gilroy's first known Guinness poster was produced in 1930. Working with copywriters like Ronald Barton and Robert Bevan, Gilroy produced more than 100 press advertisements and nearly 50 poster designs for Guinness over 35 years. He is perhaps best remembered for his posters featuring the girder carrier and the wood cutter from the Guinness for Strength campaigns of the early 1930s and for the Guinness animals. The animals, including a lion, toucan, gnu, and kangaroo, appeared, with their long-suffering zookeeper, on posters, press advertisements, show cards, and waiter trays from the 1930s to the 1960s. Gilroy continued to produce Guinness advertisements well into the 1960s even though he left Benson's employment as an in-house artist in the 1940s to pursue freelance work.

Guinness today is more focused on the psychological than upon the physical, particularly in relation to men.

Iconic Advertising Campaigns
Guinness Is Good for You 1929–63

(⊕) SEE WEB LINKS

'Good things come to those who wait' 1998–

'Surfer'

(⊕) SEE WEB LINKS

'Evolution'

(⊕) SEE WEB LINKS

'Tipping Point'

(⊕) SEE WEB LINKS

'Swimmer'

(⊕) SEE WEB LINKS

HJ Heinz

(⊕) SEE WEB LINKS

Henry John Heinze, son of Lorenz Heinze of Bavaria who emigrated to the US, was born in 1844. He began the company selling horseradish from the family vegetable patch to his neighbours. Later, they started putting ground horseradish into bottles.

In 1869 he took a partner and founded the firm of Heinz (dropping the 'e') and Noble that sold bricks and horseradish. The company flourished and two years later Heinz opened a food-processing factory where bottled horseradish and bottled pickles were made. After a promising start, the firm was bankrupted in the depression that marked the post-Civil War period and the early 1870s. Heinz borrowed $3,000 from his brother John and his cousin Frederick to relaunch as F & J Heinz. The new firm introduced tomato ketchup, pepper sauce, vinegar, apple butter, fruit jellies, and mincemeat to the US market. In 1886 he visited London and persuaded the famous firm of Fortnum & Mason to sell his goods in the UK, still at that stage the world's richest market.

In 1888 Henry bought out his brother's interests, re-named the firm HJ Heinz & Company and then bought a new site and started planning to build a new factory.

It was in 1896 that he originated the famous '57 Varieties' slogan which became one of the more famous brand signatures in the world of fast-moving consumer goods. Corporate folklore at Heinz has it that, in 1896, Henry John Heinz noticed an advertisement for '21 styles of shoes'. He decided that his own products were not styles, but varieties. Although there were many more than 57 foods in production at the time, because the numbers 5 and 7 held a special significance for him and his wife, he adopted the slogan '57 Varieties'. So, in fact the number 57 isn't related to the number of products offered by Heinz.

In 1928, it was decided to produce a canned food that became the flagship of the Heinz company, baked beans in tomato sauce. The introduction of baked beans was so successful that it was followed by spaghetti and a variety of soups. During the Second World War the Heinz factory produced food for the armed forces. Heinz became a listed public company in 1946 and continued its global expansion.

HJ Heinz & Company today is an enterprise involving more than 45,800 people in over 200 major locations worldwide, with leading brands on three continents, offering a lot more than 57 varieties—actually more like 5,700 different products in total. It is the world's largest tomato producer.

Iconic Campaign
57 Varieties 1896–
(((⊕))) SEE WEB LINKS

Luxury Goods
De Beers
(((⊕))) SEE WEB LINKS

The marketing of diamonds is one of the more instructive cases of the 20th century: the power of a sustained marketing campaign and how it shaped the public perception of diamonds as a desirable gift is most revealing.

The market for diamonds has never been characterized by free, dynamic, and open competition. Everything about the diamond industry is manipulated: supply, pricing, processing, marketing, and retailing. The leader of the diamond industry is De Beers, a company that produces half of the world's high-quality diamonds.

De Beer's 'A Diamond is Forever' advertising campaign, which started in the 1940s, was to become one of the most effective and far reaching of the 20th century. It enabled De Beers to manipulate demand as well as supply of diamonds. With the help of their advertising agency, they created a mindset, which later swept the world, in which diamonds came to be perceived, not simply as precious gems that could be traded according to volatile market prices, but as an inseparable part of our emotional life. Most specifically, diamonds became a significant love token, marking the engagement that could lead to married life. It is now difficult for courting couples to contemplate engagement without, at some stage, discussing the purchase of a diamond solitaire ring. Anything less would appear to devalue the courtship, and be a less than permanent token. The size of the diamond, or its number of carats, was somehow perceived to signify the grandeur of the affection. It was a potent place to occupy in the mass consciousness.

Although the first record of a diamond engagement ring dates back to 1477, before the 1940s, diamonds were generally not held in such high esteem and did not hold such a cherished place in the minds of women. The idea of a long historical tradition of giving a diamond ring for an engagement was a post-war invention. The giving of diamonds to mark an engagement had been around since the 19th century, but it was a low key, optional activity. In Germany, Austria, Italy, and Spain, the notion of giving diamond rings to commemorate an engagement was not even entertained. On the eve of the Second World War, Germany saw diamonds as important for industrial and military purposes, given that it is the world's hardest substance. In the UK and France, before the war, diamonds were perceived as a jewel for the upper classes. In America, the gift was usually confined to a lower quality, inexpensive diamond. Diamond sales had actually been declining in America since the early 1920s, both in quantity and value.

The man who decided to change the pattern of demand for diamonds was Harry Oppenheimer of De Beers. Oppenheimer was at the time concerned by the post-depression collapse of diamond prices, despite the best efforts of the DeBeers cartel to manipulate prices by control of supply. He selected the NW Ayer advertising agency in New York to achieve this extraordinary piece of marketing manipulation.

NW Ayer, following extensive research came up with a plan to change the attitude of the American public towards diamonds. It was a long-term strategy—to change a mind set and behaviour pattern—rather than an attempt to drive short-term sales of diamonds. Therefore, marketing of diamonds was essentially an appeal to emotions, rather than a focus on the gemstone itself. Through multiple messages and images the world would begin to perceive diamonds as the jewel of romance, esteem, and enduring love.

As a result of the sustained marketing campaign, the diamond market started to develop a curious pattern: although the diamond is for female decoration, the market is mainly composed of men as buyers—90% of all diamonds are bought by men for women. The wearers are almost always women; women rarely buy diamonds either for themselves or for others. Moreover, women are rarely involved in the selection or purchase of the diamond. The reaction of the woman, rather than the object itself, is the primary driver in the male purchasing decision. The element of surprise following the presentation of the diamond ring to the woman, and the gushing delight as it is received is an abiding mental image, portrayed in many films and television shows.

The result of the first 40 years of marketing was that Ayer helped De Beers expand its sales of diamonds in the United States from $23 m in 1939 to over $2 bn by 1980. In the same period, expenditure on diamond advertising for De Beers in North America increased from $200,000 a year to $10 m.

How did they do it? Celebrity endorsements, primarily. Ayer sought out the glamorous role models who were able to influence the purchasing habits of Middle America. In the 1940s, movie stars had a huge bearing on American society. The agency began negotiations with Hollywood to use diamonds in the titles of their movies. Movie scripts started to include the leading men using diamonds to make marriage proposals. News stories and society photographs were planted that emphasized the link between diamonds and romance. In 1946, the agency began a weekly service called Hollywood Personalities, which published stories in 125 leading newspapers with descriptions of the diamonds worn by major movie stars. In 1947, the agency produced portraits of socialites showing off their diamond rings for recent engagements. Nationwide lecture tours were organized to introduce high school girls to different ranges of diamonds and to start to plant the idea in the minds of the young. Fashion designers were encouraged to use diamonds in their new creations. The British royal family was even used to enhance the status of diamonds: for example, Oppenheimer presented Queen Elizabeth II with prize diamonds during her trip to South Africa.

The De Beers advertising campaign continued unabated during the Second World War: Ayers promoted the message that diamonds were contributing to the war effort and, consequently, buying diamonds was equated with patriotism. By 1941, the campaign was starting to show results: the sale of diamonds had increased by 55% in the United States. After the war, the Ayer agency focused upon the millions of American servicemen returning from the war.

The American market for diamonds was around 70 million people in the immediate post-war period. The agency, on behalf of De Beers, sought to influence men to buy more, and bigger, diamonds in the name of an invented 'tradition' that was linked emotionally to romance. In 1948 an Ayer copywriter came up with the legendary and enduring slogan: 'A Diamond Is Forever.' Within a year, it became the official signature of De Beers. In the 1950s, the era of conspicuous consumption in America, NW Ayer used the new medium of television to influence American public opinion. Famous actresses and other celebrities displayed diamonds to the television audience. A diamond not only became a way of legitimising a romance, of finding and keeping a man, it also became a status symbol in a status-hungry culture. The more the carats, the deeper the love, the more enduring the relationship, the greater the prestige. A famous song of the time stated, 'diamonds are a girl's best friend'.

During all this time the agency also promoted the idea that De Beers diamonds were authentic and that they were made from the rarest stones. This enabled them to fend off the challenge of synthetic diamonds (such as the process developed by GE in the 1950s). In the 1960s the agency proposed the global expansion of the idea that they had so successfully nurtured over a 20-year period in the United States. They proposed the invention of the same 'tradition' in other countries where it did not previously exist. Japan, Germany, and Brazil were targeted. Within ten years, De Beers succeeded even beyond its most optimistic expectations in creating a billion-dollar-a-year diamond tradition in Japan. Many Japanese believe that giving diamonds as a love token is part of an ancient Japanese tradition. Once the international market had provided expanded sales, the agency promoted the idea of buying a second diamond ring as a symbol of 'renewal' of marriage and of long-term love. These became known as 'later in life' diamonds. This came at a time as diamond production expanded and there was a risk of flooding the market.

With the production of diamonds of smaller caratage in the Soviet Union (which De Beers distributed), the company now had to make small diamonds respectable. The average size of a diamond, which was one carat in 1939, fell to one-quarter carat by the late 1970s. The consequence of this was to diminish the market for large diamonds, which came to be seen by the American consumers, who had become gradually accustomed to the idea of buying smaller diamonds, as gaudy and brash. Conversely, the demand for smaller diamonds started to outstrip supply.

Today, the diamond market is a low growth market, and in recent times the diamond mining industry has come under greater scrutiny for its abuse of diamond mine workers, its unethical political practices, and its manipulation of supply. De Beers has taken the decision to re-invent itself as a luxury goods company.

Iconic Campaign
A Diamond Is Forever NW Ayer, 1940s

SEE WEB LINKS

The campaign that effectively invented the diamond solitaire as the engagement ring of choice and established it as a symbol of eternal love. Prior to this campaign, love had been symbolized by all different manner of tokens and gemstones, few of which were as expensive as a diamond.

Steinway Pianos

Ray Rubican developed the famous slogan under contract to NW Ayer & Son. He noticed that almost all the greatest pianists and most of the great composers since Wagner had used Steinway pianos. Steinway had not exploited these excellent references: in fact most of Steinway's ads up to 1919 consisted of photographs of ladies sitting at pianos in lovely drawing rooms. The phrase 'The Instrument of Immortals' was developed. Steinway were initially sceptical. However, they agreed to run it once. The ad brought an immediate response. Although Steinway initially considered commercial slogans to be vulgar, they reconsidered and Steinway sales went up almost 70%. 'The Instrument of Immortals' remained the Steinway hallmark for decades.

Steinway has since this time been regarded by practitioners and the public as the world's greatest piano maker.

Notable Campaign
The Instrument of the Immortals 1919

Montblanc

SEE WEB LINKS

One of the best examples of high-quality, branded, luxury-goods companies is Montblanc.

Founded by the stationer Claus-Johannes Voss, the banker Alfred Nehemias, and the engineer August Eberstein in 1906, the company began as the Simplo Filler Pen company producing upmarket pens in the Schanzen district of Hamburg.

Their first model was the Rouge et Noir in 1909 followed in 1910 by the pen that was later to give the company its new name, the Mont Blanc. The fountain pen known today as the Meisterstück or Masterpiece was produced in 1925. Today the Montblanc brand is on other goods besides pens: watches, leather goods, and personal accessories.

The company was acquired by Dunhill in 1977, following which lower price pens were dropped and the brand was used on a wide range of luxury goods other than pens. Today Montblanc forms part of the Richemont group. Its sister companies include luxury brands Cartier, Van Cleef & Arpels, Chloé, and Baume et Mercier. Since 2000, Montblanc has manufactured all the components for Montegrappa and Cartier branded pens.

A trademark identified with Montblanc is the white stylized six-pointed star with rounded edges, representative of the Mont Blanc snowcap from above, the symbol being adopted in 1913. The number '4810', the mountain's height in metres, is also a commonly recurring theme.

Recently, it has been suggested that the logo be updated—by removing the name and using the star only. The star is also referred to as an edelweiss, an indigenous perennial that grows in the alpine forests and mountains of Europe.

Political and National Government Campaigns

Arguably, marketing has always been part of the political process in both the East and the West; whether through the use of state-controlled propaganda, party-funded advertising or, more recently, political-message management; marketing techniques are now an integral part of politics and political power.

Here is a range of important political campaigns that used the major media of their day to advance their party and candidates:

Republican Party Presidential campaign for Dwight Eisenhower
I Like Ike 1952
Eisenhower, the Supreme Allied Commander during the latter stages of World War II, captured the White House at a time when the USA had become the undisputed richest and most powerful nation on earth and had become hysterical about the threat of the USSR and was rabidly anti-communist.

This slogan appeared on millions of election campaign buttons and posters and in songs. With its alliteration, it was simplistic, but devastatingly effective.

British Conservative Party campaign poster
Labour Isn't Working Saatchi and Saatchi, 1978
A campaign that introduced the power of advertising into the world of British politics, seen to have been a decisive contributor to the downfall of the Labour government and the beginning of 18 years in power for the Conservatives under Margaret Thatcher, who became Britain's first woman prime minister. The campaign actually began before the general election of 1979, and was given greater poignancy when Labour called the election during the chaos of the infamous 'winter of discontent'.

The irony is that the supposed dole queue featured in the ad was, in fact, a group of Young Conservatives from Hendon, who were asked to participate in the shoot. Only about 20 of them turned up, and Saatchi & Saatchi, which became the ad agency of choice for the Conservatives for the next 9 years, had to reproduce images of the same people to create the impression of a snaking queue.

The campaign cost only around £100,000, but gained huge media attention, particularly amplified by the reaction of outraged Labour cabinet ministers.

After the election of 1979, Lord Thorneycroft, Tory party treasurer at the time, claimed that the poster had 'won the election for the Conservatives'.

Barack Obama Presidential campaign 2008

Just as John F Kennedy had used the emerging power of television to defeat the untelegenic Richard Nixon in the 1960 US presidential campaign, Barack Obama and his election team used the new power of the Internet as a political medium to triumph against John McCain in the 2008 presidential election.

The Obama campaign built a groundswell of political support and donations using the Web and social media. He continued to use 'old media' such as campaign rallies, broadcasts, and television advertising—but these were subordinated to the main Internet campaign, which became a national movement of volunteers, supporters, and donors.

Text messages were used over mobile phones to provide regular messages and to make requests. Facebook (Obama's Facebook page had 2.6 million 'friends' and 161,000 active users), YouTube (14.5 million hours spent watching official Barack Obama campaign videos), Twitter (123,00 'followers'), and the official website (3.2 million made donations via the campaign website) were the main web instruments used in the campaign—usage and engagement of which could be measured directly by the Obama team, unlike more traditional advertising. Obama was mentioned in 500 million blog postings (compared to McCain's 150 million) for the duration of the electoral campaign. It was also far less costly than the traditional 'pay for TV advertising' which had become the mainstay of American political campaigns since Kennedy-Nixon. Unlike Kennedy, Obama controlled the medium and therefore the message; unlike Kennedy in 1960, Obama achieved a landslide win.

National Government War campaigns

UK Army recruitment poster WWI
Your Country Needs You 1914
((🌐)) SEE WEB LINKS

The resolute face of Kitchener pointing at potential recruits had a massive effect on the British psyche, sending thousands of young volunteers to the slaughter of the trenches. Kitchener drowned, and conscription was introduced in 1916, the volunteer force having been largely wiped out since the beginning of hostilities. The poster campaign remains one of the enduring icons of the 20th century.

US War Department poster WWII
Loose Lips Sink Ships 1941–45
((🌐)) SEE WEB LINKS

With German and Japanese submarines patrolling American waters after 1942, there was huge concern over security and the need for secrecy to protect shipping. German U-boats had made a devastating raid on American fleets in the Atlantic and, of course, there was also Pearl Harbour.

This poster was part of a campaign to discourage loose or careless talk about all military matters, both in the public and in the private domain.

UK recruitment poster WWI
Daddy, what did you do in the Great War? Savile Lumey 1916
((🌐)) SEE WEB LINKS

A poster commissioned by the British Parliamentary Recruiting Committee in 1915. By 1915 the mood had changed from naïve patriotism to a sense of duty and dark resolution. This ad focused on creating a guilty conscience in those who shirked the call to arms. The little girl has apparently put her father on the spot: was he a 'shirker' during the war, or did he enlist and 'do his bit'? The look on his face suggests he was one of the men who may have elected not to serve his king and country.

A contemporary response quoted by Eric Partridge in his *Catch Phrases* was 'Shut up, you little bastard. Get the Bluebell and go and clean my medals'.

UK Ministry of Agriculture poster WWII
Dig For Victory 1940–45

(⊕) SEE WEB LINKS

An outstanding example of a public information campaign resulting in positive action. At a time of endangered food supply, the UK started the war with 850,000 allotments and ended with 1.4 million and became almost self-sustaining in food.

Places

One of the dominant forms of marketing has become the marketing of specific places—cities, regions, countries. Initially the main reason was to attract tourists and foreign currency; additionally the new target is the international, or 'inward', investor to bring direct investment and, potentially, employment to the area.

New York State Department of Commerce
I Love New York 1977
The most famous campaign in repositioning a city started when New York was in severe decline in the 1970s, facing bankruptcy, and bedevilled by high crime rates. New York, from the 1980s onwards, rebuilt its reputation as one of the world's most dynamic cities.

Host Cities and the Olympic Games
One of the principal marketing instruments in the 21st century for an individual city is to win the right to host the summer Olympic Games. As well as being seen to embrace the ideals of the Olympic movement, a city, usually backed by the national government, uses the Olympics to stimulate awareness of their city in the world, to encourage investment in local facilities and infrastructure, to create jobs, and to stimulate economic growth, either through tourism or inward investment. Increasingly, the Olympic games are awarded to host cities in recognition of their rising economic power.

The bidding process run by the Olympic Committee for the award of the Olympic Games is itself a major marketing activity involving the world's media and thousands of local, state, regional, and national government officials and huge expenses. Juan Antonio Samaranch, former IOC president, and the architect behind making the Olympic Games more open to commercial marketing opportunities, suggested in 1993, 'Marketing has become an increasingly important issue for all of us in the Olympic Movement. The revenue derived from television sponsorship and fundraising help to provide the movement with its financial independence.'

The spiralling costs of hosting an Olympics have led to an economic case that the Olympics have to result in more than a short-term injection of media attention, the patriotic gratification of having staged a successful games, and tourism, and the emphasis is now placed on the 'Olympic legacy'—the benefit derived once the visitors have departed and the benefits to the city of the new sports facilities, the infrastructure, and the long-range impact on tourism and inward investment.

The most successfully hosted Olympics of modern times—the Beijing Olympics of 2008—announced the dramatic re-entrance of China on to the world stage as a major power. It clearly helped in 'marketing' China, and Beijing in particular, to a world largely unfamiliar with it.

Given the Olympics is the most heavily viewed sporting event on earth, the awareness of the host city is always significantly increased, but awareness (a quantitative measure) must be distinguished from image enhancement (a qualitative measure) because image can be both positive and negative. Some cities do not always enhance their image as a result of hosting the Summer and Winter Olympics: examples include heavy financial loss (Montreal, 1976); building delays (Athens, 2004); terrorism or bomb detonations (Munich, 1972; Atlanta 1996); country or government boycotts (Montreal, 1976; Moscow, 1980; Los Angeles, 1984; Seoul, 1988); ambush marketing (Atlanta, 1996); weather problems (Calgary, 1988; Nagano, 1998); and suggestions of financial or bidding process impropriety (Sydney, 2000; Salt Lake City, 2002). The LA Olympics of 1984—and the Winter Olympics of Salt Lake City and Lillehammer—are so far the only games known to have made a profit, as opposed to losses, or simply to break even (Sydney).

Professional Services

Services are an increasingly large portion of the GDP of advanced economies and rising each year. Professional services are among the most profitable of these services. The marketing of professional services presents a paradox: professional services are among the oldest forms of organized business activity in history, and marketing is among one of the least established business disciplines—yet the marketing of professional services is one of the most under-developed and elusive business activities to which marketing discipline is applied.

Professional services firms, with a heavy emphasis on individual relationships, small-scale client entertainment, and discrete sponsorship have not recorded many iconic campaigns as have existed in mass consumer product and services organizations. However, the marketing ethos is starting slowly to take hold in even the most old-fashioned professional services firms.

Accenture

(((⊕))) SEE WEB LINKS

Accenture, a brand that was born on the first day of 2001, has already established global recognition in a relatively short time period. Accenture is the pioneer in professional services brand and image building, having adapted the techniques of consumer marketing in the 1990s to differentiate it from its accounting parent Arthur Andersen.

The antecedents of Accenture's brand building were unique: it was formerly the consulting practice of the accounting firm Arthur Andersen and was separated to form an independent business unit. In a bold and unprecedented step the firm began, in 1989, to market itself as an organization that helped companies apply technology to create business advantage. It became a top quality consultancy brand by the end of the 1990s. In a decade it had achieved the extremely difficult task of positioning itself in the information technology professional services market space. It had, simultaneously, created a separate identity from its accounting roots with Arthur Andersen.

In order to build this new identity, the firm had taken the pioneering step of using consumer marketing techniques to develop and build a professional services brand. It was the professional services industry's first large-scale advertising campaign used to promote name, market positioning, and brand image. Before this, the professional services category had formal rules that prevented advertising, and was known for its outmoded and archaic approaches. Most professional services firms chose not to advertise, feeling it was inappropriate, or even unprofessional.

Between 1990 and 2000, as the market for technology, systems integration, and management consultancy boomed, so the firm grew from an accounting firm's offshoot into the world's largest management and technology consulting organization.

On August 7, 2000, Accenture was notified of the successful outcome of arbitration against Andersen Worldwide and Arthur Andersen. As part of the final award that released Accenture from all further obligations to Arthur Andersen and Andersen Worldwide, Accenture was required to cease using the Andersen Consulting name by December 31, 2000.

This confronted the 11-year-old firm with a branding challenge on a gargantuan scale. After spending an estimated $7 bn building their brand over a decade, the company now had to find, implement, and introduce to the world a new name in a matter of months. Never before had a rebranding of such scope been implemented over so short a timeframe.

The rebranding as Accenture—the largest rebranding initiative ever undertaken by a professional services firm—was successfully implemented across 47 countries in just 147 days. Accenture launched worldwide on January 1, 2001. The name Accenture was invented by an employee following an internal competition, and is a fusion of 'accent' and 'future'. Accenture planned a two-phased marketing strategy for introducing itself to its global audience. The aim of both phases was to surround the company's target audience—including its 40,000 clients and prospects, 70,000 employees, 1.5 million potential recruits, as well as worldwide press and media—with messages informing them about the new name and new positioning. As well as rebranding, the objectives included a desire to reposition the company in its target markets, focusing on its ability to deliver innovative solutions to its clients across its breadth of services in Consulting, Technology, and Outsourcing. Another objective was to transfer brand equity to Accenture (which was important because the company became a public corporation later in 2001) and to eliminate residual confusion with Arthur Andersen. Ironically, in the same period, its former parent, Andersen, which had opposed the separation, collapsed in a welter of financial scandals triggered by that of Enron. The Accenture rebranding was not only highly successful; in retrospect, it was an act of extraordinary business prescience.

Personal Care Products
Mouthwash (Listerine)
Notable Campaign
'Often a bridesmaid, never a bride' Milton Feasley, of Lambert and Feasley, 1925

((⊕)) SEE WEB LINKS

This famous ad campaign appeared in magazines such as *Ladies' Home Journal*.

The now famous slogan, 'Often a bridesmaid but never a bride', quickly became an adage, still in use today. Many people believe that it is an old saying.

'Edna's case was really a pathetic one. Like every woman, her primary ambition was to marry. Most of the girls of her set were married—or about to be. Yet not one possessed more grace or charm or loveliness than she. And as her birthdays crept gradually toward that tragic thirty-mark, marriage seemed farther from her life than ever.

She was often a bridesmaid but never a bride.

That's the insidious thing about halitosis (bad breath). You, yourself, rarely know when you have it . . . '

(Ad caption from the 1925 ad for Listerine that introduced the American public to halitosis.)

Hair colourant (Clairol)
Notable Campaign
Does she . . . or doesn't she? Shirley Polykoff, 1956
A tantalizing question during the early days of the sexual revolution. Sex became a major part of advertising after this campaign.

The first Miss Clairol ads were originally written, 'Does she . . . or doesn't she? Hair colour so natural only her mother knows for sure!' However, Clairol was concerned about alienating the older generation that the word was changed to 'hairdresser'. The final ad read, 'Does she . . . or doesn't she? Hair colour so natural only her hairdresser knows for sure!' Polykoff insisted the models in the Miss Clairol ads resemble the 'girl next door' rather than the high-glamour women typically portrayed in 1950s ads. The idea was to make hair colouring respectable and mainstream. The print ads typically included a child to undercut the sexual undertones, making it clear that respectable women coloured their hair, not just women of easy virtue as was believed at the time. Also, showing the mother's hair next to the child's hair emphasized the precise colour match by comparison.

Clairol's sales increased by an amazing 413% in just six years. More than 50% of adult US women began using hair colour, up from 7% prior to Polykoff's Miss Clairol campaign. Through her ads, Shirley Polykoff helped transform Clairol from a small business (a tiny division of Bristol-Myers) to a huge international brand by assisting in the creation of a hair-colouring industry.

Pears Soap
'Cleanliness is next to Godliness' 1880

(⊕) SEE WEB LINKS

This was the brainchild of Thomas Barratt, the son-in-law of Andrew Pears, inventor of the famous soap. Barratt was an early advertising genius. He persuaded prominent skin specialists, doctors, and chemists to give glowing testimonials to Pears Soap. Such endorsements were boldly displayed in magazines and newspapers, handbills, and on posters. Lillie Langtry, a highly popular actress of the day, cheerfully gave Barratt a commendation for Pears Soap. Barratt entered the lucrative American market by persuading the enormously influential religious leader Henry Ward Beecher to equate cleanliness, and Pears Soap in particular, with Godliness. Barratt promptly bought up the whole of the front page of the *New York Herald* to display the glowing testimonial.

Retail
IKEA

(⊕) SEE WEB LINKS

Founded in Sweden by Ingvar Kamprad, IKEA, a home furnishing retailer, has grown from the most unlikely local circumstances to become both a global brand and a retailing phenomenon. IKEA is headquartered in Amhult (known locally as IKEA town) in a forest in southern Sweden. Kamprad started his first furniture catalogue in 1951 and was an early user of flat packing, which was devised in the 1950s. Since it opened its first store outside Sweden in 1963, IKEA has grown to have 170 stores in 22 countries, employs 70,000 people, and uses 2000 different suppliers around the world. Their famous catalogue, which has 7000 photographs in each edition, runs to 110 million copies annually, making it one of the world's most widely circulated publications. It consumes around 50% of IKEA's total marketing budget. It does not target any particular market segment and is distributed randomly. Such a lack of classic segmentation has not impeded IKEA: their worldwide customer base is estimated at 260 million.

IKEA has capitalized on the post-war market trends of demand for home living design, wide range of choice, and customer self-service and self-help. Its global brand is built around a combination of their design skill, their products, their stores and the marketing of all of these via their catalogue. The IKEA success formula is based on simplicity in the design of its furniture and then packing the furniture into flat packs (first done in 1956) for its retail outlets that enable the consumers to transport it and assemble it themselves. (Also since the 1950s onwards the majority of consumers have cars that can carry IKEA flat packs back to their homes.) Flat packing also enables IKEA to make major cost savings, both in terms of storage and delivery, which are passed on to customers in

Appendix 2

terms of lower prices. IKEA's giant stores are usually based near large urban centres where there is a high demand for home furnishings. This gives IKEA huge cost advantages and appeals to the consumers' home design needs. Also, IKEA's retail stores are very innovative: they give consumers ideas for home design and decoration; they display entire room concepts rather than just the individual furniture components. IKEA also provides wide choice with an average of 10,000 lines available in each store, of which 20% are changed each year. However, IKEA only employs around 15 permanent designers supplemented by 80 freelance designers around the world. The designers are constantly employed in thinking through innovative ideas—from furniture design to new ways of flat packing that are based on what customers need for convenience and quality.

Sports Equipment and Apparel Brands
Adidas

SEE WEB LINKS

The Adidas brand logo
The 'Trefoil' was adopted as the corporate logo in 1972. In 1996, it was decided that the Trefoil would only be used on heritage products such as the classic running shoes. The Adidas Equipment line was launched in 1991. In January 1996, the Three-Stripes brand mark became the worldwide Adidas corporate logo. This logo is used in all advertising, printed collateral and corporate signage.

Beginning as a cobbler in Herzogenaurach, Germany, Adidas founder Adolph Dassler, built one of the world's most popular and well-known brands of sports shoes and apparel. Growing up in poverty-stricken post-World War I Germany, Adolph (nicknamed Adi) joined his family in making and selling homemade house slippers. Dassler began producing training shoes in 1920 when he was only 20 years old. He later began to manufacture soccer, tennis, and running shoes. To ensure that each shoe would be both safe and performance-enhancing, Dassler used his own athletic experience and the input of doctors, trainers, coaches, and other athletes to guide the design of his shoes. Dassler's athletic shoes were first worn in Olympic competition in 1928. Henceforth, Adidas shoes and equipment were used by Olympic athletes and national soccer teams. Jesse Owens wore Adidas track shoes during his spectacular Olympic performance in Berlin in 1936, where he earned four gold medals. Armin Hary was the first athlete to run the 100m sprint in 10 seconds, also wearing Adidas shoes. In 1949, Dassler created the first soccer shoe with moulded rubber studs and, for the first time, adopted the trademark three stripes. The German National team won in the 1954 World Cup final wearing Adidas soccer boots with screw-in studs, which enabled the game to be played under vastly different conditions without slipping.

One of Dassler's goals in producing athletic shoes was to design them according to each sport's specific demands, a goal that resulted in more than 700 patents among which were nylon soles and running spikes. Today Dassler is known as the founder of the modern sporting goods industry.

Nike

SEE WEB LINKS

Nike revolutionized sports marketing in the 20th century, although its underlying business is sports apparel, footwear, and equipment.

The name Nike derives from a goddess of Greek mythology who sat beside Zeus and who was a winged emissary who represented him to commemorate victory in battles. The famous 'swoosh' logo was created by a student Caroline Davidson in 1971 and it represents the wing of the Goddess Nike. She was paid $35 for her work by Phil Knight who had commissioned her to design it. The logo first appeared on a sports shoe in 1972.

Phil Knight had been an athlete himself, and, together with Bill Bowerman, an athletics coach at the University of Oregon who needed lighter, better quality running shoes for his runners, they started the business (originally called Blue Ribbon Sports), as a small-scale operation in Oregon, selling imported running shoes from the back of cars. The running shoes were manufactured in Japan (ironically called 'Tigers') and only branded with the Nike 'swoosh' after 1972 for US distribution.

Knight benefited from the changing attitudes to sport and exercise. Mass participation in gyms, jogging, and sports generally, which began in the 1970s and which flourished in the 1980s and 1990s created worldwide demand for low cost, high quality sportswear. By the mid-90s Nike had revenues of nearly $7 bn and was regarded as an iconic global brand.

Part of the success of Nike was their advertising campaigns as well their sponsorship of individual sportspeople (for example Michael Jordan, Tiger Woods, Venus Williams) and teams (the Brazil football team).

Example Campaign
Just do it 1988
(⊕) **SEE WEB LINKS**

One of the more successful advertising campaigns of the later 20th century. It appealed to the mood of the times for action, particularly sporting action, to achieve some purpose in life without hesitation and deliberation. The slogan, combined with the Nike 'swoosh' logo, became a global icon.

Travel
Virgin Atlantic
(⊕) **SEE WEB LINKS**

Virgin Atlantic was born in the 1980s. Richard Branson, the British entrepreneur, had already created a successful brand with the Virgin Group, particularly in the music business. He had founded the group when he was 20 as a mail-order record company and shortly after opened a music shop in London's main shopping thoroughfare, Oxford Street. The original brand slogan of these stores was 'Cheap and nasty'. A music studio was built in Oxfordshire in 1972, where one Mike Oldfield recorded his massively successful album *Tubular Bells* for the Virgin Records label. This album sold 5 million copies and was the catalyst for Virgin Records, which signed a range of successful artists, including The Rolling Stones, Culture Club, Janet Jackson, Peter Gabriel, Simple Minds, and The Human League.

Virgin was to become one of the six biggest record companies in the world. By the early '80s the Virgin Group was well established. Branson developed the idea of operating a Jumbo Jet passenger service between London and New York in 1984. Freddie Laker had already tried to create a low-cost transatlantic airline to rival the incumbents, but this ultimately failed.

An aircraft was found, staff were recruited, licences obtained and, thanks in a great part to Richard's infectious enthusiasm, the airline took off on deadline. On the 22 June 1984 a plane packed with friends, celebrities, and the media set off for Newark, New York. Since then, Virgin Atlantic has become the second largest British long-haul international airline, operating services out of London's Heathrow and Gatwick to 18 different destinations all over the world, from Shanghai to the Caribbean. Virgin Atlantic has won numerous awards for its customer service.

In 1992, Branson consolidated and, selling Virgin Music for $1 bn to Thorn EMI, he invested the profits back into Virgin Atlantic. In December 1999 Branson signed an agreement to sell a 49% stake of Virgin Atlantic to Singapore Airlines to form a unique global partnership. The deal valued Virgin Atlantic at a minimum of £1.225 bn. In 1999, the combined sales of the different Virgin holding companies were around £3 billion.

Avis

SEE WEB LINKS

When you're only No. 2 you try harder. Or Else. 1963

SEE WEB LINKS

The first campaign to promote the No. 2 market position (against Hertz's No. 1 position). This was a new technique at the time and gave Avis a platform to advance their customer service.

The Rise of Online Brands

The rise of the Web in the late 20th century ushered in a new era in direct marketing, advertising, and brand building. The Web enabled new commercial business models to be created, both for traditional as well as new products and services. A direct consequence of the web revolution was a new model for marketing. The Web enabled several new approaches to marketing: micro-segmentation of buyers and consumers, niche product and service providers were given the opportunity to expand their operations without the usual high marketing and sales costs; consumers became stronger—they had been given access to information that they could use ahead of the purchase of products, which had the effect of increasing competition and driving down prices; whole industries, which had traditionally relied on a physical intermediary, media agencies, such as bookselling, music distribution and retailing, insurance selling, travel agency, and stockbroking—moved online and were transformed forever. Traditional media, particularly print media, declined, and with it the ability to charge high prices for media placement and advertisements followed. Marketers had to learn to have continuous conversations with their customers, interacting with them, being sensitive to the shift in power to their much better informed and opinionated consumers; content was generated as much by the end user as by the producer; the ability of consumers to publish themselves on the Web and to discuss products with other users, meant that marketers began to lose their century-long ability to remain in control of the marketing message that they had created for mass audiences whom they had hitherto sought to influence and manipulate. Familiar forms of advertising and media placement declined as the use of the Web and its various applications started to displace and overtake old norms.

After the bursting of the 'dot.com' speculative bubble in the early part of the 21st century, leading web-enabled company brands, with good business models, emerged to rival the world's leading commercial brands.

Many of the early pioneering sites on the Web, initially founded in garages and student rooms, which had robust business models and focused on an unmet market need, have become major international corporations and brands, and have brought enormous wealth to their founders. Some have succeeded by transferring traditional commercial models (bookselling, auctions, printed student yearbooks) onto the Web and revolutionizing them; others have made businesses out of the technological possibilities that only existed because of the Web (online communities, search engines). Many, in classic corporate practice, have become acquirers of other online companies with less robust business models than themselves.

Here are five of the leading web company brands who have played a transformational role in changing and creating commercial business models and the conduct of marketing.

Amazon.com

Amazon.com is among the major successes of those Internet businesses founded in the 1990s. Its principal innovation was to bring the power of the Web to traditional business models (initially bookselling and later the marketing and distribution of a wide range of goods and services). Although now seen as a veteran of web-enabled businesses, in its relatively short life Amazon.com has mastered traditional marketing technique as well as modern ones: combining customer centricity, a vast range of choice, lower prices, self service, and convenient ease of use, Amazon is a classic combination of 'old world' skills with 'new world' techniques.

Amazon.com was launched in 1995, typically from a garage, by Jeff Bezos and was mainly focused on selling books. Bezos saw the World Wide Web could offer customers the convenience of browsing a selection of millions of book titles in a single view. Amazon.com was successful early, and came through the dot.com disaster at the turn of the century intact because it had a robust business model.

Since its inception Amazon.com has consistently enlarged the choice of goods and services offered to customers and expanded its ability to deliver from a worldwide set of warehouses. It has also used technological innovation to get closer to its customers. For example, Amazon.com offers a personalized shopping experience for each customer by allowing them to simulate a real-life visit to a bookstore in which they can browse books before buying ('Search Inside The Book'); they have made it very easy for customers to part with their money with their very convenient 'shopping basket' and checkout using one-click shopping; they also have intelligence software systems that analyse individual customer's preferences and buying patterns and offer them related goods ('Listmania' and 'Wish List').

Amazon.com has also opened itself up to other businesses and developers. Amazon.com is primarily an e-commerce platform, and for the past decade has made this available to other vendors. Thousands of world-class retail brands and individual sellers use the Amazon.com e-commerce platform as a sales and distribution channel ('Marketplace', 'Advantage', 'Amazon Services'). Independent software developers also work on Amazon.com's applications ('Amazon Web Services'). Launched in July 2002, the AWS platform exposes Amazon technology and product data that enables developers to build applications on their own.

Google.com

Google.com has become the dominant information search engine organization of the Internet. In the process of establishing its dominance in the information age, Google has also become one of the world's leading brands. With each year its search engine becomes increasingly sophisticated; its applications are able to track the intentions of users and to organize information around these intentions. Google also has a robust business model, and derives its revenues from a unique form of self service, results-based advertising, which it pioneered and which now threatens traditional media advertising models.

Google began life as a federally funded research programme (Digital Library Project) at Stanford University in 1996 led by PhD students Larry Page and Sergey Brin. Focused on the mathematics of web-page linking, Page and Brin developed the PageRank algorithm, which is at the heart of the Google search system. This algorithm transformed the way in which online searches are done.

Originally the search engine used the Stanford website. The domain *google.com* was registered on September 15, 1997. *Google Inc.* was incorporated on September 4, 1998 in a garage in California. The name 'Google' originated from a misspelling of 'googol' which refers to the number represented by a 1 followed by one-hundred zeros. The verb 'to

Google' was added to the *Oxford English Dictionary* in 2006, meaning 'to use the Google search engine to obtain information on the Internet'.

Usage of the Google search engine grew exponentially from its time of launch. With its growing URL index and database, the company was able to extend its services, which in turn helped to feed its own intelligence on searchers' intentions and investigations. The first Google index in 1998 had 26 million pages; by 2000 it reached the one billion mark; by 2004, 8 billion. By 2009, Google was indexing more than a trillion URLs.

By 2001 Google was available in 26 languages and in that same year started to offer image searching. 2005 was a breakthrough year for Google's extended services: for example, Google Reader, its feed reader, and Google Earth, a satellite imagery-based mapping service which combined 3D buildings and terrain with mapping capabilities for the entire planet were launched. In 2006 Google acquired the popular YouTube, which vastly extended its multimedia library assets. With various technical upgrades to its technology in 2007, Google enabled multimedia indexing (such as maps, books, and videos) to be displayed on a search results page. Google Analytics gave users the ability to measure the quality and impact of websites as well as their marketing campaigns. AdSense for mobile provided sites optimized for mobile browsers with the ability to host the same ads as standard websites. A content-targeted advertising service, enabling publishers to access Google's network of advertisers was then followed by Site Targeting, an Adwords feature giving advertisers the ability more accurately to target their ads to specific content sites. Google's Website Optimizer is a free website-testing tool with which site owners can continually test different combinations of website content (such as images and text), to see which ones yield the most sales, sign-ups, leads, or visitors. In 2009 Google started to test interest-based advertising on partner sites and on YouTube. This kind of tailored advertising allows ads more closely related to what people are searching for, and it gives advertisers an efficient way to reach those who are most interested in their products or services. Further developments in mobile advertising are also planned.

Google's meteoric rise and its funding model also challenged the traditional advertising model. Page and Brin had always been opposed to the dominant Internet advertising model of the 1990s, which was the pop-up banner advert on a website. The banner ad market started to decline rapidly after the 'dot.com' disaster in 2001–02. Having initially tried this method of advertising, Google replaced it and started selling ads associated with search keywords which were kept separate from the search terms (i.e. down the right-hand side of the search results page). Keywords came to be sold on a self service basis, with a combination of price bid and click-through. Adwords launched in 2000, with 350 customers. By 2002 it became a pay-per-click option, which Google adapted from other providers of pay-per-click at the time. Adwords uses keywords to precisely target ad delivery to web users seeking information about a particular product or service. With pay-per-click pricing, advertisers only pay when an ad is clicked on. However, Google's version of the click-through rate differed from that of other services at the time (such as Overture) who gave highest listing to the highest bidder: but this meant that an advertiser could bid their way to the top of the ranking with an irrelevant ad, and if no one clicked on it, then nobody could make any money from the advertising.

Google did not invent either search- or auction-based pay-per-click advertising—their innovation was in taking it to a new level and approaching these existing methods in a different way. Google did something different—introducing mathematics and measurable relevance into advertising—which in turn affected how marketers think about the return on advertising. Google measured the ad's relevance by the click-through rate it received and turned this into a ranking algorithm. So if an ad with a lower bid per click got clicked more often, it would rank higher. Also, the model was a flexible cost (unlike traditional media buy): advertisers can specify a maximum daily budget for their ads. Once the budgeted amount is spent, an ad is dropped for the rest of the day. This methodology was to have a major impact on both the method of advertising and also on Google's profitability as a company.

Wikipedia.com

The prime purpose of Wikipedia.com is to be a free online encyclopaedia, with the content being provided by volunteers.

Wikipedia, a name suggested by Larry Sanger, was launched on its own domain, wikipedia.com, on 15 January 2001. Wikipedia was initially conceived as a feeder project for Nupedia, a concept developed by Jimmy Wales and Larry Sanger, to produce a free online encyclopaedia. Nupedia was, however, too slow in production. So the concept of creating a faster process was advanced by Sanger as a counterpart to Nupedia, based upon the use of volunteer contributors, without expert editorial review, and using only a peer review process. Wikipedia.com was born from these discussions. The new model quickly eclipsed its parent. The project passed 1,000 articles around 12 February 2001 and by 2002, there were 40,000 articles. Wikipedia reached a million articles in 18 languages by 2006.

It saw the democratization of knowledge and the use of the Web not only to widen access but also to enlarge the number of producers to the non experts.

Major encyclopaedias, such as the *Encyclopaedia Britannica*, were still in printed hard copy; Microsoft's *Encarta*, published in 1993, was available on CD-ROM, and hyperlinked. Richard Stallman described the usefulness of a 'Free Universal Encyclopedia and Learning Resource' in 1999.

Open collaboration and communal governance based in 'wiki' software is an article of faith.

eBay.com

eBay.com was founded in 1995 as AuctionWeb in San Jose, California, by Pierre Omidyar, at the beginning of the 'commercial' phase of the Internet. eBay is not only successful in moving a classic commercial form online, but it is also a successful business model. Initially an online auction site, eBay expanded from its original format to include standard shopping, online classified advertisements, online event ticket trading, and online money transfers and other services.

By 1997, the site had hosted 2,000,000 auctions, compared with 250,000 during the first year of its existence. The company officially changed the name of its service from AuctionWeb to eBay in September 1997. Originally, the site belonged to Echo Bay Technology Group, Omidyar's consulting firm. Omidyar had tried to register the domain name echobay.com, but found it already taken so he shortened it to his second choice, *eBay.com*. Meg Whitman was hired as eBay President and CEO in March 1998. eBay went public on September 21, 1998, making Omidyar a billionaire.

As the company expanded product categories beyond collectibles into almost any saleable item, business grew quickly. In February 2002, the company purchased iBazar, a similar European auction website founded in 1995 and then bought PayPal on October 14, 2002. In late 2009, eBay completed the sale of Skype for $2.75 bn, but retained 30% equity in the company.

eBay is now a global company. Meg Whitman decided to step down to pursue a political career.

Facebook.com

By 2010 Facebook.com's list of participants was greater than the population of the USA, having only been launched as a social networking website in February 2004. In March 2010 more people visited Facebook than Google. It has become the world's leading social network site.

It was founded by Mark Zuckerberg, a psychology student with skills in computer programming, with his college roommates at Harvard, Eduardo Saverin, Dustin Moskovitz, and Chris Hughes. The website's membership was initially limited to Harvard students (Harvard at the time did not have an online photographic record of its own). Zuckerberg had hacked into Harvard's computers to retrieve ID photos of various dormitories on the campus and was subsequently charged by the Harvard authorities with breach of security, violating copyrights, and violating individual privacy, and faced expulsion. However, the charges against him were dropped. It was immediately successful: within 24 hours of its campus launch, 1,200 Harvard students had signed up, and after one month, over half of the undergraduate population had a profile.

It was originally launched as Thefacebook.com, but Zuckerberg dropped the definite article from its name after purchasing the domain name facebook.com in 2005 for $200,000. The name Facebook derives from the photo sheets given to students at the start of the academic year by American school and university administrations with the intention of helping students to get to know each other and the staff.

Facebook expanded beyond Harvard to other colleges in the Boston area, then to all Ivy League universities in the US. It later included any university student, then any high school students, and, finally, membership was extended to anyone aged 13 and over. In 2005 it reached UK universities. In 2006, the network was extended beyond educational institutions to anyone with a registered e-mail address. It remained free to join and makes money through advertising. By 2010 it had spread worldwide and had 400 million active members.

Appendix 3
Some notable British and American advertising slogans

Slogans promoting products and services

Access takes the waiting out of wanting
Access credit card, UK, c.1973

Access—your flexible friend
Access credit card, UK, 1981

I like Aeroplane Jelly . . . Aeroplane Jelly for me,
I like it for dinner, I like it for tea
Originally sung by five-year-old Joy King, it began in 1938 and was in use in the 1980s

That'll do nicely, Sir!
Television advertisement for American Express card, UK, late 1970s onwards

Don't leave home without it
American Express card, USA, 1981

Apple—The Power to Be Your Best
Apple Corporation, USA, 1986

You too can have a body like mine
Charles Atlas body-building courses

The greatest show on earth
Barnum and Bailey's circus, from 1881

Worth a guinea a box
Beechams pills, c.1940

That's a h**1 of a way to run a railroad!
Slogan for the Boston and Maine Railroad, derived from a cartoon, c.1932, showing two trains about to collide. A signalman comments: Tch-tch—what a way to run a railroad!

Bounty—The Taste of Paradise
Long-running slogan for Bounty chocolate bars

Alas! My poor brother
Caption to a picture of a sorrowful bull looking at a jar of Bovril meat extract, 1896

The two infallible powers. The Pope and Bovril
Bovril meat extract, late 1890s

I hear they want more
One apprehensive bull to another, 1903; Bovril meat extract

Bovril—prevents that sinking feeling
Bovril meat extract, 1920

Let the train take the strain
British Rail, 1970

Inter-City makes the going easy, and the coming back
British Rail, from 1972

This is the age of the train
British Rail, 1980

We're Getting There
British Rail, 1980s

It's good to talk
British Telecom, 1994

And all because the lady loves Milk Tray
Cadbury's Milk Tray chocolates, 1968 onwards

Everyone's a fruit and nutcase
Cadbury's Fruit and Nut chocolate, 1964 onwards

Perfume worth 9 guineas an ounce
Camay soap, c.1956

You'll look a little lovelier each day
With fabulous pink Camay
Camay soap, c.1960

Milk from contented cows
Carnation Milk, 1906

Is it true . . . blondes have more fun?
Lady Clairol, c.1965

It's the real thing
Coca-Cola, 1970

I'd like to buy the world a Coke
Coca-Cola, 1971

Things go better with Coke
Coca-Cola, 1963

Cool as a mountain stream
Consulate menthol cigarettes

If we don't have the lowest fare, we probably don't fly there
Continental Airlines, USA

Don't just book it—Thomas Cook it
Thomas Cook Travel Agents

Thank Crunchie it's Friday
Crunchie chocolate bars

Trust Dettol to protect your family's health
Dettol antiseptic/disinfectant, 1978

Kills all known germs
Domestos bleach, 1959

I'm only here for the beer
Double Diamond beer

Drinka Pinta Milka Day
British Milk Marketing Board, 1958

Go to work on an egg
British Egg Marketing Board

Happiness is egg-shaped
British Egg Marketing Board

You can rely on the lion
British Egg Marketing Board

The Esso sign means happy motoring
Advertising jingle for Esso, UK, 1950s

Put a tiger in your tank
Esso, USA, 1964

You only fit double glazing once, so fit the best
Everest Double Glazing, UK

Now hands that do dishes can be soft as your face
Jingle for Fairy washing-up liquid

Say it with flowers
Advertisement for the Society of American florists, late 1920s

High o'er the fence leaps Sunny Jim
'Force' is the food that raises him
Force breakfast cereal, 1903

They're g-r-r-r-eat!
Long-running slogan for Kellogg's Frosties cereal

Desperation, Pacification, Expectation, Acclamation, Realization
Fry's Chocolate, UK, post-First World War, on advertisements featuring the 'five boys'

The greatest motion picture ever made
Promotional slogan for the film Gone with the Wind, *1939*

Guinness is good for you
Guinness, c.1930s

My goodness, my Guinness
Guinness, c.1930s

Pure Genius
Guinness, 1994

Don't be vague—ask for Haig
Haig whisky, c.1936

Happiness is a cigar called Hamlet
Hamlet cigars, UK

Does she . . . or doesn't she?
Clairol, 1950s

If you want to get ahead, get a hat
UK Hat Council, 1965

Heineken refreshes the parts other beers cannot reach
Heineken lager, 1975 onwards

Beanz means Heinz
Heinz baked beans

Make today a Heinz Souperday
Heinz soups, 1968

Let Hertz put you in the driver's seat
Hertz car rental, 1962

It beats as it sweeps as it cleans
Advertising slogan for Hoover vacuum cleaners, 1919

Horlicks guards against night starvation
Horlicks milk drink

It's fingerlickin' good
Kentucky Fried Chicken Co., USA, 1950s

You press the button, and we'll do the rest
Kodak cameras and film

Never knowingly undersold
John Lewis stores, c.1920

The mint with the hole
Life-Savers, USA, 1920; Rowntree's Polo mints, UK, from 1947

Lucozade refreshes you through the ups and downs of the day
Beecham Foods, c.1978

Nine out of ten screen stars use Lux toilet soap
Lux soap, USA, late 1920s

Out of the strong came forth sweetness
Lyle's Golden Syrup; from the Bible, Judges 14:14

Test drive a Mackintosh
Apple Corporation, USA, 1984

Chocolates with the less fattening centres
Maltesers chocolates, UK, 1965

A Mars a day helps you work, rest and play
Mars bars, from 1960

The right one
Martini, UK, 1970

Any time, any place, anywhere
Martini, UK, 1970s

For Mash Get Smash
Smash instant mashed potato

Good to the last drop
Remark made by Theodore Roosevelt, 1907, about Maxwell House coffee; later used as an advertising slogan

Just Do It
Nike, 1993

Murray Mints! Murray Mints!
Too-good-to-hurry-Mints
Advertising jingle for Murray Mints, UK, from late 1950s

Naughty but nice
Slogan promoting the sale of cream cakes

All human life is there
Slogan promoting the News of the World

Mean! Moody! Magnificent!
Promotional slogan for the film The Outlaw, 1943

We are the Ovalteenies
Happy girls and boys
Advertisement for Ovaltine

Oxo is British—Made in Britain—By a British Company—with British Capital and British Labour
Early advertising slogan for Oxo, UK

Oxo gives a meal man-appeal
Oxo, 1958

Ask the man who owns one
Packard, USA, 1902

Keep that schoolgirl complexion
Palmolive Soap, 1917

Since when I have used no other
Pears Soap, 1884

He won't be happy till he gets it
Pears Soap

Top breeders recommend it
Pedigree Chum dog food, UK, 1964

The tea you can really taste
Brooke Bond PG Tips

P-p-p-pick up a Penguin
Penguin chocolate biscuits

You'll wonder where the yellow went
When you brush your teeth with Pepsodent
Advertising jingle for Pepsodent toothpaste, USA, 1950s

Persil washes whiter—and it shows
Long-running Persil soap powder slogan

Everything you hear is true
Pioneer hi-fi equipment, 1970s

Player's please
John Player and Sons cigarettes

What is home without Plumtree's Potted Meat? Incompleat [*sic*]
Early 1900s

Someone, somewhere wants a letter from you
Post Office campaign, 1960s

Snap! Crackle! Pop!
Kellogg's Rice Crispies, USA, c.1928

It's a lot less bovver with a hover
Qualcast Lawnmowers, UK

Don't forget the fruit gums, Mum
Rowntree's Fruit Gums, 1958 onwards

Have a break, have a Kit-Kat
Rowntree's Kit-Kat chocolate bars, from c.1955

They laughed when I sat down at the piano. But when I started to play!
Advertisement for the US School of Music, 1920s

Sch ... you know who
Schweppes mineral drinks, 1960s

Some day all watches will be made this way
Slogan used by Seiko for its first quartz watches, late 1960s

Man invented time—Seiko perfected it
Seiko watches, 1980s

Complete satisfaction or your money cheerfully refunded
Selfridge's department store

The customer is always right
Selfridge's department store

You can be sure of Shell
Shell UK, c.1931

Senior Service satisfy
Senior Service cigarettes

Every picture tells a story
Advertisement for Sloane's Backache and Kidney Pills, showing someone bending over in pain

Can you tell Stork from butter?
Stork margarine

You're never alone with a Strand
Strand cigarettes

Tell 'em about the honey, Mummy
Kellogg's Sugar Puffs

Tetley make tea-bags make tea
Tetley's tea

Top people take the Times
Slogan promoting The Times *newspaper, 1957*

Which twin has the Toni?
Toni home perms, USA, 1951

Treats. Melt in your mouth, not in your hand
Treats chocolates

Tunes help you breathe more easily
Tunes throat lozenges

Virginia is for lovers
Tourist board slogan, Virginia, USA

You've come a long way baby
Virginia Slims cigarettes

Think small
Volkswagen, USA, from c.1959

Stop me and buy one

Wall's ice-cream, 1922

They came as a boon and a blessing to men,
The Pickwick, the Owl, and the Waverley Pen
Waverley pens

Where's the beef?
Wendy's Hamburgers

Breakfast of champions
Wheaties cereal, USA, 1950

Eight out of ten cats prefer Whiskas
Whiskas catfood, 1970s

We're with the Woolwich
Woolwich Equitable Building Society, UK, from late 1970s

Nothing over sixpence
Woolworth stores, UK, from 1909

Let your fingers do the walking
Yellow Pages, from American Telephone and Telegraph Company, 1960s

Slogans promoting political parties and social change

One man, one vote
Campaign run by Major John Cartwright (1740–1824) against plural voting

No taxation without representation
In use before the American War of Independence, 1775–83

Liberté! Egalité! Fraternité!
Liberty! Equality! Brotherhood!
French Revolution, 1793

Ulster will fight, and Ulster will be right
Ulster Volunteers opposed to Irish Home Rule, 1913–14, from a letter by Lord Randolph Churchill, 1886

Votes for Women
Suffragette Movement, 1905, in Emmeline Pankhurst, My Own Story *(1914)*

Are we downhearted? No!
World War I, based on a remark of Joseph Chamberlain

Your King and Country need you
World War I

Kraft durch Freude
Strength through joy
German Labour Front, 1933

Ein Reich, Ein Volk, Ein Führer
One realm, one people, one leader
Nazi Party, 1934

Dig for victory
Ministry of Agriculture, 1939

Is your journey really necessary?
World War II

Careless talk costs lives
British Ministry of Information, World War II

A bayonet is a weapon with a worker at each end
Pacifist movement, 1940

Coughs and sneezes spread diseases
Ministry of Health, c.1942

No names, no pack drill
Used frequently in both World Wars

With thumb in bum and mind in neutral
US Navy catchphrase, 1940s

Fair shares for all
Labour Party; devised by Douglas Jay, 1946

The family that prays together stays together
Devised by Al Scalpone for the Roman Catholic Family Rosary Crusade, 1947

I Like Ike
US button badge, first used in 1947, to support Eisenhower

Keep Britain tidy
British government, 1950s

Ban the bomb
Current from 1953 onwards. Made famous by the CND

Better red than dead
British nuclear disarmament movement; 'Better dead than red' was also in common use

Life's better with the Conservatives
Conservative Party, 1959

Make love, not war
Common in the mid-1960s

Flower Power
Hippy slogan, 1960s

Let's go with Labour
Labour Party, 1964

In your heart you know he's right
Goldwater Presidential campaign, 1964

Don't ask a man to drink and drive
Road safety campaign, 1964

Thirteen Wasted Years
Unofficial Labour Party slogan prior to 1964 General Election

Prosperity with a Purpose
Conservative Party, 1964

Let's Go With Labour For The New Britain
Labour Party, 1964

Think For Yourself—Vote Liberal
Liberal Party, 1964

Black is beautiful
US civil rights movement, 1966

I'm backing Britain
Slogan, 1968; campaign to support UK economy after devaluation of sterling

Would you buy a used car from this man?
Campaign slogan directed against Richard Nixon, 1968

Power to the People
Black Panther movement, 1969

Out of the closets and into the streets
Gay Liberation movement, USA, c.1969

Burn Your Bra
Attributed, erroneously, to the feminist movement, USA, 1970s

It smells like you're kissing an old ashtray
Health Education Council anti-smoking campaign, c.1970

Yesterday's men (they failed before!) [Of the Conservatives]
Labour party, 1970

What a Life!
Liberal Party, 1970

A Better Tomorrow
Conservative Party, 1970

Now Britain's Strong—Let's Make It Great To Live In
Labour Party, 1970

Clunk, Click, every trip
Road safety campaign promoting the use of seat belts, 1971

Dull it isn't
Recruiting advertisement for the Metropolitan Police, 1972

England Expects—Scotland's Oil
Scottish National Party, 1973

Let Us Work Together
Labour Party, 1974

Change the Face of Britain
Liberal Party election manifesto, 1974

Putting Britain First
Conservative Party, 1974

Scotland a Nation Once Again
Scottish National Party, 1977

Labour isn't working
Conservative Party, 1978

Lavorare meno—Lavorare tutti
Work less—work for everybody
From a collection of slogans used by students and workers during the 1970s demonstrations

Be all you can be
Scottish Health Education Council, 1980s

Choose Life, Not Drugs
Scottish Health Education Council, 1980s

Britain is Great Again, Don't Let Labour Wreck It
Conservative Party, 1987

Don't Die of Ignorance
Department of Health Aids campaign, 1987

Meet the Challenge, Make the Change
Labour Party, 1989

Green Policies in a Nutshell
Green Party, 1992

Independence in Europe: Make It Happen Now
Scottish National Party, 1992

Changing Britain for Good
Liberal Democrat Party, 1992

It's Time to Get Britain Working Again
Labour Party, 1992

The Best Future for Britain
Conservative Party, 1992

Good Health is Good Business
Health and Safety Executive, 1993

Appendix 4
Web links

Finding marketing resources on the Internet

(((⊕))) SEE WEB LINKS

The Internet has a vast amount of information on marketing and related subjects available to academics, professionals, and students alike. Finding reliable data should not be difficult although a few points need to be taken into account. The material should be up to date. Small organizations and departments within academic institutions sometimes encounter funding difficulties and are unable to continue with their researches. Make sure to look at the 'Last updated' section of the main website page before using any data. Information should be obtained from websites run by universities, research institutes, and other reputable organizations. Websites maintained by individuals may not be up to date and comprehensive. It is also possible that the prejudices of those maintaining the websites will be reflected in the content and list of links.

A selection of useful websites for students of marketing

General Marketing Terms and Resources
• An extensive list of mainly Internet marketing terms. A–Z listing.

Chartered Institute of Marketing
• The website of the Chartered Institute of Marketing has a list of marketing terms, quite UK-centric, in their Knowledge Hub section. Includes case studies and research papers.

The Marketing Society
• The website of the Marketing Society, the UK's leading marketing association.

Biz/ed
• Marketing resources on this UK business education website.

American Marketing Association
• Website of the American Marketing Association. Includes also a resource library.

KnowThis
• A virtual marketing library, part of the WWW virtual library, with articles, tutorials and many useful links. Relevant topics on marketing.

Quirk's Marketing Research Review
• Contains a glossary of useful marketing related terms. Term or definition search.

Glossarist
• Various glossaries around specific areas of marketing.

Hackers, Hits and Chats: An E-Commerce and Marketing Dictionary of Terms
• An e-commerce list of marketing terms.

MarcommWise marketing glossary
• Glossary of marketing communications terms.

Department of Marketing, Monash University
• The Monash University dictionary of marketing terms (Don Bradmore).

Business Link
• Practical tips for online marketing.

Marketing Teacher
• Marketing basics at the introductory level, particularly good for people new to marketing.

Consumer Behaviour: The Psychology of Marketing
• Introduction to marketing.

Website Tips
• Definitions of marketing acronyms.

Good Marketing Ideas
.• Marketing ideas and strategies for beginners.

The Marketing Research Association
• A self-managed, not-for-profit organization providing programmes and services for market research professionals.

Advertising, Brand, and Public Relations Terms
• Important website on advertising.

4As
• American Association of Advertising Agencies.

All About Public Relations
• Public relations organizations and associations.

Brand Channel
• Brand and advertising terms.

CIPR
• UK's Chartered Institute for Public Relations—resource, research, and learning section.

H.A.T.
• History of classic British advertising on an online archive.

Google Webmaster is also an excellent resource for those practitioners wishing to understand how to optimize their searches and to market their websites.